Educational Administration

The Developing Decades

Edited by

LUVERN L. CUNNINGHAM

WALTER G. HACK

RAPHAEL O. NYSTRAND

Proceedings of a Career Development Conference
Sponsored by
The University Council for Educational Administration
and The Ohio State University

McCutchan Publishing Corporation
2526 Grove Street
Berkeley, California 94704

© 1977 by McCutchan Publishing Corporation

Library of Congress Catalog Card Number 76-27956
ISBN 0-8211-0226-5

Printed in the United States of America

Educational Administration

THE NATIONAL SOCIETY
FOR THE STUDY OF EDUCATION

Series on Contemporary Educational Issues
Kenneth J. Rehage, Series Editor

The 1977 Titles

Educational Administration: The Developing Decades, Luvern L.
 Cunningham, Walter G. Hack, and Raphael O. Nystrand, Editors
Early Childhood Education: Issues and Insights, Bernard Spodek
 and Herbert J. Walberg, Editors
*The Future of Big-City Schools: Desegregation Policies and Magnet
 Alternatives,* Daniel U. Levine and Robert J. Havighurst, Editors

The National Society for the Study of Education also publishes Yearbooks which are distributed by the University of Chicago Press. Inquiries regarding all publications of the Society, as well as inquiries
about membership in the Society, may be addressed to the Secretary-
Treasurer, 5835 Kimbark Avenue, Chicago, IL 60637. Membership in
the Society is open to any who are interested in promoting the
investigation and discussion of educational questions.

Preface

The chapters in this volume were presented as papers at a conference entitled "Educational Administration Twenty Years Later: 1954-1974," which was held at The Ohio State University, April 27-30, 1975. The general purpose of this conference was to assess developments in the knowledge and practice of educational administration during this twenty-year period and to identify directions for research, leadership, and preparation for educational administration in the years ahead.

The idea—and theme for the conference—was first proposed by Jacob W. Getzels in a December 1973 conversation with Jack Culbertson of the University Council for Educational Administration (UCEA). Recalling the 1954 meeting of the National Conference of Professors of Educational Administration (NCPEA) as a benchmark event that marked the beginning of emphases on the behavioral sciences in educational administration, Getzels pointed to the need for intellectual "stock taking" of developments since that time. At about the same time, Roald F. Campbell, Luvern L. Cunningham, and Raphael O. Nystrand of Ohio State were speculating about the desirability of renewing national attention on research in educational administration. They also spoke with Culbertson who informed them of

Getzels's idea and indicated his intention of advancing the stock-taking notion for consideration by others in the field.

Culbertson convened an initial meeting to consider a stock-taking conference in New Orleans in February 1973 and a second meeting in Columbus, Ohio, in June of that year. Those participating included Jacob W. Getzels, Roald F. Campbell, Andrew W. Halpin, Max G. Abbott, Donald J. Willower, and H. Thomas James. With the suggestions and support of this group, Culbertson sought reactions from a panel of twenty selected leaders in this and other countries during the summer of 1973. These efforts led to a preliminary prospectus, based largely on an initial outline prepared by Getzels, and a search for a host agency to continue the planning and to hold the conference.

In the fall of 1973, the academic faculty of educational administration at Ohio State agreed to host the conference and proposed that it be held as a means of recognizing Roald F. Campbell's outstanding contributions to the field. A steering committee was formed at Ohio State to refine conference plans and carry out the program. This group, consisting of Culbertson, Cunningham, Nystrand, Walter Hack, and Fred Frank (UCEA) prepared the program in consultation with the original ad hoc group convened by UCEA.

The conference was planned on the assumption that the proceedings would be published. Papers were sought that would both provide a commentary on the most significant developments during the decades under review and suggest directions for the future. Topics for presentations were organized around four themes: the context of administrative inquiry and practice from 1954 to 1974, the changing nature of practice during those years, the changing nature of administrative study over this period, and projections for the future. In order that the conference and publications would pay as much attention as possible to future implications of the recent past, contributors to the first three themes were invited to include a future-oriented code to their presentations.

An essential part of the format of the conference was group discussion of the respective papers. Indeed, the schedule allowed only time for presenters to summarize the main ideas of their papers in anticipation that these ideas would be elaborated more fully in the discussion sessions.

During the late 1970s the field of educational administration is in some intellectual disarray and is seeking either affirmation of the directions taken in recent years or indications of appropriate alternative futures. Our objective in identifying conference participants was to engage people who could help the field reflect critically about developments of the past twenty years and contemplate the implications of these developments for the future. We enthusiastically commend the papers to readers of this volume. We do so, however, with the caution that one should not expect to find consensus or unanimity of perspective among them. Indeed, there was some disagreement among participants as to whether the events of the two decades could be interpreted better as those of a field in the turmoil of adolescence or one in the rattle of old age. Our bias, as reflected in the title of this volume, is toward the former. As the field moves toward greater maturity, it is useful to consider the teachings of the past. The authors of this volume provide both scholars and practitioners with considerable assistance in this endeavor.

The leadership of UCEA was central to both the substance and logistics of this conference. Many of the professional developments referred to in the conference papers were given impetus or support from UCEA during the decades under review. This conference was one such event. Considering UCEA's contributions to the field, it was natural and appropriate that the organization be seen as a sponsoring agency for the conference. Jack Culbertson played a central coordinating role in formulating the conference and engaged the network of professors from UCEA in suggesting and critiquing program ideas. Such widespread and thoughtful participation is of great value to conference planners. Culbertson and the UCEA staff were active and helpful contributors through the full range of conference activities. We were aided immeasurably by their presence and greatly appreciated their assistance.

The conference was made possible by a grant from the Martha Holden Jennings Foundation, to which we are grateful. The views expressed in the conference papers are those of the authors and editors and do not necessarily represent those of the foundation, UCEA, or Ohio State.

We wish to acknowledge the support and assistance provided by our colleagues at Ohio State. We particularly appreciate the assistance of William Bainbridge, Frank Cody, Michael Elsberry, Joann Horton, Nancy Pitner, Jill Hake, Debbie Drasylko, and Lorraine Presson with conference logistics and preparation of the manuscript. We are proud too that this conference and its published proceedings pay tribute to our friend and colleague, Roald F. Campbell.

Luvern L. Cunningham
Walter G. Hack
Raphael O. Nystrand

Contributors

Edwin M. Bridges, Stanford University

Roald F. Campbell, Salt Lake City, Utah

Wayne M. Carle, Texas Southern University

W. W. Charters, Jr., University of Oregon

Robert Cummings, Stanford University

Luvern L. Cunningham, The Ohio State University

Donald A. Erickson, Simon Fraser University

Robin Farquhar, University of Saskatchewan

Alan K. Gaynor, Boston University

Keith Goldhammer, Michigan State University

Jacob W. Getzels, University of Chicago

Daniel E. Griffiths, New York University

Andrew W. Halpin, Tucson, Arizona

Laurence D. Haskew, University of Texas at Austin

Andrew E. Hayes, University of North Carolina at Wilmington

Glenn L. Immegart, University of Rochester

Virla R. Krotz, California State Board of Education

Virginia D. Nordin, University of Wisconsin at Madison

David B. Tyack, Stanford University

Bernard C. Watson, Temple University

Contents

Part I

KEYNOTE, TRIBUTE, AND RESPONSE

Chapter 1 of this volume contains the keynote delivered at the conference by Jacob W. Getzels. It focuses upon the intellectual significance to educational administration of the period from 1954 to 1974. Getzels refers to the period as a new era marked by the recognition of educational administration as a domain of study as well as a domain of practice. The early conceptualizations during this period emphasized psychological and sociological approaches to synthesizing the perspectives of scientific management and human relations that were dominant during the first half of the century. By the mid-1960s, however, the press of social issues and citizen protest had produced a shift in both scholarly and lay interest toward other perspectives, including law and economics. A consequence of this shift was the emergence of a thesis of accountability in educational administration. Looking to the future, Getzels warns that, if it continues, this emphasis will have harmful effects upon educational practice and scholarship.

Roald F. Campbell was an outstanding contributor to both practice and scholarship during the period from 1954 to 1974. He was a participant in the pivotal 1954 conference and coedited one of the benchmark volumes that grew out of that meeting. Professor

Campbell retired as Novice G. Fawcett Professor of Educational Administration at The Ohio State University in 1974. In recognition of this event and his distinguished career, UCEA and Ohio State joined to sponsor the 1975 conference in his honor. Luvern L. Cunningham, a friend and colleague at both Chicago and Ohio State, offered a tribute to Professor Campbell at the conference banquet. It comprises Chapter 2 and is presented in continuing recognition of his remarkable impact upon the field of educational administration.

Chapter 3 contains Professor Campbell's address given at the conference banquet. It deals briefly with the past and then offers comments on the implications of contemporary social and professional developments for the future of educational administration. Pluralism, declining enrollments, teacher organizations, state governance, emphasis on outcomes, and the deification of administrative practice are identified as factors that will influence the future. Viewing the latter as a form of anti-intellectualism, Campbell calls for renewed emphasis on the study and application of social science in administration. He cautions, however, that this will require multi-faceted and specialized approaches in order to be of use and appeal to practitioners.

1. Educational Administration
Twenty Years Later, 1954-1974

JACOB W. GETZELS

Certain events—which seem at the time merely academic—become benchmarks in a field of study and practice. The event in itself may not solve anything; in fact it often does not. But it achieves something more important: it raises the right questions, poses the crucial problem. And in so doing the event produces resounding repercussions for years to come.

The famous Solvay Conference on Physics at Brussels in 1911, for example, was such an event. As Banesh Hoffman describes the meeting in his biography of Einstein, "Although the discussions were learned and lively and long, the problems did not yield their secrets. They bided their time and the Solvay Conference seemed to have solved nothing. Nevertheless, it was to have resounding repercussions."[1]

In social science, the International Congress at New Haven in 1929 was another such event. It was here that, after thirty years of advocating connectionism, Thorndike announced: "I was wrong."[2] As a matter of fact, he was not as wrong as he thought, but the meeting provides a benchmark in the decline of connectionism and the rise of Gestalt influence in psychology and education.

More recently at the annual meeting of the American Psychological Association in 1950, to cite a final instance, Guilford raised the problem of the relation between intelligence and creativity.[3] He pointed out that, although there had been hundreds of studies of intelligence each year during the preceding quarter century, there had been fewer than 200 studies of creativity during the same period. The meeting did not solve the enigma of intelligence and creativity. But it did pose the problem. Within a dozen years, there were more than 200 studies of creativity in a single year, and the concepts of convergent and divergent thinking had become commonplaces.[4]

The 1954 meeting of the National Conference of Professors of Educational Administration (NCPEA) at Denver was a similar event. Although the problems that were posed did not yield their secrets and the meeting seemed at the time to have settled nothing, it was to have resounding repercussions. We had little idea of the repercussions the problems posed there would have, or that the meeting would one day, twenty years later, serve as the focal point, or at least the point of departure, for another meeting.

What I should like to do, then, in these introductory remarks to the present meeting, is to comment briefly on each of the following topics: the primary conceptions of educational administration before 1954; the significance of the 1954 meeting; the repercussions that followed from it; a number of central issues in the field as they appear today; and, finally, the possible impact of one of the issues on the work of the university and more especially on the work of the professor of educational administration—a topic I had not intended to include but to which I was compelled as it emerged in preparing these remarks.

Thesis and Counterthesis:
Scientific Management and Human Relations

The predominant view of administration during the first quarter century or so was, of course, one that emphasized "scientific management." It held that excellence in management was "knowing exactly what you want men to do, and then seeing to it they do it in the best and cheapest way."[5] Among the principles of administration were: management should take away from the worker responsibility for planning the work, it should measure productive effort by time and motion study, and it should set incentives before the worker in order to stimulate desirable effort on his part. Numerous treatises and textbooks—those by Bobbitt, Cubberley, Strayer and Reeder, among others—applied the principles to educational administration. Cubberley, for example, in his enormously influential *Public School Administration* insisted that the administrator must plan the educational policy but would "find it wise to keep the policy to himself."[6]

It would be a mistake to see, as some do, scientific management as merely the aberration of deluded or self-serving men, or as a perverse accident. The principles of scientific management, however ill taken they may seem to us today, were isomorphic with the prevailing system of values and conception of human nature of the time. This system determined the relation between worker and employer, pupil and instructor, teacher and administrator.

The system of values was built on four pillars. The first pillar was based on a *work-success ethic*; values of material achievement took precedence over values of human being. The second pillar, which was based on a *future time orientation*, affirmed that "time is money" and "a penny saved is a penny earned" and stressed that time should be used as frugally and efficiently as money itself. The third pillar emphasized *competitive individualism*, which epitomized the maxim "the race is to the swift" and stated that the primary responsibility was to oneself rather than to any collectivity. The fourth pillar, based on *Puritan morality*, marked respectability, thrift, self-restraint, and cleanliness as the signs of common decency and sloth a sin second only to idolatry.[7]

The dominant conception of the human being was that he was by nature an empty organism responding only to pleasure and pain, reward and punishment. The person himself would do nothing unless impelled by the carrot of incentive or the goad of authority. It was no aberration or accident that the classroom of the time took the form it did. The teacher was placed in front of the room, the pupils sat in rigid rows facing him, and gold stars were dangled before the pupils, since it was presumed children would not think or learn or do anything useful without the prod of incentive or authority.[8]

Given this value system and conception of human nature, what could be a more sensible and practical classroom structure and arrangement of pupils and teacher? And given the same system and conception, what could be a more sensible and practical administrative structure and arrangement of teacher and principal than one similarly based on the primacy of incentives and authority as advocated by scientific management?

Every point has its counterpoint, every thesis engenders its own counterthesis.[9] If scientific management is considered the thesis in administration during the first quarter century, then human relations developed as the counterthesis during the second quarter century. The creed of the counterthesis was that human relations was the "warp and woof" of an organization and that all those in it should "evoke each other's ideas, come to see each other's viewpoints, and integrate their viewpoints in pursuit of the common goal."[10] Support for the conception of management based on human relations was provided by a number of studies, notably the Hawthorne experiments, and even more so by the famous investigation of children's reactions to different types of leadership. The terms "democratic," "autocratic," and "laissez-faire" became everyday words; human relations and group dynamics, which in a sense were launched by this study, took firm root in the language if not always in the practice of educational administration.[11]

There was an outpouring of treatises and texts from this point of view. Implicit in all was the dictum stated explicitly in one text: The primary responsibility of the educational administrator is to facilitate interaction in the faculty group so that "all individuals affected by any decision should have a share in determining its character and form."[12] This was a far cry from scientific management's principle of separation of planning from performance and Cubberley's admonition to the school administrator that he would be wise to keep his plans and policies to himself.

Just as it would be a mistake to see the thesis of scientific management as the aberration of deluded or evil men, so it would be a mistake to see the counterthesis of human relations as only the inspiration of more sophisticated and virtuous men. Like scientific management, the view of human relations was also isomorphic with the prevailing system of values and conception of human nature—but an altering system of values and an altering conception of human nature.

The work-success ethic was giving way to an ethic of *sociability*; the American ethos shifted from Main Street to Madison Avenue, and the model for our young changed from the hard-working Horatio

Alger hero to the affable young man in the grey flannel suit. Future time orientation was giving way to *present time orientation*; the former national slogan "a penny saved is a penny earned" was replaced by the new slogan "buy now, pay later." Competitive individualism was giving way to *adaptive conformity*; inner-direction was transformed to other-direction; self-made man became organization man. And Puritan morality was giving way to *moral relativism*; morality became a statistical rather than an ethical concept; virtue was whatever the group one belonged to thought was virtuous.[13]

The dominant conception of the human being was transformed from one of the connectionist empty organism to one of a dynamic social organism. In a sense, Watson's and Thorndike's images of human nature were replaced by Freud's and Lewin's. The authority-centered classroom, with its rigid straight rows where everyone could face only the teacher, became, at least ideally, the group-centered classroom, with the movable chairs and circular arrangements where everyone had to face everyone else.[14] There was more than an accidental parallel between the teacher's management of pupils through sociometry and the administrator's management of teachers through group dynamics and human relations; an emphasis on the *interpersonal* aspects of organized behavior replaced the former emphasis on the *impersonal* aspects.

Synthesis and Repercussions:
The Study of Educational Administration

If, for convenience, scientific management, with its stress on impersonal authority, is considered the thesis of the first era, and if human relations, with its stress on personal interaction, is viewed as the counterthesis of the second era, then the third era—the era catalyzed if not inaugurated by the 1954 meeting—may be considered the attempt at a synthesis.[15] There was not one formulation of the period that did not try to integrate the impersonal and personal aspects of organizations and administration into a unified scheme.

The synthesis proposed by Chester Barnard, who had published that remarkable treatise *The Functions of the Executive* in 1938,[16] was rediscovered, or really discovered. So far as I could find, virtually no text in educational administration before the 1950s mentions the work; by the 1960s hardly a text does not mention it. Barnard conceived of an organization, whether industrial or educational, as involving production or impersonal forces and humane or personal forces. The function of the executive was to coordinate these forces in order to maximize both effectiveness, the accomplishment of organizational purpose (the aspect stressed by the thesis of scientific management), and efficiency, the satisfaction of individual purpose (the aspect stressed by the counterthesis of human relations).

Similar syntheses were developing specifically in educational administration and were set forth at the 1954 meeting. Some scholars even point to a single "brief but provocative and influential monograph," having its genesis at the meeting and published in 1955, which "can be identified as the herald of this new era" [and] "pointed the way for much of the work which has followed."[17] This seems to attribute too much to a single work or event, but there is no doubt that the meeting is a benchmark of the new era. New conceptions of educational administration synthesizing the preceding ones were in the making as the content of *Administrative Behavior in Education,* sponsored by NCPEA and published in 1957, was to show.[18]

I shall cite only two instances; there were perhaps other more notable ones. One conception visualized administrative behavior as involving the now familiar dimensions, initiating structure and consideration. In initiating structure, the administrator lets the staff know what is expected of them and sees to it that they are working up to capacity (once more note the similarity to aspects of the thesis of scientific management). In consideration, the administrator is friendly, approachable, and gets staff approval on important matters before going ahead (once more note the similarity to aspects of the counterthesis of human relations). Effective leadership involves the synthesis of initiating structure and consideration.[19] Another conception visualized the school as a social system and perpetrated the dreadful jargon of nomothetic and idiographic dimensions, the former referring to the formal structure of roles and expectations in the organization, the latter to the informal patterning of personalities and dispositions. A nomothetic style of administrative behavior places emphasis on the production requirements of the system akin to the mode of scientific management. Idiographic style places emphasis on the personal requirements of the individuals akin to the mode of human relations. The so-called transactional style synthesizes the two.[20]

This third period in administrative thought has been variously called the theoretical era, the social science era, the behavioral science era, the social systems era, or the social psychological era. The terms are quite descriptive. But the transformation was more profound than mere reference to theory, behavioral science, or social psychology would suggest. The essential shift was from conceiving of educational administration as a domain of action only to conceiving of it as a domain of study also.[21] The shift moved the focus of effort from an orientation based on solutions, where experienced administrators gave answers to questions of "how to do it" to an orientation based on inquiry, where problems were posed and understanding was sought regarding the phenomena of administration in their own right. Two successive *Yearbooks* on administration published by the National Society for the Study of Education (NSSE), one before the 1954 meeting and one after, dramatically illustrate the transformation. Five of the nine people responsible for the 1946 *Yearbook* were practicing state school officers or school superintendents; none of the fifteen people responsible for the 1964 *Yearbook* held these positions.[22]

The transformation had repercussions—manifest effects—on research in educational administration and the literature to prepare administrators. There is, of course, always the question of how large or small an effect is, and opinion on this may differ. But however the magnitude is assessed, there is no doubt that there was a significant change in the character of research and the literature. During the first half of the century research consisted mainly of status studies and collections of opinion. Little research dealt with testing theoretical propositions; virtually none involved the concepts and methods of the behavioral sciences.[23] One need only compare the content of dissertations and journals of the 1930s and 1940s with those of the 1950s and 1960s and especially the articles in preceding journals in administration with those in the present *Journal of Educational Administration* and *Educational Administration Quarterly* to see the changes in the literature. The very existence of these publications reflects the changes symbolized by the 1954 meeting. As one observer put it, "The current excitement arises from the fact that within recent years educational administration has become a field of study and of development as well as a vocation."[24]

The most fascinating change—at least for me—was in the literature used to prepare administrators. I have already commented that before 1950 virtually no texts mentioned Chester Barnard's work; virtually no texts after 1960 did not refer to it. The change was not merely in people but in the fundamental point of view. Virtually none of the texts before 1950 referred to theory; virtually none of those after 1960 did not refer to it. It is, however, most telling—and, as I said, fascinating—to follow the gradual introduction of the new ideas emerging in the theoretical treatises and research reports from the study of educational administration through several editions of the same authors' text intended for the preparation of administrators. In a sense, this analysis has the logic and rigor of a controlled experiment; we are keeping authorship constant and observing the repercussions of an idea on the field over time.

Let me illustrate the point by referring only to the so-called nomothetic-idiographic model—not because it is the most notable instance of the point I am making, but because I happen to be most intimately acquainted with this model. Consider a text that went through two editions. In the first edition there are two references of a sentence each, one of which describes the formulation as "very limited."[25] In the second edition, eight years later, the references are lengthy, the framework is presented in some detail, and it is described as "a model . . . which has been extremely fertile . . . [and] has already become a classic . . ."[26] I am not pointing out the merit of any particular model, least of all this one. I am suggesting, rather, that there are manifest changes in the literature. When commentators assert, as some so avidly do, that there have been no changes, they are not only mistaken but they do a disservice to the field and to the scholars who are incorporating the changes in their work.[27]

Consider another instance, this time from a text that went through three editions. In the first edition, the last chapter was entitled "Toward the Emergence of a Theoretical Framework for the Study of School Administration."[28] It dealt hesitantly with theory and its value for administrators as if the author did not yet know whether to place his bets on the emerging idea. There is nothing hesitant about the second or third editions. In the second edition, published seven years after the first, the chapter originally entitled "Toward the Emergence of a Theoretical Framework . . ." has been firmly retitled "A Theoretical Framework for the Study of Educational Administration." Note, if you will, the emphasis on the study of educational administration. Indeed, the text goes further and now adds a chapter entitled "Models in Educational Administration," which ends with this passage: "Improvements in and new approaches to school administration depend on the development and use of models. . . . The professor of educational administration can be conceptualized in terms of the administrator-scientist who develops and tests models."[29] Shades of the 1954 meeting! For it was said then that a similar remark could only be made by the Young Turks, the designation given to those advocating this point of view.

I turn to a last example—this from a text that has gone through four editions. The Foreword to the first edition states quite directly the authors' view of what is needed for the preparation of administrators, "We feel that serious examination of and thought about one's own experiences and those of other people dealing with similar problems is of vital importance to anyone who wishes to gain a real understanding of the administrative process."[30] Forewords to succeeding editions are of a different order. In the fourth edition it is stated, "The book is built on the conviction that one develops an understanding of educational administration as one examines *concepts* and relates them to actual experiences."[31] Here is the crucial change. In the first edition understanding of educational administration comes from relating one's experiences to the experiences of others. In succeeding editions understanding is said to come from relating one's experiences not only, and perhaps not even primarily, to the experiences of others but to theoretical concepts as well. If one assumes Barnard to be the patron saint of the 1954 meeting, or at least of the Young Turks, here are some provocative numbers quantifying the repercussions over the years for those who are convinced only by numbers. The index to the first edition gives only reference to Barnard, the index to the second edition gives three, to the third five, the fourth seven.[32] In the first edition Barnard's views are allotted exactly one sentence; by the fourth edition they receive an exposition of several pages.

The Thesis Again: Accountability

The emphasis of the 1950s and 1960s on the sociological and psychological study of administration within the school as a social system was in a state of decline by the turn of the decade. This is not to say that work had ceased and it was time for an obituary, but rather that the field no longer seemed to have the original vitality. Neither can it be said that the work had not been fruitful nor that there were no residual effects. On the contrary, as we saw, there were substantial changes in conception, research, and preparation in educational administration. The development was almost a classic case, similar to the one described in *The Structure of Scientific Revolutions*.[33] The very success of the social psychological paradigm, to say nothing of its failures, led to its decline; the paradigm was incorporated into the lore, vocabulary, and common sense of the field. By 1970 there were few texts that did not deal with behavioral science theory, the school as a social system, and educational administration as a field of study as well as a vocation.

Circumstances outside the school were also forcing a reconsideration of the study and practice of educational administration. The middle and late 1960s were times of social unrest. The struggle over civil rights, inequality of opportunity, Vietnam, the new pluralism, the effects of inflation, and the increasing skepticism of citizens as to whether they were getting their money's worth for the taxes they were paying—all these factors were impinging on the schools. The study and practice of administration, which had faced inward upon relations within the school system, necessarily turned its focus outward to relations of the school system to other systems with which it was inextricably bound—political, legal, and economic systems, among others.

The social psychological synthesis was fragmented into a number of new theses. The field moved toward politics, law, economics, even the humanities, and one wonders what the consequences might have been if the movement toward the humanities had "taken." The primary activity, however, was in economics; this movement did "take," for reasons that are fairly obvious. As one economist explains, "More than any other social scientists, [economists] are willing and eager to *use* their models toward practical ends . . ."[34] What is even more important, he points out, economists are able to provide their client with predictions and will translate their findings into *cost-benefit* terms, which may be applied to taking an account of the effectiveness of what one is doing.

Promises of this kind from the "hard" of the otherwise "soft" social sciences and humanities gave impetus and legitimacy to the emergence of *accountability* as the salient new thesis in educational administration. More than this, educational accountability was part of the increased demand for social responsibility laid upon all institutions, private as well as public, in the late 1960s.[35] In this sense, education was only joining the accountability movement in business as it had joined the scientific management and human relations movements in other years. Some say more simply and cynically that the federal government made money available for the application of accountability to the schools, and everyone took a piece of the action. With an irony he could not foresee at the time, President Nixon announced in a special message on educational reform to Congress in 1970: "School administrators and school teachers alike are responsible for their performance, and it is in their interest as well as in the interests of their pupils that they be held accountable."[36]

If the analysis, begun earlier, of alterations in the system of values and conceptions of the learner is pursued further, other reasons for the egregious rise of the accountability thesis may also be adduced. The hedonistic and relativistic values of the 1950s seemed, during the turbulent 1960s, to be altered to values stressing social responsibility, educational relevance, personal authenticity, and moral commitment.[37] Life was more serious; citizens not only wanted a hand in determining what the schools were teaching their children but they also held the schools responsible for the actual effects on their children. And in some quarters conceptions of children were altered from those that regarded pupils as having unequal capacities to learn to those that viewed them as having equal capacities to learn if only the right instructional methods and contingencies of reinforcement were applied. As one proponent of this view said, "Up to 95% of our students can learn much of what they are taught to the same high levels typically reached by only our best students . . . [if we] provide each student with the time and quality of instruction he needs to demonstrate this mastery."[38] Since 95 percent of our children can learn up to levels typically reached by only our best students if only the quality of instruction and reinforcement is appropriate, then surely someone should be held accountable if all 95 percent of the children who are presumed equally able to learn do not learn equally.

Whatever the reasons, there was a spectacular rise of accountability as a major thesis in educational administration during the first years of the 1970s. In the late 1960s, none of the texts with which I was acquainted even mentioned the term, and I was astonished when Luvern Cunningham wrote unabashedly in 1969, "We will hear much more about accountability. It will become a household word much as the IQ or the whole child."[39] I did not believe him; I agreed with those who said it was only a "buzz word." But by 1970 others were writing, "Clearly a new educational movement is underway. The school systems of America are entering what the *Washington Post* has termed 'An Age of Accountability.' "[40] In 1972 the book entitled *Accountability in American Education* opened with the lines: "The age of accountability is dawning in American education and could well become one of the most important educational movements in the decade of the 1970s."[41]

This may be an exaggeration, and accountability may still turn out to be only a buzz word. Yet in the near term, consider the following data compiled from the *Education Index*.[42] Up to 1969 the *Education Index* records no articles with titles carrying the word "accountability." In the volume covering 1969-1970, four such articles appear. By the following year the quantity of material had become so large, a special category called "Accountability in Education" had to be set up; between July 1970 and December 1971, 88 titles appeared in this category. Henry Dyer estimated that, if this rate continued, by 1979 the *Education Index* would index well over 1,000,000 articles on accountability, give or take 100,000 or so. This is, of course, facetious. Nonetheless, ERIC shows the following entries under "Educational Accountability": 1969—0; 1970—1; 1971—42; 1972—101; 1973—112. By way of comparison over the same years, the entries under "Educational Experiments" were: 1969—35; 1973—21; under "Educational Equality," 1969—9; 1973—10.

Accountability was no mere academic matter important only to contributors to journals cited in ERIC and the *Education Index*. By 1974, thirty states had passed legislation requiring some form of educational accountability. Other states introduced accountability through executive order or other means. In any case, by 1974 most state education agencies had established or were developing programs for achieving accountability.[43] To be sure, many of the laws and programs are still ineffectual. But their intent is serious. Indeed, the education committee of a certain state legislature came up with a bill that read in part as follows: "If the performance of any school district on any test approved by the state board of education . . . does not equal or exceed the national performance average for such a test for two successive years, said school district shall not receive any further state financial assistance . . . until such time as said school district has achieved such national performance average."[44]

Consider for a moment the effect if all states passed laws that all their districts must exceed the national average. And consider the assumption that the way to upgrade education through accountability is to withhold funds from the schools whose students are falling furthest behind. As Dyer comments, "In the old educational theology it was generally supposed that the way to promote learning in the young was to beat the devil out of the students; the new educational theology seems to hold that the same purpose can be accomplished more efficiently by beating the devil out of the educators."[45]

A number of consequences flow from a stress on administrative accountability, as Ralph Spencer cogently points out.[46] Educational administration will be pushed in the direction of applying theories of business management; schools will overmeasure that which is measurable and neglect that which is not measurable but which may be at the very heart of education; precise statements of objectives, procedures, and standards of performance will be written down, thus increasing bureaucratization; efforts will increasingly be made to demonstrate favorable results for the sake of the "corporate image," and to manage the news and suppress results which may be seen as damaging to the institution's accountability stock; there will be an emphasis on functions of internal control through hierarchical supervision; as accountability increases, conflict due to clashes with other simultaneous movements will increase, notably with collective bargaining and with the drive toward professionalism by teachers, to mention only two forces that now run counter to accountability.

To this list I should like to add a seventh consequence of a somewhat different order. The focus of investigations will move rapidly from research on educational and administrative processes to the evaluation of products. That is, we will inspect inputs and evaluate outputs and neglect what goes on in between. I did not realize how rapidly this change in educational inquiry was taking place until I looked into the program of the annual meeting of the American Educational Research Association (AERA) for 1974. What engaged the interest of educational scholars was startling. The program listed no fewer than thirty-eight separate sessions on evaluation and another five on accountability. By way of comparison, science education had two sessions, counseling five sessions, reading—mind you, reading—had sixteen sessions, theory no sessions, and higher education five sessions. In addition, research itself—which presumably is what AERA is about and which included six separate subheads like methodology, development, management, needs, organization, and utilization—had only forty-six sessions as compared to forty-three sessions for the various aspects of evaluation and accountability.[47] As someone remarked at the meeting, the research enterprise in education seems to have moved from pursuing inquiries to passing judgments.

Accountability at the University: The Work of the Professor in Educational Administration or Otherwise

The notion of accountability is invading the university too, and one increasingly hears the terms cost effectiveness, evaluation, and accountability used in relation to the professorship, including the professorship in educational administration. Try as I might, I find it impossible to apply the ordinary notions of cost effectiveness and accountability to the work of a university; their use here seems to me mistaken in the extreme.

Consider an actual incident.[48] Professor Subrahmanyan Chandrasekhar of the University of Chicago is one of the world's most distinguished astrophysicists. During the mid-1940s he drove, week after week, some 100 miles between Yerkes Observatory, located in Wisconsin, and the university proper to meet a class of only two students. This was apparently a cost effectiveness nightmare. Ten years later in 1957 the whole class won the Nobel prize in physics; the two students were Tsung-Dao Lee and Chen Ning Yang, who discovered the violation of the principle of parity, one of the great achievements of science in the twentieth century. Was this the result of considering cost-effectiveness? Accountability? How could that be determined at the time?

Moreover, how, in all seriousness, can any notion of accountability be applied to an idea—to such ideas as Darwin's natural selection, Einstein's $E=MC^2$, Freud's interpretation of dreams, Mendel's experiments in genetics, Piaget's stages of cognitive development, or Skinner's teaching pigeons to be superstitious, to say nothing of Galileo's cosmology? Just how much are these ideas worth, and how could their benefit have been determined at the time they were formulated?[49]

Indeed, in each of these cases—and hundreds more could be mentioned—the accounting of benefit by the contemporary accountants was mistaken in the extreme. Darwin was hounded as an anti-Christ; Freud was vilified as having a dirty mind; Einstein was said to be dealing only with impractical abstractions (who thought in 1905 of atomic energy?); Mendel was neglected for a generation; Piaget, whose first work was published in the 1920s, seemed to have no application to anything; and Skinner was only making pigeons superstitious (and what could that have to do with the technology of teaching or behavior modification in humans?). And Galileo was almost burned at the stake for a truth which we now take for granted but which he himself had to recant in order to save himself from the supposed exponents—shall I say experts—of accountability of his day.

It is clear that the simple imperative and self-evidently virtuous notion of accountability is not so simple as it appears or as its exponents would have us believe. To be sure, educational administrators should be responsible for producing educational results, and university professors should be held responsible for producing scholarly results. How can anyone be opposed to responsibility or to being held accountable? But exactly *who* should do the accounting, *what* it is that should be accounted for (what are productive scholarly results?), and *when* the accounting should be made are questions that are unanswered. And when questions of both method and theory are unanswered they tend to be settled by expediency rather than by principle.

As only one example, let me demonstrate the difficulty encountered in determining *when* a decent estimate of accountability can be made. R. P. Feynman, a Nobelist in physics, is describing his work on quarks. He comes to a point where he needs a mathematical formulation to move the work forward. He writes, "In fact, the equations [needed] ... were written down over 20 years ago by Yang and Mills, who saw no application of them but published them because they looked so beautiful and symmetrical."[50] Feynman then adds—

and this is my point regarding the *when* of accountability of intellectual products that seem to have no immediate application—". . . sometimes the truth is discovered *first* and the beauty or 'necessity' of that truth seen only later."[51]

All would-be accountants of the scholarly enterprise should contemplate and savor this statement: The truth is discovered first and the necessity or utility of that truth may be seen only later. I know of no better description of what basic work in the university, at its characteristic best, is about—whether in physics, mathematics, political science, the history of education, or educational administration. For, if the truth is not discovered first, it may not be there when the practical necessity for it arises later. Assume, for example, that Yang and Mills's equations, which self-confessedly had no practical application when they were formulated, were not available when Feynman needed them. And this, of course, is the danger of the current anti-intellectual standards of accountability, which hold only to the immediate and material consequences measurable by the available criteria of evaluation.

Accountability as presently formulated has been taken entirely from methods and theory in business—methods and theory which, however applicable to business corporations or even elsewhere in education, are not applicable to the scholarly work of a university. As Alfred North Whitehead told the American Association of Schools of Business years ago, "The modern university system will be successful only if the ultimate authorities . . . remember that universities cannot be dealt with according to the rules and policies which apply to the familiar business corporation."[52]

What then are the distinctive characteristics and functions of the university and its work in educational administration? Asked of any other institution, "What is it about? What does it do? What does it produce?," the answer is relatively simple. The work of a factory, a store, a hospital may be described as providing solutions to manifest problems—problems that have already been identified and formulated. The accounting system of inputs and outputs, profits and losses, costs and benefits can be applied, usually at once. The work of a university cannot be described so simply. The work of a university (whether in the classroom, the laboratory, or the field) lies distinctively, as does that of no other institution, in making explicit that which is problematical—in exploring enigmas still needing formulation as problems, to say nothing of solutions.[53]

This engagement with the enigmatic rather than the apparent, with the ultimate rather than the immediate, with the fundamental rather than the pragmatic, renders the university liable to the charge that it is not doing anything, not producing anything. It is especially vulnerable to this charge when the principal criteria of worth become analysis of cost benefit and the standard of value is the pay-off. One can judge the cost benefit, the pay-off, of an answer that is produced, of a solution that can be applied. But how does one measure the cost benefit of a problem that is found—a problem, moreover, that may not be solved in one's own lifetime? How, for example, does one measure the cost benefit of the problems that were raised at the 1954 meeting, problems which altered the study and vocabulary of educational administration, even if they themselves were not solved? Or even if the problem is solved, as in the case of Yang and Mills's mathematical equations, how does one measure the cost benefit when the solution has utility only a generation later?

The prior question "Need one *find* problems?" may be raised. Is not the universe already teeming with dilemmas at home and abroad, in the arts and the sciences, in economics and in education? The world is, of course, teeming with dilemmas. But the dilemmas do not present themselves automatically as *problems* capable of resolution or even of sensible contemplation. They must be posed and formulated in fruitful and often radical ways if they are to be moved toward solution. And this, it seems to me, is the work of the university, whether in astrophysics or educational administration. As Einstein put the issue: "The formulation of a problem is often more essential than its solution, which may be merely a matter of mathematical or experimental skill. To raise new questions, new possibilities, to regard old questions from a new angle, requires imagination and marks real advance in science."[54] And, I would add, in all activity of any worth.

It is exactly this activity—the identification of where problems lie and questions are still needed, and not only the solution of problems already identified—that is the distinctive work of the university in all areas of inquiry it chooses to undertake, including, of course, educational administration. The products of such work, like the problems themselves, often seem esoteric or, as the saying goes, merely academic, and their value is not measurable by the popular criteria of the moment. But they bear fruit in knowledge which illuminates our experience and, in due course, often in applications of the greatest practical utility.

Consider an instance or two. The invention of the electric dynamo from which we get today's power and light would not have been possible if someone had not posed the prior problem, a problem that surely did not trouble anyone in any immediately practical way: What is the nature of electromagnetic induction? Quite typically, many of Faraday's contemporaries looked upon his formulations with skepticism and considered them useless. In fact, Gladstone, then the Chancellor of the Exchequer, interrupted Faraday in his description of his work to ask impatiently, "But after all, what use is it?" Faraday's response was, "Why, Sir, there is every probability that you will soon be able to tax it."[55] In our own time the invention of the polio vaccine would not have been possible if someone had not posed the prior, apparently useless, problem: What is the nature of the mammalian cell, and can it be maintained outside the living organism?

There are those who argue that such instances may hold true in the physical and biological sciences but not in the social sciences, and surely not in education. One must beware of analogies. Yet what would the present curriculum look like if Thorndike and Woodworth had not posed the problem: What is the nature of transfer of training from one subject to another? Recall the role of Latin and Greek in the training of the faculties of the mind—training that seemed so sensible and practical. Or what would the attitude toward gifted children be today if Terman had not posed the problem: What is the nature of giftedness and its relation to later achievement? Recall that precocious children, the so-called "quiz kids," were looked upon as "queer kids," and the rule was to hold them back since "early ripe, early rot." And, more recently, what would the preparation of administrators be like if Lewin and his colleagues had not posed the problem: What is the nature of different types of leadership and their effect on the behavior of individuals and the dynamics of groups?

I have, I am afraid, sounded as if the work of the university professor is unplanned, hit or miss, and irresponsible—as if any problem will do—and he is not held accountable. Nothing is further from the case. The system of accountability in fundamental scholarship is strict and ruthless, surely more severe than in any other professional work. It is a system internal to the work itself, as much a part of the work as the procedures and results. It is a system composed of one's colleagues within the university and in universities far beyond, a system of journal editors and anonymous referees, of skeptical attitudes and devastating public review, of recognition, indifference, and humiliating rejection.

Today there is pressure on the university and on certain elements in it, of which educational administration is a prime target, to turn away from exploring fundamental enigmas and to deliver technical services, to advocate policies rather than formulating problems, and to deal with practical necessity rather than with conceptual uncertainty. The pressure has its source not only in the real difficulties facing education but in an unhappy confluence of anti-intellectualism and financial stringency; it takes many forms—the call for assembly-line efficiency, the application of businesslike management, and, above all, the accounting of results not by their contribution to fundamental and ultimate knowledge but by their immediate and material consequences.

No one can—or should—deny the need for services and policies and for dealing with immediate necessity. The university professor of educational administration cannot and should not neglect these; it would be as much a disaster if the academy became a cloister as if it became a marketplace. Yet there are other individuals and other institutions that can also provide services and policies and deal with immediate necessity, and perhaps do these things just as well. If, however, through the imposition of inapplicable notions of assembly-line efficiency, businesslike management, and accountability of the "input-output" type, those in the university are not permitted to behave distinctively in its mode, who else will ask the fresh questions or explore the fruitful enigmas? The necessity for such questions, as in the case of Yang and Mills's equations, the structure of mammalian cells, or the effects of different styles of leadership on group performance, may not be seen until later, but without them how will the later dilemmas be resolved?

The 1954 meeting on educational administration was notable because it raised memorable questions and posed crucial problems—questions and problems with resounding repercussions to this day. It can only be hoped that twenty years hence the same may be said of the 1975 meeting at Ohio State: it raised memorable questions, posed crucial problems.

Notes

1. B. Hoffman, *Albert Einstein: Creator and Rebel* (New York: Viking, 1972), 97.

2. E. R. Hilgard and G. H. Bower, *Theories of Learning* (New York: Appleton-Century-Crofts, 1966), 25.

3. J. P. Guilford, "Creativity," *American Psychologist* 5 (September 1950), 444-454.

4. J. W. Getzels and J. T. Dillon, "The Nature of Giftedness and the Education of the Gifted," in R. M. W. Travers (ed.), *Second Handbook of Research on Teaching* (Chicago: Rand McNally, 1973), 689-731.

5. F. W. Taylor, *Shop Management* (New York: Harper & Row, 1911), 21.

6. J. W. Getzels, J. M. Lipham, and R. F. Campbell, *Educational Administration as a Social Process* (New York: Harper & Row, 1968), 23-30.

7. J. W. Getzels, "Changing Values Challenge the Schools," *School Review* 65 (Spring 1957), 92-102.

8. J. W. Getzels, "Images of the Classroom and Visions of the Learner," *School Review* 82 (August 1974), 527-540.

9. This view of the development of administration was called to my attention in an unpublished paper by Chung-il Yun, to whom I am grateful; see also R. G. Owens, *Organizational Behavior in Schools* (Englewood Cliffs, N.J.: Prentice-Hall, 1970).

10. H. C. Metcalf and L. Urwick, *Dynamic Organization: The Collected Papers of Mary Parker Follett* (New York: Harper & Row, 1940), 14.

11. Getzels *et al.*, *Educational Administration as a Social Process*, 36-39.

12. W. A. Yauch, *Improving Human Relations in School Administration* (New York: Harper & Row, 1949), 40.

13. See Getzels, "Changing Values."

14. See Getzels, "Images."

15. The terms thesis, counterthesis, and synthesis are, of course, shorthand designations for the three eras. The periods so demarcated were by no means as sharply defined as the necessarily schematic account unavoidably implies; at any given time it was a question of relative emphasis rather than the all-or-none presence or absence of a particular point of view. See n. 9, above.

16. C. Barnard, *The Functions of the Executive* (Cambridge, Mass.: Harvard University Press, 1964), originally published in 1938.

17. T. J. Jenson and D. L. Clark, *Educational Administration* (New York: The Center for Applied Research in Education, 1964), 59.

18. R. F. Campbell and R. T. Gregg, *Administrative Behavior in Education* (New York: Harper & Row, 1957).

19. A. W. Halpin, *Theory and Research in Administration* (New York: Macmillan, 1966).

20. J. W. Getzels and E. G. Guba, "Social Behavior and the Administrative Process," *School Review* 65 (Spring 1957), 423-441; see also Getzels *et al.*, *Educational Administration as a Social Process*.

21. See, for example, the early paper by J. W. Getzels significantly entitled "A Psycho-Sociological Framework for the Study of Educational Administration," *Harvard Educational Review* 22 (Fall 1952), 235-246; also, A. P. Coladarci and J. W. Getzels, *The Use of Theory In Educational Administration* (Stanford, Calif.: Stanford University Press, 1955).

22. Compare N. B. Henry (ed.), *Changing Conceptions in Educational Administration*, Fifty-fifth Yearbook of the National Society for the Study of Education, Part II (Chicago: University of Chicago Press, 1946), with D. E. Griffiths (ed.), *Behavioral Science and Educational Administration*, Sixty-third Yearbook of the National Society for the Study of Education, Part II (Chicago: University of Chicago Press, 1964).

23. R. G. Owens, *Organizational Behavior*, 16.

24. V. Miller, *The Public Administration of American School Systems* (New York: Macmillan, 1965), 545.

25. E. L. Morphet, R. L. Johns, and T. L. Reller, *Educational Organization and Administration: Concepts, Practices, and Issues*, 2nd ed. (Englewood Cliffs, N.J.: Prentice-Hall, 1967), 67-68.

26. E. L. Morphet, R. L. Johns, and T. L. Reller, *Educational Administration: Concepts, Practices, and Issues* (Englewood Cliffs, N.J.: Prentice-Hall, 1959), 66.

27. For other evidence of change in educational administration over a period of years, see R. F. Campbell, "Educational Administration—A Twenty-five Year Perspective," *Educational Administration Quarterly* 8 (Spring 1972), 1-15.

28. S. J. Knezevich, *Administration of Public Education* (New York: Harper & Row, 1962).

29. S. J. Knezevich, *Administration of Public Education*, 2nd ed. (New York: Harper & Row, 1969), 537.

30. R. F. Campbell, J. E. Corbally, and J. A. Ramseyer, *Introduction to Educational Administration* (Boston: Allyn and Bacon, 1958), vi.

31. R. F. Campbell, E. M. Bridges, J. E. Corbally, R. O. Nystrand, and J. A. Ramseyer, *Introduction to Educational Administration*, 4th ed. (Boston: Allyn and Bacon, 1971), xvi. Italics added.

32. Campbell *et al.*, *Introduction to Educational Administration*, 46; 2nd ed. (1962), 452; 3rd ed. (1966), 464; 4th ed. (1971), 451.

33. T. S. Kuhn, *The Structure of Scientific Revolutions* (Chicago: University of Chicago Press, 1962).

34. A. Daniere, "The Syntax and Substance of Economics," in J. Culbertson, R. Farquar, B. Fogarty, and M. Shibles (eds.), *Social Science Content for Preparing Educational Leaders* (Columbus, Ohio: Charles E. Merrill, 1973), 171.

35. J. W. Getzels, "On the Transformation of Values: A Decade after Port Huron," *School Review* 80 (Winter 1972), 505-518, especially 516-517.

36. Cited in R. W. Hostrop, *Managing Education for Results* (Homewood, Ill.: ETC Publications, 1973), 3.

37. See Getzels, "On the Transformation of Values."

38. J. H. Block, "A Description and Comparison of Bloom's Learning for

Mastery Strategy and Keller's Personalized System of Instruction," in Block (ed.), *Schools, Society, and Mastery Learning* (New York: Holt, Rinehart, & Winston, 1974), 17.

39. L. L. Cunningham, "Our Accountability Problems," in L. H. Browder (ed.), *Emerging Patterns of Administrative Accountability* (Berkeley, Calif.: McCutchan, 1971), 59.

40. L. M. Lessinger, "The Powerful Notion of Accountability in Education," in Browder (ed.), *Emerging Patterns,* 64.

41. F. J. Sciara and R. R. Jantz, *Accountability in American Education* (Boston, Mass.: Allyn and Bacon, 1972), 3.

42. H. S. Dyer, "School Evaluation: A Realistic Response to Accountability," *North Central Association Quarterly* 46 (Spring 1972), 390-396.

43. P. Hawthorne, *Legislation by the States: Accountability and Assessment in Education* (Denver: Cooperative Accountability Project, Report No. 2, Bulletin No. 3100, November 1974), 1.

44. Cited in Dyer, "School Evaluation," 395.

45. *Ibid.,* 395.

46. R. L. Spencer, "Accountability as Classical Organization Theory," in Browder (ed.), *Emerging Patterns,* 88-90.

47. American Educational Research Association, Annual Meeting Program for 1974, 227-232.

48. J. T. Wilson, "Introductory Remarks: The Nora and Edward Ryerson Lecture," *University of Chicago Record* 9 (1975), 92.

49. This section is based in part on J. W. Getzels, "Basic Research and Accountability," a paper delivered at the Symposium on Accountability Implications for R & D Management, American Educational Research Association Annual Meeting, Chicago, April 19, 1974.

50. R. P. Feynman, "Structure of the Proton," *Science* 183 (February 15, 1974), 610.

51. *Ibid.*

52. Cited in E. H. Levi, "The Integrity of Universities," address at ceremonies marking the twentieth anniversary of Hebrew Union College, Los Angeles, Feb. 12, 1974.

53. This section is based in part on J. W. Getzels, "Problem Finding," the 343rd convocation address, University of Chicago, *University of Chicago Record* 7 (1973), 281-283.

54. A. Einstein and L. Infeld, *The Evolution of Physics* (Cambridge, Mass.: Cambridge University Press, 1947), 95.

55. S. Chandresekhar, "Shakespeare, Newton, and Beethoven or Patterns of Creativity," *University of Chicago Record* 9 (1975), 107.

2. Roald F. Campbell:
Teacher, Leader, Learner

LUVERN L. CUNNINGHAM

In this chapter I will try to give voice to the thoughts of those who attended the conference on which this book is based and reflect the sentiments of UCEA and The Ohio State University in their co-sponsorship of the conference.

The conference was convened to honor Roald Fay Campbell—teacher, scholar, leader, learner. And, indeed, this was our intent. But in fulfilling that intent, we shared our admiration for Roald with our love for Della and our affection for other members of their family.

There is, in instances such as this, a temptation to be anecdotal, to be humorous, to be reportorial, to be historical, to be nostalgic. Despite reminders to myself to avoid all of the above, I have succumbed in part to each. And I have done so knowing Roald's disposition for getting on with important matters, for deciding, for acting, for avoiding the sentimental, for confronting the issues, for the application of intelligence to the questions of the day. And I have done so knowing Della's patience for Roald's disposition for getting on with it, for acting, for deciding, for avoiding the sentimental, for confronting issues.

I have thought from time to time about the features of our common experience, about the singular nature of my respect for

him, about the attributes of his statesmanship. We have been colleagues at two major universities, the University of Chicago and The
Ohio State University; we have survived the perils of joint authorship; we have served together on the committees of many doctoral
students; we have joined in the study of educational problems in several school districts; we have even been each other's dean; and I have
had the unusual challenge of succeeding him in two or more major
responsibilities.

A few nights before the conference was held, I was flying to San
Francisco. About eight miles above the continental divide I heard an
interview with Charlie Pride, the talented black country and western
singer, a person who has earned the respect of the country and western devotees across America. And I was reminded of Roald. Those of
you who know of Charlie Pride know how powerfully expressive his
country and western music is. You know of its basic, earthy qualities.
You know that it carries the sentiments of a large segment of rural
and small-town America. You know, too, of his devotion to the basic
tenets of American beliefs, his noncompromising position on quality
in human performance, his unflagging pursuit of equality, his frequent commentary on human rights, his reference to being the same
as all Americans on the inside, permanently tanned on the outside.

And I heard Roald in those words. I heard Roald's devotion to
excellence, to integrity, to the permanence of truth, to the rejection
of prejudice and discrimination, to patience in the achievement of
such noble and enduring objectives.

Roald the Leader

Roald "has been there and done it all," in the simplicity of the
contemporary. He earned his Ph.D. at Stanford. He has been a
teacher, a superintendent, a professor, a chairman, a dean. He directed the Laboratory School at the University of Utah. He was dean
of the Graduate School of Education and chairman of the Department of Education at the University of Chicago, and prior to that
served as director of the Midwest Administration Center at Chicago
and most recently as Novice G. Fawcett Professor of Educational
Administration at The Ohio State University.

He has earned the respect and applause of his colleagues. These
recognitions have come in many forms. He is a charter member and

one of the founding fathers of the National Academy of Education. He served as president of AERA in 1969-1970 and has been editor of *School Review*; the first editor of *Educational Administration Quarterly*; UCEA board member; lecturer in Australia and Pakistan; consultant; member of the Cleveland Conference; chairman of Mayor Daley's Committee to Nominate Candidates for the Chicago Board of Education; and chairman and member of hosts of local, state, and national committees, commissions, panels, and field study groups. He was recently chairman of an important panel of the National Institute of Education charged with examining the future of educational laboratories and research and development centers and is the author of many, many publications—books, monographs, articles, essays, research reports, field studies, and policy memoranda.

The books and monographs that Roald has written and cowritten have had a major influence on the field of educational administration. Within his writings there are themes and continuities. He and John Ramseyer published a fine volume in 1955 titled *The Dynamics of School-Community Relations* that foreshadowed many of the serious issues of citizen participation that we are confronting today. *Administrative Behavior in Education,* coedited with Russell Gregg in 1957, was a landmark volume and caused substantial new interest in examining the value of the social sciences to the field of educational administration. His textbooks have been widely used and, in their way, helped shape the thought and perspectives of students in our field. The 1963 monograph *Nationalizing Influences in Secondary Education* (with Robert Bunnell) was read thoughtfully by scholars and practitioners throughout the country for its insightful assessment of the impact of the large-scale curriculum movements upon the nation's schools. "The Folklore of Local School Control," a 1957 article in *School Review,* has been quoted repeatedly (and reprinted) since its appearance. In 1967 Gerald Sroufe and Donald Layton, with Roald, published *Strengthening State Departments of Education.* In 1974 the series of volumes on state governance of education (written with Tim Mazzoni, associate director of the governance project, and others) appeared, and in 1976 *State Policy Making for the Public Schools* (written with Mazzoni) was published. And there were dozens of other important contributions.

Roald's writing, like his speech, is clear, pointed, documented, and always substantive. He is a fine teacher of writing too, as I can testify, and President Corbally has also benefited from Roald's sensitive but forceful blue pencil.

Roald the Teacher

The giftedness of Roald's teaching is near legend. Students and colleagues, professionals and laymen issue testimony to Roald the teacher. His classes are noted for their quiet seriousness, for their unflagging exhibition of excellence, for their consistent devotion to quality in individual performance, for their theoretical attributes and simultaneous respect for practice.

Similarly, his counsel with students about dissertations or other research interests, his skill in involving students in research or field problems, his guidance of field experiences, his sensitivity and clarity in delegating responsibility to students—each of these associations with students is marked by high expectation, by discomfort with shabbiness, by constructive suggestion, by respect for the integrity of the learner, by the buttressing of confidence, by readiness to support students years after their campus associations.

I recall so vividly Roald's work with graduate students at the University of Chicago. In 1958 when I arrived there as an awkward assistant professor, he was in the midst of nourishing the dissertation interests of Loren Downey, Roger Seager, and Alan Slagle. Room 328 was their favorite workplace. Andrew Halpin, Philip Jackson, Conrad Briner, and Jacob Getzels became involved along with many others. Dow McCarthy, Rod McPhee, and Tom James dropped in too. The research interests of Downey, Seager, and Slagle became the interests of us all; we became joint inquirers; we became stakeholders; we wished the inquiry well. Three dissertations emerged, a fine device for gathering data was perfected (Task of Public Opinionnaire), and a widely cited monograph, *The Tasks of Public Education* was written by Downey, Seager, and Slagle. And making it happen was Roald. The story could be repeated many times with other names, other research themes, in that and other settings.

Roald the Learner

Teaching and learning, learning and teaching, two sides of the same, each the face of the other. Great teachers are great learners and great learners are great teachers. Roald possesses an almost insatiable appetite for learning. He learns through research, reading, writing, and human association. He enters a new learning arena with gusto, acquires a solid knowledge base, and pursues inquiry with remarkable openness.

It would seem to be axiomatic that a scholar/teacher would also be a learner. It is not for some. But for Roald, his learning has been exacting. He has consistently searched for new understandings, for extending and modifying his own cognitive map, for locating new concepts, new ideas, new ways of viewing events. He has in the parlance of synecticists "made the ordinary strange and the strange ordinary."

Inquiry. Search. Data. Concepts. Frameworks. They are the tools of his learning trade. He has focused his inquiry on *the persistent* and *the emergent* problems of education. Examination of his professional searching reveals themes and foci. A *persistent theme* has been his inquiry into the problems and issues of educational governance in the United States. The most recent example is his extensive study of governance of education at the state level. Another persistent theme has been the relationship between schools and their settings. Still another theme is the constitutional and legal issues that free and constrain American education.

He has examined the dominant influences that mold and shape the institution of education, especially those that have national significance. He has been interested consistently in the professorship in educational administration. He has devoted time to the nature and theory of administration itself, especially its existence as a social process. He has involved and stimulated many of us toward that end. A strong collegial association was formed by Jacob Getzels and James Lipham in that regard. The three, under the leadership of Getzels, published *Educational Administration as a Social Process* in 1968. Roald has been persistent in his devotion to the improvement of practice through the application of knowledge—closing the gap between theory and practice. He has the utmost respect for the practitioner—the leader on the firing line. You find him consistently in their midst.

In regard to *the emergent,* he completed a penetrating analysis of performance contracting a few years ago, the best review in the literature of this short-lived venture in American education.

Many remark about his gift for synthesis. He possesses the ability to gather large amounts of data into his perceptual field, to apprehend salient themes, to give voice to them, and, consequently, to provide direction for us all. A remarkable attribute, indeed.

Earlier I used the word gusto to describe Roald's approach to learning. It applies equally well to his bowling style, to his work around the yard and in the flower beds, to his tenor singing voice, to his planning of professional events. Gusto!

Although Roald has left us at Ohio State (and earlier, the University of Chicago) he is not the kind of individual who retires. After a quarter at the University of California at Santa Barbara, he began teaching in British Columbia. And his chapters arrived on time for the revision of *Introduction to Educational Administration*.

Closing

Each of us has his or her own cherished view of the Campbells —Della and Roald. That perspective has been shaped by a blend of personal and professional associations spanning the years. Some have been privileged to know Roald, to have sampled the strength of his intelligence through his writings, to have witnessed and admired his will, to have learned from him through collegial and student relationships, *to have received his hand in friendship*. Others have been privileged to know Della, to have been lifted by her laughter, to have shared her interest in the arts and literature, to have listened with affection to her resolute beliefs about the importance of every human being, to have joined with her in her respect and admiration for educational institutions, *to have received her hand in friendship*. And others of us have been privileged to know them, to have engaged with them in thoughtful conversation, to have walked with them in their gardens, to have been guests in their home, *to have received their hands in friendship*.

In closing, and with a proper bow to poetic license, let me share these sentiments:

If I were Jonathan Seagull
And I could live my life
A second time, I would
Soar. I would repeat my
Apprenticeship, my training, my

Agony of success. But I would
Look for the rugged beauty of the
Wasatch, Idaho and Utah, especially
Where they join. Where the jewel,
Bear Lake nestles within
Its mounting, a symbol
Of unity geological. Where
The vastness of the West, sage and
Sand are punctuated by the grandeur
of granite. I would soar high
Above that majesty. I would plummet
Earthward, focusing on the expanses,
The hamlets, the villages, the farms
And I would see the people, their
Nobility, their freedom. And they
Would wave to me, earning the doff
Of my wingtip as I pull out and
Sail high and free. They with me,
Free.
And I would lift with the wind
To plummet again. My soul pitched
To the magnificence, to the search
For meaning, for understanding. That land,
A land, exacting and dry, that
Nourished a people. A people vibrant,
Tough and willed, people who turn their
Faces to the wind, people who challenge
Despair and ennoble the land with
Their love, people who caress the
Landscape and strengthen themselves,
And I would learn of their number,
Of those who spread their wings,
And live afar.
And I would smile, because I sensed why
They learned to fly. To leave their
Land, and share, their
Gentle tensil, the fight for right, the
Elegance of simplicity, the exquisite
Joy of truth at first

Recognition.
Climbing high and pulling hard,
I would take note of two of these people and their symbols,
Of their reverence and triumph, of their love and
Expression.
Two of that land and theirs, who
Ventured south and west,
From the jewel.
They paused and grew on the
San Andreas, returned to the
Wasatch, and left again.
For the east, and Ohio's
Land Grant. On to the
Midway at Kimbark and
Back to the Olentangy
Westward to the Wasatch.
And Home.

3. Educational Administration:
A Personal View of Its Future

ROALD F. CAMPBELL

If my contribution to the field has been in any way significant or unusual, I am inclined to ascribe most of it to the times and to the people with whom I have had the good fortune to be associated. First, as to the times. My own lifetime, 1905 to 1975, spans the period in which educational administration emerged as a field of study and of practice. I became a teacher of grades 7 and 8, and concurrently the principal, of a four-teacher elementary school in 1925. Most years since then I have been a teacher, an administrator, or a teacher of administration. Just being around for fifty years would seem to have much to do with this recognition.

As to people, let me mention a few. For some reason Della Jones found me to be a suitable partner, and we were married in 1931. In all of my nomadic wanderings—to Brigham Young University and Stanford for graduate study; to Moore and Preston, Idaho, where I served as a superintendent of schools; and to the University of Utah, Ohio State University, University of Chicago, and back to Ohio State where I served as a professor—she has been a constant companion. In our association she has been caring, generous, perceptive, constructively critical, but always supportive whether in disappointment or achievement.

I appear to have been most fortunate in the longevity genes I inherited and in the girl I encountered on a college campus many years ago. But fortuitous circumstances may be even more pronounced in the next events I shall mention. Asael Lambert, a professor at BYU whom I came to admire, went to Stanford for a doctoral program. His example, perhaps more than anything else, convinced me that I too might leave the protective environment of the Rocky Mountains and try my hand at Stanford where a whole new world was opened. Walter Cocking, father of the National Conference of Professors of Educational Administration, for some unexplainable reason invited me, when I was at the University of Utah, to be one of seventy professors from across the nation to attend the Endicott Meeting in 1947. Perhaps Cocking thought that at least one representative should come from that vast expanse between Iowa and California. I must have seemed no worse, nor better, than anyone else he might have chosen. Not long after the Endicott Meeting came the Kellogg program and the establishment of eight regional centers in the United States and one in Canada. Harold Fawcett, Dan Ikenberry, Ward Reeder, John Ramseyer, and others at Ohio State found me suitable for a position on that campus. That move had much to do with projecting my future professional activities, including the coeditorship of the *Administrative Behavior* book. Perhaps my biggest move came in going to the University of Chicago in 1957 as director of the Midwest Administration Center. Frank Chase was central to that appointment, and he extended professional and personal support to me for my thirteen years at Chicago. It is obvious that the circumstances of the time and assistance from a number of key people had much to do with the transition of a kid from a rural hamlet in southern Idaho, whose initial college work was done nearby at a struggling college, to metropolitan Chicago and the research atmosphere of one of the world's great universities.

The story does not end here, however. A number of my former colleagues and students including Vern Cunningham, Jack Corbally, Roy Larmee, and Fred Staub induced a tired dean to accept the Fawcett professorship and return to Ohio State University. For over four years I had the great luxury of doing just what I pleased. My sponsors may have understood even better than I that freedom to do as one pleases does not change the habits of a lifetime. Although I have not mentioned many other circumstances of time and people, including parents who were better educated than they were schooled and who extended great moral support even when they could provide little financial support, these reflections must stop. I hope, however, that they make the point that propitious circumstances and the influence of scores of people were the major factors in the development of my career.

Let me now shift from ruminations about my own life to some personal views about the field of educational administration, perhaps even hazarding a few guesses about the future of the field. I realize that prophesying is dangerous, perhaps even foolish, because several of the major papers of the seminar are directed to the future. Even so, here are a few thoughts.

To begin with, our field is not a basic discipline in the sense that economics or psychology are disciplines. Nor is the field a professional discipline, as Broudy[1] uses the term, in the way that pathology or endocrinology are professional disciplines. Educational administration is first of all a field of practice, and many of us here have also tried to make it a field of study. Any form given to an applied field of study makes a large number of people uncomfortable. Many practitioners prefer recipes or affirmation rather than having their behaviors or their organizations submitted to examination. Many academics have difficulty understanding a field that appears to borrow from psychology, sociology, economics, political science, and other disciplines.

But practitioners and scholars alike may not appreciate the demanding criteria imposed upon an applied field. These criteria have been well suggested by Argyris[2] in his discussion of behavioral science research. He contends that such research should be both applicable and applied. To be applicable, knowledge must be relevant, pertinent, and germane. But to be applied, that knowledge must actually be used. Thus, those of us in an applied field have the obligation to generate or organize knowledge that is applicable and to use or encourage the use of such knowledge. These two demands would seem to challenge the best that both practitioners and professors can bring to the task.

Even the acceptance of this challenge should not blind us to the forces that help shape the field. Elsewhere,[3] I have suggested that there have been at least three major approaches to educational administration during this century: scientific management, human

relations, and social science utilization. In each of these periods the
field has been shaped by many forces such as the socioeconomic impact of the larger society, managerial developments in industry,
movements in the larger field of education, and the influence of a
few key professors. Without attempting full documentation, I would
like to point out that from about 1910 to 1930 scientific management flourished largely because society had accepted efficiency as a
major goal, Frederick Taylor and others became famous conducting
time and motion studies in industry, the measurement movement
came to flower in education, and George Strayer at Teachers College
was willing to organize a graduate course around any operational task
in a school system. Callahan[4] has provided us with a rather good description of this period.

In time, this preoccupation with job analysis apparently helped
stimulate a counteremphasis. From about 1930 to 1950 human relations became the watchword. Again, note some of the external influences. In the larger society were economic collapse, depression, and
war. At least during the depression, and as expressed in New Deal
measures designed to combat it, we came to value people more than
business efficiency. Moreover, Elton Mayo had to conclude from his
Western Electric studies that productivity was affected more by
internal motivation of workers than by external working conditions.
While the progressive education movement had begun earlier, it was
during this period that we heard much about the "whole child."
Dewey had obviously eclipsed Strayer at Teachers College. Perhaps
even more indicative was the rash of books about human relations or
democracy in educational administration.[5]

Then came the 1950s and the 1960s. Here I must tread lightly
for many of the prime movers were at the conference on which this
book is based. In any case, science, even social science, had become
important to government and business. The National Science Foundation was actually established in 1950. Chester Barnard seemed to
be the harbinger of a new movement. Even as president of the New
Jersey Telephone Company he found time to deliver the Harvard lectures, which later became his book,[6] and to suggest the two dimensions of effectiveness and efficiency. He gave the latter term a new
twist but in any case one dimension was job oriented and the other
was person oriented. It was also in this period that the national curriculum programs were established, with generous federal support,

and each discipline set out to seek its own structure, if one may borrow from Bruner.[7] As for professors, I hesitate to name names, but groups of professors at a number of institutions became important contributors: the leadership studies at Ohio State University, the work of the Midwest Administration Center at Chicago, the Social Science Research Center at the University of Michigan, the Harvard Business School, the Center for Higher Education at Berkeley, to name but a few. I wish only to make the point that the applied field with which we are concerned has always been formed in large measure by a number of external forces. This will probably continue to be the case. I would thus like to name at least a few developments in the larger society and in the profession that may help shape administration in the years to come.

Those social and professional developments that seem particularly pertinent to me are:

1. Pluralistic cultural values will continue.

2. For some years the school will be a declining industry.

3. Teachers organizations will exercise a significant role in educational governance.

4. States will become more important in the governance of education.

5. The stress on educational outcomes will continue.

6. For a time at least, the deification of administrative practice, as contrasted to administrative thought, will persist.

Space permits only a brief exploration of each of these points. The pluralistic nature of our culture seems to need little explanation. Each of us has noted the demise of the "melting pot" notion. We no longer have a homogeneous set of values, perhaps we never did, but in any case the dominant group in our culture made it appear that the whole culture espoused a particular set of values. We now recognize more clearly than in the past that the values of groups vary in terms of many dimensions such as age, occupation, income, race, national origin, and religious affiliation. Our recognition of this diversity appears to be a step forward. But we have not yet learned how to cope with such differences.

Declining school enrollments, particularly at the elementary-school level, has become a trend in most school districts. For the country as a whole, enrollments in grades 1 to 8 in public and non-public schools over a three year period fell from about 34,000,000 to

31,000,000 pupils.[8] These figures do not reflect the more rapid decreases found in many of the larger cities, particularly in central parts of these cities. The most painful recognition of this condition to date has been the closing of schools in many of our school districts. Such action runs counter to the American ethic of bigger and better, and many citizens have not yet come to terms with such a notion.

The power of teachers organizations is well supported. In the twelve states included in the Governance Project[9] teachers' organizations were, with few exceptions, the most influential interest group in education, always exceeding the administrators' organization and in all but one or two cases exceeding the school board organization in their influence with the governor and the state legislature. Teachers had shown that they could elect legislators just as earlier in New York and elsewhere they had shown that they could elect local school board members. Teachers, moreover, aspire to even more influence, a clear example of which is the drive to establish a professional practice board in each state, with most members made up of teachers.

The advent of more state control in education stems from at least two developments. First, the President and the Congress, as explicitly expressed in the President's Commission report,[10] continue to question the role of the federal government in education and to push functions and financing back to the state level. Even in the Rodriguez case,[11] the U.S. Supreme Court took a similar position in declaring education not a "fundamental interest," albeit by a vote of five to four. The other move for state control derives largely from the ever-growing budget demands for schools and colleges. Education allocations are now a major part of the entire state budget, hence no governor or state legislator can ignore such demands. It is obvious that the quest for reform in state school finance, even to the extent of full state assumption, gives further impetus to state jurisdiction.

The disposition of educators to deal chiefly with processes is less and less acceptable to a skeptical public. The public wants more data on educational outcomes. This, in part, is what the whole accountability movement is about. Perhaps even more significant is the development and continuation of the National Assessment program. For the first time we have nationwide data on the achievement of students and adults in ten separate subject areas and by age, sex, race, region, type of community, and level of schooling of parents. These data raise questions that must now be addressed.

Finally, we are experiencing what Hofstadter[12] called anti-intellectualism. Many practitioners in administration see little value in administrative theory or few ways in which universities and scholars can be useful to them. Instead, great stress in some quarters is being placed on best practice as opposed to any analytic framework. It is unfortunate that "best" often seems to be expressed in terms of survival. If a superintendent of schools can survive all the forces that surround him—his board, the teachers' organization, the business community, the public media, the minority groups, the state legislature, and the Department of Health, Education, and Welfare—he is considered successful and his behavior is to be emulated. This position seems to be given concrete expression in the staffing of the workshops sponsored by the National Academy for School Administrators. Most of the instructors are superintendents. I do not deny that practitioners can contribute to the solution of the very complex situations in which most administrators now find themselves, nor do I suggest that useful analytic approaches can be offered by all professors. I only wish to point out that administrative survival is often valued more highly than administrative analysis. Appropriate analysis may suggest that some practices and even some practitioners should be eliminated. Moreover, if professors have no applicable knowledge or no way of making that knowledge usable to practitioners, perhaps they, too, should be eliminated.

I have suggested, by way of summary, that the profession will be confronted with cultural pluralism, a declining school population, teacher power, more state control, a concern about school outcomes, and a fair dose of anti-intellectualism. What does all of this mean for educational administration, particularly for professors of educational administration?

To begin with, as March[13] has pointed out in considerable detail, we are a declining industry. With the decline in school enrollments, the demand for school principals and school superintendents will decrease, a condition that has a number of implications for our field. Perhaps most significant is the fact that we are being confronted by a condition that has even larger social ramifications. Our longtime adherence to "the-bigger-the-better" philosophy has come to an end. We are being forced to think in qualitative rather than quantitative terms. I hope we can meet such a challenge.

We also appear to have a new cult of efficiency in education, as James[14] has noted. The push for systems analysis—whether for input-output analysis, planning-programming-budgeting systems, organizational development, or network analysis—seeks to make organizations more rational and efficient. This is not, however, merely a revival of Taylorism and scientific management. Systems concepts and practices are more sophisticated and complete than they were in the early part of this century. With respect to their application to educational organizations, there is the further impetus supplied by the accountability movement and technical advancement in skills of evaluation and measurement, particularly as developed by the National Assessment Program.

A revival and revision of scientific management does not, however, mean that the emphasis on human relations has no place. If we are, indeed, to cope with a pluralistic culture, we need to know more not less about people—their values and their motivations. If we are to deal productively with teachers' organizations, we need to recognize that much of that interchange should be influenced by what we know about individual needs, morale, and commitment to the goals of organizations. While we cannot reconstruct the industrial environment in which Mayo did his Western Electric experments, neither can we deny that workers are more productive when their motivation is internal rather than external.

We come then to the emphasis on social science in administration. Has that movement lost its relevance? Not in my view. We need to make more not less use of the concepts of social science, as we proceed to develop the field of educational administration. In the 1950s and 1960s we borrowed heavily from social psychology because we had a number of social psychologists who did seminal thinking in the field of educational administration. For a time it even became fashionable to speak of structure and consideration or, heaven help us, nomothetic and ideographic. It is unfortunate that many users of these terms did not fully comprehend what they were talking about. Moreover, some professors and some practitioners apparently assumed that a new vocabulary was a substitute for an analysis of the phenomena. The social-psychological models were useful in thinking about internal organizational behavior; they had less to say about external organizational behavior. We need insights not only from social psychology but also from political science and economics if we are to comprehend matters external to organizational well-being. Moreover, if we are to understand pluralistic cultures, the disciplines of history, philosophy, and anthropology would seem to provide useful insights.

But none of these disciplines come ready-made for educational administration. Their frameworks, concepts, and research findings become useful only when thoughtfully adapted to our own field. In addition, if applicability is a criterion, we will have to be concerned not only with valid knowledge but also with the processes of intervention and the uses of that knowledge. The adaptation and conveying of applicable knowledge will require the efforts of professors who pursue the challenge that exists in relating the concepts of one or more disciplines to organizational behavior in education. In order to deal with the many disciplines noted above, major universities will obviously require a faculty of diverse interests and strengths.

All of this may suggest that the field of educational administration can no longer chase a single rainbow. Achievement of tasks, though important, is not enough. Human relations, though crucial, are not all-encompassing. For educational administration to borrow from one or two disciplines, although suggestive, does not include all of the phenomena. The field is more sophisticated and complex. We may be on the threshold of developing some professional disciplines within the general field of educational administration. At present, some of these specializations may be described as organizational behavior, the economics of school finance, or the politics of education, but we may develop more appropriate designations as we continue to work with them. Perhaps even the current anti-intellectualism of practitioners will wane when professors demonstrate more clearly a competence in at least one aspect of the phenomena surrounding the establishment, operation, and evaluation of educational institutions.

Notes

1. Harry S. Broudy, *The Real World of the Public Schools* (New York: Harcourt Brace Jovanovich, 1972), 86.

2. Chris Argyris, *The Applicability of Organizational Sociology* (London: Cambridge University Press, 1972), 82.

3. Roald F. Campbell *et al.*, *Introduction to Educational Administration*, 4th ed. (Boston: Allyn and Bacon, 1971), ch. 4.

4. Raymond E. Callahan, *Education and the Cult of Efficiency* (Chicago: University of Chicago Press, 1962).

5. For instance, G. Robert Koopman *et al.*, *Democracy in School Administration* (New York: Appleton-Century-Crofts, 1943).

6. Chester I. Barnard, *The Functions of the Executive* (Cambridge, Mass.: Harvard University Press, 1938).

7. Jerome S. Bruner, *The Process of Education* (Cambridge, Mass.: Harvard University Press, 1960).

8. U.S. Bureau of Census, *Statistical Abstract of the U.S., 1974* (Washington, D.C.: U.S. Government Printing Office), 110.

9. Roald F. Campbell and Tim L. Mazzoni, Jr., *State Policy Making for the Public Schools* (Berkeley, Calif.: McCutchan, 1976), ch. 5.

10. President's Commission on School Finance, *Schools, People, Money: The Need for Educational Reform* (Washington, D.C.: The Commission, 1972).

11. *San Antonio Independent School District* v. *Rodriguez*, 411 U.S. 1 (1973).

12. Richard Hofstadter, *Anti-Intellectualism in American Life* (New York: Knopf, 1963).

13. James G. March, "Analytical Skills and University Training in Educational Administration," *Journal of Educational Administration* 12 (May 1974), 17-44.

14. H. Thomas James, *The New Cult of Efficiency and Education* (Pittsburgh: University of Pittsburgh Press, 1969).

Part II

THE CONTEXT OF
CONTEMPORARY PRACTICE

The case has been made that the period from 1954 to 1974 was a discrete and significant one in the field of educational administration. In the process of stock taking, an initial concern is that of assessing the context within which administrative inquiry and practice occurred.

Context may, of course, be viewed from various perspectives. Those who planned the conference upon which this book is based and the scholars who presented papers agreed that a useful format would be one that reviewed the historical developments, the philosophical and political issues of the period, the judicial interpretations and actions on key problems, and, finally, the responses and actions of educational institutions themselves.

David Tyack and Robert Cummings examine public school leadership before 1954. Two dominant interpretations of the profession of school administration are identified. An initial view is that of evolutionary professionalism characterized by the struggles of early superintendents to prove their competency and expand their authority as administrative scientists. The conventional alternative view is that best articulated by Raymond Callahan in his *Education and the Cult of Efficiency,* in which school administrators were portrayed as being particularly vulnerable to business influences of the day and thus capitulated to business applications of scientific management.

From their own analysis Tyack and Cummings posit a third interpretation. Rather than characterizing the period as one of professional control versus political control, they view it from the perspective of gradually shifting political and organizational contexts for educational decision making. As political linkages and institutional structure change, new promise is offered for today's roles of leadership in the schools.

A description of the most relevant issues that confronted administrators over the two-decade period is developed by Bernard C. Watson. His examination reveals two discrete but harmonic themes: America's confrontation with the reality of pluralism and the disenchantment with the conventional values and trappings of the American dream. Watson concludes that the most crucial challenge facing school administrators is that of reorienting their perspectives and behaviors to relate to the reality of pluralism and to the shift in values in order that the schools may achieve their lofty goals.

An obvious and important element in the context of educational administration from 1954 to 1974 is the role and influence of the courts in society in general and the schools in particular. Virginia Nordin sees the confrontation between the law and the schools as a systemic conflict. Two self-contained and operating systems dedicated to the preservation of a democratic society are locked in open conflict in matters of individual rights and institutional authority. The courts, in their concern for the constitutional rights of individuals, have limited the authority of schools and, in some cases of equity, have intervened in the administration of schools. To date, the courts are using the schools to reform society. Administrators, according to Nordin, are well advised not only to understand the decisions of the courts but also to learn how these decisions can best be put into practice.

Donald A. Erickson observes that the schools themselves during the twenty years after 1954 responded erratically to forces within and around themselves. The absence of directed and systematic change is attributed to the lack of validated causal models for guidance in policy in schools. This void in turn resulted from, at least partially, the empirical inquiry dominating research in educational administration, and school administrators who were insensitive to the demands and potentialities of policy-oriented research. Erickson concludes that evidence compiled from research over the era from 1954 to 1974 suggests there is a need for a profound paradigmatic shift in studies of educational administration. There is a potential for new work regarding causal models of school effects; the possibility remains, however, that this movement could abort like so many other "breakthroughs" of the past.

4. Leadership in American Public Schools Before 1954:
Historical Configurations and Conjectures

DAVID B. TYACK AND ROBERT CUMMINGS

Every person is a historian, using memory to make sense of the present. Members of occupations construct understanding of their roles from collective memories. Marines are exhorted to carry on the traditions of the Corps; Catholic bishops carry out their daily tasks in a Church shaped by almost twenty centuries of rich institutional memory; and school administrators, too, have a sense of the past which influences their beliefs and behavior, whether that past is consciously articulated and analyzed or simply taken for granted.[1]

What we propose is to analyze briefly two dominant interpretations of the profession of school administrator and then to suggest a third account as an alternative, which we believe to be more accurate. The first view we call evolutionary professionalism; we focus on Ellwood P. Cubberley as one of its chief spokesmen. The second is Raymond Callahan's interpretation of school administration as a capitulation to business efficiency, a history he has called "an American tragedy." In both of these interpretations training programs for school administrators play a highly significant role; for Cubberley it is positive and for Callahan negative. Our own interpretation suggests that formal instruction in administration has had relatively marginal impact on the development of the superintendency. Instead, we concentrate on the changing political and organizational context for decision making in public education and on the social characteristics of people who rose to the top of the system.

Evolutionary Professionalism: Cubberley

Until the publication of Callahan's influential study *Education and the Cult of Efficiency* in 1962, the dominant interpretation of the history of the superintendency was one based on evolutionary professionalism. One of the clearest expositions of this view was Cubberley's *Public School Administration* (1916). According to Cubberley, school administration came of age as a profession in the twentieth century. Prior to that time there were many gifted amateurs and pioneers who struggled to create the conditions under which expert executives might one day run schools according to an emerging science of education, free from the kinds of politics that had crippled superintendents in the past. Cubberley saw the city as the chief battleground for enlightened leadership and portrayed in vivid language the old-style ward boards and the large central school committees that perpetually meddled in the everyday administrative affairs of the schools, treating the early superintendents as clerks. He applauded the changes at the turn of the century which reduced the size of city school boards and introduced a new norm of board behavior, namely that the lay members should restrict themselves to "legislative functions" and turn the actual running of the schools over to experts whom they employed as superintendents. These new executives were to be trained in the science of education in university professional schools. As Cubberley saw it, the field of educational administration was rapidly changing from an intuitive trade or one based on common sense into a specialized profession, the principles and factual base of which were rapidly being discovered by the process of scientific inquiry.[2]

The story was thus a tale of optimistic evolution: freeing the schools from "politics" and turning them over to scientific experts. From training the new administrator would gain a clear sense of "what ought to be done, and why." Looking back in 1925, Cubberley saw the years since 1900 as "a great creative period" in which training in educational administration had changed from guesswork to statistically based scholarship. The handful of schools offering largely undergraduate instruction in education had grown into hundreds of colleges and universities providing increasingly specialized study, and the scanty literature on schooling had mushroomed. As universities generated new educational principles and practices, the school survey movement spread innovations in systems across the nation, for the survey became "an important form of educational engineering, by means of which the administrative problems of a school system may be determined" and the performance of schools measured against the new standards. Cubberley was confident that in time the superior efficiency of trained experts would persuade state legislatures to require specialized certification of administrators.[3]

Within the ranks of administrators and university professors of education there were but few dissenters to Cubberley's interpretation of evolutionary professionalism. In the 1930s Jesse Newlon and a few others criticized the narrowly focused training and conservative mentality of administrators. John Dewey attacked the superficial scientism of much educational research. Numerous critics decried lax admission standards and trivial courses in administrative programs. But few disagreed with Cubberley's basic assumptions or his faith in the power of professional training.[4]

The Cult of Efficiency: Callahan

This benign interpretation was abruptly challenged, however, by Callahan's important study *Education and the Cult of Efficiency.* The very changes that Cubberley had applauded as signs of scientific management in education—cost accounting, pupil accounting, expansion of vocational schooling, and the various statistical measures of "efficiency"—Callahan portrayed as "capitulation." "I was surprised," he wrote, "and then dismayed to learn how many decisions they made or were forced to make, not on educational grounds, but as a means of appeasing their critics in order to maintain their positions in the school." Cubberley's "great creative period" thus became "an American tragedy" to Callahan because schoolmen emulated business to save their own skins. Vulnerable to attack from the public and especially from their employers—the local school boards—superintendents adopted the lingo and practices of those with high status in the society—businessmen—and betrayed their earlier tradition of educational administrators as scholar-statesmen. A few sturdy souls held out against the cult of efficiency, as did Superintendent William Maxwell of New York, but most fell in step in the march led by university educationists like Cubberley of Stanford University, George Strayer of Teachers College at Columbia University, and Franklin Bobbitt of the University of Chicago.[5]

Callahan derived two implications for policy from this tragic story. The first was to make superintendents less vulnerable by making them less dependent on the local electorate and local board. The second implication was to improve the training of school administrators so that they would deserve this greater power. "To this end schools and colleges of education will have to raise their standards of admission and improve the quality of their programs of graduate studies for school administrators. To grant autonomy to poorly educated individuals would be dangerous; to produce highly qualified individuals and then place them in a weak, insecure, vulnerable position is senseless."[6]

In retrospect it is apparent that the similarities between the Cubberley and the Callahan interpretations are probably more important than the differences. Both deplore the vulnerability of the superintendent and want to take the schools out of "politics"; both want autonomy for the trained expert; both attribute great importance to training. They differ chiefly on their evaluation of "scientific management." We doubt very much that Cubberley would accept Callahan's account of why schoolmen welcomed it. Rather than viewing scientific management as "capitulation," Cubberley saw it as the logical corollary of the corporate model of school governance. Since school boards were to operate on the model of successful large businesses—a tenet widely accepted by schoolmen in the early twentieth century—the principles of scientific management would naturally apply to both kinds of organization. Most schoolmen were not frightened or coerced into this notion of efficiency; they welcomed it with genuine admiration, for it gave them useful tools and high status by analogy with business executives. It was the pioneer superintendents of the nineteenth century that Cubberley saw as especially "vulnerable"—men who worked "often against tremendous obstacles, often in conflict and contest to the end of their careers, and often by the sacrifice of much that men hold dear."[7]

An Alternate Interpretation

If one steps outside the Cubberley-Callahan framework of interpretation, it is possible to approach the issues from other directions.
Rather than treating "vulnerability" and "school politics" as a
"problem" to be overcome by more power to the professional, one
can assert that all forms of public control of schools are "political"
and examine just how the political and organizational context of
decision making changed over time. One can ask just how great an
impact specialized training in administration actually has had on the
beliefs and behavior of school superintendents. And one can ask if
the personal and social characteristics of administrators may not have
been at least as important in explaining their careers as other factors.
(It is interesting to note, for example, that when Callahan reports the
reasons superintendents themselves gave for their dismissals, they
cited such matters as marital status, religion, and age.) Recent research by scholars such as Richard Carlson casts severe doubt on the
importance of professional training and indicates the importance of
religion and other "nonprofessional" variables.[8]

As a result of pondering such questions and searching for evidence to answer them, we would like to suggest an alternate interpretation of the superintendency in the century before 1954. We have
called our essay "configurations and conjectures," because much of
what we have to say is still speculative, although based on the best
data we could find. We can summarize our central argument in three
statements:

1. There have been significant changes in the external governance and internal organization of school systems; these alterations
did much to transform the job of the school superintendent.

2. The personal and social characteristics of superintendents
have been relatively uniform, so far as we can determine, over the
last hundred years and have probably been crucial determinants in
the selection and performance of superintendents.

3. In comparison with political and organizational context and
general social characteristics, formal training in educational administration has had marginal impact on the character of educational leadership.

Political and Organizational Contexts for Decision Making

Over the last hundred years major shifts have occurred in the political linkages between school systems and communities and in the organizational character of schooling. There have been significant transformations in the ideology, structure, and behavior of school boards; in the functions of schooling; and in the size, functional specialization, and complexity of operation of school systems. These political and systemic changes have greatly modified the task of leadership in American education. The first phase we shall examine—roughly the period before 1890—was a time when the bureaucratic system-building of the superintendents tended to conflict with the pluralistic politics of active lay boards of education and when the goals of schooling were relatively simple and clear-cut. The second phase—beginning about 1890—saw the consolidation of rural and village schools and the centralization of control of urban schools, a great growth in specialization of function and hierarchy in school structures and more ambitious and ambiguous goals for formal education.[9]

During the nineteenth century, most school board members thought it their responsibility to administer the schools. Lay committeemen often examined pupils, inspected privies, chose textbooks and methods of teaching penmanship, certified and selected teachers, and decided on the myriad details of running the schools. As cities grew in size, central and ward boards of education generally shared these duties. Large central boards of education often subdivided themselves into many subcommittees to transact the complicated tasks of running what was becoming a large enterprise. When urban boards found that they had difficulty in keeping track of the daily operation of the schools, they commonly appointed a person called "superintendent" to classify children, observe teachers, and keep records on attendance, punctuality, and performance in examinations—work which lay board members thought themselves capable of doing if they only had the time. Often preempted from making key decisions—hiring staff, determining curriculum, planning policy—superintendents were primarily clerks or factotums. Schoolmen and lay reformers frequently complained about lay "meddling" and corruption, but the norm of active lay administration remained powerful.

During most of the nineteenth century the goals of schooling in cities were relatively straightforward: teaching the three R's and socializing children to patterns of behavior in school that it was thought would prepare them for participation in newly emerging urban institutions. A report in 1874 stated with blunt clarity a consensus of leading educators: "military precision is required in the maneuvering of classes. Great stress is laid upon (1) punctuality, (2) regularity, (3) attention, and (4) silence, as habits necessary through life for successful combination with one's fellowmen in an industrial and commercial civilization."[10] As late as 1900 the typical child remained in school only about five years. Schooling thus played a much smaller part in determining life chances than is the case in the twentieth century. If one judges by the school reports, the superintendents as well as the pupils were accountable for relatively precise tasks—making sure the students got to school on time, ensuring strict discipline and observance of school rules, keeping accurate records, and measuring academic output.

With the maturing and consolidation of corporate enterprise at the turn of the century came a concurrent shift in thinking about the proper roles of school boards and superintendents. In rural areas reformers sought to consolidate schools and put them under the direction of appointed expert county superintendents. An alliance of members of the business and professional elites in the cities, linked together with university leaders, wished to substitute a fully developed corporate model of school administration for haphazard decision making by lay board members and their superintendent-agents. This model was simple in its basic outline, though seldom realized in all its purity. The city board was to be small rather than large, serving the whole city rather than wards, composed of "nonpolitical," "successful" men (women were thought inferior as board members), operating in a committee of the whole rather than in a subcommittee, transacting its business expeditiously and in gentlemanly fashion, with no speeches to the galleries. Such a plan of decision making required that most decisions be delegated to the superintendent, who was to be given substantial power to take the initiative and establish agendas as chief executive. The political coalition for charter revision closely resembled the elites which more generally dominated urban "progressivism." As Samuel Hays has noted, efficiency and expertise were slogans characteristic of political reform in many domains during the early twentieth century.

As school systems grew in size and complexity (secondary education mushroomed in the twentieth century) educational functions grew more complex and vague. Students stayed in school longer, and schooling became more crucial in determining one's career in a society increasingly attuned to educational credentials. The craze for "social efficiency" among reformers vastly broadened the purposes of schooling. By 1918, for example, in the influential statement of the "Cardinal Principles of Secondary Education," educators declared that schools should be responsible for developing nothing less than "1. Health. 2. Command of fundamental processes. 3. Worthy home membership. 4. Vocation. 5. Citizenship. 6. Worthy use of leisure. 7. Ethical character."[11] Diffuse and noble goals had been voiced since the days of Horace Mann (who skillfully sold the common school as panacea), but now schoolmen tried to institutionalize manifold purposes.

One result of the expanded functions of the school was specialization, a differentiation of the older relatively uniform system into separate divisions and roles. In the cities there now appeared academic tracks and specialized programs, compulsory attendance officers and experts in child accounting, medical examiners and school health programs, and intelligence testing experts and vocational counselors to sort children for tracks in school and occupations in later life.

As new layers of bureaucracy developed and new departments proliferated in the big systems, the span of control grew too large for one superintendent to master. Accordingly, much day-by-day decision making gravitated to middle levels of administration. In survey after survey superintendents reported that they and their staff of experts were gaining greater initiative vis-à-vis the school board in most key domains. The days of the large lay board, "meddling" in administrative detail, with only one agent between them and the building principals, had given way to a new corporate system, at least in the larger cities. So set became the new norms of nonparticipation in administration by school boards that superintendents after 1920 would decry as illegitimate the kinds of lay influences regarded as customary a generation earlier.

As the political and organizational contexts for decision making gradually shifted over time, superintendents' conceptions of their roles subtly changed, though continuities can be found in each

period. Many of the common school pioneers of the 1840s and
1850s had taken an evangelical view of their task: like Mann, they
tried to arouse the conscience of their fellow citizens, to persuade
them to translate their generalized faith in education into an abiding
support of the public school. It is no coincidence that many of the
leaders in the movement, especially in the West and South, were
Protestant ministers.[12] After 1900, however, as the corporate model
of school decision making took hold, the business executive became
the favored role-conception of superintendents. They talked of differentiation of plant, cost accounting, personnel management, and
"stockholders" (citizens). Such palaver probably appealed to the
businessmen who predominated on boards of education. But despite
the attempt to develop indices of "efficiency," the goals of education were too fuzzy for precise accounting of administrative success,
and the analogies to business executives were imperfect at best. Even
in the big cities a number of superintendents still maintained an
interest in improving curriculum and in classroom instruction. In
small cities and towns, as will be seen, superintendents often continued to supervise teachers and to perform quasi-clerical tasks.[13]

No single role-conception such as that of the business executive
could encompass the manifold duties of school leaders. As we shall
see in examining normative discussions of professional training of administrators, role conflict and role ambiguity pervaded the lives of
superintendents. Was the superintendent to be a "democratic leader"
and, if so, *how* in a hierarchical school system that was often, as
Willard Waller said, a "despotism in a state of perilous equilibrium"?
If the superintendent was to be an educational expert, how was he to
be judged a success or failure? (It was easier to judge the success of a
surgeon by the recovery of his patients, a businessman by the profit
he made, or a lawyer by the cases he won for his clients.) Even
though superintendents often had to be skillful political negotiators
both within and without the school system, one role-conception
assiduously denied was that of politician. As Wallace Sayre notes, the
notion of the "nonpolitical" nature of the common school was too
serviceable a myth to endanger. A study of the social characteristics
and career lines of superintendents will help to explain how they
reacted to ambiguity of roles and to the changing contexts of decision making.[14]

Social Characteristics and Career Lines of Superintendents

Unlike the political and organizational context for decision making in schools, which changed markedly during the last one hundred years, the social characteristics of superintendents appear to have remained quite constant, at least in this century. Our data on superintendents in 1899, the surveys of superintendents made by the American Association of School Administrators, and Frederick Bair's detailed study of approximately 850 superintendents in 1934 together reveal a consistent (although still quite sketchy and incomplete) portrait of the typical head administrator in school districts: a white male in his mid-forties from a rural background who rose from the ranks in a lifelong career devoted to schools. In Bair's sample almost all were native born (98.5 percent), 90 percent were of Anglo-Saxon background (one-half had ancestors who immigrated before 1800). Ninety percent of them were church members, almost all Protestant (of 823 who answered this question only six had Roman Catholic fathers, and none were Jewish). They were also disproportionately Republican, then as now, and men of moderate to conservative social philosophy.[15]

The portrait is an interesting one. Almost all superintendents were male in a profession that was 85 percent female in 1920. Almost all were native born, mostly Anglo-Saxon, when the United States was a nation of immigrants from dozens of lands (in 1910, 40 percent of the citizens were first or second-generation immigrants). They were overwhelmingly Protestant in a religiously pluralistic nation. And most (even a large percentage of those who superintended large city schools) were raised in rural areas at a time when the country was undergoing rapid urbanization. They were middle-aged career educators in a sea of youngsters and mostly young teachers.[16]

This is an interesting portrait, but probably not a surprising one. In most respects superintendents matched leaders in other occupations, though they probably came from lower social strata (Bair found that two-thirds of the parents of the superintendents he studied had gone no further than elementary school, and half of the fathers were farmers).[17] Superintendents had to enter their careers through the relatively low-status occupation of teacher, unlike many other occupations where one might enter at a higher level.[18] Superintendents also tended to match the characteristics of the school boards that hired them: mostly male Protestants in the higher reaches of the occupational structure.[19] Several studies have shown that sex, race, religion, marital status, and social philosophy are important variables in board selection of school leaders. The very ambiguity and diffuseness of the goals of schooling, and the difficulty of measuring "success," have probably reinforced the tendency to give weight to diffuse characteristics of high status like "proper" ethnicity, maleness, or mature age. Even height was important: like most other leaders, superintendents were taller than average. In addition, for a superintendent to be a member of a respectable church and to have a stable marriage might have been comforting signs of reputability if not guarantees of respectability. Like the banker's conservative dress, such social characteristics were an outward measure of safe leadership in a risky enterprise. In short, the consistency of social attributes of superintendents has not been a historical accident; it has been important to be the right man at the right place at the right time with the right attributes. The importance of ascribed characteristics such as race or sex is not the invention of advocates of affirmative action.[20]

What effects did the social characteristics of superintendents have in their careers, in their perspectives and performance? Here one enters an especially speculative realm, and we shall suggest some possible consequences of maleness, of rural and native born origins, and of lifelong socialization in one institution, the public school.

Maleness, like whiteness, was almost everywhere essential to selection as superintendent. A few women might gain low status jobs as county superintendents, driving their Model T's along dusty roads from one rural school to another, but in practically every well paid superintendency men held sway. Hierarchy within the school relied heavily on the dominance of men in the outside society: the male boss symbolized authority. And to the degree that people advanced within the school system through sponsorship of aspiring teachers by administrators above them, the bond of gender in an "old boy" network probably linked the persistent males in a feminized occupation (it is significant that Phi Delta Kappa was exclusively male).[21]

It was not only within the schools, however, that maleness was an asset. The schoolboards were mostly male, and many of the influential community organizations to which superintendents belonged were frequently closed to women. The superintendent of the Madison, Wisconsin, schools wrote that the administrator "who devotes some time to the Rotary Club, the Kiwanis Club, and other organizations for men will find the professional incrustation within which he has insulated himself violently perforated." He told of a western superintendent who admired the "empire builders" in the local Chamber of Commerce and who "hunted with them, fished with them, and became their friend and companion. When the time came to direct the schools into some new and untried enterprise, these men threw their mighty enthusiasm into the project not because they were advocates of the educational principle upon which the experiment was based, but because they wanted their friend to win."[22]

It is likely that the rural upbringing of superintendents also deeply influenced their conception of their task. In 1933 over one-third of superintendents in cities with more than 100,000 population graduated from high schools in communities smaller than 2500; 68 percent of all superintendents that year had grown up in communities with less than 5000 people. Scholars have noted how often educational leaders have glorified a rural upbringing and seen the city chiefly as a source of social problems. It is likely that superintendents raised in rural areas would have gained little firsthand knowledge of the city child's life out of school and would have seen the role of the school, as did Cubberley and many other trainers of administrators, as a countervailing influence. Overwhelmingly native born, Anglo-Saxon, Protestant, raised in the comfortable provincialism of the small town, the school administrator was likely to regard his own social values and patterns of belief and action as self-evidently correct. Cultural differences, where they existed, were to be eradicated by campaigns of "Americanization." Persistence in deviant ways was apt to be taken as evidence of depravity or deprivation. And superintendents who had seen the dream of success realized in their own careers (many of them had read success and hero stories as children, Bair reports) were likely to see America as a land of opportunity for all but the "ne'er-do-wells." In short, their own lives had taught them to be true believers.[23]

Furthermore, superintendents were among the very few leaders who had essentially spent their entire lives under the socializing influences of the same institution (a parallel might be Roman Catholic bishops trained in parochial schools and sent at an early age to the seminary). Constant familiarity may not breed contempt but it may tend to dampen wonder and experiment. Many observers have commented on the very long time it takes for major innovations to be put into wide practice. It is possible that the lifelong exposure to conventional wisdom and processes by those at the top of the system may have something to do with this institutional conservatism; at least some have alleged that this is true of American bishops. Perhaps some strong intervention in the lives of schoolmen might have redirected their course as leaders. Was graduate training such an intervention?[24]

Impact of Professional Training on Superintendents

It is no small task to assess the impact of graduate training on the superintendency. From one point of view, the history of the graduate training of superintendents is encouraging, as indicated later in the statistics cited on degrees. In such programs administrators were exposed to many new standardized techniques of child accounting, sanitation, budgeting, public relations, curriculum development, and the design and maintenance of buildings. Professors sometimes played important roles as sponsors in placing their graduates in successive superintendencies. But it is easy to attribute too much importance to training in comparison with the cumulative effect of the influences thus far described.

Under certain conditions specialized training might have considerable impact on the subsequent careers of graduates. One way is the transmission of particular skills or knowledge clearly needed in a distinct occupation—for example, in electrical engineering. Another way professional programs have an effect is to ration entry into an occupation as medical schools do with their restrictive admission and limited output. A third model of influence might be to provide intense socialization to the distinct norms of a group—for example, at West Point or a Jesuit seminary.[25]

Graduate training in educational administration fits none of these models very well. There is intense argument and considerable diversity in practice concerning the skills or knowledge necessary for superintendents.[26] Unlike medical schools, programs in educational administration have generally not been selective in admission nor has certification seriously narrowed the pool of candidates eligible for positions, at least until the last generation. Furthermore, the way in which most administrators have pursued their professional training—sporadically, in summer or evening courses over a number of years—makes it unlikely that graduate work alone provided the kind of intense socialization needed to produce major changes in occupational behavior. On the contrary, for most administrators graduate training was a low-risk, low-gain enterprise that probably reinforced their pre-existing social characteristics and occupational socialization.

The general educational trend for superintendents has been one of rapidly rising attainment, though the relative increase in schooling has been less than in the case of teachers. The percentages of superintendents with no college degree fell from 13 percent in 1923 to 4 percent in 1933 to .2 percent in 1952, while comparable figures for those with master's degrees rose from 32 percent in 1923 to 57 percent in 1933 to 79 percent in 1952. The number with doctorates remained stable at 3 percent from 1923 to 1933 but increased sharply to 15 percent in 1952.[27] Whereas in 1905 only one state had special credential requirements for superintendents, by 1939 twenty-five states had some kind of administrative or supervisory certificate.[28]

Superintendents typically earned their degrees by taking courses while they were employed in the schools. A comprehensive survey of superintendents in 1923 showed that only one-quarter had pursued graduate study fulltime for a year or more.[29] When Harold Hand studied the professional lives of superintendents in eight states at the end of the 1920s, he found that 80 percent did not earn a B.A. until they had taught for five or more years, began their master's degree at age twenty-nine, and completed it at age thirty-four or thirty-five. Aspiring teachers or principals could prepare for the possibility of a higher position without losing a paycheck.[30] In 1931 a leading professor of educational administration concluded that since school boards generally hired superintendents the way they had in the past—before specialized training—there was "little hope for the immediate success of any educational plan that might contemplate educating young men and women for superintendencies in the belief that persons so educated may hope for an immediate appointment to an executive position of any consequence."[31] For the average superintendent advanced training was not a narrow and essential passageway into high status, as it was for a physician. Rather it was a minor detour that might give him a shortcut on the main highway of promotion through experience and through being at the right place at the right time with the right friends and the right social attributes.

Numerous experts called for more rigorous selection of students in administrative training programs. In 1941, after the widely publicized oversupply of educators during the great depression, two observers visited training programs and expressed their dismay at the "indifference which national organizations of school administrators on the one hand, and professional schools offering training programs on the other hand, have displayed in the establishment of entrance requirements." In most schools all that was required, they said, was a B.A. and cash to pay tuition.[32] As Richard Carlson has noted, standards in admissions continued to be a serious problem thirty years later.[33]

Testimony and evidence on the quality of training of educational administrators was often depressing. In 1921 a study of the leading graduate departments of education reported that 75 percent had fewer than ten faculty members, and that in half of these schools fewer than 50 percent of the professors had doctorates. Many did not even have master's degrees. Their normal teaching load exceeded twelve hours per week. And these programs were the cream of the crop.[34] In 1931 Fred Engelhardt lamented that almost every college or university that trained teachers felt itself capable of preparing superintendents of schools.[35]

From 1910 through 1954 professors of educational administration vigorously debated about what sort of curriculum gave the best training for the superintendency. Arguments basically centered around preparing them pragmatically for the job as it was or giving them a broad perspective that would help them to adapt the schools to changing circumstances. To one familiar with post-1954 debates, discussions of the importance of theory and social sciences and the need for internships have a familiar ring.[36] And so it goes.

Following Franklin Bobbitt's theory of curriculum construction some experts contended that professors should scientifically study what superintendents actually do—through analyses of their duties and how they spend their time—and then prepare them for these tasks. Fred Ayer, professor at the University of Texas, represented this view: "It seems obvious that vocational training should be closely related to the actual duties which workers are called upon to perform." He studied what superintendents reported they actually did in 1926-1927 (and since the respondents were mostly graduate students in prestigious universities, it seems likely that their positions were not much below average, though they were often in small school systems). The results were enlightening. In addition to the expected duties of attending board meetings, making reports, and supervising teachers, 80 percent of the superintendents reported that they went to the post office daily; and each week half of them operated the mimeograph machine, 18 percent wrote "literary gems on the blackboard," 93 percent inspected toilets, and 93 percent inspected the janitor's work. Most of them said that they were interested in curriculum, but this often meant talking with salesmen and selecting textbooks rather than rethinking the course of study. When asked what they did for their own professional improvement, 73 percent said that they read religious literature weekly. All in all, superintendents were overwhelmed with the tasks of keeping the buildings clean and warm, child accounting, business management, and keeping the board and parents happy. It was an anxious vocation and a busy one. To those professors who believed that training programs should prepare men for specific tasks, such studies as Ayer's legitimized units or courses in budgeting, heating and ventilating, managing janitorial services and sanitation, writing publicity releases, and record keeping.[37]

Other professors argued that "administrivia" could be learned on the job and claimed that superintendents needed, above all, to be educational and community leaders, functions that required a background in educational philosophy, curriculum theory, social sciences, and educational policy. The most articulate advocate of this broad based training was Jesse Newlon, professor at Teachers College. His book *Educational Administration as Social Policy* was a sustained attack on the drab scientism and conservative social theory he found endemic in the training of administrators. Through analysis of the contents of textbooks and courses in educational administration he concluded that most graduate instruction concentrated on the *how* of such subjects as budgeting, plant design and maintenance, personnel management, and public relations. It virtually ignored "critical examination of educational and social implications of the structure and procedures discussed." He found in works on administration an *implicit* theory of society: "It is a confused mixture of the prevailing laissez-faire social and economic philosophy and the philosophy of business efficiency, with a vague democracy and Christian idealism."[38]

In Newlon's analysis of the training of educational administrators, as well as in observations by scholars like Ralph Tyler, there emerges a criticism of educational administration that strongly resembles John Dewey's attack on inbred scientism in education. Much of the research in educational administration became isolated from scholarship in other fields and sought quantification of the obvious, in Dewey's words, as if statistics "were a magical guarantee of a scientific product."[39] This raw empiricism lacked the power of unifying interpretive theories. "Theory," said Tyler in 1946, "seeks to organize, to interpret, and to give direction to the practice of school administration."[40]

Because of intellectual disarray, low admission standards, sporadic enrollment in courses, and the marginal importance of professional training to most school boards, specialized training in administration probably had little impact on the careers of most superintendents. It is likely, however, that under certain circumstances graduate study did have a significant influence in the lives of some administrators. Even critics like Newlon did concede that graduate study sometimes did help to spread new standardized methods of child accounting, budgeting, sanitation, and "in general, a much more orderly and efficient management of schools." In addition, it appears that some professors of educational administration developed networks of influence in their regions—or even nationally, as in the case of George Strayer at Teachers College—in which they could sponsor the mobility of favored graduates. Such influence, of course, required school boards to seek and honor the advice of the "barons." In cities where the "corporate model" of school governance was strong—in other words, where "successful men" on school boards turned the running of the schools over largely to the superintendents —graduates of university programs sometimes had an opportunity to put into practice new ideas they had learned in professional training. School surveys linked professors and graduates and often served as vehicles of reform, for the survey design was like a template of approved education, a set of standards imposed from the top down. Thus under special conditions professional training may have made an important difference in superintendents' careers and performance on the job.[41]

Epilogue

We have briefly analyzed two dominant interpretations of the history of leadership in American schools and proposed an alternate way to understand this history. We doubt that professional training has had quite the influence that pioneers like Cubberley hoped or that critics like Callahan feared. We see the political problems of American schools as entailing more complex issues than the "vulnerability" of the educational expert. We also believe that advocates of affirmative action are correct when they point out the continuing and historic fact that status characteristics like sex and race (and class and religion, for that matter) have been important in determining who became superintendents.

The experience of the last decade has no doubt shaped our interpretation. In recent years the older consensus on the "nonpolitical" model of education has shattered. Women and minorities have made people newly aware of conscious or unconscious bias in the rationing of privileged positions in our society. And lately there have been numerous studies questioning the impact of many forms of schooling.

We believe it is important to have a realistic understanding of possible reform of educational leadership through improved training. We do not mean to suggest, however, that better programs in educational administration would not make a difference. First, graduate schools can actively recruit different kinds of people whose varied backgrounds will help them to adapt schools to the learning styles of our pluralistic population; there is, in our view, no one best system of education nor one best kind of superintendent. Second, and related to the first point, graduate schools can use their power of accrediting and sponsoring students to provide occupational mobility for people traditionally excluded from leadership. Third, training programs can give potential leaders an accurate knowledge of the nature of power in our society, examining "serviceable myths" and painful dilemmas alike, and can help educators to discover the limited but important ways in which schools can promote social justice. These are not heroic aspirations, but accomplishing these tasks well would ultimately make a difference in American education.

Notes

1. Carl L. Becker, *Everyman His Own Historian: Essays on History and Politics* (New York: F. S. Crofts, 1935).

2. Ellwood P. Cubberley, *Public School Administration: A Statement of the Fundamental Principles Underlying the Organization and Administration of Public Education* (Boston: Houghton Mifflin, 1916), 83-84.

3. *Ibid.*, vi, 130; Ellwood P. Cubberley, "Public School Administration," in I. L. Kandel (ed.), *Twenty-Five Years of American Education: Collected Essays* (New York: Macmillan, 1924), 177-195.

4. Jesse H. Newlon, *Educational Administration as Social Policy* (New York: Scribner's, 1934); John Dewey, *The Sources of a Science of Education* (New York: Liveright, 1929).

5. Raymond E. Callahan, *Education and the Cult of Efficiency* (Chicago: University of Chicago Press, 1962), "Preface," 7-8.

6. *Ibid.*, "Preface."

7. Cubberley, *Public School Administration*, 130; Aaron Gove, "The Trail of the City Superintendent," *NEA Addresses and Proceedings*, Thirty-ninth Annual Meeting, Charleston, S.C., 1900, 214-222.

8. Callahan, *Education and Cult*, 207; Richard O. Carlson, *School Superintendents: Careers and Performance* (Columbus, Ohio: Merrill, 1972), ch. ii.

9. Rather than providing extensive documentation for this section we refer the reader to the notes for chapters ii-iv in David B. Tyack, *The One Best System: A History of American Urban Education* (Cambridge, Mass.: Harvard University Press, 1974).

10. Duane Doty and William T. Harris, *A Statement of the Theory of Education in the United States as Approved by Many Leading Educators* (Washington, D.C.: U.S. Government Printing Office, 1874), 14.

11. Commission on the Reorganization of Secondary Education, *Cardinal Principles of Secondary Education* (Washington, D.C.: U.S. Government Printing Office, 1918), 10-11.

12. David B. Tyack, "The Kingdom of God and the Common School: Protestant Ministers and the Educational Awakening in the West," *Harvard Educational Review*, 36 (Fall 1966), 447-469.

13. Larry Cuban, "School Chiefs under Fire: A Study of Three Big-City Superintendents under Outside Pressure," unpublished Ph.D. dissertation, Stanford University, 1974, ch. v.

14. Raymond E. Callahan, *The Superintendent of Schools: An Historical Analysis* (Bethesda, Md.: ERIC Document Reproduction Service, 1967); Wallace S. Sayre, "Additional Observations on the Study of Administration: A Reply to 'Ferment in the Study of Organization,'" *Teachers College Record*, 60 (Oct. 1958), 73-76.

15. David B. Tyack and Robert Cummings, "The American Urban School Superintendent in 1899: Some Statistical Data," compiled from information contained in the *Journal of Education*, 50 (Dec. 7, 1899), 374-380; NEA, Department of Superintendence, *The Status of the Superintendent* (First Year-

book; Washington, D.C.: NEA, 1923); NEA, Department of Superintendence, *Educational Leadership* (Eleventh Yearbook; Washington, D.C.: NEA, 1933); American Association of School Administrators, *The American School Superintendency* (Thirtieth Yearbook; Washington, D.C.: AASA, 1952); Frederick Haigh Bair, *The Social Understandings of the Superintendent of Schools* (New York: Teachers College, Columbia University, 1934); Newlon, Educational Administration, 128-130; Carlson, *School Superintendents*, 34-35. Most of these surveys contain errors in sampling, bias in self-reports, and other defects, but they still offer largely consistent and useful data.

16. E. P. Hutchinson, *Immigrants and Their Children, 1850-1950* (New York: Wiley, 1956), 3; Sol Cohen, "The Industrial Education Movement, 1906-17," *American Quarterly*, 20 (Spring 1968), 95-110; Tyack, *One Best System*, 59-65, 255-268.

17. Bair, *Social Understandings of Superintendent*, ch. vii; Newlon, *Educational Administration*, ch. vii.

18. Bair, *Social Understandings of Superintendent*, ch. vii; Carlson, *School Superintendents*, 20-22.

19. Carlson, *School Superintendents*, 29-34; George S. Counts, *The Social Composition of Boards of Education* (Chicago: University of Chicago Press, 1927).

20. Carlson, *School Superintendents*, 32. On some effects of ambiguity of goals, see Michael D. Cohen and James March, *Leadership and Ambiguity: The American College President* (New York: McGraw-Hill, 1974).

21. Suzanne Estler, "Women as Leaders in Public Education," unpublished paper in *Studies in Educational Leadership*, Stanford University, School of Education, 1974; Grace C. Strachan, *Equal Pay for Equal Work: The Story of the Struggle for Justice Being Made by the Women Teachers of the City of New York* (New York: B. F. Buck, 1910).

22. Charles S. Meek, "How Shall the Superintendent Spend His Time?" *NEA Addresses and Proceedings*, Fifty-ninth Annual Meeting, Des Moines, Iowa, 1921, 730-731; "How Do Women Rate?" *Nation's Schools*, 37 (March 1946), 45.

23. Bair, *Social Understandings of Superintendent*, ch. vii; Dana F. White, "Education in the Turn-of-the-Century School," *Urban Education*, 1 (Spring 1969), 169-182; Marvin Lazerson, *Origins of the Urban School: Public Education in Massachusetts, 1870-1915* (Cambridge, Mass.: Harvard University Press, 1971), ch. i.

24. Cuban, "School Chiefs under Fire," ch. v.

25. For recent studies of the impact of training, see the chapter by Edwin Bridges in this volume.

26. Cubberley, "Public School Administration"; Newlon, *Educational Administration*.

27. Tyack and Cummings, "American Urban School Superintendent in 1899"; NEA, Department of Superintendence, *Educational Leadership*, 108; AASA, *American School Superintendency*, 447.

28. John Lund, *Education of School Administrators* (U.S. Office of

Education, Bulletin No. 6, 1941; Washington, D.C.: U.S. Government Printing Office, 1942), 85; AASA, *Standards for Superintendents of Schools: Preliminary Report of the Committee on Certification of Superintendents of Schools* (Washington, D.C.: AASA, 1939).

29. NEA, Department of Superintendence, *Status of Superintendent*, 25, 29.

30. Fred Engelhardt, "The Professional Education Program for School Executives," *American School Board Journal*, 83 (November 1931), 49-51.

31. *Ibid.*, 51.

32. Lund, *Education of School Administrators*, 22.

33. Carlson, *School Superintendents*, 23-25.

34. Leonard V. Koos, *Standards in Graduate Work in Education* (U.S. Bureau of Education, Bulletin No. 38, 1921; Washington, D.C.: U.S. Government Printing Office, 1922), 17-18.

35. Engelhardt, "Professional Education Program," 51.

36. Cubberley, "Public School Administration"; Frank E. Spaulding, *et al.*, *The Aims, Scope, and Methods of a University Course in Public School Administration* (Iowa City: National Society of College Teachers of Education, 1910); George D. Strayer, "Job Analysis and the Problem Attack in the Training of Superintendents of Schools," in National Society of College Teachers of Education, *Studies in Education* (Fifteenth Yearbook; Chicago: University of Chicago Press, 1927), 146-154; Newlon, *Educational Administration*; Asael B. Murphy, "Training the City Superintendent," *School Executives Magazine*, 51 (March 1932), 291-293.

37. Fred C. Ayer, "The Duties of Public-School Administrators," *American School Board Journal*, 78 (Feb. 1929), 39; 78 (Apr. 1929), 39; 78 (May 1929), 52-53; 79 (Oct. 1929), 33-34, 136; 78 (June 1929), 60.

38. Newlon, *Educational Administration*, 93.

39. Dewey, *Sources of a Science of Education*, 50.

40. Ralph W. Tyler, "The Role of University Departments of Education in the Preparation of School Administrators," in William C. Reavis (ed.), *Educational Administration: A Survey of Progress, Problems, and Needs* (Chicago: University of Chicago Press, 1946), 36, 31-45.

41. Newlon, *Educational Administration*, 87-88; Hollis L. Caswell, *City School Surveys: An Interpretation and Appraisal* (New York: Teachers College, Columbia University, 1929); Robert L. Rose, "Career Sponsorship in the School Superintendency," Ph.D. dissertation, University of Oregon, 1969.

5. Issues Confronting Educational Administrators, 1954-1974

BERNARD C. WATSON

The Reality of Pluralism

During the twenty-year period from 1954 to 1974 this nation was confronted with a number of critical issues: war, civil rights activity, equal opportunity, civil disorders, and a growing mistrust of public institutions. An examination of the critical issues reveals two primary themes. The first is characterized by America's confrontation with the reality of pluralism, a confrontation brought on by the demise of the myth of the "melting pot" and a consequent quickening of the struggle for equality waged by various ethnic and minority groups. The second theme is characterized by a crisis in meaning precipitated by a growing disillusionment regarding many aspects of American society and the consequent challenges to societal values and institutions.

The themes are obviously interrelated, each helping to define and dramatize the many aspects of the other. Equality—of rights and opportunities—is a basic tenet of the American system and of the American dream, which promises upward social and economic mobility for those who achieve. But the realities in America have not always been consistent with the promises. While the have-not minorities protested both the arbitrary restrictions on their mobility and the circumstantial constraints that developed as a consequence of generations of discrimination and deprivation, the "haves" of the majority were faced with the realization that the American dream itself was more a nightmare to many Americans.

These two decades saw many of the traditional assumptions concerning the integration of racial and ethnic groups into American society severely challenged and openly refuted. The expectation that ethnic and racial groups would be assimilated or Americanized socially, economically, politically, and culturally into the mainstream with a consequent lessening or elimination of ethnic and racial identities took a thorough and probably richly deserved beating. The civil rights movement led by blacks and other minorities was extended by the struggle for rights and recognition waged by women and students. These struggles forced at best a second look at the "melting pot" theory and at worst forced many to discard it as Panglossian and counterproductive. Rather than producing a homogenization or dilution of the various ethnic and racial identities, the twenty-year period gave rise to a resurgence of support and respect for the value and uniqueness of these identities. Instead of an evolutionary process of assimilation, there were conflict and confrontation, both physical and ideological. It became obvious to all that America was not color blind; nor was it blind to ethnic differences, age differences, or sex differences. And although the civil rights movement often focused on specific rights (such as voting and public accommodations), the fundamental thrust was to force American society to acknowledge in a new way the pluralistic nature of its population and to challenge the nation to eliminate policies, practices, misconceptions, and stereotypes that enabled these differences to be used as the basis for inequality and the denial of fundamental rights. For many Americans, the primary issue of the two decades centered around the extent to which the nation would acknowledge and accommodate its pluralism.

Perhaps the most significant factor in the broadening of the issue of equality was America's rediscovery of poverty, a rediscovery forced on the American conscience by the 1963 March on Washington led by Martin Luther King, the urban riots, and Michael Harrington's book, *The Other America*. Although for many the American dream had become the American reality of affluence, or at least material comfort, for others there were poverty and bare subsistence.

In 1960, 9,000,000 families and 9,000,000 unrelated individuals lived below the poverty level as defined by the U.S. Department of Labor.[1] But, in the 1960s, unlike the 1930s, the problems of poverty and unemployment were not so much problems of the masses but of particular classes of people—most notably blacks (41 percent of whom lived below the poverty line in 1965),[2] Mexican-Americans, Puerto Ricans, youth, and women. While many white Americans were successfully pursuing the dream—increasing the years of education, becoming trained to find places in the now predominantly white-collar job market, moving to the suburbs, and accumulating a moderate amount of material luxuries—blacks, particularly those who had migrated to Northern cities from the South in record numbers after World War II, were caught in a cycle of poverty and urban decay. This was also the case with Puerto Ricans who had migrated to the mainland, Mexican-Americans, and the rural poor, both white and black. Despite the fact that blacks had made their most rapid economic advances between 1965 and 1970, the rediscovery of poverty and deprivation not only overshadowed the gains but accentuated the sense of futility and entrapment felt by a large segment of the black population.

The assault of the civil rights movement on the *de facto* segregation of the North, which enlarged the issue of equality from a regional to a national one and from an issue of rights to an issue of opportunity as well, was an attack on the economic disparities that were the real causes of entrenched and continuing inequality and institutionalized discrimination. The issue of equality of opportunity thus became the framework in which many of the social issues of the period were perceived. Discriminatory housing practices which allowed whites to control the suburbs and concentrated blacks in the cities, urban decay and the diminishing financial base of the cities, the rising crime rate and welfare rolls, and the increasingly inadequate job training and education in the cities—all became critical aspects of the perpetuation of inequality. The commitment to equality, then, meant not only acknowledging the rights of the minority populations but also taking aggressive measures entailing substantial resources of society to overcome the historic and well-established patterns of discrimination. Such steps required major changes in policy and practice for most of the economic, political, and social institutions of the nation.

Also required were major changes in the composition of and

access to policy-making levels in all of these institutions and organizations. The issues of equality and pluralism are fundamentally issues centered on who is allowed or has the right to participate in the development and promulgation of policy. It is at the policy levels that provisions for continued equality of opportunity may be safeguarded while assuring that the needs and interests of all groups are effectively represented. Thus, pluralism highlighted not only the issue of equal rights and equality of opportunity but of adequate representation on policy levels as well. Thus demands for representation at the policy-making level represented a challenge to monopolistic control of social, economic, and political institutions by the majority, a control that had too often prevented representation or reflection of minority views.

Finally, the challenge of pluralism was a challenge not only to current practices and conditions but to popular attitudes as well. A key factor in the development of the solidarity of minority groups was promotion of a positive identity which heightened the consciousness of group membership and reinforced positive aspects of their uniqueness. A logical consequence of positive group identity was a renewed attack upon the popular stereotypical misconceptions that frequently served as a rationale for continued inequality.

The Younger Generation

If two major themes of America's last twenty years were the confrontation with pluralism and the disruption of traditional values, goals, and institutions, the phenomenon of the younger generation was a pivotal point between the two. Student activism and the revolt of youth focused on both themes and generated critical questions related to the role of youth in society.

Student activism and rebellion became a phenomenon and a crisis in the 1960s. Amidst affluence, anxiety, social malaise, an unpopular war, a generation gap developed into a veritable cultural revolution. Youthful reactions to societal conditions polarized between dropping out to pursue counter life-styles on the one hand and becoming militantly involved in changing the direction, values, and leadership of society on the other. Young people appeared to be unified in a common demand that recognition of the rights of youth to self-expression and self-determination be ensured—the right, in some respects, to "do their own thing." Thus emerged the crisis over students' rights and power, a crisis that is part of the problem of pluralism in that it challenges the larger society to acknowledge the needs, interests, and desire for self-determination of another minority element. The question of student rights and power became an issue for the schools, which were challenged to recognize the constitutional rights of students and their right to be represented in policy-making bodies. Exacerbating the issue not only for schools but for the larger society as well was the need to recognize a new age of majority.

The mood of the younger generation, a mood of anger, rebelliousness, and despair, developed in part from the rejection by many young people of some traditional values, the recognition of the hypocrisy represented by the gap between the country's ideals and the reality of its conditions, and a widespread suspicion and lack of faith in the leadership in society.[3] Among the consequences of this state of mind among many youth, especially college and high school youth, were the growth of the drug culture, the creation of alternative life styles, and later—during the early 1970s—the less dramatic but more widespread tendency to withdraw their emotional involvement from social and political matters and channel feelings into their private lives where there were more control and less frustration.[4]

The virulence and depth of youthful discontent with society became problematical for a larger society which pondered whether these were transitional moods of a younger generation, perhaps early indications of a basic malaise or the onset of a transitional period for society.

The American Dilemma and the Crisis of the American Dream

The crisis of pluralism and equality is a major aspect of what Myrdal called "the American Dilemma"—the separation between American ideals and the reality of American life. In the past twenty years, America has had to wrestle not only with the gap between reality and the ideal but also with the prospect that traditional American goals and values have, in some ways, gone sour. Out of this challenge to traditional values came a crisis in meaning, a crisis that involved questioning authority and uncertainty about the permanence and superiority of traditional institutions in American life.

The crisis of values, given momentum by the disaffection of youth and exacerbated by the increasingly negative aspects of rampant technology and bureaucratization of society, precipitated a crisis in meaning for many Americans. The context of American society had changed. The conditions that had in the past supported and reaffirmed the traditional values and beliefs now seemed to negate them. In an increasingly technological society, work for many was becoming dehumanizing, success seemed to demand an enormous price, and leisure was too often a process of submersion in media. It appeared that the cost—to individuals, institutions, and the environment—of maintaining a highly complex, technological society was too high.

Unquestioned acceptance of common political values also became suspect. The Vietnam War challenged the traditional definitions of patriotism; the spread of political corruption and the widening of the credibility gap seemed to make a mockery of democratic principles, and humanitarianism became suspect as its institutionalization demoralized and dehumanized its clients.

Morality became more and more utilitarian and individual, not based on traditional values. Among the consequences were "the sexual revolution," changing attitudes toward marriage and divorce, a shift toward developing standards of morality based on individual need, and a temporary retreat by society from efforts to legislate morality.

As traditional values were questioned, America experienced a crisis of authority as traditional social institutions, caught between traditional and emergent values, were challenged as to their continuing viability. Church, school, family, and government were accused of irrelevance, and the basic values they represented were brought into question; consequently their ability to provide leadership and authority was seriously undermined, while alternative structures developed.

This crisis of American values had created a sense of anxiety, a malaise, a faltering of the country's spirit. Traditional values had produced a sense of well-being, a structure of meaning, and a form of stability. As traditional values were challenged and questioned, America faced the necessity of redefining priorities, establishing new directions, and, in the process, critically examining its institutions and its leadership.

Impact on the Schools

Virtually all of the issues with which Americans struggled in the period 1954 to 1974 had a profound impact on the schools, an impact that went far beyond the traditional reflex responses to changes in the larger society. The very nature of the issues of pluralism, equality, equal opportunity, and traditional and emergent values focused a glaring spotlight on the schools precisely because schools and education have always been an acknowledged pathway to economic and social mobility as well as key facilitators of the "Americanizing" concept. Indictments of the schools, generated by these issues, came from sources external to the schools and challenged what appeared to be monopolistic control of education by educators and the middle class. Every aspect of schooling—from governance, financing, student and employee personnel practices (hiring, assigning, promoting, testing, evaluating, disciplining, and so on), curricular content, school-community relations, and policy making came under attack.

If schools were seen as major contributors to the problems and issues outlined previously, they were also viewed as prime vehicles for developing solutions to the problems. Consequently, instead of merely reacting to problems in society, the schools were vigorously *acted upon* by many other forces within society. One result has been the development of new priorities, policies, and powers—in short, a new context—within which the schools must operate, a context that differs radically from the context of the schools of the 1940s. Perhaps the most striking and significant aspects of the new context are the demythologizing of education—putting to rest the fiction that education is apolitical—the unprecedented involvement in education by the courts and the federal government, the balkanization of school personnel, and the mobilization of client (students and community) interest and power.

The cornerstone of political mythology in education had been the assumption of state legal control accompanied by relatively unrestricted local autonomy. Federal grants to education had flowed through the state to the local level with little doubt that the educational objectives would be achieved. Local areas, with consent from the state, levied taxes to support educational needs. But a strong political alliance between rural and suburban factions in the state legislatures stymied the increasingly urgent urban demands for new sources and structures for fiscal support of education. Traditionally, the states granted considerable autonomy to local districts and both presumed, until the late 1950s, that educational programs were adequate for the needs of all the students.[5] While the states set broad guidelines and local districts developed their own rules of governance and management, the courts accepted "reasonableness" as the rationale for regulations and procedures and interfered little, if at all, in the activities of local districts.

This tranquil picture of local control with relatively little political disruption was shattered under the pressures of the past twenty years. The issues of rights and opportunities presented a new lens through which virtually every aspect of education was reexamined and reevaluated. The exposure of the failures of schools to deal equitably and effectively with *all* students mobilized many sectors of society whose previous inactivity had been viewed as acceptance of the political mythology. With poverty and equality as national issues and schools as a highly valuable and presumably viable vehicle to bring about reform, federal involvement in education took on unprecedented forms. And, while attempts at reform were being generated at the federal level—with the high watermark of activity occurring in Johnson's "Education Congress"—the complexity and intricacies of the issues of equal opportunity were exacerbated by the growing volume of court cases dealing with education.

The new era began with the 1954 Brown decision and accelerated at a phenomenal rate[6] primarily because advocates of equality and civil rights charged, and the courts agreed, that much educational policy developed under state law was not in conformity with federal constitutional requirements. In order to promote equality and the protection of constitutional rights, the courts found themselves involved in setting up criteria for policy making in many areas of education.[7] Between 1959 and 1973 emerged what has been called an era of education under the supervision of the courts.[8]

Three landmark decisions illustrate the impact of the equality issue on three major areas of educational concern: racial segregation and discrimination, school financing, and personal rights. The 1954 Brown decision and subsequent rulings outlawed intentional racial segregation; the Supreme Court decision in the Tinker case (1969) eliminated the criteria of reasonable exercise of power in judging school rules and practices and placed the burden on schools to prove (in First and Fourteenth Amendment cases) that "the prohibitions they imposed are necessary because of conduct that interferes materially and substantially with school operations."[9] In the Rodriguez case (1973), the Supreme Court refused to characterize education as a "fundamental interest," and the court would not rule on financing programs for education, thus throwing the issue back into the state courts and legislatures.[10]

Under the same banner of equality of opportunity that involved the courts in educational matters, the federal government also moved into a more powerful position in education. The combination of Title VI of the Civil Rights Act of 1964 and Title I of the Elementary and Secondary Education Act of 1965 presented schools with unprecedented federal financial aid to be used in nondiscriminatory ways and to be targeted on the poverty areas. The Civil Rights Act also empowered the Attorney General to file suit for the desegregation of public schools. In addition to direct aid to education, the federal government, through the antipoverty legislation, had, by July 1965, 239 community action programs throughout the country, 209 of which involved education in some way.[11] The very passage of the ESEA had changed the context of education—federal monies brought with them a degree of federal guidance and control as well as increased burdens on educators to create and carry out programs that would serve the poor and disadvantaged.

One of the adjuncts of increased federal involvement in education was the concept of client advocacy, a concept which contributed to the mobilization of community powers in education.[12] Client advocacy emphasized participation by the poor and minorities in the delivery of services. In effect, it supported the idea that services be delivered with their participation. No longer could schools provide services for the poor. Federal programs encouraged client advocacy first through the use of aides in the schools and then by providing for client membership on committees advising educators. Client or parent involvement escalated with demands for control over central educational decisions, through community control or decentralization. Along with client advocacy came increased demands for educational accountability. Both client and federal involvement in the schools underwent major modifications in the late 1960s as several assumptions upon which the attack on poverty and inequality were based

were proven to be of questionable validity. The first assumption—
that educators had the knowledge to solve the problems of the disadvantaged if only the schools had adequate resources—was challenged by lack of results and the tendency of local districts to use the
funds in traditional programs or to meet the spiraling costs of basic
educational needs. The second assumption that the state education
associations would work with local districts to provide leadership in
programming and in bringing about compliance with judicial and federal stipulations regarding nondiscrimination was also challenged, as
many states looked the other way while local districts continued discriminatory practices and lost federal funds.[13]

The power of both the state and the local districts to control
education had ultimately been challenged. Judicial and federal decisions raised serious questions as to the ability of the states to provide
leadership in what was increasingly seen as a problem of national
scope that needed national direction, federal funds, and the imprima-
tur of a national priority. A New Jersey superior court judge, giving
his opinion in the Cahill case, questioned the supremacy of local control, which he observed is sometimes "control for the wealthy, not
for the poor."[14] This decision challenged the sanctity of local control
when used to shield discriminatory practices.

Balkanization of the System

Within the school structure itself, economic and professional
pressures were precipitating an internal realignment of power which
resulted in the balkanization of the system. Indictment of the
schools for failure to respond to the needs of all the clients rested
heavily on school personnel, particularly the teachers, who saw themselves increasingly in a vulnerable public position of accountability
but with little direct power over educational policies. Seeking protection, representation, and power, teachers turned to unionization and
organization, a process that found state and local education authorities unprepared to deal with the full implications of the new development. School boards—amateur negotiators—faced professional bar-
gainers representing teacher organizations, and, without protective
regulations from state agencies, bargained away many management
prerogatives along with salaries and fringe benefits. Administrators
and nonprofessional personnel likewise sought the safety of a union

organization that would present a stronger front in the battle for dwindling resources and a protective shield against the criticisms being leveled at education. At the same time, student activism generated additional demands for the internal reorganization of power as students sought representation in policy decisions.

Student activism and the issue of pluralism combined with the crisis in values to generate indictments against the content as well as the process of education. The failure of the schools to educate a significant segment of the population led many to believe that the schools were locked into an outmoded system of pedagogy that did not meet the full needs of any of its students. Schools were challenged to develop new content and methods of instruction that would address the affective as well as cognitive needs of the students. Schools were urged to encourage more flexibility, creativity, and individuality, to become more relevant to students' needs and interests, and to help students develop meaningful personal values amid the changing and conflicting values of society. At the same time, the basic value structure of education was being questioned. The authority and viability of the schools to maintain a leadership role in society were questioned by those who saw schools as instruments for perpetuating class dominance and discrimination through a paper meritocracy.[15]

In what was really a very short period of time, American schools had to adjust to a new context of policy making and governance, balancing all of the new participants and priorities while they tried to create effective responses to major societal problems whose roots lay within and outside the immediate sphere of education. The task fell most heavily on the shoulders of school administrators whose positions in the school hierarchy and in the interstices between school and society made them the agents through which the currents of change were translated into the schools.

Impact on the Administrator

The critical issues of the past twenty years have created new dimensions of the school context that every educational administrator has had to confront. As schools have become big business, a focal point for political activity, and a vehicle for social reform, administrators have had to adjust, expand, and reinterpret their roles to fit into the new context. The responses of individual administrators have been a function of their abilities, flexibility, insight, and often, fundamentally, their capacity for survival. Reflection is frequently a luxury in the midst of pressing needs for action; most administrators have been confronted with problems and new modes of action for which they have had no previous preparation but with which they have had to deal. This has been true of both the superintendency and the principalship.

Although the responsibilities and functions of the superintendent and the principal are different—the superintendent dealing with school boards, politicians, and the community at large as well as with the full range of the educational hierarchy; the principal with the faculty, students, and parent community of an individual school —there is a common denominator in their quandary as administrators: increased problems and responsibilities on the one hand and a curtailment of power on the other.

This development is clearly reflected in the popular image of educational administrators: the principal, beset with seemingly insoluble problems ranging from discipline to curriculum and besieged by demands from students, parents, teachers, and community; the superintendent struggling to remain afloat amidst political vicissitudes and capricious school boards, cajoling out of the public purses enough money to keep the school system operating and, it is to be hoped, effective. There are, of course, significant exceptions to these images. But the popular currency of these profiles, heavily reinforced by the testimony of principals and superintendents in the educational literature, points to fundamental problems created or exacerbated by the crises of the past two decades.

Many see the educational administrator as an important element in the solution of educational problems. If this is an accurate perception, and indeed it should be, then it is necessary to make it possible for administrators to deal with the problems of education. Whether or not administrators can in fact deal with educational problems appears to be intimately involved in the role definitions and self-concepts of the administrator. Many of the changes in school context have had direct impact on the nature of the roles of superintendents and principals. The impact has altered the traditional descriptions of these roles, but the development of new roles for the superintendency or principalship is still in its nascent stages. This situation has created severe problems for educational administration in all of its aspects, from recruiting and training to on-the-job performance. First, let us consider how the traditional administrative roles have been altered by the impact of the critical issues of the past twenty years.

Problems of Superintendents

As a result of societal pressures during the past two decades and the subsequent altering of the school context, superintendents have had to adjust their priorities and their roles to deal with the politicization and balkanization of the schools, increasingly active school boards, pressures from the community at large, and an increasingly complex and expanding bureaucracy. The positioning of the schools in the center of many of the recent critical issues of society, competition among many public institutions for funds and priority consideration by political powers, and the open acknowledgment of the interrelationship between education and politics have, in many respects, turned the superintendency into a political position.

While, in theory, the traditional relationship between the superintendent and the school board was to have been that of administrator to policy maker, in actuality, many superintendents either made policy or controlled the policy-making process. This situation developed as a result of the myth that most educational decisions were technical decisions that should be handled by experts in the field of education. The superintendent, as the top technical expert in education, was thus allowed, without the interference of school boards, the public, or politicians to make many of the policy decisions for the school district. Under the pressures of the past twenty years, however, the notion that education belonged to the experts dissolved and was replaced by open politicization of the problems and policies of education. Areas that superintendents had previously viewed as apolitical—anything from curriculum to student placement—became highly volatile political issues. With the politicization of these issues came greater accountability of the superintendent to taxpayers, school boards, and politicians as well as a curtailment of the previously unchallenged power of the superintendent. As Nolte describes,

A long thread of research (Coleman, Jencks, and so forth) in recent years had unraveled much of the traditional cloak of the educational "expert," exposing superintendents to the critical eyes of a public disenchanted with PhDs and with schools that don't teach children the three Rs, yet cost $1,000 a year per pupil to operate. Upshot: The previously sacred, politically sanitized waters of public education have become what many superintendents see as dirty political pools.

Vis-à-vis school boards, politicians and citizens pressure groups, superintendents are losing some of their traditional executive authority (but not their responsibility) as more and more educational issues are being hastened into the political and legal arenas.[16]

A concomitant of the politicization of education has been a heightened vulnerability of the superintendent's position to the political vicissitudes inherent in school boards and the larger community. Such vulnerability has been described in the somewhat euphemistic phrase "Superintendent's Shuffle"[17] which refers to the rapid turnover among school superintendents. Many attribute this phenomenon to the dwindling power of the superintendent and the multiplication of the problems with which he must deal.[18] The turnover, or shuffling of superintendents from one city to the next, is often a function, immediately, of the conflict between superintendents and more active school boards. School boards are themselves political animals —appointed or elected—and, as their compositions change, so might their tolerance for or acceptance of a particular administrator. As one administrator recounted, he served one year as superintendent in a district, was fired after that year was over, was rehired again six months later when a new school board came into office, and, two years later, was fired again after yet another power shift in the school board.[19]

Presumably neither school boards nor superintendents are pleased with this type of revolving door administration. Both must adapt to the political nature of education by redefining roles so as to balance educational expertise and public-controlled policy. In the meantime, such a precarious atmosphere exacts a heavy toll on educational leadership. As one former superintendent has advised, "If a superintendent is innovative, he can expect to stay only three years ... the first year you learn, the second year you make recommendations, and the third year you get out."[20]

It is obvious that, to stay alive, superintendents have had to acknowledge the political facts of life and have had to become adept at political behaviors not only for their own survival but for the prosperity or survival of the educational programs under their jurisdic-

tion. However policy decisions are allocated within the school hierarchy, the ultimate power lies in the political arena. Superintendents
and other school administrators have found themselves becoming
politicians and public relations representatives, developing power
bases within the community to garner support for educational objectives.

In addition to the problems presented by politicization, superintendents have also been severely jolted by the ramifications of balkanization within the schools. Whereas he was previously at the apex
of a united hierarchy of educators, the superintendent, with the
onset of collective bargaining and organization of virtually all personnel within the schools, now found himself without portfolio. The
question of where the superintendent fit into the bargaining process
was debated extensively in the professional literature. While it appeared that the superintendent had landed fairly solidly on the managerial side of the bargaining table, it also appeared that this was only
the beginning of the problems of superintendents as they related to
balkanization, a phenomenon that further illustrates the problem of
increased responsibilities and reduced power. For example, demands
for equal educational opportunity required that experienced and
well-qualified personnel be placed in schools in slum areas as well as
in suburban areas. In addition, civil rights laws and federal stipulations required minority hiring and affirmative action programs to
work toward a faithful reflection of the pluralistic nature of the community within the school staff. Concurrent with these demands,
however, restrictions on the exercise of authority by superintendents
and other administrators were developing in the form of union contracts which dealt not only with salaries and fringe benefits but also
with teacher assignments, transfers, hiring and firing, tenure, class
size, nonteaching duties of the faculty, assignment of teacher aides,
and the like. Thus, superintendents, as well as others in the administrative hierarchy, had to work to achieve societally established objectives within curtailed parameters of power and in conjunction with
policy and procedures they may have had little or no part in formulating. In addition, then, to acquiring skills in politics and public relations, superintendents have also had to become adept at dealing with
all of the factors that unionization of school personnel entails.

Other problems abound. With the consolidation of school districts, many superintendents find themselves in charge of large, some-

times unwieldy, bureaucracies with a proliferation of specialists whose talents must be integrated effectively into the bureaucratic structure. Large bureaucratic structures begin to take on characteristics of their own: survival techniques, internalized norms that defend the status quo against change, co-optation, and the like. Superintendents must add to their bag of tricks a knowledge of organizations and the skills to deal within their context in order to achieve educational objectives.

What of the superintendent, then? He or she is trained and equipped as an educator for a role traditionally protected by the stamp of "expert," finds that the whole context of his or her operations has changed, and discovers that he or she must develop the skills of politician, labor arbiter, public relations expert, or systems analyst, to name but a few. It is understandable that, in the midst of flux, vulnerability, and role confusion, those who are in the position of superintendent find themselves questioning the appropriateness of their training, abilities, and effectiveness, if not their sanity. The traditional role of the superintendent has been drastically altered, but the alteration in the role is merely a reflection of the changed role and function of education brought about by changes in society. Education is no longer construed as comprising simply curricula, textbooks, students, and faculty. Although many educators have long understood this, all, from the superintendent down to the classroom teacher, must now be prepared to operate in this new context of understanding in which the problems of education and the skills needed to cope with them are not necessarily the traditional problems or skills of education or educators. The new conceptualizations of roles and functions have been difficult to achieve, and the changes reverberate throughout the hierarchy. Many superintendents are consumed by the day-to-day struggle for survival. Said one superintendent, "I couldn't even tell you which high school would close tomorrow. My greatest leap into the future was to plan for next week's board meeting."[21] In such a situation educational leadership— effectively planning for tomorrow's schools—becomes a scarce commodity. Superintendents have not only had to reassess their own roles, but also reevaluate the roles of others in the educational hierarchy in the attempt to promote the development of educational leadership. One indication that new educational leadership has rarely emerged is the fact that few superintendents or principals have changed their concept of the role of principal from that of middle management administrator to that of educational leader.

Problems of Principals

Recent surveys of principals and superintendents have revealed that their problems, as perceived by those in the field, are increasingly similar. The major difference is that their roles are played out in slightly different contexts. Like the traditional role of the superintendent, that of the principal is dissolving, and his or her powers are being redefined in the midst of mounting pressures, problems, and vulnerability. The traditional images of the principal as housekeeper, "big daddy," teacher's protector, "superteacher," or foreman[22] are no longer viable in light of new developments in education. The bureaucratically based concept of the principal as middleman—a kind of substitute role definition—is doing little to solve the problems of education that turn on the lack of effective educational leadership.

The issues of the past twenty years have changed the role of the principal vis-à-vis the students, faculty, and the community. Discipline has been consistently identified by the American public as the major problem in schools, as revealed in Gallup polls. Indeed, accounts of a day or a week in the life of an urban school principal[23] make it quite clear that this problem consumes much of the principal's time. But a great number of court decisions have placed the burden of responsibility on the schools for proving justifiable those restrictions placed on students in areas covered by the First and Fourteenth Amendments. These decisions have made many administrators wary of exercising their authority. This occurs simultaneously with increased demands that schools deal effectively with the problems of delinquency, vandalism, drugs, and other antisocial behaviors. Simultaneously the open challenges to authority so prevalent in this period and the popular and plentiful criticism of schools have contributed to the erosion of the principal's power.

Balkanization, of course, has had repercussions on the behavior of principals as well as superintendents. Unionization frequently left principals out in the cold—separated from the body of teachers but not included on the management team of negotiators. For many principals who saw themselves as superteacher, or big daddy, to a school faculty, this separation, and the consequent and predictable antagonism between labor and management, meant significant changes in definitions of roles and behavior. Like superintendents, principals have had to develop skills in handling educational issues with an eye to union regulations, due process, and considerable curtailment of their former power over the assignment and activities of their faculty and even in the selection of educational programs.

The principal's role in relation to the community has also been changed. Principals have had to become adept at handling school-community relations, which have become increasingly volatile. With a more active and volatile school community and demands for more effective participation in policy making in education by all public sectors, principals have been faced with the task of integrating these elements effectively into the governance of schools. These pressures for community participation in educational decisions did not develop in the past two decades. They have long been standard procedure in middle-class communities. But the pressure for participation by the poor and minority groups has been a new phenomenon, greeted often with suspicion, fear, or resentment. Such participation is essential to the diversification of the orientation of schools and their ability to reflect, understand, and deal positively with the pluralistic nature of society. Principals have been faced with the problems of (their own or other) opposition to the encouragement of such community participation.

In the midst of societal and organizational upheaval, principals have been expected to keep their eyes on the real mission of the schools—to educate the students. To do so, however, principals must be able to develop a positive climate in the schools, be flexible enough to make room for innovative programs and alternative methods of education, and sufficiently discerning and aware of the short- and long-range needs of society to be able to distinguish between "politically inspired educational innovation (and) innovations which truly prepare an individual for a productive, adjusted life in an increasingly complex world."[24]

The sum of all of the responsibilities adds up to an enormous job for school principals and a very new and different role in the education complex. As the American Association of School Administrators observed:

... school administrators cannot afford to be in the untenable position of trying blindly to apply traditional concepts to the new and changing circumstances.

School administrators must reassess, and when appropriate, reshape and redesign their leadership role, using all the intelligence, insight, and understanding which can be brought to bear. Many old established traditions and processes will no longer suffice.[25]

Internal Pressures—The Basis of the Role Conflict

There are, however, many administrators—superintendents and principals alike—who are still attempting to apply the traditional roles and modes of behavior in a school context that, we have seen, is radically different from that which nurtured and validated the traditional forms. The general assessment is that the principalship has changed very little in the last forty years.[26] This situation takes its toll not only on the achievement of educational progress—the responsibility of administrators which should have priority but which has somehow become lost in the turmoil of daily survival—but also on administrators in the form of internal conflicts between perceived goals and responsibilities on the one hand and inadequate time, training, or talent to be effective in achieving these goals and responsibilities on the other. As long as roles remain frozen at about 1940, the internal pressures will continue to build with severe implications for all of education.

The freezing of these roles appears to depend in large measure on the pressures of a bureaucratic hierarchy and the presence of what many perceive to be an immovable and unchangeable system which reinforces the status quo and rids itself of the disturbing elements. Thus, the principalship, overwhelmed by and immersed in maintenance duties, is often perceived by superintendents and principals as a middle-management position in the educational hierarchy. The emphasis is on administration, but all of the problems that the principal faces demand effective educational leadership. The skills demanded are highly varied, but many administrators find that the tools with which they have been equipped are valuable only in maintaining the status quo. How to reconstitute the role to enable the administrator to become an educational leader becomes a top priority. The key, if there is one to unlock the chains that many administrators feel bind them, is how administrators view themselves and the system and the situation in which they must function. William Wayson has stated the problem:

People who have not succeeded in changing the principalship, or who have never tried, often argue that the role of the principal makes change impossible. Roles and role expectations are perhaps the second most important variable in determining what anyone does; in the case of the principalship, they hold a low second place to *what the principal perceives those expectations to be and which ones he chooses to meet.* There are no permanent, fixed, and universally agreed on role expectations for the principalship . . . . No one should be denied the recognition that in the final analysis it is he himself who chooses, for whatever reasons, to do what he does; yet thousands of American principals have been denied that recognition, and that accounts for most of their insecurity and much of their failure. It is possible to teach people to understand and recognize the impact of what others expect them to do. And it is possible for principals to become skillful at weighing the costs and benefits of choosing one expectation over another—always with the knowledge that they must make the choice. The great variability in how principals function is proof enough that they do much to determine their own roles.

The constraints on the principal, like constraints on most people, arise primarily from the way he chooses to view himself, his world, and his role. To transform his role, he must see himself and his surroundings in a different way. Of course there are constraints in the external world, but they are far less restraining than many principals assume. Inasmuch as the problem lies in the incumbent's perception of his job, that is where interventions should be directed.[27]

Bringing about changes in perception is a difficult task, and a number of conditions in the system itself seem to work against this result. The indoctrination against a sense of autonomy and creativity begins early, since many administrators have advanced through the ranks of teaching and have adopted a mode of behavior that accommodates to bureaucratic norms. "Ways of doing things gain validity with longevity: the length of their utilization is cited as proof of their effectiveness . . . . Newcomers enter as novices and are taught by tribal elders 'how it is done around here.' . . . By the time they are eligible for promotion, they have incorporated these priorities and taboos into most of their thinking . . . . When new and creative responses are demanded, the bureaucrat looks inept, feels paranoid, and becomes defensive."[28]

It is understandable, then, that the reactions of such individuals to the new rigors and demands on administrators have frequently been negative and defensive. Types of such defensive reactions will help to illustrate the problems of administrators and the subsequent problems they create for the field of education. There are those who meet the pressures from clients and administration with the tactic of "keeping peace at any price—including the sacrifice of their professional integrity." They may play community against administration or vice versa; they may learn the current rhetoric, without risking actual changes in their schools or with only superficial changes, and quickly advance up the ladder before the absence of positive results in the school becomes obvious. The principal may attempt to develop a power base among community activists, students, or parents. Such an advocacy role supports them in dealing with a central office that seeks to avoid confrontation and controversy as much as possible. Still others have championed one innovative program, gaining for themselves reputations as innovators, which insulates them from criticisms. To protect against their vulnerability, still others have sought the safety of unions or professional organizations. Whatever the mode of defensive reaction, schools under the control of principals who take such recourse gradually and ultimately deteriorate.[29]

It is difficult, indeed, after exposure to the experience of an urban school principal, for one to imagine how administrators can do anything other than simply survive. There are, however, administrators who have responded to the pressures and crises of recent times in a creative, effective way, and the fact that they have been able to do so seems to depend to a great degree on their perception of themselves and of the system. This type of administrator sees himself not as a middle-management man locked into a system, but as an autonomous individual who will work with the system when possible but in spite of the system when necessary in order to accomplish the goals of creating a humane and workable learning environment. What is most significant is that he or she deals with educational problems in a way exemplified by the late Marcus Foster, who considered all problems, whatever their source or nature, to be educational problems. The power to handle these problems in an innovative way means that the principal does not invest the system with oppressive powers that may or may not exist. A cardinal rule is never ask permission of the system because superiors are likely to disapprove of a proposal whose results are not guaranteed. This type of principal will acknowledge and accept the necessity of creating power bases outside the bureaucracy rather than relying on his position within the school hierarchy. To feel autonomous and capable, then, in the midst of many problems, the principal must be able to draw on a variety of skills. He must be politically sophisticated to develop the necessary power sources without being controlled by them. He must be discerning and informed to make curricular and instructional choices that have a valid and substantial relationship to the needs of the students. Finally, he must be broad in his vision in order to accept any problem that interferes with the educational process as one that he must deal with, whether it be a traditional "educational" problem or not.

A major problem, however, is how to recruit and train individuals so that they become educational leaders rather than administrators. Procedures concerning recruitment and training have been affected by the changes in the last twenty years, but the sad fact is that the training of administrators is still in the stage of Model T.[30]

Recruitment and Training of Administrators

The issues of equality and pluralism have added new guidelines and priorities to the process of administrative recruitment. Pluralism and increased educational understanding have called attention to the variety and uniqueness of needs, priorities, and problems of individual schools. Individual schools and school districts are not interchangeable parts, and assignment of administrators on the basis of who is next in line for a promotion or transfer is counterproductive to the achievement of educational objectives. The capabilities, talents, personality, style of leadership, and concerns of the individual administrator must be matched with the needs and nature of the school. Otherwise there is the risk of destroying potentially fine administrative talent and undermining the progress of the school as well.[31]

Pluralism and equality have also altered recruitment practices through restrictions against discriminatory personnel practices and, more positively, through affirmative action programs. Affirmative action in administrative recruitment has sought to place more minorities in administrative positions, but problems and inadequacies have developed around the execution of these programs. Certain defense mechanisms have been employed in the recruitment and hiring procedures with the result that the real impact of affirmative action programs has been somewhat diluted. The first mechanism has been to plead scarcity of qualified candidates from minority groups. A survey in 1970,[32] however, indicated that not many school districts had seriously attempted to find black administrators. A second mechanism has been to place minorities in federally funded programs that have a limited life span and that are usually not positions of power in the traditional school hierarchy or to place them in positions in the lower echelon with very limited power. The number of minorities in school administrative positions is growing slowly, but compliance with the law and the full use of the potential administrative resources in these areas have not yet become realities.

Even with full utilization of the potential of minorities, recruitment of educational administrators has and will continue to become increasingly difficult in the face of competition from the business community. The new framework of education requires administrators with capabilities, knowledge, and dedication that also make them prime candidates for positions in business management with potentially greater monetary reward and upward mobility. School administration may find fewer individuals turning to that field because the ceiling for advancement is quite low—there are just so many positions for superintendents and those who attain that level tend to monopolize it.

Changes in the roles of administrators have quite naturally changed the criteria used for recruitment of new administrators. A report on research in 1972 indicates actual or desired changes in criteria used to screen candidates for principal preparation programs. The study observed:

Modal responses indicate a need for placing *greater* importance on the following criteria: exhibits charismatic personality, communicates a sense of social mission, displays social sensitivity, shows commitment to educational and social reform, shows willingness to take risks and tolerate ambiguity and stress, has had work experience outside of education, has had strong academic background in technical managerial skills.
A tendency is also indicated toward placing *less* importance on standardized IQ test scores.[33]

Ultimately the problems of recruitment, role definition, and changes in context are dependent upon administrative training programs, but it is perhaps in this aspect of an administrator's career that the least amount of change has taken place. The new problems of schools demand leadership, but training programs are still placing the heaviest accent on administrative and maintenance functions.

Even though the importance of administrative leadership in bringing about change is generally accepted, a large majority of educational leaders continue to carry out *only* those tasks which relate to efficiently and effectively maintaining the existing system. What is more frightening, however, is the fact that the vast majority of young entry-level administrators do not appear to be performing any differently than their predecessors. It is this "new blood" which, it could reasonably be expected, should provide leadership for significant educational change.[34]

Insights as to what should constitute the new training programs come from the training schools themselves, administrators in the field, and experimental programs. The previously cited critique of administrative training identifies some of the sources of the problems. Many administrators were being advanced to the ranks directly from the classroom without adequate preparation; their training and strengths were not in leadership but in tasks of organizational maintenance. While many of those promoted from the ranks of teachers have had some graduate training, "the majority of the initial graduate programs (master's degree) in educational administration apparently have not adequately provided them with the understandings and skills and/or necessary support systems for them to perform their duties effectively, except in administrivia, i.e., in the usual organizational maintenance task areas."[35]

A survey of all colleges and universities having graduate departments in educational administration indicated that professors see principals spending the greatest portion of their time on improvement of instruction. These departments stressed that preparation should include current knowledge of curricular developments, acquaintance with the effects of out-of-school socioeconomic milieu of the student, and human awareness or sensitivity training. Most professors felt that the general balance between subject fields should remain unchanged with some addition of preparation in industrial relations, the humanities, political science, and business administration.[36]

A survey of twenty-four metropolitan school principals that same year (1972) indicated that the highest priority was given to administrative problems. They were followed by the need for more understanding of the foundations of education to provide a background against which to test the adequacy of traditional assumptions of education and to develop new assumptions, as many of these traditional ones were no longer relevant. The third priority was the supervision of instructional and curricular development, followed by the desire for some knowledge of counseling, educational psychology, and research methods and statistics. The major conclusions from the study were that the principal's role had expanded to include many of the problems traditionally dealt with by superintendents, that training programs would have to accommodate the differences in individual needs and problems of administrators, and that principals would have to learn to work effectively with the team concept in order to handle all of the problems they confronted.[37]

Training of administrators is also being given assistance in the changes in administrative theory in education. Previous emphases of administrative theory—on efficiency and performance of tasks; on democracy with stress on human relations, group dynamics, and permissiveness[38]—have been integrated into a broader, more comprehensive concept of administrative theory. Educators acknowledge that the administrative problems in their sphere are similar in nature to administrative problems in any area; thus in their own training educators have been able to borrow from the large body of administrative theory and to integrate insights provided through the expanded knowledge of the behavioral sciences. As the body of administrative knowledge increases and administration itself becomes more of a science, administrators must develop a high level of professional responsibility.

It is important to differentiate between the science of administration and the policy decisions in education. Science is concerned with getting a closer "fix" on reality. Science deals with what "is" and the meaning of what is. Policy deals with what ought to be, with goals and directions. Goal-setting behavior of people may be studied scientifically, and indeed knowledge is necessary to perspicacious goal-setting, but the goals themselves are not the product of science. Moreover, the scientist may be motivated by his own values in deciding what to study, but his study per se must meet a public (other scientists) and not a private criterion.
. . . the administrator needs not only some knowledge of the science of administration but also some convictions about the ethics of administration. In practice he should be able to apply his scientifically derived insights ethically. This is a most difficult assignment in a pluralistic culture such as ours.[39]

Some of the most intensive efforts to meet the needs for a new breed of administrator are coming from special programs created to recruit and train top-level educational personnel. One of the major recruitment problems centers on the lack of determined criteria for identifying potential administrators with the right leadership abilities. The National Program for Educational Leadership sponsored by the U.S. Office of Education attempted to expand the talent pool by recruiting school administrators from positions of leadership in the fields of law, social work, the ministry, business, industry, and government service. New efforts to provide support for those already on the job are evidenced in the Superintendents' Training Program, sponsored by the Rockefeller Foundation, which takes mid-level administrators and gives them one year of on-the-job training with two different superintendents.

Other innovative programs attempt to integrate new sources of content for administrative training. Two areas of particular emphasis in the inclusion of new content are the arts and humanities and futurism. The latter area reflects efforts to provide administrators with a comprehensive view of the future that is not available through the traditional disciplines. A third area of new content draws on the management and information sciences and provides instruction in systems analysis, operations research, data retrieval, and the like.

New programs are also seeking to develop more appropriate instructional methods, particularly in the development of simulation approaches that are now focusing on the processes of administration rather than on a single role such as elementary school principal, emphasizing the concept of the administrative team, and working more and more in the area of value analysis and clarification. Many of the efforts to create new training experiences have been developed within an interorganizational framework implementing the cooperation of a number of universities, such as the University Council for Educational Administration, which includes nearly fifty leading universities in the United States and Canada.[40] These programs and others—the Consortium for Educational Leadership (Ford Foundation) and the Fellowship for Managers of Educational Change—acknowledge the need for new approaches to problems of recruitment and training of administrators in education.

The most critical challenge ultimately facing school administrators is that of being prepared to deal with tomorrow's problems in tomorrow's schools. The question is how to plan educational policies of the future by packaging them into the educational training of today. The changes of the past twenty years occurred so fast and encompassed so much that schools and administrators are only beginning to catch up with the implications for their own operations and behaviors. If, however, education is to reflect the pluralistic nature of society, if it is to adjust effectively to changes in values, and if, at the same time, it is to fulfill the highest priority of providing quality education to all of its students, then the field must have administrators who are capable of not merely maintaining the schools but leading them into the future.

Notes

1. Gresham M. Sykes, *Social Problems in America* (Glenview, Ill.: Scott, Foresman, 1974), 199.

2. Levitas Mitchell, *America in Crisis* (New York: Holt, Rinehart, Winston, 1969), 38.

3. This is a brief summary of a Sykes examination of "The Crisis of Meaning," Sykes, *Social Problems*, ch. viii.

4. Quoted from Yankelovich by Robert Chander in *Public Opinion* (New York: R. R. Boroken Company, 1972), 54.

5. John F. Hughes and Anne O. Hughes, *Equal Education* (Bloomington: Indiana University Press, 1972), ch. iv.

6. The greatest increase in court cases was on the federal level: there were 112 cases on the federal level in the period between 1946 and 1956 compared with 729 cases between 1956 and 1967 and 1,273 cases between 1967 and 1971. Significantly, the number of state court cases declined from 7,091 in the 1946-1956 period to 3,691 in 1956-1967 and 2,237 between 1967 and 1971. See John C. Hogan, *The Schools, the Courts, and the Public Interest* (Lexington, Mass.: D. C. Heath, 1974), 7.

7. For example: dress codes, school paper censorship, corporal punishment, suspension, expulsion, student pregnancy, admissions and graduate requirements, school financing, etc. See Hogan, *Schools, Courts, and Public Interest*, ch. v. The courts also exercised their powers to reopen schools closed to avoid desegregation; require tax levying for support of schools; assign teachers and students to specific schools to achieve racial balance; require special programs for the underprivileged; enforce student and teacher rights of freedom of expression. (*Ibid.*, 10.)

8. *Ibid.*, 9.

9. *Ibid.*, 85.

10. *Ibid.*, 73.

11. *Federal Role in Education* (Washington, D.C.: Congressional Quarterly Service, 1967), 3.

12. Hughes and Hughes, *Equal Education*, ch. vi.

13. *Ibid.*

14. Hogan, *Schools, Courts, and Public Interest*, 155.

15. See the radical critics' proposals to "deschool" society; i.e., Ivan Illich's writings.

16. M. Chester Nolte, "How Fast is the Power of the Superintendents Slipping Away?" *The American School Board Journal* (September 1974), 43.

17. "The 'Superintendent's Shuffle' Lames and Maims—Just Ask an Ex-Schoolman," *The American School Board Journal* (September 1974), 44-45.

18. *Ibid.*, 44.

19. *Ibid.*

20. *Ibid.*

21. *Ibid.*, 45.

22. Bernard C. Watson, "Teacher Militancy and Collective Negotiations," in Richard W. Saxe (ed.), *Perspectives on the Changing Role of the Principal* (Springfield, Ill.: Charles C Thomas, 1968).

23. See for example Luvern L. Cunningham, "Hey Man, You Our Principal?" *Phi Delta Kappan* (November 1969), 123-128.

24. James E. Bruno, "Emerging Issues in Education: An Overview and Perspective," in James E. Bruno (ed.), *Emerging Issues in Education* (Lexington, Mass.: Heath, 1972), 24.

25. Forrest E. Conner, *School Administrators View Professional Negotiations* (Washington: American Association of School Administrators, 1966), "Preface."

26. Harold J. McNally, "Summing Up," *National Elementary Principal* 54 (September-October 1974), 11.

27. William Wayson, "A Proposal to Remake the Principalship," *National Elementary Principal* 54 (September-October 1974), 34.

28. William Wayson, "A New Kind of Principal," *National Elementary Principal* 50 (February 1971), 10-11.

29. See Bernard C. Watson, *In Spite of the System* (Cambridge, Mass.: Ballinger, 1974), ch. ii.

30. McNally, "Summing Up," 13.

31. Donald A. Erickson, "Forces for Change: A New Role for Principals," in Saxe, *Changing Role of the Principal*, 290.

32. "No Widespread Search for Black Teachers, Officials," *Nations Schools* 85 (May 1970), 45.

33. Neal C. Nickerson, "Status of Programs for Principals," *NASSP Bulletin* 56 (March 1972), 12-13.

34. Larry W. Hughes and Gerald C. Ubben, "New Leadership for the Secondary School," *NASSP Bulletin* 54 (September 1970), 62.

35. *Ibid.*, 63.

36. Nickerson, "Programs for Principals," 10-19.

37. Adolph Unruh, "The Metropolitan Principal: Preparation for Survival," *NASSP Bulletin* 56 (April 1972), 24-32.

38. Daniel E. Griffiths (ed.), *Behavioral Science and Educational Administration*, Sixty-third Yearbook of the National Society for the Study of Education, Part II (Chicago: University of Chicago Press, 1964), ch. i.

39. Roald F. Campbell, "Implications for the Practice of Administration," in Griffiths, *Behavioral Science and Educational Administration*, xiii, 301.

40. This synopsis draws on the summary from Robin H. Farquhar and Michael W. Martin, "New Developments in the Preparation of Educational Leaders," *Phi Delta Kappan* 44 (September 1972), 26-30.

6. Educational Administration and the Courts, 1954-1974

VIRGINIA DAVIS NORDIN

The purpose of this chapter is threefold: to identify the major court decisions impinging on educational leadership during the period from 1954 to 1974, to indicate the impact of these decisions, and to pinpoint future impingements. This is a rather tall order, considering the limitations of space. I will, however, attempt to summarize the important cases and to perceive some patterns of actions and causes for them which will help us all better understand the current interaction between the courts and the schools.

As a somewhat innocent bystander I tend to see the confrontation between the legal system and the educational system during the last twenty years as a war of worlds—two worlds both rather confident of their own intelligence, their own high moral purpose, and their own special mission to preserve the democratic system. Unfortunately, these worlds have also often had two different ideas about how this last task should be accomplished, or, if they have not precisely differed, each at least has wanted to approach the problems in its own special way. I see this systemic conflict, this unpremeditated intersection of two self-contained operating systems, as the cause of the mutual misunderstanding that has sometimes arisen. I do not really see a deep conflict in values, although the authoritarian nature of some public school administration is certainly antithetical to the courts' concern for the legal rights of the individual. Both systems wish to accomplish good for our society. Perhaps if they understand each other better, this result can be accomplished for the good of all. The emergence of the study of the interaction of law and education, in both law schools and schools of education, is a good sign.

It should be remembered that the courts are the repository of tremendous power. They are accustomed to declaring a law unconstitutional and having it wiped off the books; they are accustomed to telling the executive that certain actions are unconstitutional and having those actions stop. This power has caused many commentators to advise judicial restraint lest the power atrophy, and in the past the courts have by and large heeded this advice.

One of the manifestations of judicial restraints in the past had been the reluctance of the courts to interfere with the educational system, both public school and higher educational systems. As the Supreme Court noted in *Epperson* v. *Arkansas*,[1] "Judicial interposition in the operation of the public school system of the Nation raises problems requiring care and restraint . . . Courts do not and cannot intervene in the resolution of conflicts which arise in the daily operation of school systems and which do not directly and sharply implicate basic constitutional values."[2] This restraint, especially in higher education, is based on a respect for academic freedom, and the sense of the importance of the educational mission which ought best be left to those who understand its workings and share its high goals. It is on this last point, perhaps, that the Court has stumbled, believing that an institution that teaches and preaches about democracy and constitutional rights should also be required to put those concepts into practice. Concern of the courts with the school is more complex, however, than distaste for a lack of due process, although the courts have spent centuries in defining fair treatment under the due process clause. It is also a threat posed to the authority of the courts, and hence to the rule of law in our society. The desegregation cases, as is widely known, have been characterized by evasion of legal duties and reluctance to comply. In this the Supreme Court may itself be somewhat to blame. I do not believe, however, that the courts have wanted or have enjoyed immersion in educational administration, but rather have been forced to protect the basic legal rights expressed in our Constitution lest the democratic experiment fail.

Judge Wright's "Parting Word" from *Hobson* v. *Hansen* epitomizes this view: "It is regrettable, of course, that in deciding this case this court must act in an area so alien to its expertise. It would be far better indeed for these great social and political problems to be resolved in the political arena by other branches of government. But these are problems which seem at times to defy such solution. In such situations, under our system, the judiciary must bear a hand and accept its responsibility to assist in the solution where constitutional rights hang in the balance."[3]

In practice, the major interest of the courts has been the protection of individual rights, and this concern has been reflected in the courts by (1) desegregation cases, (2) cases upholding academic freedom, (3) cases on religious establishment and exercise, and (4) cases defining the civil rights of students and teachers. In order to implement the law the courts have been forced, reluctantly, to enter into administration. There are now some indications that they may be trying to disentangle themselves. I would like to look at the cases in the areas mentioned to determine what the courts' actions have been, how those actions have modified educational leadership, and what course the courts may take in the future. I would also like to consider how the education cases may have modified the courts and what future responsibilities educational leadership may bear in this regard.

Desegregation

It is tempting to begin and end any analysis of education and the law during the last twenty years with the desegregation cases. This is because these cases both encompass and epitomize the issues in the conflict between the schools and the courts. In addition, they fit very neatly into the time period. *Brown* I[4] was decided in May 1954 and *Brown* II[5] almost exactly twenty years ago. I have discussed elsewhere the evolution of the affirmative action power of the courts in the civil rights and desegregation cases. Affirmative action comes from the equity power of the courts. Equity, once called the Court of the King's Conscience, refers to the power of the courts to form flexible remedies in situations in which the more formal remedies of monetary damages or incarceration are inappropriate. Affirmative action, although originally a labor law term in this country, surfaced early in the civil rights cases in an attempt to define the power of the trial courts to tailor remedies to shifting situations, and to continue jurisdiction of the courts as plans were put into effect in order to monitor compliance with constitutional mandates. It is certainly the exercise of this equity power which has caused the greatest concern both to the schools and the courts. The schools have had the courts looking over their shoulders on a daily basis, and the courts have gotten into a task for which they are essentially unfitted. One commentator has noted that desegregation cases are more like labor arbitrations than like normal cases which are heard once and decided; the desegregation cases go on—through *Swann* I,[6] II, III, and so forth. Many a judicial mind must wonder whether the courts have not picked up a hot potato which cannot be put down.

The fault for the use of equity power probably goes back to the overly flexible language the Supreme Court used in *Brown* I and II, and to the reluctance of the educational establishment to do the educational planning mandated by the law. The courts thus had to step in, somewhat hesitantly, to do the planning themselves. Over and over again we see courts complaining about or at least noting the inappropriateness of this activity. Charles Black, in *The Occasions of Justice,* notes the reactions of his native Texas to *Brown* I. He asserts that if there had been a strong unqualified opinion it might have been obeyed, although reluctantly, but that the "soft" approach of the Supreme Court in essence turned the decision into a suggestion rather than the law of the land.[7]

It is in *Brown* II, the "all deliberate speed" case, that the U.S. Supreme Court defined the equitable powers of the courts to take affirmative action to eliminate illegal racial segregation in the schools and thereby predicted the tasks of the district courts for the next twenty years. In 1955 the U.S. Supreme Court delegated the primary judicial role to the U.S. District Courts. It directed them to be guided by equitable principles which are characterized by "a practical flexibility in shaping its remedies and by a facility for adjusting and reconciling public and private needs."[8] Specifically, the district courts were directed to: "consider problems related to administration, arising from the physical condition of the school plant, the school transportation system, personnel, revision of school districts and attendance areas into compact units to achieve a system of determining admission to the public schools on a nonracial basis, and reviewing of local laws and regulations. . . . They will also consider the adequacy of any plans the defendants may propose. . . . During this period of transition, the courts will retain jurisdiction of these cases."[9]

And thus the U.S. District Courts got into the business of school administration and wrestled largely on their own for the next decade and more. By 1964 the Supreme Court realized its mandate was being challenged and abandoned "all deliberate speed" for an immediate obligation. In 1968 the Supreme Court itself found it necessary to intervene again to define the desegregation process in *Green* v. *County School Board*[10] which dealt with a "freedom of choice" plan. Since resistance to the law seemed to be getting out of hand, the Supreme Court stressed the result (desegregation) rather than the means (freedom of choice) and refused to let school boards transfer to the parents the responsibility laid on them by the courts in the *Brown* cases. In 1969 the Supreme Court, in *Alexander* v. *Holmes County Board of Education,*[11] "sent the doctrine of deliberate speed to its final resting place." Then, since the school districts and their leadership had failed by and large to present merger plans, the U.S. Circuit Court of Appeals for the Fifth Circuit (covering the southern states) effectuated the Supreme Court's decision by writing its own plan for all school districts under its jurisdiction to begin the following fall term in the case *Singleton* v. *Jackson Municipal Separate School Districts.*[12] Although the courts used educational administrators as expert witnesses in these cases, the final decisions were made by the courts because the object was to protect constitutional rights, not to administer the schools. In 1971 the Supreme Court again undertook to define the responsibilities of school authorities and school districts more precisely in *Swann* v. *Charlotte Mecklenburg Board of Education.*[13] This case advanced the idea of desegregation toward the north by announcing an evidentiary presumption against the school district which came close to the idea that segregated patterns are in themselves a denial of equal protection. It was also the first busing case. In it the Supreme Court specifically reaffirmed the equitable powers of the district courts once a violation had occurred. The Court stated:

In seeking to define even in broad and general terms how far this remedial power extends it is important to remember that judicial powers may be exercised only on the basis of a constitutional violation. Remedial judicial authority does not put judges automatically in the shoes of school authorities whose powers are plenary. Judicial authority enters only when local authority defaults.

School authorities are traditionally charged with broad power to formulate and implement educational policy and might well conclude, for example, that in order to prepare students to live in a pluralistic society each school should have a prescribed ratio of Negro to white students reflecting the proportion for the district as a whole. To do this as an educational policy is within the broad discretionary powers of school authorities; absent a finding of a constitutional violation, however, that would not be within the authority of a federal court. As with any equity case, the nature of the violation determines the scope of the remedy. In default by the school authorities of their obligation to proffer acceptable remedies, a district court has broad power to fashion a remedy that will assure a unitary school system.[14]

In this case also the Court specifically rejected the contention that Title IV of the Civil Rights Act of 1964 could limit or modify the powers of the Court to apply the Fourteenth Amendment. It stated: "There is no suggestion of an intention to . . . withdraw from the courts their historic equitable remedial powers."[15] *Keyes* v. *School District No. 1*[16] extended the *Swann* requirement to northern schools, by finding that schools in the Denver area were segregated by affirmative state action which made the resulting racial patterns unconstitutional, and continued to define the equity power to deal with discrimination. The Court referred specifically to boundary gerrymandering, construction of new schools, transfers, and excessive use of mobile classrooms. It began to look as though local control, due to misuse or nonuse, had been forfeited entirely to the equity power of the federal courts. However, in 1974 in the Detroit case, *Bradley* v. *Milliken,*[17] the Supreme Court refused to consolidate suburban and urban school districts citing lack of segregationist intent when the districts were originally formed; and later in 1975 the Court refused to hear the Indianapolis case in which city and county districts were consolidated for all functions except the schools.[18] *Bradley* v. *Milliken* signals a significant change of direction by the Supreme Court, particularly in light of the discussion of emphasis on local control in the opinion and since this language does not stand alone. In *Wheeler* v. *Barrera,*[19] a case dealing with the use of Title I funds in parochial schools in Missouri, the Supreme Court strongly directed the lower court to stay out of the business of educational administration. We should also take into account in this sequence

San Antonio Independent School District v. *Rodriguez,*[20] which clearly left local control of finance intact and outside the Equal Protection clause. Justice Marshall in his dissent to *Bradley* v. *Milliken* said that the majority was "listening to the election returns." Many commentators have agreed. In all fairness, another possible reason for the Court's retrenchment, must be considered. At the very beginning, in 1955, the Court indicated that the local courts would have to become deeply involved in the administration of the public schools. While many realize that the courts have greatly interfered with educational administration, it is also true that the desegregation cases have had a major impact on judicial process. It may *not* be that the justice in *Bradley* v. *Milliken, Wheeler* v. *Barrera,* and *San Antonio School District* v. *Rodriguez* are listening to the ballot box, they may have been concerned for the survival of the judicial system. The desegregation cases have caused both statutes and Constitutional amendments to be sponsored which directly and indirectly challenge authority possessed by the judicial system since the days of *Marbury* v. *Madison.*[21] Alexander Bickel describes it as follows:

The short of it is this. The Supreme Court has held that there are cases in which the only effective remedy for school segregation is to order the busing of children below the sixth grade. In such a case, having determined that but for the busing the segregation of schools would go unremedied, if the Court should accept the command of Congress that it may not administer what it regards as the only effective remedy, the Court will have accepted a more far-reaching limitation on judicial power, a greater qualification of the power of judicial review established by *Marbury* v. *Madison*, than ever before in its history....[22]

Perhaps after twenty years of trying to impose integration on unwilling systems the courts do not wish to expose their power to further erosion. In this they may be wise. The relevant school board actions during the last twenty years have often been an exercise in how to avoid, by delay, a clear pronouncement by our highest legal authority. There is no question that this situation has undermined the authority of the courts and for this we all suffer. Our government is of laws, not men, but I wonder what conclusions students draw about the supremacy of the rule of law when, twenty years after its mandate, a Supreme Court order is widely unobeyed.

Despite the retrenchment of the Supreme Court, it seems apparent that the lower courts (and no doubt the lawyers involved), having developed some expertise in educational administration, continue to exercise it. In 1974 the concern of the NAACP Legal Defense Fund was over the statistics which indicated that larger percentages of black students than white students were being suspended, expelled, and otherwise disciplined in integrated schools (see also *Goss* v. *Lopez infra*). This issue came before the U.S. District Court in Dallas in the case of *Hawkins* v. *Coleman*[23] decided in June 1974. The opinion came after two years of litigation and two appeals to the Fifth Circuit. The case will be instructive, I think, when future relationships between educators and the courts are considered. The suit was brought by black students alleging that the student suspension rules (1) denied them due process, (2) denied them equal protection of the laws, and (3) were enforced in a discriminatory manner. The court did not find a denial of due process and did not discuss equal protection, but concluded that racism *was* the chief cause of disproportionate numbers of blacks receiving suspension and corporal punishment. The evidence the court relied on to reach this conclusion reflects the increasing sophistication of the courts, and the bar, in these matters. The first witness, an expert in statistical evaluation in education, testified that black students were being suspended more often than whites at all three levels and were receiving more long-term suspensions. Then an expert on institutional racism testified that the Dallas Independent School District fit into a national pattern of discrimination as a "white-controlled institution." This means that most decisions about distribution of resources are made by white administrators. "Institutional racism," as opposed to "personal racism," exists when the procedures of an institution are prejudiced against or unresponsive to a racial group. Institutional racism leads to hostility which leads to suspensions; conduct acceptable in a black environment may become "disruptive" to teachers unfamiliar with black environment. The next witnesses were black parents who testified as to the existence of problems predicted by the expert witnesses. This evidence was not contested. The expert on institutional racism recommended a four point program: (1) Institutional and structural change, (2) Training of teachers and counselors, (3) Training of black students, and (4) Encouragement of community programs of affirmative action.

The court found that racism was the chief cause of the disproportionate suspensions for blacks, and that an "affirmative action program" including the above four points was needed. Somewhat wearily, we may imagine, the court refused to detail the affirmative action program since "the Court has no intention of taking from the School Board or the Superintendent and other officials the running of the schools."[24] Then the court had this to say:

> It should be pointed out, however, that if there is to be progress in Dallas towards removing institutional racism there must be a change in attitude of both the School Board and the officials. There has prevailed among these officials a determination to resist every effort to make the changes which have been decreed and which they should know are inevitable. The law will be followed, says the School Board, but then only after every effort has been made to resist. There has been an utter lack of leadership in developing public opinion to accept necessary changes in the school if the law is to be followed.
>
> Cooperation on the part of the school officials with the public generally, and particularly the parents, is needed at the same time changes are made in the school system. It is the responsibility of the School Board and officials to take the lead in the development of public opinion and in obtaining cooperation.
>
> No court can decree a change in attitude. That is something within the individual. Put briefly, there must be a real effort on the part of everyone involved to accentuate the positive while at the same time eliminating the negative effects of "white institutional racism."[25]

It is obvious that this case tells us a great deal about current interaction between educational leadership and the courts. The nature of the evidence used, conclusions drawn, and remedies required shows an increasingly sophisticated understanding of educational administration along with some weariness at the continued necessity for the courts to run the schools. The courts don't want to run the schools, but, where there is no alternative to upholding the law, they will have to take action. The court's words are a strong indictment of educational leadership. Are they true? We can agree, no doubt, that the courts are using the schools to reform society and this is an increased burden on administration of education, but on the other hand, it is an appropriate one. This society presumes that we can solve most problems through better education. Can it also be presumed that educators know how to solve all problems but their own? Has sufficient attention been given to these problems in our graduate programs training educational administrators and our efforts toward continuing education and in-service training? Might efforts be better devoted to solving the problem instead of resisting it or being guided by those who resist? The need to change is a moral imperative. Can it harm us to try to fulfill it?

I would like to point out one other aspect of this issue and this case. Suspensions and expulsions are of national concern to black organizations; issues in the *Coleman* case are therefore likely to be repeated in other districts, and these cases, as others before them, will build on each other in a national campaign of test cases.

Another new but effective measure involves suing the administrative agencies in order to require them to take stronger action to effectuate desegregation through *writs of mandamus*. This was resulted in two decisions startling in their widespread effect. *Adams* v. *Richardson*[26] forced the Department of Health, Education, and Welfare (HEW) to begin active enforcement of integration of public higher education systems in eleven southern states, and *Kelsey* v. *Weinberger*[27] cut off funds under the Emergency School Aid Act to several major cities that had failed to integrate adequately their public school faculties. In the latter case the court invalidated a waiver granted by the secretary of HEW to allow these districts more time to achieve faculty integration. Women's Equity Action League and other women's groups have now picked up this idea and asked the District of Columbia District Court to issue a mandamus to HEW to enforce better Executive Order 11246, as amended by 11375, and Title IX of the Education Amendments of 1972.

While it is true that lawyers in the Office of Economic Opportunity (OEO) are no longer able to pursue education cases, there is now in existence a core group of trained and interested public service lawyers who will continue to pay attention to problems of civil rights in the schools, including those related to desegregation, discrimination, suspension and expulsion, free press, free speech, and other problems for both teachers and students. In addition, *Bradley* v. *School Board of Richmond*[28] has given them the resources to act upon these problems, at least in the desegregation cases, by allowing the award of attorney's fees and costs to the prevailing party.[29]

Academic Freedom

While the courts have shown commendable stamina and courage in the desegregation cases, I believe that during the past twenty years some of the finest hours in school law came in the academic freedom cases. These are the cases from the McCarthy era—cases that established the legal protection of academic freedom, a freedom which is not spelled out in our Constitution or statutes but which comes to us directly from the courts. Many of us probably recall those times in which the Court stood as a strong bulwark and support for individual teachers against institutions of education and others who were reflecting political pressures which demanded a witch hunt. Over and over the Supreme Court struck down overly broad, vague loyalty oaths which attempted to reach beliefs and thoughts rather than impermissible actions and which therefore impinged on academic freedom. The Court's views were summarized in *Keyishion* v. *Board of Regents* this way:

Our nation is deeply committed to safeguarding academic freedom, which is of transcendent value to all of us and not merely to the teachers concerned. That freedom is therefore a special concern of the First Amendment, which does not tolerate laws that cast a pall of orthodoxy over the classroom. "The vigilant protection of constitutional freedoms is nowhere more vital than in the community of American schools." *Shelton* v. *Tucker,* .... The classroom is peculiarly the "marketplace of ideas." The Nation's future depends upon leaders trained through wide exposure to that robust exchange of ideas which discovers truth "out of multitude of tongues, (rather) than through any kind of authoritative selection." ... In *Sweezy* v. *New Hampshire,* ... we said:

"The essentiality of freedom in the community of American universities is almost self-evident. No one should underestimate the vital role in a democracy that is played by those who guide and train our youth. To impose any strait jacket upon the intellectual leaders in our colleges and universities would imperil the future of our Nation. No field of education is so thoroughly comprehended by man that new discoveries cannot yet be made. Particularly is that true in the social sciences, where few, if any, principles are accepted as absolutes. Scholarship cannot flourish in an atmosphere of suspicion and distrust. Teachers and students must always remain free to inquire, to study and to evaluate, to gain new maturity and understanding; otherwise, our civilization will stagnate and die."[30]

The Court also refused to weaken the Constitutional protection afforded by the Fifth Amendment in *Slochower* v. *Board of Higher Education.*[31]

In the latter part of that twenty years, the courts, having exempted teachers from the impositions of McCarthyism, found it easy to extend the protection of teachers' civil rights. It allowed teachers freedom to comment as citizens on the activities of their boards and administrations,[32] to become active politically in the civil rights movement without fear of dismissal,[33] and to organize to bargain collectively without fearing for their jobs,[34] although laws prohibiting strikes have repeatedly been held constitutional.[35] The days are gone when teacher contracts contained promises to abstain from dancing, immodest dressing, and any other conduct unbecoming a lady; not to fall in love, become engaged or secretly married, or go out with young men "except as so far as it may be necessary to stimulate Sunday-school work."[36] Teachers have increasingly gone to court to insist on wide latitudes of personal freedom of behavior, and they are, by and large, successful, although the courts have not condoned active espousal of homosexuality.[37] There does seem to be a rule evolving that one moral slip is not grounds for dismissal or failure to hire. A continuing pattern of immoral behavior must be shown.

In *Cleveland Board of Education* v. *La Fleur*[38] the Supreme Court set aside arbitrary rules requiring female teachers to resign at the fifth month of pregnancy, although leaving intact provisions for a notice of return after pregnancy. The Supreme Court opinion is instructive in its view of the administrative rationale for the desire to keep the arbitrary rule. In a footnote the Court puts aside the appeals derived from lawyers pertaining to health, safety, and welfare and comments instead on the testimony concerning "social taboos" of the administrators at the trial. That footnote should remind us that "You mustn't try to fool" the "Nine Old Men."

Another significant decision in the realm of academic freedom was *Epperson* v. *Arkansas,*[39] which dealt with the teaching of evolution in the public schools. It is important, however, to remember that the essence of that holding springs from the First Amendment prohibition against the establishment of religion, although free speech is also mentioned. Subsequent cases have indicated that, on the public school level at least, there still remains wide administrative discretion in the selection of teaching materials and teaching subjects. In 1974, for example, the teaching of abortion in the public schools was held not to be constitutionally protected[40] and it is still possible to dismiss teachers for the use of inappropriate materials or language,[41] although standards of acceptability are much broader than they once were. For example, use of a four-letter word for fornication to illustrate the idea of cultural taboos was upheld under limited circumstances.[42] In that case, incidentally, Judge Wyzanski attempted to formulate rules for the future guidance of teachers and administrators, but the appeals court preferred a case-by-case balancing method. Nevertheless, the academic and personal freedom of teachers have increased substantially during the last twenty years and will undoubtedly continue to increase, though perhaps as much through bargaining efforts as through litigation.

A keystone case decided in the last double decade was *Tinker* v. *Des Moines Independent Community School District.*[43] This is the case in which the Supreme Court upheld the right of pupils to wear black arm bands to school to protest the Viet Nam war over the objections of the school authorities. The Tinker case set out the now famous "substantial disruption and material interference" test against which all subsequent questionable student behavior has been measured. Armbands were followed by buttons and by underground newspapers, as well as those not so underground. The Supreme Court was to have reviewed one of the newspaper cases during that term but dismissed it as moot because the students had graduated.[44] This decision was a small ray of light for the beleagured administrator. If the Supreme Court is going to refuse to hear cases involving students who have graduated, it will mean that the Court will hear only such suits as can be framed as class actions, since cases can rarely reach the Court while the students are still in school. And thus there may be a few less cases. The decision in the "Corn Cob Curtain" student newspaper case from the Seventh Circuit is instructive for a number of reasons. In it the court considered a detailed school regulatory code section by section and found each section a violation of the students' right to free speech and free press. What is striking to me is that the superintendent, or his attorney, obviously tried to draft the rules to follow the language in the *Tinker* case as closely as possible, yet the court still struck down every rule. The moral may be that in trying to draft rules of procedure—and this will surely be one of the court's greatest areas of concern during the next ten years—it is better to consult your conscience than your lawyer, to aim for what is fair rather than what is "legal."

It does seem evident that the courts are basically concerned with fairness to individuals, assuring that they have adequate prior notice of the nature of conduct which is unacceptable; that they understand in what particulars they are deemed to have erred; and that they be allowed to give their own side of the story before an impartial arbiter. These are the essential requirements in *Goss* v. *Lopez,*[45] the case which required a minimal amount of due process for suspensions less than ten days. Although the requirement of these standards did mean that unfettered administrative discretion as to what constitutes proper behavior for students and teachers was modified, it is difficult to believe that this modification was improper. It is, on the contrary, difficult to understand why the use of such procedures did not evolve naturally from the school systems themselves, which are, after all, supposed to be inculcating the basic values of a democratic society. We cannot teach respect for law and order when we do not practice it. That the Supreme Court feels strongly about due process is made abundantly clear in *Wood* v. *Strickland*,[46] which opens the door to the possibility of holding school officials liable in monetary damages for a conscious failure to grant constitutional due process.

A final area of consideration that leads us back to the desegregation and racial discrimination cases is that of special education: tracking, labelling, and problems of the multi-language child. Here the concern of the courts has also been with the individual. A leading case in establishing the rights of the mentally handicapped is *Hobson* v. *Hansen*[47] which was decided by Judge Skelly Wright in the District of Columbia in 1967. This case was another judicial indictment of educational administration, because it criticized not the *theory* of tracking, but the way it was actually put into *practice* in Washington, D.C. The decision, 118 pages in length and the result of a year's exclusive study by Judge Wright, attacked the culturally biased testing and classification which locks students into lower tracks without providing compensatory education in a track system precipitated by racial desegregation. The opinion was handed down in June 1967 and was to be implemented by the following October. Additional cases have led to guarantees of due process and of meaningful education for special education students. The greatest impact of these cases was to spur the passage of state legislation providing education for all educable citizens of school age.[48] Although no case regarding education of the mentally retarded has reached the Supreme Court, in 1974 the Court decided *Lau* v. *Nichols*,[49] which directed the San Francisco Unified School District to eliminate discrimination against Chinese students who did not speak English by providing them with some form of compensatory education. Interestingly, in *Lau*, the plaintiffs did not ask for specific relief, but asked only that the

Board of Education be directed to apply its expertise and rectify the situation, a stance that wisely recognizes the need for the courts to decide and the schools to administer.

A second *Hobson*[50] decision in 1971 required equalization of expenditures within 5 percent of the district mean, but in 1973 the Supreme Court handed down *San Antonio Independent School District* v. *Rodriguez,*[51] which left intact the system of local finance for school districts that had been attacked under the Equal Protection clause. In reaching this conclusion, the Court noted that "the judiciary is well advised to refrain from imposing on the States inflexible constitutional restraints that could circumscribe or handicap the continued research and experimentation so vital to finding even partial solutions to educational problems and to keeping abreast of ever-changing conditions."[52] Although *Rodriguez* did *not* require reallocation of school funds on a constitutional basis, several state courts, notably those in California and New Jersey in the *Serrano*[53] and *Robinson*[54] cases, have required a reallocation under state constitutional provisions. New legal requirements in school finance will undoubtedly modify school operations during the next decade. While the specific applications may be difficult, I do not believe the courts are wrong to require greater equalization of educational expenditures. The problem is, again, that, if the courts are forced to do work for which they are not fitted, they may not do it as well as professional administrators might.

Religious Establishment and Exercise

A final area in public school management which has been changed by the courts is that of religious exercises in the public schools. Basic societal and educational issues underlie these cases. Is it possible to teach and not to preach? Is not inculcation of values and, hence, religion an inevitable part of the teaching function? The Supreme Court has essentially reaffirmed the pluralistic presumption of society and further rejected the concept of the melting pot in these cases. Important as these and related cases wrestling with different forms of aid to parochial schools are, I do not see them as central to the conflict of styles and approaches between the courts and the schools, since they involve a third factor, religion, and therefore a separate Constitutional question with which the Supreme Court has always been involved. No review of educational law would be complete, however, without them.

From 1955 to 1975 the U.S. Supreme Court wrestled with the issues of how much and what kind of religious education could take place in the public schools. The issues involved both the intrusion of religion into public schools and the amount of support the government can give to private religious education. *Engle* v. *Vitale*[55] struck down the New York State Board of Regents' "denominationally neutral prayer" as an unconstitutional establishment of religion; in 1963 the Supreme Court interdicted the reading of Bible verses without comment and the recitation of the Lord's Prayer.[56] It was also during this period that the U.S. and state supreme courts began to determine how much, if any, support for parochial schools by way of busing, textbooks, auxiliary services, equipment, federal funds for special services, federal or state funds for building was allowed under constitutional standards. The U.S. Supreme Court has ruled that schools may not "establish religion" by holding religious exercises or instruction of any kind in the schools, although carefully circumscribed programs during released time are allowable. The extent to which state aid could go to parochial schools and colleges may become a less pressing issue now that schools and colleges are less crowded, but important guidelines have been set down and significant cases are still in litigation. The clearest development has been the three-part test from *Lemon* v. *Kurtzman* (1973)[57] regarding legislation designed to help religiously oriented institutions. It provided that: (1) The statute in question must have a secular purpose; (2) its primary effect must neither inhibit nor advance religion; and (3) it must not foster an excessive entanglement of government with religion in the sense of a comprehensive discriminating and continuing state of surveillance.

The Supreme Court has specifically disallowed reimbursement to parents and students in various forms as well as tax benefits for parents[58] while allowing loans of textbooks to private religious schools.[59] *Meek* v. *Pittinger,*[60] a Pennsylvania case, allowed the loan of books but not other instructional materials and auxiliary services such as special education instruction or the loan of equipment such as projectors which might be converted to a religious purpose. The Supreme Court also took a very strong stand for free exercise of religion in *Wisconsin* v. *Yoder,*[61] which allowed the religious beliefs of the Amish to prevail over the state compulsory attendance law, since compulsory attendance in public schools would essentially destroy the Amish religion. The court found that the compulsory attendance law "carries with it precisely the kind of objective danger to the free exercise of religion which the First Amendment was designed to prevent. . . ."[62]

During this period it also became apparent that federal aid to public schools was easier to justify constitutionally than state aid[63] and that programs of aid to colleges were more defensible than those to public schools, since students of college age are more intellectually discriminating and attendance is not compulsory.[64] A minor thesis is that aid in the form of special education seems more constitutionally acceptable. State supreme courts continue, however, to apply stricter standards than the federal courts, even in the area of individual scholarships or institutional aid to religiously affiliated colleges.[65] On the college level, the Tennessee program of tuition grants for private college attendance was struck down by a three judge district court and is presently before the Supreme Court on appeal.[66]

Civil Rights of Students and Teachers

A final area of interest in educational law during the last twenty years has been the relation between *higher* education and the courts. The recent involvement of the courts in higher education administration represents a startling change. This clash of two worlds may be even more cataclysmic than the conflict between the public schools and the courts, since it appears that higher education still does not comprehend that it is subject to law. Nor does it believe that the courts really are able and intend to modify the universities' own internal processes.

Here again, my view is the same. The courts have "impinged" substantially on educational leadership during this period. Education, however, has brought this impingement on itself to some degree by failing to exercise adequate leadership in facing the issues that really concern the courts. Despite some retrenchment by the courts, the impingement will continue unless leadership itself begins to solve the issues underlying those being raised in litigation. Although I have some sympathy with the plaint of Kingman Brewster, president of

Yale University, that the academy is being overregulated by the federal government,[67] I also feel that the academy has only itself to blame for not keeping its house in order. To me, the courts, are only asking that constitutional rights be observed in academia as elsewhere, having learned, to their surprise, that this may not happen automatically.

For example, if statistics indicate that universities have a history of discrimination, it seems to me that they cannot complain about regulations designed to overcome that discrimination, even if the regulations are complex, burdensome, and interfere with known, comfortable ways of doing things. Discrimination is wrong, and the academy could have been correcting itself instead of waiting to have change thrust upon it from without. From 1970 to 1973 the United States Supreme Court decided four cases dealing with higher education: The tenure cases, *Roth*[68] and *Sinderman,*[69] which indicated that tenured professors have a property interest in their jobs which guarantees them procedural due process within the university while untenured professors do not; the Connecticut College case on whether the local Students for a Democratic Society (SDS) chapter was entitled to recognition and how much internal due process a college was required to afford, *Healy* v. *James;*[70] and the student nonresident tuition case, *Vlandis* v. *Kline,*[71] which struck down irrefutable presumptions of nonresidence and threw financial assumptions for state universities into confusion. Given previous history, this is an unprecedented intervention into university decision making. Although the Supreme Court set aside any consideration of the requirements for affirmative action in admissions in *De Funis* v. *Odegaard,*[72] a similar case will undoubtedly be placed before the Court in the next ten years. I believe there has been a slight tinge of outrage in these cases since the courts, along with the rest of society, have traditionally assumed that higher education was above reproach and of the highest moral standards, and that, since these institutions were leading society, the courts did not need to worry about the enforcement of constitutional rights within their confines. When cases were increasingly brought that indicated that school and college systems did not indeed always protect constitutional rights and were not in the forefront of society in this regard, the courts did not hesitate to bring the educational system up to the standards set for the rest of society.

Let us hope that Justice Douglas' comments on the health of university life, in *Healy* v. *James*, are too pessimistic, but they do not bode well for future confrontations:

The present (SDS) case is miniscule in the events of the 60's and 70's. But the fact that it has to come here (to the Supreme Court) for ultimate resolution indicates the sickness of our academic world, measured by First Amendment standards. Students as well as faculty are entitled to credentials in their search for truth. If we are to become an integrated adult society, rather than a stubborn status quo opposed to change, students and faculties should have communal interests in which each age learns from the other. Without ferment of one kind or another, a college or university (like a federal agency or other human institution) becomes a useless appendage to a society which traditionally has reflected the spirit of rebellion.[73]

If the courts begin more and more to pass on questions of higher education, college and university administrators and their governing faculties will begin to see, explore, and understand the concerns of the courts. Particularly because of the constitutional issues and reflections of current social policy, it seems likely that, in its attempts to enforce the latter, the courts may violate some of the most cherished rules and values of academic life such as institutional autonomy. The possibilities and resultant problems of legal enforcement should be recognized, and institutions should begin to deal with the problems in their own ways to avoid the heavy-handed attentions of the courts.

Future Trends

In trying to assess the sweep of the law through the channels of education during the last twenty years, and to draw some conclusions, I am overwhelmed by the magnitude of the task. Reviewing the cases in this short space gives me the sensation of looking out a window of a fast train. It is therefore necessary to try to indicate some trends. While the most important concept to keep in mind is the interaction between law and education, the impact of legal thinking on administration will be of increasing significance. In the past twenty years the courts and the legislatures have told the schools: (1) that they may not discriminate by segregating their school systems according to race, either by law or by fact; (2) that they may not teach religion in the public schools, or force students to seek religious instructions elsewhere during certain school periods; (3) that they may not impinge on the free speech or the constitutional rights of teachers and that they may not impinge on the constitutional rights of students, except to the degree necessary to carry forth a proper educational purpose; and (4) as an overriding directive, that they must be fair. They must exhibit fairness in all the programs of education and in the process and procedures taken to expel students, to fire teachers, or any other action with implications for individual rights. And the courts have said that the schools must be fair, not only by their own traditional ways of doing things, but by the general standards held by our society and held by our Constitution and laws. In this rondelet, the schools have asked the courts why they are trying to run the schools; the courts have replied that they are *not* trying to run the schools but only enforce Constitutional rights; the schools have replied that the courts' style of enforcing Constitutional rights is impinging on educational leadership, and the courts have replied that educational leadership is incapable of comprehending the Constitutional mandate, which means devising a plan that encompasses good educational planning *and* constitutional law. The courts' only expertise and mandate is in applying the law, which they must continue to do.

In this exchange I believe the courts rightly have the last word. It is true that the courts are using the schools to reform society, but that in itself is a left-handed compliment. Most other institutions do not have that capacity. We would be much farther down that road if, rather than studying and teaching the law with a view toward understanding how to avoid compliance and resist impingement, we approached it with a desire to understand the basic constitutional mandates and to put them into practice in our schools and in our world.

In short, I do not really see the courts impinging on educational leadership, but rather, sometimes reluctantly, carrying out their Constitutional mandate. I believe educational leadership is best advised to understand not just the *requirements* of court decisions but also the *reasons* for them so they may anticipate and join in future developments of the law of education.

In the next ten years the courts will no doubt continue to expand the individual rights of students and teachers, particularly women and girls. I have not discussed Title IX of the Educational Amendments of 1972, because it has not yet generated any opinions, but the elimination of sex discrimination in the public schools will be a major focus for the next ten years. Public school finance may be forced to shift its base and, for the first time, higher education and public school education may be competing in the legislative halls for the same budgetary dollar. New Constitutional means of supporting private education may put a further strain on school finance and put educational administration into the context of competition. Affirmative legal duties to educate the community in the necessities and practicalities of social progress may emerge. Above all, the courts will continue to press administrators to devise their own solutions, so that the courts may withdraw from active involvement in the schools.

My approach to the historical relation between law and education in the last twenty years and its portent for the future thus lead me to the following conclusions:

1. There is increasing interaction between the courts and the schools and, more recently, between the courts and the colleges.

2. This is likely to remain the case, particularly given the present litigiousness of the American people.

3. The courts will hold schools and colleges to at least as strict a standard as the rest of society.

4. Administrators ought to anticipate decisions of the courts in order to maintain their own leadership mandates.

5. It is extremely important for educational administrators to see as their duty upholding the rules of law in this country, in order that they teach respect for the law and maintain the strength of the rule of law and hence the strength of the free government of our society.

Notes

1. *Epperson* v. *Arkansas,* 393 U.S. 97, 89 S. Ct. 266, 21 L. Ed. 2d 228 (1968).

2. *Ibid.,* 393 U.S. at 101.

3. *Hobson* v. *Hansen,* 269 F. Supp. 401, 517 (D.C.D.C. 1967).

4. *Brown* v. *Board of Education of Topeka,* 349 U.S. 294, 75 S. Ct. 753, 99 L. Ed. 1083 (1955).

5. *Brown* v. *Board of Education of Topeka,* 347 U.S. 483, 74 S. Ct. 686, 98 L. Ed. 873 (1954).

6. *Swann* v. *Charlotte-Mecklenburg Board of Education,* 399 U.S. 926

(1969), 400 U.S. 802 (1969), 402 U.S. 1 (1971), 402 U.S. 43 (1971), 403 U.S. 912 (1972).

7. Charles Black, *The Occasions of Justice* (New York: Macmillan, 1963), 152.

8. *Brown* v. *Board of Education* 349 U.S. at 300.

9. *Ibid.*

10. *Green* v. *County School Board*, 391 U.S. 430, 88 S. Ct. 1689, 20 L. Ed. 2d 716 (1968).

11. *Alexander* v. *Holmes County Board of Education*, 396 U.S. 19, 90 S. Ct. 29, 24 L. Ed. 2d 19 (1969).

12. *Singleton* v. *Jackson Municipal Separate School Districts*, 419 F. 2d 1211 (5th Cir. 1970).

13. *Swann* v. *Charlotte-Mecklenburg Board of Education*, 402 U.S. 1, 91 S. Ct. 1267, 28 L. Ed. 2d 554 (1971).

14. *Ibid.*, 402 U.S. at 15.

15. *Ibid.*, 402 U.S. at 19.

16. *Keyes* v. *School District No. 1*, 413 U.S. 921, 93 S. Ct. 2686 37 L. Ed. 1043 (1973).

17. *Bradley* v. *Milliken*, 418 U.S. 717, 94 S. Ct. 3112, 41 L. Ed. 2d 1069 (1974).

18. *U.S. and Donny Buckley* v. *Board of School Commissioners of Indianapolis*, 503 F. 2d 68 (1974).

19. *Wheeler* v. *Barrera*, 417 U.S. 402, 94 S. Ct. 2274, 416 Ed. 2d 159 (1974).

20. *San Antonio Independent School District* v. *Rodriguez*, 411 U.S. 1, 93 S. Ct. 1278, 36 L. Ed. 2d 16 (1973).

21. *Marbury* v. *Madison*, 5 U.S. 137, 2 L. Ed. 135 (1803).

22. Alexander M. Bickel, "Education in a Democracy: The Legal and Practical Problems of School Busing," 3 *Human Rights* (1973) 53, 58. See also Alex M. Bickel, *The Supreme Court and the Idea of Progress* (New York: Harper & Row, 1970); Philip B. Kurland, *Politics, the Constitution and the Warren Court* (Chicago: University of Chicago Press, 1970).

23. *Hawkins* v. *Coleman*, 376 F. Supp. 1330 (1974).

24. *Ibid.* at 1338.

25. *Ibid.*

26. *Adams* v. *Richardson*, 351 F. Supp. 636 (D.C.D.C., 1974).

27. *Kelsey* v. *Weinberger*, 363 F. Supp. 521 (D.C.D.C., 1974).

28. *Bradley* v. *School Board of Richmond*, 416 U.S. 696, 94 S. Ct. 2006, 40 L. Ed. 476 (1974).

29. *Alyeska Pipeline Service Company* v. *The Wilderness Society*, 421 U.S. 240, 44 L. Ed. 2d 141, 95 S. Ct. 1612 (1975).

30. *Keyishion* v. *Board of Regents*, 385 U.S. 589, 603, 87 S. Ct. 675, 683, 17 L. Ed. 2d 629, 640 (1967).

31. *Schlochower* v. *Board of Higher Education*, 350 U.S. 551, 76 S. Ct. 637, 100 L. Ed. 692 (1956).

32. *Pickering* v. *Board of Education*, 391 U.S. 563, 883 Ct. 1731 (1968).

33. *Johnson* v. *Branch*, 364 F. 2d 177 (4 Cir. 1966).

34. *McLaughlin* v. *Tilendis*, 398 F. 2d 287 (1968); *Indianapolis Education Association* v. *Lewallen* (7th Cir. 1969); *Hanover Township Federation of Teachers* v. *Hanover Common School Corp.*, 318 F. Supp. 757 (N.D. Ind. 1970).

35. *Hortonville Education Association et al.* v. *Hortonville Joint School District No. 1 et al.*, 66 Wis. 2d 469 (1975); *Lawson* v. *Board of Education of Vestal Cent. Sch. Dist. No. 1*, 315 NYS 2d 877 (1970); *Board of Education* v. *N. J. Educational Association*, 247 A2d 867 (1968); *Pinellas County Classroom Teachers Association* v. *Board of Public Instruction*, 214 So 2d 341 (1968).

36. Quoted in Louis Fisher and David Schimmel, *The Civil Rights of Teachers* (New York: Harper & Row, 1973), 1.

37. *Sarac* v. *State Board of Education*, 249 Cal. App. 2d, 57, 57 Cal. Rptr. 69 (1967).

38. *Cleveland Board of Education* v. *La Fleur*, 414 U.S. 632 94 S. Ct. 791, 39 L. Ed. 2d 52 (1974).

39. *Epperson* v. *Arkansas.*

40. *Mercer* v. *Michigan State Board of Education*, 379 F. Supp. 580 (D.C. Mich, 1974).

41. *Lindros* v. *Governing Board of Torrance School District*, 25 C.A. 3d 38 (1972).

42. *Mailloux* v. *Kiley*, 323 F. Supp. 1387 (D Mass 1971).

43. *Tinker* v. *Des Moines*, 393 U.S. 503, 89 S. Ct. 733, 21 L. Ed. 2d 731 (1969).

44. *Jacobs* v. *Board of School Commissioners* 490 F2d 60 (1973), cert. denied (1974).

45. *Goss* v. *Lopez*, 419 U.S. 565, 95 S. Ct. 729, 42 L. Ed. 2d 725 (1975).

46. *Wood* v. *Strickland*, 43 LW 4293 (1975).

47. *Hobson* v. *Hansen.*

48. Wisconsin Statutes, Chapter 89.

49. *Lau* v. *Nichols*, 414 U.S. 563, 94 S. Ct. 786, 39 L. Ed. 2d 1 (1974).

50. *Hobson* v. *Hansen*, 269 F. Supp. 401, aff'd. sub nom *Smuck* v. *Hobson*, 408 F. 2d 175 (D.C. Cir. 1969).

51. *San Antonio* v. *Rodriguez.*

52. *Ibid.*, 411 U.S. at 43.

53. *Serrano* v. *Priest*, 361 F. 2d 474 (C.A. Cal 1974).

54. *Robinson* v. *Cahill*, 119 N.J. Super. 40 (1972).

55. *Engle* v. *Vitale*, 370 U.S. 421, 82 S. Ct. 1261, 8 L. Ed. 2d 601 (1962).

56. *Abbington School District* v. *Schempp*, 374 U.S. 203, 83 S. Ct. 1560, 10 L. Ed. 2d 844 (1963).

57. *Lemon* v. *Kurtzman*, 403 U.S. 602, 91 S. Ct. 2105, 29 L. Ed. 2d 745 (1971).

58. See *Committee for Public Education* v. *Nyquist*, 413 U.S. 756, 93 S. Ct. 2955, 37 L. Ed. 2d 948 (1973); *Levitt* v. *Committee for Public Education*, 413 U.S. 472, 93 S. Ct. 2814, 37 L. Ed. 2d 736 (1973).

59. *Board of Education* v. *Allen*, 392 U.S. 236, 88 S. Ct. 1923, 20 L. Ed. 2d 1060 (1968).

60. *Meek* v. *Pittinger*, 374 F. Supp. 639 (1973).

61. *Wisconsin* v. *Yoder*, 406 U.S. 205, 92 S. Ct. 1526, 32 L. Ed. 2d 15 (1972).

62. *Ibid.*, 406 U.S. at 218.

63. *Wheeler* v. *Barrera*.

64. *Wheeler* v. *Barrera; Americans United for Separation of Church and State* v. *Dunn*, 384 F. Supp. 714 (M.D. Tenn. 1974); *State ex rel. Warren* v. *Nusbaum* 64 Wisc. 2d 314 (1974).

65. See, e.g., *Nebraska* v. *Swanson*, 192 Neb. 125, 219 N.W. 2d 726 (1974).

66. *Americans United for Separation of Church and State* v. *Dunn*.

67. Speech at American Bar Foundation, Chicago, February 22, 1975.

68. *Board of Regents of State Colleges et al.* v. *Roth*, 408 U.S. 564, 92 S. Ct. 2701, 33 L. Ed. 2d 548 (1971).

69. *Perry* v. *Sindermann*, 408 U.S. 593, 92 S. Ct. 2694, 33 L. Ed. 2d 570 (1971).

70. *Healy* v. *James*, 408 U.S. 169, 92 S. Ct. 2338, 33 L. Ed. 2d 266 (1971).

71. *Vlandis* v. *Kline*, 412 U.S. 441, 93 S. Ct. 2230, 37 L. Ed. 2d 63 (1973).

72. *De Funis* v. *Odegaard*, 416 U.S. 312, 94 S. Ct. 1704, 40 L. Ed. 2d 164 (1974).

73. *Healy* v. *James*, 408 U.S. 169, 197, 92 S. Ct. 2338, 2354, 33 L. Ed. 2d 266, 288 (1971).

7. An Overdue Paradigm Shift in Educational Administration,
Or, How Can We Get That Idiot Off the Freeway?

DONALD A. ERICKSON

Several speakers at the conference on which this book is based demonstrated that political constraints, legal requirements, administrative roles, and other important facets of schooling shifted significantly between 1954 and 1974. But some characteristics of educational institutions seem virtually immutable.

In 1911 Thorndike wrote that educators were tired of uniformity and would henceforth individualize. Sixty-one years later, Glaser complained that "time goes by with still only recognition of the problem and as yet no directions toward solution realized." In 1928 Thayer applauded "the passing of the recitation." Forty-one years later, Hoetker and Ahlbrand reviewed extensive evidence that the recitation was still pervasive in the classroom.[1]

What follows, however, is not another fugue on the beloved theme, "Resistance to Change in Schools."[2] The tenor of that motif, I fear, is to accent symptoms more than causes. To confuse the figure further, I think the school is less like a stubborn ox and more like a sightless person on a freeway. As the blind man fumbles down the median strip, drivers curse him for impeding traffic and bellow instructions about leaving the road. But he gets a rundown feeling whenever he complies. So he clutches the median markers compulsively, feigning forays to distant green fields when the curses sound especially truculent. Several travelers comment eloquently on his "mindlessness"; some note that he "adopts innovations" slowly and superficially; others demand that "change agents" work him over; and passing federal agents thrust money into his hands with hints of more to come, hoping gratitude or greed will lure him off the highway in keeping with published guidelines.

The analogy is overdone. A more cautious approach might be to say: Historians may some day explain that much vacuous, erratic behavior by the school in this century was predictable, since the institution was simultaneously threatened and denied the feedback it needed to defend and improve its performance. Its leaders would have loved to do better, but they didn't know how. Perhaps the best documented example of the vulnerability and irrationality of a blind institution is found in Callahan's remarkable treatise, *Education and the Cult of Efficiency,*[3] though I think Callahan put too much stress on local support and control as explanatory variables and too little on the lack of an adequate knowledge base. Hospitals that are subject to much local purview do not pirouette, like schools, to every piper's tune. Medicine can marshall evidence for its procedures. In the menacing years depicted by Callahan, schools responded with shocking mindlessness to the deified business ethic by feigning efficiency. Given their primitive technology, the efficiency was superficial, even self-defeating. Once the danger passed, the charade was abandoned, though the current accountability movement is educing similar tendencies.

The "alternative schools" movement may be interpreted somewhat similarly. The private free schools that spearheaded the movement were created almost entirely by middle-class white parents,[4] the segment of society supporting public education most reliably in the past. It appeared for a time that the private free schools would spread like wildfire, obliterating white middle-class support for public schools. In this light, the suddenly popular public alternative schools may be viewed as mainly the result of an effort to defuse and discredit the demand for unconventional alternatives, especially among middle-class whites. Many private free schools were bribed into the public fold, and many others collapsed when forced to compete without benefit of similar lucre. Public school officials are accused of discouraging, impeding, and neglecting their own "alternatives," many of which seem phony to begin with. We should not be surprised if the announcement soon comes forth, "We tried that, too, and it didn't do any good."

Lacking evidence of educationally effective structures, what more can we expect? Custodial demands alone are overwhelming in many schools. Among the steady parade of bright new ideas, most exact a heavy toll in energy and time. Few produce what their advocates promise, and when they fail, we almost never know why. Until our strategies begin to pay off in achievement of goals, the syndrome of the blind man on a freeway will probably persist. Educators will distrust their critics, who most often seem unrealistic and wrong, will rely on intuition and conventional wisdom, and will ward off challenges through pantomimes painfully perfected.

Now conjure up another scenario. Suppose that available findings[5] and conceptualizations[6] concerning the capabilities of computer-assisted instruction (CAI) had been followed up with adequate field experiments. Suppose the experiments had produced appreciable gains in student learning at negligible or reduced cost (since teacher salaries have been spiraling rapidly while electronic slaves have grown cheaper), by combining CAI with adjustments in pupil-teacher ratios or number of subject matter specialists. Or suppose, in line with the work of Salomon and Achenbach,[7] repeated findings on field experiments that focused on theory had shown that student tutors could be used to foster basic cognitive improvement among both tutors and those being tutored, for negligible or reduced fiscal outlays. Could the Luddites have blocked fundamental change in schools during the past two turbulent decades? I doubt it very much.

As these examples imply, the lack of validated casual models for policy guidance in schools may be partially attributed to the major thrust of empirical inquiry between 1954 and 1974 in the field generally described as educational administration. The lack may also be partially attributed to the fact that school administrators (whom we trained) were insensitive to the demands and potentialities of policy oriented research.

In discussing this view, I plan to approximate an adversary procedure. First, I am going to sketch a gloomy picture, with scholars appearing as villains. Second, I will present a more positive, encouraging assessment, featuring scholars in white hats. Finally, I intend to hazard a brief opinion of what is "really" going on, and what might be facilitated with effort on our part.

This routine of thesis-antithesis-synthesis is adopted, not for the

sake of Hegel or humor, but because I could find no stable balance
between my elation and my despair. Some auguries look very favorable, but some difficulties appear equally formidable, and there is
abundant ground for discomfort in the smugness found by Campbell
and Newell and Sroufe.[8] The negative and positive sides of my analysis are both presented, then, in order that readers may draw their
own conclusions, to some extent independent of the outlook finally
expressed here.

The Case for Pessimism

When the modern "theory movement" in educational administration gained major impetus, around 1954, it could have carried us
in any one of several directions. Halpin expressed the emphasis essential to acquisition of an adequate knowledge base: "The ultimate
criteria of administrator 'effectiveness' should be expressed in terms
of group or organizational achievement. . . . Whenever an intermediate criterion is posited, it must be . . . recognized only as a stop-
gap. . . . *Let it be emphasized again that if one fails to establish the
relationship between the behavior of the administrator and syntalic
measures of the organization's 'effectiveness,' he evades the most
fundamental research issue at stake.*"[9]

Halpin was alluding specifically to research on administrative
behavior, but the point applies with equal force to any area of organizational research in education. Until we forge clear connections
between the dynamics under study and school outcomes, our work
may build scholarly reputations and contribute to general theories in
various disciplines, but it won't lend much succor to the superintendent in search of productivity.

This is not to say that every organizational study in education
must utilize criterion variables reflecting achievement of goals. The
primary purpose of some work should be to establish relationships
between organizational phenomena and achievement of goals, whereas other work should explain those phenomena. To state the issue
another way: Some studies would be designed mainly to specify and
demonstrate, usually in sociopsychological terms, how individuals
respond (i.e., the attitudes, skills, and understandings they develop)
to organizational conditions in schools (e.g., conditions facilitating
friendship across socioeconomic or racial lines; particular mechanisms of student selection and control; attractiveness and availability

of extracurricular roles; mechanisms to recruit, retain, and motivate teachers with specific competencies; particular combinations of instructional media; various approximations of "mastery learning" or "adaptive environment" models). Other studies would focus largely on the internal and exogenous variables that can be manipulated to produce organizational conditions shown to be conducive to valued school outcomes. If each of the two branches of this two-pronged strategy were executed in awareness of the other, we would be spared many trivial investigations that now clutter our journals.

For several reasons, Halpin's call for inquiry into the determinants of organizational achievement[10] was widely ignored. One reason is that in schools, unlike some other organizations, it is difficult to obtain clear evidence of organizational effects. This is because, to do so more than peripherally, the researcher must identify, in student behavior over short or long terms, the unequivocal results of school structures and processes, despite the powerful influence of genetic and environmental factors. With the ultimate, ideal criteria of organizational effectiveness ostensibly out of reach, many students of educational organization settled for intermediate criteria, such as ratings of administrative effectiveness by presumed experts, numerous permutations of climate and morale, and judgments by researchers as to the nature of the "good" or "healthy" organization (e.g., the greater the number of innovations during a three-year period, the better the school system). On many occasions, measures of educational "input" were regarded as measures of "output" (e.g., schools that consumed greater quantities of scarce resources were presumed to produce greater student achievement). Unfortunately, such an approach means that the consequences for achievement of goals instituting a change in inputs or organizational arrangements cannot be estimated. Worse still, one can envision situations in which almost any input would be related inversely to valued outputs. In another spate of studies, done mainly by economists, certain school inputs (e.g., expenditures) were related directly to certain purported outputs (e.g., lifetime earnings), without attention to the organizational transformations in the intervening "black box."[11] Except when serving as propaganda, these inquiries were practically useless to school administrators concerned with organizational effectiveness, for they revealed virtually nothing about the consequences of organizational arrangements.

Perhaps the most important reason for the existence of policy studies that are irrelevant (and thus responsible, to an extent, for the syndrome of the blind man on a freeway) is the pronounced and growing prevalence of work preoccupied with disciplinary concerns. It is widely assumed, apparently, that our task as scholars is to use schools and other educational settings as handy laboratories for testing, revising, and elaborating upon conceptual material valued by social psychologists, sociologists, anthropologists, linguists, economists, and political scientists. Similarly, many researchers seem part of an interdisciplinary effort to understand organization and administration in the abstract, with little regard for such specific settings as education. As Corwin[12] points out, organizations may be examined from a number of standpoints, not all of which demand criterion variables that measure achievement of goals. Quite defensibly, for instance, one may investigate the internal adjustments of organizations confronted with various environmental constraints. But researchers in education have selectively adopted models of organizational inquiry, avoiding paradigms that require assessment of the achievement of goals (probably because such assessment seems so difficult). There is, for example, some reputable work in industry on connections between morale and productivity, but no parallel investigations exist in education. We may be a long time producing a reliable basis for educational practice if we keep focusing most of our effort on phenomena that have no demonstrated relevance to educational outcomes or to variables administrators can manipulate to improve student learning.

To be sure, there are many examples in history of scholars who were completely disinterested in practice but whose "basic" findings nevertheless had a profound salutary effect on human affairs. Coleman's seminal work on the "adolescent society"[13] was produced because of his concern for contextual analysis rather than education, as he explicitly indicates. But must we rely on these occasional happy accidents to advance educational practice?

I reluctantly mention a third possible explanation for inquiry that is off focus. In some universities the notion seems to exist that research designed to produce implications for practice is necessarily inferior. I think this sentiment is ridiculous, as the following example may demonstrate. In several respects, my argument parallels the efforts of such scholars as Carroll and Gage[14] who approximately a decade ago sought to counteract the practice then prevalent among students of learning to neglect determinants of learning *in schools.* Carroll observed that it was difficult to synthesize research concerned with maturation, individual differences, learning, thinking, motivation, and social development "into an integrated account of the process of *school learning*." He then proposed a model of "factors affecting success in *school learning*" [italics added] that had a pronounced impact on later inquiry.[15] Similarly, Gage complained that "theories of learning [merely] deal with the ways in which an organism learns." He called for theories of *teaching*, which would delineate "the ways in which a person influences an organism to learn."[16] The new models of instruction, teaching, and school learning did not produce inferior research. On the contrary, I suspect most scholars acquainted with the area would characterize the paradigm shift as particularly catalytic.

To paraphrase Carroll, it is difficult to synthesize current findings on administrative behavior, teacher morale, organizational climate, and a score of other widely researched concepts into an integrated conception of how educational goals can be organizationally facilitated. Our condition is worse than the one Carroll and Gage were endeavoring to ameliorate. Theories of learning—while not as useful as theories of instruction to those who had to teach, develop curricula, or train others to do so—were at least proximate. Much research and training is at best tangential and often merely conjectural with respect to the goals our institutions strive to achieve.

I believe we must counterbalance the preoccupation with process and structure in their own right. We need intense work on causal models linking process and structure to student behavior and long-term accomplishment. We must produce theories of *educational* organization, *educational* production (cf. Herriott and Muse[17])— bodies of "technical knowledge about the systematic design and conduct of education, based upon scientific research."[18] It is not enough to announce, "There is nothing so practical as good theory." One must specify *what* theory is useful for what purposes.

The assumption in much research and training seems to be, "Theoretical ferretting into group and organizational phenomena is sure to make the educational administrator more effective." On the contrary, if the school administrator is to be more than a human relations oilcan, fiscal funnel, or public relations pitchman, he will need theory concerned with school *productivity*. Many organizational arrangements might be conceived to keep the money flowing, the community mollified, and the staff harmonious and content. But which of these, if any, will facilitate goal achievement? In the absence of evidence concerning organizational prerequisites of productivity, universities might well revert to the old practice of letting retired superintendents run training programs while scholars "do their thing." From where I stand, executives in training can learn much more from James Redmond than from Talcott Parsons. Or better still, perhaps, much time now spent on organizational theory in training programs might be devoted to various aspects of instructional theory and curriculum.[19]

My comments concerning research are not a plea for the atheoretical. Similarly, I am not here concerned with studies done under severe time constraints to illuminate pressing policy issues—a mode of reconnaissance discussed provocatively by Coleman[20]—though I think these pursuits also need more attention. Nor am I suggesting that the bulk of our work during the past two decades has been useless. I am urging a focus that may give more meaning to organizational studies in education.

To illustrate: Spady has produced dramatic evidence, much in line with findings from Schwartz, that the extra curriculum may be a far more powerful aspect of schooling than is generally recognized.[21] In Spady's exploration, which has unusual longitudinal features, high school extracurricular participation is strongly associated with college plans, even when an impressive array of correlates is controlled. In addition, extracurricular involvement is a potent predictor of college success. Participants in high school extracurricular roles in Spady's sample have a 37 percent greater chance of fulfilling their college aspirations than have nonparticipants, after academic performance, intrinsic motivation, and perceptions of peer status are taken into account. Spady's findings, tentative though they may be until further rummaging is done, cast entirely new light on evidence from the "ecological psychologists" at Kansas.[22] When that group first published data suggesting that forces inducing committed participation in extracurricular activities were much stronger in small schools than in large schools, and that proportionate student participation varied accordingly, organizational theorists had reason to be interested, but there was no great rejoicing at annual meetings of school administrators. If the findings of Spady and Schwartz[23] hold

up, however, inquiries already conducted into the apparent consequences of school size (along with efforts to deal with several ambi-
guities, such as rural and urban differences between small and large
schools) may assume an importance no one anticipated. I think further knowledge from the literature on school effects will throw a
dramatic spotlight on other organizational studies that now seem
unexciting, while some favorite areas of investigation will pale by
comparison, and sectors thus far utterly neglected will move toward
the top of our agenda.

The redirection suggested here is not a return to the particular
emphasis in Halpin's classic statement.[24] In 1957 the most prominent
thrust in our field was toward a theory of *administrative behavior*
that might predict organizational achievement. That focus embodied
an exaggerated conception of the administrator's impact (education's
Great Man conception of human affairs). Today there is more discussion of administrative powerlessness,[25] in keeping with evidence
showing that far more variance in student achievement and aspiration
is associated with classrooms than with schools or school systems.[26] Many writers claim that the school executive makes a profound difference. No trustworthy evidence seems available to demonstrate this difference, however, perhaps because success comes so
seldom that it washes out in all sizable samples.

If medical science had been constructed on the same Great Man
assumptions, its guiding theories would relate to the physician's personal patterns of behavior. The medical literature might be laden
with discussions concerning the physician's "democratic versus
authoritarian" bedside manner; his relative emphasis on "communication, discussion, compliance," etc., in diagnostic decision making;
and the degree of "initiating structure" and "consideration" in his
relationships with nurses and hospital administrators. It is fortunate
for us all that budding MDs spend most of their time studying treatments found effective for combatting disease. Though not totally
irrelevant, findings about the physician's personality and behavior are
a long way from serving as an effective base for medicine. Similarly,
the achievement of organizational goals seems far more dependent
upon the procurative and allocative strategies embodied in system
design, modification, and administration than upon the decision-
making styles and interpersonal orientations of executives, though
these styles and orientations are not totally irrelevant.

In the effort to help administrators survive occupationally and as human beings, however, I view these studies of administrative problems and behavior as critical. The world of the school administrator is tough, and often vicious. If our graduates enter that arena aware of what their personal dilemmas may be, and equipped with habits of inquiry and reflection that lend perspective, they will more likely endure and experience individual success. I have written a little along this line myself.[27] To any school executive seeking sanity and self-understanding I would commend the work of Bridges; Carlson; Getzels, Lipham, and Campbell; Halpin; Hemphill; Lucietto; McKague; Miner; Powers; Trask; and Wolcott, to mention just a few examples.[28] Knowledge of political realities, sociological dynamics, finance and economics, and other areas covered in our training programs will also help graduates survive—and help them contribute to the survival and smooth functioning of their organizations. But goal achievement is something else. Different bodies of knowledge meet different needs. To contend that studies predominating in this field between 1954 and 1974 provided no adequate basis for outcome-oriented organizational strategy in education is not to disparage them for other important purposes. It is good to prevent suicides, even in ineffective organizations. And current work (e.g., Bridges' analyses of various implications of time in administrator behavior) may considerably facilitate the use of findings relevant to policy, as they become available.

In one of his provocative papers, Hills[29] reminds me of Getzels's contention that the major impact of theory is often produced indirectly. That is, theory may fail to yield directly discernible implications for practice and yet may influence practice by altering one's basic conceptions of human affairs. I agree, though the relationship should hold less frequently as we make more progress in the social sciences. And Getzels himself calls for *theory on the topic of concern,* not just any theory. When analyzing change in schools, he asks for "conceptions dealing systematically with the nature of change."[30] Even if we have to settle largely for the indirect benefits discussed by Getzels, the theory needed to illuminate questions of school productivity seems most likely to eventuate from the two-pronged research approach outlined earlier—from inquiries into the consequences of various organizational arrangements, as largely exhibited in student behavior, and from investigations of the internal and environmental conditions (sociological, political, economic, anthropological, legal, etc.) that produce and modify those organizational arrangements.

Be sure, however, that even the most successful research along the lines suggested here will not be enough, in and of itself, to get the blind man off the freeway. Within my lifetime, at least we can hope for little more than a collection of theories, each clarifying a special slice of reality and embodying its own special limiting assumptions. There will still be much need for "the arts of the practical and eclectic"[31] which provide "temporary and tentative bridges . . . between useful parts of bodies of knowledge in the course of their application to practical problems."[32] But that fascinating issue cannot be pursued within the limits of the present chapter.

To generate the "useful parts of bodies of knowledge" that are relevant to policy, we need data that school systems are not famous for producing.

Among scholars whose writings on research relevant to policy I have recently examined are D. T. Campbell; Campbell and Stanley; Caro; Chase; Coleman; Cooley; Dyer; Emrick, Sorensen, and Sterns; Grant; Gilbert and Mosteller; Hanushek and Kain; Hilgard; Levine; Light and Smith; Michelson; Moynihan; Rohwer; and Shulman.[33] There is considerable agreement that more large-scale surveys, roughly of the nature of *Equality of Educational Opportunity* (EEO)[34] will be needed. But the performance of our graduates in providing data for that investigation is not comforting, a point Jencks documents in some detail.[35]

Despite the Congressional mandate behind EEO and the notable stature of the researchers, only 55 percent of school districts in the intended sample provided even minimally satisfactory cooperation.[36] Adequate cooperation (defined here as returning data for student, teacher, and principal for each school) was forthcoming from only 40 percent of the districts. Twenty-five major school systems declined to participate in any way—including those in Boston, Chicago, Columbus, Hartford, Los Angeles, and Wilmington. Among the systems refusing to provide test data on pupils, though forwarding some information from principals, were Buffalo, Cincinnati, Cleveland, Indianapolis, Kansas City, Peoria, Sioux Falls, Steubenville, and Syracuse. Grossly inaccurate responses were rampant. Many principals in big cities checked items indicating their schools were located in small town, rural, and suburban settings, with the best explanation, apparently, being carelessness. Principals seemed so eager to view their schools as serving "a general cross section" that they often gave seriously distorted estimates of parental socioeconomic status. Teachers and principals frequently disagreed concerning the presence or absence of grouping according to ability, and even, to a major extent, as to the average number of pupils in a class. Responses of principals concerning serious problems in their schools possessed reliabilities estimated at .28 and .36.

Quite apart from the lack of cooperation among administrators that frequently mars important studies, Dyer observes that school systems are not set up to provide accurate, comparable information on such apparently straightforward matters as enrollment, expenditure per pupil, quality of school plant, and "hundreds of other types of 'basic' data in common use."[37] Dyer thinks we can scarcely begin decent studies relevant to policy until we find ways of making school district records useful for policy considerations, a point advocates of performance budgeting have been emphasizing for years.

There is also considerable agreement among scholars interested in policy questions that large-scale surveys are not enough, given the massive problems of interpretation in nonexperimental educational research[38] and the tendency of school systems in the nation as a whole to experiment within a very narrow range.[39] George Box is quoted as observing, most aptly, "To find out what happens to a system when you interfere with it, you have to interfere with it (not just passively observe it)."[40] In my view, the writer contributing the most to this area of discussion is Donald T. Campbell.[41] Campbell sees typical laboratory experiments in education as relatively trivial, since the settings are so dissimilar to school contexts, and since the work is severely limited by the researcher's ability to corral subjects (typically, college sophomores) for an hour or so. He describes administrators as gatekeepers of the milieus (schools and school systems) in which most of our investigations should occur. Campbell argues persuasively that each important policy intervention in an educational system should be made in such a way (e.g., by means of random assignment to treatments, "staged" innovations, unobtrusive measures, interrupted time-series and regression discontinuity designs) that its consequences will be documented as a contribution to professional knowledge. But he notes that school administrators have a habit of committing themselves too strongly to proposed solutions to risk evidence of failure, and he observes that they need to be persuaded as to the advantages of randomization and other devices of experimental intervention.

Rather than adding several paragraphs on the aversion of educational administrators and their professional organizations (notably, the American Association of School Administrators) to evidence that seems at all sensitive (National Assessment and voucher experiments are good examples), I will assume you are aware of this propensity. On the other hand, I have found no adequate national study of the responses of school leaders to large-scale surveys and more limited field experiments; it would therefore be hazardous to generalize too freely about the patterns mentioned here.

Even so, the evidence has me puzzled. Purportedly, we have acquainted administrators-in-training with empirically derived theory and basic issues of research design for more than twenty years. Yet many administrators seem oblivious to the most minimal requirements of a field of applied theory. They garner their information in a form irrelevant to the most essential policy issues, they withhold cooperation from vital studies, they fear evidence that might prove current practices inadequate. What applied field deserves even a quasi-scientific label under these circumstances? Is part of the problem the existence of a pseudo-scholarly mystique in some universities? Does this mystique suggest that if would-be school officials do obeisance for a few months to research gurus in graduate schools—no matter how little these gurus know about the educational effects of school organization—they will have done their due to scholarship? Does theory that is only speculatively and indirectly relevant to educational goal achievement constitute a hidden curriculum? Does it effectively teach administrators that research in schools need not ask sensitive questions about goal effectiveness and thus should be tolerated only when innocuous?

The Case for Optimism

A more positive case can also be made. Considering the minor impact of our research in the past, the limited interest and cooperation of administrators should surprise no one; if we become more effective, they may lend us more help. Furthermore, as Donald

Campbell observes,[42] many administrators are imbedded in such sensitive political situations that they must avoid negative evidence to survive; perhaps we can do something about that. Scholars are examining the reasons why school executives resist field experiments.[43] Promising techniques are emerging that are designed both to reduce the threat our work often poses and to avoid the methodological flaws of much previous inquiry. Some implications for training are rather clear. If our own theory becomes more pertinent to policy, and if we involve students extensively in the planning and study of policy interventions conceived as experiments (along the general lines sketched out by Campbell[44]), we might produce a generation of administrators who view themselves as life-long contributors to professional knowledge. They might show a commitment to careful experimentation, rather than to "solutions" scooped up on the latest pilgrimage to Atlantic City. To hasten that day, as Campbell suggests, we should probably declare a moratorium on studies used to evaluate individual administrators and concentrate on "comparison of alternatives realistically available to the administrator, to neither of which he is unalterably committed."[45]

In retrospect, it is also evident that the disciplinary orientation that earlier was disparaged in some respects produced important benefits. After having examined studies over the past decades, I believe the influence of the disciplines considerably enhanced the rigor of our designs and conceptualizations. Much organizational inquiry conducted during past years may turn out, as I suggested earlier, to be directly relevant to achievement of goals once the necessary evidence is in.

The source of most of my optimism on the topic of this chapter relates, however, to the vistas revealed by several recent studies—studies that may prove, in the long run, to be harbingers of a new era, exemplars of a paradigm shift. The EEO survey,[46] though considerably lacking in organizational perspective and handicapped by the rough proxies available in school systems to measure conceptually specified variables, was probably the most critical breakthrough. I do not, however, wish to demean previous work in the same genre. EEO was a powerful assault upon the fog-generating assumption that organizational inputs in education could, for all practical purposes, be regarded as measures of school output. Coleman and his colleagues demonstrated that the connection between input and output was problemmatic. Communities could not simply assume that by increasing school resources in keeping with conventional wisdom they would promote greater student learning. A new question was raised in the national consciousness: What arrangements in schools *do* have an impact on valued outcomes?

In the years since EEO, many able scholars have been attracted to the study of school effects, including some associated at least peripherally with administrative training programs.[47] The critiques, reanalyses, and apologetics triggered by EEO are generally provocative. Among my own favorites are Hanushek's reanalysis and reviews and critiques by Jamison, Suppes, and Wells; Guthrie; Spady; Wiley; and Herriott and Muse.[48] We have learned much in a few years about the partitioning of variance in cases of multicollinearity. Fascinating discussion and application of measures ("elasticities," "beta-coefficients," etc.) have facilitated policy considerations.[49] Work on the dimensioning of instructional processes in Follow-through "Planned Variation" studies[50] has applicability, I believe, to our field. Cooley emphasizes what we should have known all along—that educational "innovations" generally represent recombinations of strategies long practiced in outstanding schools and classrooms, and therefore should be studied, not as discrete inventions, but as "packages" representing variation along common dimensions. Even when innovations turn out to be nonevents,[51] investigation of the variation along the common dimensions may reveal a lot concerning classrooms and schools. Numerous other contributions from "post-Coleman" studies of school effects could be mentioned.

For present purposes, however, the most important inquiries are those connecting organizational variables, conceived in the light of reasonably sophisticated organizational theory, to valued school outcomes.

Spady's study on the consequences of extracurricular involvement has already been mentioned.[52] Numerous inquiries had previously lent credence to the view that the student's status among peers was related to plans for college. Perhaps open recognition of an individual's worth encourages higher aspirations. But student status is probably influenced by official allocations of rewards and punishments, especially insofar as the extra curriculum's "Big Men on Campus" are concerned.[53] Spady reasons that the extra curriculum may also function as an arena for the development of competencies important for success in college and later occupational endeavors.[54] E. Q. Campbell and Schwartz suggest, similarly, that many extra-curricular activities inspire more student commitment than the classroom typically elicits.[55] The classroom often provides little immediate gratification, and its structure often implies that the student's usefulness to society is merely potential. The extra curriculum's down-to-earth qualities, its activities immediately consequential to student and adult communities, and its demand for student capabilities not required in classrooms, may make it a superior learning context for some purposes.

Even apart from the extra curriculum, many questions remain unanswered concerning organizational conditions that affect student social relationships, which in turn have been traced rather compellingly to apparent consequences in aspiration and achievement.[56] Much inquiry is needed to discover how organizational arrangements facilitate the development of friendship (rather than antagonism) among newly integrated individuals and groups. We also need to know how they affect the balance of influence in friendship dyads (through allocations of status or authority, for instance), how they affect the direction and intensity of norms in school-wide or subgroup "cultures," and in what way they determine how individuals are affected by such norms. These are only a few of the issues that need clarification in the general area of Spady's work.[57] Moreover, when we learn how to shape student social relationships in schools, new experimental designs will be feasible. By manipulating social relationships, we could obtain far more conclusive evidence of their effects on valued school outcomes.

The most important feature of Spady's study, then, may be the almost virgin territory it opens up. Spady provides a long overdue effort, informed by organizational theory, to comprehend the structural dynamics which, partly by modifying student social relationships, may affect the achievement of organizational goals. The related inquiries of Anderson and Tissier and of Schwartz are also important, and scholars contemplating sorties into this area can obtain conceptual assistance from Ausubel and Ausubel, Dreeben, Bidwell, Boocock, Spady, and Bain and Anderson.[58]

Bidwell and Kasarda have contributed another trailblazing effort to explicate the effects of organizational variables.[59] They report several findings supporting a model in which organizational variables are mediating influences between community characteristics and student achievement. Attention only to directly observable relationships of fiscal resources indicates little payoff for educational goals, but indirect statistical connections suggest that monetary inputs affect student behavior in a substantially indirect manner by influencing staff characteristics. Furthermore, when its apparent impact on teacher qualifications is controlled, the educational level of the parent risk population has only minor consequences for reading achievement. The Bidwell and Kasarda study is only exploratory, but it offers tantalizing leads for further investigation. It suggests that organizational variables will be critical explanatory components in any adequate causal model of school effects.

Heyns attempts to compensate for the previous lack of attention to organizational influences in studies on schooling and social stratification.[60] She makes the incisive argument that inquiries ignoring the unequal allocation of resources to students *within* schools, as most school effects studies have done, are in no position to conclude that resources are distributed in a substantially equal manner, or that unequal apportionment would not matter. Her data suggest that both counselors' encouragement of college plans and counselors' time (defined in terms of number of student visits) are unequally allotted among high school curricular streams in favor of the college-preparatory group, in a manner virtually independent of grades, ability, and socioeconomic background when curriculum placement is controlled. Student educational aspiration (a school output variable) is more dependent on curriculum placement than upon self-reported grades or tested verbal ability. There is, however, no conclusive evidence to indicate the extent to which the relationship is attributable to the effects of aspiration on curriculum placement, the effects of some unmeasured variable on both aspiration and curriculum placement, or some combination of these possibilities.

Finally, the consequences of *time* as a manipulable organizational variable are revealed by Wiley.[61] Wiley thinks one prominent reason for the frequent finding that differential school practices have few, and generally small, effects on student achievement is that the *duration* of the child's exposure to the practices was not properly taken into account. An analogy would be a study of the properties of various medicines without attention to dosages. Wiley finds *pronounced* effects of time in school on verbal ability, reading comprehension, and mathematics achievement. His work meshes admirably with numerous causal models of school learning, particularly those building on Carroll's ovarian statement.[62] Wiley's analytic approach permits policy decisions to be based on estimates of the amount of learning in a given subject area that may be expected from a given time increment. School executives could make explicit cost-effectiveness decisions by comparing these estimates with the marginal outlays required to effectuate the time increments.

It is obvious that any sampling of studies as brief as the foregoing must be partial and inadequate. I have necessarily glossed over many critical issues, even those relating to the few investigations discussed here. The matters are developed more satisfactorily in the volume, *Educational Organization and Administration.*[63]

Conclusions and Suggestions

Suppes and Morningstar, Fletcher and Atkinson, Salomon and Achenbach, Spady, Schwartz, Anderson and Tissier, Bidwell and Kasarda, Heyns, and Wiley,[64] all published since 1969, could be interpreted as indicating a profound paradigm shift in studies of educational organization. We could be leaving an era in which structure and process were studied mostly as a way of adding to disciplinary domains, and we could be entering a period of exciting new work on theories of *"educational* organization," *"educational* production," and the "design and conduct of *education.*" Our priorities may be governed increasingly by causal models of school affects developed, revised, and extended through empirical inquiry.

On the other hand, this inchaote movement could abort, much like the "advent" of individualization in 1911, the "passing" of the recitation in 1928, and a hundred other "breakthroughs" heralded by fanfare in past decades. Despite recent progress, we face enormous difficulties. Viewed over a period of ten or twenty years, the work on school effects, with but few exceptions, is distinguished by contradictory evidence.[65] The school outcomes to be considered are multitudinous, different segments of society disagree in ranking and valuing them, and most instruments now available exhibit serious shortcomings.[66] We still confront the general lack of cooperation from school districts considered earlier. It is still possible to argue that the complexities of education will simply not yield to our empirical probings.[67]

At the moment, however, I am inclined toward the view that a fundamental paradigm shift is in process, that it represents enormous opportunities for my field, and that it deserves all the encouragement we can give it. In articles to be published elsewhere, I plan to discuss at some length the concepts and strategies that seem available for exploitation. Within the space available here, let me merely mention four general approaches:

1. A national (and perhaps international) effort should be launched to design and disseminate new systems for acquisition of data for schools, systems designated to facilitate field experiment, large-scale surveys, and, through them, the acquisition of a reputable base of knowledge for a field still floundering after all these years. Important suggestions have been made in this regard by Dyer and by D. T. Campbell.[68] Since such a system will probably not enjoy widespread adoption, perhaps universities and other centers of educational research should cultivate consortia composed of school systems that *are* interested in leading the way to reasonably scientific policy making. I have broached this idea to one national organization of schools, and considerable enthusiasm has been indicated in response.

2. The time has obviously come, I submit, for a fundamental, sweeping reassessment of our training programs. My previous suggestions may warrant some weighing in this connection.

3. New lines of communication should be opened up between scholars interested in the strategies of organizational research emphasized here and students of instructional processes. The interaction between these traditionally separate domains could be mutually productive. The latter group has developed causal models and research techniques we might profitably emulate and adapt, while their conceptualizations, I am convinced, would gain explanatory power through addition of organizational components. Shall we begin with a conference sponsored by the University Council for Educational Administration, or with a symposium at a meeting of the American Educational Research Association?

4. The frontier organizational work now conducted in relatively scattered fashion by scholars identified earlier might progress more swiftly through concerted effort at one or two centers. One remembers, in this connection, the early leadership studies at The Ohio State University, the focus on the Getzels model at the University of

Chicago, pupil control ideology investigations at Pennsylvania State University, studies of bureaucracy at the Ontario Institute for Studies in Education, recent work on innovation at the Center for the Advanced Study of Educational Administration, and many other significant group efforts. There is some evidence that at the present time breakthroughs in the social sciences are achieved disproportionately by teams,[69] though I doubt that the contributions of the individualistic scholar will be entirely suspended.

Notes

1. E. L. Thorndike, *Individuality* (Boston: Houghton Mifflin, 1911); R. Glaser, "Individuals and Learning: The New Aptitudes," *Educational Researcher* 1 (June 1972), 5-13; V. T. Thayer, *The Passing of the Recitation* (Boston: D. C. Heath, 1928); J. Hoetker and W. P. Ahlbrand, "The Persistence of the Recitation," *American Educational Research Journal* 6 (March 1969), 145-167.

2. My assigned topic at the conference on which this book is based was "The Nature of Schools and Other Educational Organizations: 1954-74." For the sake of parsimony, I often refer in this chapter merely to "schools," but the characteristics discussed seem applicable to all educational organization. The implications may be particularly serious for public institutions.

3. R. E. Callahan, *Education and the Cult of Efficiency* (Chicago: University of Chicago Press, 1962).

4. G. Graubard, *Free the Children* (New York: Pantheon Books, 1972); B. S. Cooper, *Free School Survival* (Sarasota, Fl.: Omi-Print, 1975).

5. P. Suppes and M. Morningstar, "Computer-Assisted Instruction," *Science* 166 (1969), 343-350; J. D. Fletcher and R. C. Atkinson, "An Evaluation of the Stanford CAI Program in Initial Reading," *Journal of Educational Psychology* 63 (1972), 597-602.

6. R. M. Gagné, "Educational Technology and the Learning Process," *Educational Researcher* 3 (January 1974), 3-8.

7. M. K. Salomon and T. M. Achenbach, "The Effects of Four Kinds of Tutoring Experience on Associative Responding," *American Educational Research Journal* 11 (Fall 1974), 395-405.

8. R. F. Campbell and L. J. Newell, *A Study of Professors of Educational Administration* (Columbus, Ohio: University Council for Educational Administration, 1973); G. E. Sroufe, "Nova's Ed.D. Program for Educational Leaders: Looking Backward, Looking Forward," *Phi Delta Kappan* 56 (February 1975), 402-405.

9. A. W. Halpin, "A Paradigm for Research on Administrator Behavior," in R. F. Campbell and R. T. Gregg (eds.), *Administrative Behavior in Education* (New York: Harper and Row, 1957), 155-199. Italics in original.

10. *Ibid.*

11. Compare H. Levin, "A Cost-Effectiveness Analysis of Teacher Selection," *Journal of Human Resources* 5 (1970), 24-33.

12. R. G. Corwin, "Models of Educational Organization," in F. N. Kerlinger (ed.), *Review of Research in Education 2* (Itasca, Ill.: F. E. Peacock, 1974), 247-295.

13. J. S. Coleman, *The Adolescent Society* (New York: Free Press, 1961).

14. J. B. Carroll, "A Model for School Learning," *Teachers College Record* 14 (1963); N. L. Gage, "Theories of Teaching," in *Theories of Learning and Instruction,* Sixty-third Yearbook of the National Society for the Study of Education, Part I (Chicago: University of Chicago Press, 1964).

15. Carroll, "Model for School Learning," 723-733.

16. Gage, "Theories of Teaching," 268-285.

17. R. E. Herriott and D. H. Muse, "Methodological Issues in the Study of School Effects," in F. N. Kerlinger (ed.), *Review of Research in Education 1* (Itasca, Ill.: F. E. Peacock, 1973), 209-236.

18. Gagné, "Educational Technology."

19. R. Jean Hills, "The Preparation of Administrators: Some Observations from the 'Firing Line,' " *Educational Administration Quarterly* (Autumn 1975), 1-20.

20. J. S. Coleman, *Policy Research in the Social Sciences* (Morristown, N.J.: General Learning Press, 1972).

21. W. G. Spady, "Status, Achievement, and Motivation in the American High School," *School Review* 79 (May 1971), 379-403; H. Schwartz, "Open Curtain—Open Mind," *Administrator's Notebook* 21 (1973), 1-4.

22. For example, R. G. Barker and P. V. Gump, *Big School—Small School* (Stanford: Stanford University Press, 1964).

23. Spady, "Status, Achievement, and Motivation"; Schwartz, "Open Curtain—Open Mind."

24. Halpin, "Paradigm for Research."

25. E. M. Bridges, "Administrative Man: Origin or Pawn in Decision Making?" *Educational Administration Quarterly* 6 (1970), 7-25; D. A. Erickson, "Moral Dilemmas of Administrative Powerlessness," *Administrator's Notebook* 20 (1972), 1-4.

26. For example, studies cited in B. Anderson and R. M. Tissier, "Social Class, School Bureaucratization and Educational Aspirations," *Educational Administration Quarterly* 9 (Spring 1973), 34-49.

27. D. A. Erickson, "Forces for Change in Principalship," *Elementary School Journal* 65 (November 1964), 57-64; "Moral Dilemmas."

28. E. M. Bridges, "A Model for Shared Decision Making in the School Principalship," *Educational Administration Quarterly* 3 (Winter 1967), 49-61; Bridges, "Administrative Man"; R. O. Carlson, *Executive Succession and Organizational Change* (Chicago: Midwest Administration Center, University of Chicago, 1962); J. W. Getzels, J. M. Lipham, and R. F. Campbell, *Educational Administration as a Social Process* (New York: Harper and Row, 1968); A. W. Halpin, *The Leadership Behavior of School Superintendents* (Chicago: Midwest Administration Center, University of Chicago, 1959); A. W. Halpin, "Muted

Language," *School Review* 68 (1960), 85-104; J. K. Hemphill, "Personal Variables and Administrative Styles," in D. E. Griffiths (ed.), *Behavioral Science and Educational Administration*, Sixty-third Yearbook of the National Society for the Study of Education, Part II (Chicago: the Society, 1964), 178-198; L. L. Lucietto, "Speech Patterns of Administrators," *Administrator's Notebook* 17 (1970), 1-4; T. R. McKague, "LPC—A New Perspective on Leadership," *Educational Administration Quarterly* 6 (1970), 1-14; J. B. Miner, "The Managerial Motivations of School Administrators," *Educational Administration Quarterly* 4 (Winter 1968), 55-71; T. E. Powers, "Administrative Behavior and Upward-Mobility," *Administrator's Notebook* 15 (1964), 1-4; A. E. Trask, "Principals, Teachers, and Supervision: Dilemmas and Solutions," *Administrator's Notebook* 13 (1964), 1-4; H. F. Wolcott, *The Man in the Principal's Office* (New York: Holt, Rinehart, and Winston, 1973).

29. Hills, "Preparation of Administration."

30. J. W. Getzels, "Creative Administration and Organizational Change: An Essay in Theory," revision of paper presented at conference on "Frontiers of School Leadership," Center for Coordinated Education, University of California, Santa Barbara, January 1968, 5.

31. J. J. Schwab, "The Practical: A Language for Curriculum," *School Review* 77 (November 1969), 1-23; J. J. Schwab, "The Practical: Arts of Eclectic," *School Review* 79 (August 1971), 493-542.

32. Schwab, "Practical: Arts," 502.

33. D. T. Campbell, "Factors Relevant to the Validity of Experiments in Social Settings," *Psychological Bulletin* 54 (1957), 297-312; "From Description to Experimentation: Interpreting Trends as Quasi-Experiments," in C. W. Harris (ed.), *Problem in Measuring Change* (Madison: University of Wisconsin Press, 1963), 212-242; "Administrative Experimentation, Institutional Records, and Nonreactive Measures," in J. C. Stanley and S. M. Elam (eds.), *Improving Experimental Design and Statistical Analysis* (Chicago: Rand McNally, 1967), 257-283; "Reforms as Experiments," *American Psychologist* 24 (1969), 409-429; D. T. Campbell and J. C. Stanley, "Experimental and Quasi-Experimental Designs for Research on Teaching," in N. L. Gage (ed.), *Handbook of Research on Teaching* (Chicago: Rand McNally, 1963), 171-246; F. G. Caro, "Issues in the Evaluation of Social Programs," *Review of Educational Research* 41 (April 1971), 87-114; F. S. Chase, "Educational Research and Development in the Sixties, The Mixed Report Card," in Committee on Education and Labor, House of Representatives, *Educational Research: Prospects and Priorities*, Appendix 1 to Hearings on H.R. 3606 and Related Bills to Create a National Institute of Education before the Select Subcommittee on Education (Washington, D.C.: U.S. Government Printing Office, 1972), 1-37; Coleman, *Policy Research*; W. Cooley, "Assessment of Educational Effects," address at 1974 Annual Meeting of American Educational Research Association, April 15, 1974; H. S. Dyer, "Some Thoughts about Future Studies," in F. Mosteller and D. P. Moynihan (eds.), *On Equality of Educational Opportunity* (New York: Random House, 1972, 385-422; J. A. Emrick, P. H. Sorensen, and M. S. Stearns, *Interim Evaluation of the National Follow-Through Program, 1969-71: A Technical Report* (Menlo Park, Ca.: Stanford

Research Institute, 1973); G. Grant, "Shaping Social Policy: The Politics of the Coleman Report," *Teachers College Record* 75 (December 1973), 17-54; J. P. Gilbert and F. Mosteller, "The Urgent Need for Experimentation," in Mosteller and Moynihan (eds.), *On Equality of Educational Opportunity,* 371-383; E. A. Hanushek, and J. F. Kain, "On the Value of *Equality of Educational Opportunity* as a Guide to Public Policy," in Mosteller and Moynihan (eds.), *On Equality of Educational Opportunity,* 116-145; E. R. Hilgard, "The Translation of Educational Research and Development into Action," *Educational Researcher* 1 (July 1972), 18-21; D. M. Levine, "Educational Policy After *Inequality*," *Teachers College Record* 75 (December 1973), 149-179; R. J. Light and P. V. Smith, "Choosing a Future: Strategies for Designing and Evaluating New Programs," *Harvard Educational Review* 40 (1970), 1-28; S. Michelson, "The Association of Teacher Resourceness with Children's Characteristics," in A. M. Mood (ed.), *Do Teachers Make A Difference?* (Washington, D.C.: U.S. Government Printing Office, 1970); D. P. Moynihan, "Sources of Resistance to the Coleman Report," *Harvard Educational Review* 38 (1968), 23-26; W. D. Rohwer, Jr., "Decisive Research," *Educational Researcher* 1 (July 1972), 5-11; L. S. Shulman, "Reconstruction of Educational Research," *Review of Educational Research* 40 (June 1970), 371-396.

34. J. S. Coleman et al., *Equality of Educational Opportunity* (Washington, D.C.: U.S. Government Printing Office, 1966).

35. C. S. Jencks, "The Quality of the Data Collected by *The Equality of Educational Opportunity* Survey," in Mosteller and Moynihan (eds.), *On Equality of Educational Opportunity,* 437-512.

36. In the subsample considered by Jencks (1972), 13% of the districts were entirely uncooperative, 14% returned one or more principal questionnaires but no student data, and 28% returned questionnaires for some schools only.

37. Dyer, "Some Thoughts about Future Studies."

38. Compare Herriott and Muse, "Methodological Issues."

39. Hanushek and Kain, "Production of Education."

40. Gilbert and Mosteller, "Urgent Need for Experimentation."

41. Campbell, "Factors Relevant to the Validity of Experiments"; "From Description to Experimentation"; "Administrative Experimentation"; "Reforms as Experiments."

42. *Ibid.*

43. See especially Campbell, "Administrative Experimentation"; "Reforms as Experiments."

44. *Ibid.*

45. Campbell, "Administrative Experimentation," 178.

46. Coleman, *Equality of Educational Opportunity.*

47. C. E. Bidwell, "Schooling and Socialization for Moral Commitment," *Interchange* 3 (1972), 1-27; J. W. Guthrie, "A Survey of School Effectiveness Studies," in Mood (ed.), *Do Teachers Make a Difference?* 25-51; Levin, "Cost-Effectiveness Analysis."

48. E. Hanushek, "The Production of Education, Teacher Quality, and Efficiency," in Mood (ed.), *Do Teachers Make a Difference?* 79-99; D. Jamison,

P. Suppes, and S. Wells, "The Effectiveness of Alternative Instructional Media," *Review of Educational Research* 44 (Winter 1974), 1-67; Guthrie, "Survey of School Effectiveness Studies"; Spady, "Impact of School Resources"; D. E. Wiley, "Another Hour, Another Day: Quantity of Schooling, A Potent Path for Policy," *Studies of Educative Processes*, No. 3, University of Chicago, July 1973, in W. H. Sewell, R. M. Hauser, and D. L. Featherstone (eds.), *Schooling and Achievement in American Society* (in preparation); Harriott and Muse, "Methodological Issues."

49. G. G. Cain and H. W. Watts, "Problems in Making Policy Inferences from the Coleman Report," *American Sociological Review* 35 (1970), 228-242; Hanushek, "Production of Education"; Levin, "Cost-Effectiveness Analysis"; Wiley, "Another Hour, Another Day."

50. Cooley, "Assessment of Educational Effects."

51. W. W. Charters and J. E. Jones, "On the Risk of Appraising Non-Events in Program Evaluation," *Educational Researcher* 2 (November 1973), 5-7.

52. Spady, "Status, Achievement, and Motivation."

53. Compare Coleman, *Adolescent Society*.

54. Spady, "Status, Achievement, and Motivation."

55. E. Q. Campbell, "Adolescent Socialization," in D. A. Goslin (ed.), *Handbook of Socialization Theory and Research* (Chicago: Rand McNally, 1969); Schwartz, "Open Curtain—Open Mind."

56. E. Q. Campbell and C. N. Alexander, "Structural Effects and Interpersonal Relations," *American Journal of Sociology* 71 (1965), 284-289; J. McPartland, "The Relative Influence of School Desegregation and of Classroom Desegregation on the Academic Achievement of Ninth Grade Negro Students," *Journal of Social Issues* 25 (1969), 93-102; E. L. McDill, L. C. Rigsby, and E. Meyers, Jr., "Educational Climates of High Schools: Their Effects and Sources," *American Journal of Sociology* 74 (1969), 567-586; A. M. Greeley and P. H. Rossi, *The Education of Catholic Americans* (Chicago: Aldine, 1966); R. Wax, "The Warrior Dropouts," *Transaction* 4 (1967), 40-46; I. Weinberg, *The English Public Schools* (New York: Atherton, 1967); Spady, "Impact of School Resources."

57. Spady, "Status, Achievement, and Motivation."

58. Anderson and Tissier, "Social Class"; Schwartz, "Open Curtain—Open Mind"; D. R. Ausubel and P. Ausubel, "Ego Development among Segregated Negro Children," in H. A. Passow (ed.), *Education in Depressed Areas* (New York: Bureau of Publications, Teachers College, Columbia University, 1963), 109-141; R. Dreeben, *On What Is Learned in School* (Reading, Mass.: Addison-Wesley, 1968); Bidwell, "Schooling and Socialization"; Sarane S. Boocock, *An Introduction to the Sociology of Learning* (Boston: Houghton Mifflin, 1972); Spady, "Impact of School Resources"; R. K. Bain and J. G. Anderson, "School Context and Peer Influences on Educational Plans of Adolescents," *Review of Educational Research* 44 (Fall 1974), 429-445.

59. C. E. Bidwell and J. D. Kasarda, "School District Organization and Student Achievement," *American Sociological Review* 40 (1975).

60. B. Heyns, "Social Selection and Stratification within Schools," *American Journal of Sociology* 79 (1974), 1434-1441.

61. Wiley, "Another Hour, Another Day."

62. Carroll, "Model for School Learning."

63. Donald A. Erickson, *Educational Organization and Administration*, American Educational Research Association Readings in Educational Research, Merlin C. Wittrock (ed.) (Berkeley, Ca.: McCutchan, in process).

64. Suppes and Morningstar, "Computer-Assisted Instruction"; Fletcher and Atkinson, "Evaluation of the Stanford CAI Program"; Salomon and Achenbach, "Effects of Four Kinds of Tutoring Experience"; Spady, "Status, Achievement, and Motivation"; Schwartz, "Open Curtain—Open Mind"; Anderson and Tissier, "Social Class"; Bidwell and Kasarda, "School District Organization"; Heyns, "Social Selection"; Wiley, "Another Hour."

65. Compare Jamison, Suppes, and Wells, "Effectiveness of Alternative Instructional Media."

66. R. M. Gagné, "Policy Implications and Future Research: A Response," in Mood (ed.), *Do Teachers Make A Difference?* 169-173.

67. C. D. Hardie, "Research and Progress in Education," in H. S. Broudy, R. H. Ennis, and L. I. Krimerman (eds.), *Philosophy of Educational Research*, American Educational Research Association Readings in Educational Research, Merlin C. Wittrock (ed.) (New York: John Wiley and Sons, 1973), 87-101.

68. Dyer, "Thoughts about Future Studies"; Campbell, "Administrative Experimentation" and "Reforms as Experiments."

69. K. W. Deutsch, J. Platt, and D. Senghaas, "Conditions Favoring Major Advances in Social Science," *Science* 171 (1971), 45-459.

Part III

THE CHANGING
NATURE OF PRACTICE

During the period from 1954 to 1974 the practice of educational administration changed in many ways. As chapters in the preceding sections make clear, these changes were generally linked to contextual developments. In the opening chapter of Part III Keith Goldhammer speaks directly to these events in analyzing the changes in the role of the school superintendent between 1954 and 1974. Schools, he says, became more politicized on one hand and more restricted by the courts and Congress on the other. Goldhammer emphasizes the growing importance of coordination, orchestration, and negotiation in the face of conflicting perspectives as hallmarks of the contemporary superintendent. While he focuses only upon the superintendency, his analysis may also be applicable to other administrative roles, including the principalship.

Another perspective on practice during the period is gained by reviewing the activities of professional associations, foundations, state education agencies, and the federal government. These ancillary institutions, as Laurence Haskew terms them, often reflect the concerns and emphases of the field. Haskew notes a theme of social responsiveness among these institutions during the period under review. He avers, however, that the emphasis upon activism during the last half of the period served to vitiate whatever focus an earlier emphasis on study may have encouraged.

It has become commonplace to suggest that the kinds of developments described by Goldhammer and Haskew require a "new breed" of leader to cope with them effectively. As Haskew points out, funding institutions invested a substantial portion of their educational dollars in an effort to identify or prepare such leaders. In his examination of preparation for leadership, Edwin Bridges notes that the field requires abilities like those discussed by Goldhammer but asserts that programs to prepare leaders based at universities may be dysfunctional. By overemphasizing the heroic aspects of leadership and neglecting the reality of organizational impediments to change, these programs may encourage future leaders to act in ways that will lead to future disappointment. Moreover, the university setting and reward structure differ so greatly from situations of field leadership that the behaviors students adopt to succeed in the former may be to their detriment in the latter.

By 1974 educational administration had become a very complex and controversial arena. Few people were satisfied with the state of the field. As part of the broader press for activism and accountability, people outside the field asked why schools could not be managed more efficiently or respond more effectively to particular issues. Practitioners decried mounting pressures from outsiders and sought ad hoc solutions to the problems of the day. Scholars were criticized for focusing their attention on describing problems rather than proposing ways to remedy them. To many, it seemed that the pressures upon the field had mounted at a pace too great for those within it to adapt in systematic ways. As a consequence, practitioners continued to rely heavily upon intuition, past experience, and ad hoc advice in day-to-day situations, although the problems they faced differed substantially from those of 1954.

8. Roles of the American School Superintendent, 1954-1974

KEITH GOLDHAMMER

Social roles are shaped by many factors. They are formed by the expectations that relevant individuals have for them; by their social and cultural settings; by people who exert influence upon the role holder; by the technology related to the functions of those roles; by history and precedent; and by unique events. There are commonalities among the different individuals who hold the roles, and there are also unique characteristics determined by the values, personalities, and objectives of those individuals. Administrative roles are complex configurations of any number of factors, and it is difficult to determine the commonalities because there are so many pertinent variables that must be considered.

It would be impossible in a short chapter to attempt to draw a comparison between two time periods with respect to the changing roles of all administrative positions in education. This chapter, therefore, will focus upon one administrative role, namely, that of the superintendent of schools.

The University Council for Educational Administration (UCEA) was generated as a response to an attempted revolution. The revolution was a grand design to establish a science for educational administration in place of the folklorish base which predominated prior to

1950. It was a part of a movement to improve the quality of administration, particularly as related to the superintendency, and to understand better all of the forces that impinged upon the superintendency and made it the unique administrative position it was. It came at a period when the superintendency was at the center of tremendous social ferment in the United States—a ferment that, in and of itself, was to become a dominant force in shaping the roles of superintendents.

Factors Affecting the Superintendency in 1954

The year 1954 will be remembered primarily for the Supreme Court's decision on school desegregation. Knowingly or not, the court established the point from which a new era in American society would be dated. Not only schools but American society itself would be different from this point on. It was inevitable that a key social position such as the school superintendency would be among those factors most affected by the changing value structures in American society. Older superintendents will recall the days before 1954 and nostalgically ruminate about what it was like when they didn't have to be concerned about so many uncontrollable variables; when their major job was "education," and no one in the community expected, or possibly would even tolerate, policies that introduced school operations into the arena of social action and social policy. The schools were seen as isolated enclaves within the mainstream of American society, but in the twenty years following the Supreme Court's decision of 1954 they would be shaken by violent cataclysms. These idyllic enclaves would discover that they were not only connected with, but even possibly the central focus of, controversy within the mainstream. One can perhaps best see the changes that have taken place in the roles of the superintendency by isolating some of the factors that have shaped the superintendency both in the era before 1954 and in the present day.

Prior to 1954 the school was a first-line gatekeeper for social mobility. The acquisition of the proper school credentials enabled an individual to rise above his more humble social class origins and climb the ladder which permitted him to achieve increasingly higher levels of social status. Without these credentials, an individual's opportunities for such mobility were greatly restricted. Greater access to higher education through federal scholarships and the GI bill made it possible for members of the working class to enter professional schools and obtain the credentials necessary for their emergence into the prestigious levels of stratified society.

In this milieu the school had control over the dispensation of a great social benefit which parents wanted for their children. The school could exact its proper price for the rewards it had to bestow upon those it found worthy. It demanded conformance. It required polite behavior. It required that the parents of the children who were to be its beneficiaries keep it sheltered and protected from the mainstream conflicts of the broader society of which it was a part. School teachers and administrators were viewed as the instruments through which children of the lower and middle classes would be able to advance socially and economically and bring honor to their parents.

By 1954 it was apparent that American society was about to enter a period of severe transition. Prior to 1950 those who described the American scene were still mainly captivated by what appeared to be the monistic homogenization of American social structure. The prosperity after World War II seemed to affect all classes of society equally, so that few would not benefit from the increasing advantages of this mighty technological society. But one grave error was made in the analysis. Most of the interpreters of American life failed to see the impact of universal education upon the current society. Groups that had formerly been denied freedom of access to the highest levels of the school system were now beginning to benefit from it. And a universal improvement in the level of education of the masses caused them to question the economic and social elitism that still prevailed. By 1954 there was an emerging militant pluralism—a recognition of the power of groups to demand that society provide for them the means through which they could achieve greater access to all available opportunities and rewards. Social paternalism was being questioned, and the right of leaders to command was fading away.

In spite of the movement of society toward a greater acceptance of pluralism, and involvement of all groups in the decisional structure, the school organization remained basically autarchical. In spite of the fact that in the 1940s and early 1950s teachers in the United States upgraded their qualifications and developed greater professional capabilities, there were no fundamental changes in the administrative hierarchy. Autarchical paternalism was not compatible with the degree to which teachers had acquired professional capability and their deep concern for involvement in the decisional structure of the school. Teachers wanted a voice in making their economic rewards commensurate with their professional responsibilities. Teachers were beginning to reject subservience as unbecoming to their advanced professional training and capabilities. But by 1954 there were still relatively few school districts in the United States where teacher power had emerged to compel bargaining contracts. Personnel policies were established by school boards with the advice of the superintendent and with or without the consent of the teachers affected. The emerging new professionalism was, however, an indication that school boards and superintendents could no longer consider teachers as powerless, subordinate hired hands.

The age of information technology was in its infancy. Relatively few school districts could afford computers or had the technical capability to use computer technology effectively as an aid to administrative processes. In general, the old-line administrator still carried most of the information he needed for his decision making "in his hip pockets." The day was soon to come, however, when even the school district of moderate size would have access to more information about its operations and requirements than could be digested by a single human being. The school administrator was faced with a technological revolution, which would require him to become increasingly dependent upon the information systems and specialists who were carving out new roles in the administrative team.

Prior to 1954 school politics were dominated by individuals who were naive about the use of power and indifferent to its acquisition. Typically, individuals who were active in school affairs were second or third line influentials in the community. Only rarely was a school board election the object of considerable political conflict within a given community. Even in large cities there was a tendency for school boards to be self-perpetuating entities; members found recruits for open positions or relied upon self-appointed "blue ribbon" committees to make nominations of "acceptable" candidates. School board membership was a matter of civic service rather than a representation of particular interest groups. Superintendents were prepared to deal with school boards that could readily arrive at a consensus and that produced little internal conflict. The literature on relationships between superintendents and school boards dealt with the problems of avoiding conflict rather than the containment or use of conflict as an administrative device.

School board members were disorganized and, in most places in the United States, highly dependent upon the expertise of the super-intendent and his staff in order to conduct their business. School board associations were just emerging and were dominated by admin-istrators rather than by board members. Very frequently school board associations were subordinate to professional organizations and viewed their roles as supportive.

The community in which the school administrator worked gen-erally accepted certain stereotypes that produced relatively homo-geneous expectations about teaching, the functions of the schools, and the roles of teachers and administrators. The schoolmarm or master was assumed to be dedicated to simplistic values related to the education of children. The role of the school was to teach the three R's and to make children behave. Teachers were considered self-effacing individuals, dedicated to pursuing the interests of others and indifferent to their own. The school was expected to lay a foun-dation for success in life, but the real test of an individual's capabili-ties would come through involvement in the economic affairs of society.

Implications for the Roles of the Superintendent in 1954

The implications of these forces upon the roles of the superin-tendent can best be seen in four categories of his responsibilities: executive, manager, educator, and public relations officer.

Executive. The superintendent of schools was viewed as the head of the hierarchical organization of the schools and the final authority for the maintenance of all systems within the school orga-nization. He was considered to be the "boss" and the dispenser of rewards and punishments to all personnel within the system. One of his greatest concerns was that of being policy advisor and interpreter of the actions of the board both to the community and to the school staff. Although the literature was replete with distinctions between policy making and execution, assigning the former to school boards and the latter to superintendents, the distinction was never clear in the operating role of the superintendency. Most boards would not have been able to make policy without the technical and professional advice of the superintendent. The smaller the community in which he operated, the greater was the superintendent's difficulty in keeping the school board clear of executive functions. Never totally sure of exactly where to draw distinctions, most superintendents endeavored to involve their boards in administration. Superintendents seemed to feel a primary obligation to be the board's executive before the faculties and the community. It was the duty of the superintendent to interpret school needs to the board, to the community, and to the staff and to describe for the staff the regulations, privileges, responsibilities, and limitations under which they worked based on the policies and values of the community and the school board. The superintendent was expected to run a tight ship and be accountable to the school board and the community for everything that happened concerning the schools. His reputation both with the community and with the profession was dependent upon the degree to which he could maintain smooth, harmonious operations within the school and in the relationships of the school with the community.

Manager. As manager of the school enterprise, the superintendent was assumed to have expertise in several areas.

Probably the most important evaluation of the superintendent concerned the way in which he managed the financial affairs of the school system. Regardless of the size of the system and the availability of technical expertise in financial matters, the superintendent who wanted to win the respect of the power elites within the community had to demonstrate his prowess in managing financial affairs, economizing on operations and expediting the business.

The 1940s and 1950s were periods of growth in enrollments for most school systems within the United States, and, as a result, most school districts were faced with massive programs for the construction of new buildings. The superintendent was considered to be the expert on school buildings. He had to make final recommendations to the school board relative to the acceptance or rejection of architectural plans, contractual relationships, and the acceptance or rejection of new construction. Since capital construction required dramatically large amounts of public funds, the superintendent had to demonstrate that he could manage the construction program without frills, waste, or ostentation.

The third aspect of the superintendent's responsibility as manager related to his administration of personnel. In the last analysis, he was responsible for the employment of all personnel, both professional and supportive, in the school organization. Although he might administer through subordinates, both staff members in the central office and principals of schools, he had to set the standards, recommend policies to the board, and establish the principles upon which human relationships would be maintained. The most complex problems of personnel were brought to him for resolution. His success depended upon the extent to which he could make that resolution. In cases of legal conflicts, he was the defendant of the school system and had to protect its interests as well as that of the school board. Personnel within the school district recognized him as the ultimate "boss."

The fourth aspect of his operation as manager concerned his ability to give leadership to the support programs (or auxiliary services) of the school system. As another phase of his role, he was the person who was ultimately held accountable for the effective and economical operation of the support services, and the provision of the necessary supplies and amenities for operating the schools. In the small school district he was the purchasing agent, and in the largest school districts he was the final authority before taking contracts and major purchases to the school board. If he was not presumed to have expertise in these matters, he was expected to judge the expertise of subordinates.

All of these facets of his role as manager had to be orchestrated into a grand design that led to the economical, efficient, and effective operations of the school enterprise. These were the terms in which his accountability was best expressed.

Educator. In addition to his other roles, the superintendent of schools was also assumed to be the educational authority—"Mr. Education"—within the community. It was his obligation to assist the board and the staff in the selection of educational objectives and the formulation of appropriate instructional programs necessary to meet these objectives. He was expected to be able to distinguish between effective and ineffective educational programs and to install the most effective programs with the least expenditure of public funds. When educational issues arose, he was the final mediator of conflicts and interpreter of both professional and community expectations for the proper education of all children. His responsibility was to see that learning took place so that children acquired the ability to advance to higher levels of educational or occupational attainment. If dislocations occurred, he was expected to pinpoint the nature of the failing and introduce remedial action.

Public Relations. As head of the school system, the superintendent was its spokesman. He addressed the community on behalf of both the school board and the professional staff, and interpreted school programs, needs, and accomplishments. He was expected to be visible to the public and a participant in important activities of the community. His presence demonstrated that the schools were serving the needs and desires of the community as interpreted by influential groups within it. The superintendent had some contact with the media and frequently appeared before the public to convey information about the schools' programs.

In the last analysis, the superintendent was viewed as the leader whose activities made a fundamental difference in the successful operations of the schools. On his shoulders rested the final responsibility. Even though it was the school board that made policy and represented the community within the school organization, it was the superintendent who really stood at the head of the school organization and had to coordinate all of the efforts.

Factors Affecting the Superintendency in 1974

By 1974 some of the emerging trends noted in 1954 had fully developed, and, for the most part, the superintendent had to cope with a significantly different milieu.

There could now be no question that the schools were a key public agency within an aggressively pluralistic society. Sometime after 1954 the American ideal of the melting pot disintegrated. Diverse cultural groups within each community no longer wanted to be entirely homogenized into the mainstream. Each group not only wanted to maintain its own values and cultural perspectives but also demanded that its unique concerns be reflected in the policies and programs of all governmental agencies, including the public schools. In the 1940s educators proclaimed that the schools should serve the needs of all of the children of all of the people. The schools were now faced with the added necessity of providing diverse and differentiated programs to satisfy all of the components of the pluralistic community. Not only were they required to deal with fragmented values and a diversification of needs, but they also had to give assurance that there would be no denigration of the culture of any group within the society. School personnel could no longer rely upon the safety of conformance to a dominant value system. The pluralistic society required recognition of the legitimacy of different perspectives and the obligation of the schools to provide programs that were congruent with all of them.

The pluralistic society necessitated a different emphasis on the social role of the school than administrators were accustomed to dealing with. After the 1954 Supreme Court decision on school desegregation the recognition came that public schools were an instrument of social policy and no longer isolated enclaves within the broader society. The schools could not be used by superior agencies of governance as instruments for the accomplishment of social objectives. Schools were now increasingly involved in effecting social change. Social issues previously of little concern to the schools became, by law and the interpretation of the Constitution, major problems with which school boards, administrators, and teachers had to contend. These were great issues, which could not be resolved simplistically or quickly. As a consequence, schools—and, in particular, leadership within them—became focal points of controversy. School administrators had to learn to live with conflict on major issues, which could only be resolved by working in collaboration with other social and governmental agencies.

After 1954 the schools were a frontline agency for resolving discrimination in American society. Various action groups now became militantly involved in school politics and internal school affairs. Most of these action groups had platforms that they wanted to achieve, which they felt could be accomplished either within or through the public schools. Heretofore voiceless segments of the community now became vocal and demanded that school officials give attention to the issues that concerned them. The great problem for the school administrator was that he could not remain neutral. Policy that would appease one group would antagonize another. Even failure to act was viewed as a commitment to one point of view and an instrument to be used by one group against another. The effective school administrator had to learn how to contain conflict, how to manage conflict, and how to negotiate and win compromises among contending forces.

New legal restraints were also placed upon the schools and the freedom of action of school administrators. Schools now became involved with programs sponsored by the federal government. To participate in these programs and to gain federal funds for their operation, school districts had to abide by the guidelines prescribed by Congress or federal administrative agencies. Almost all of these programs tended in some ways to regulate both policies and operations within the schools. Federal courts determined local policy through their power to enforce constitutional provisions and government regulations. School boards and administrators could use the courts to delay the implementation of federal regulations, but most of them recognized that the day would inevitably come when delay was no longer tolerable and the courts would use increasingly severe sanctions to enforce conformity. Beyond the government and the courts, power groups had learned how to use federal regulations and the court system effectively to achieve their ends.

Among the influences changing the character of the customary arenas in which educational administrators operated, the new pluralism impelled groups of employees to demand greater consideration for their unique interests, to form unions or other active associations, to employ professional representatives, and to force recognition of their right to involvement in the processes of decision making. Gone was the old model for decision making, in which the superintendent collected information, formulated a proposal for a policy, and then presented his recommendation to the board for action. Policies now had to be developed by negotiation and bargaining with various groups. The attention paid to the forms of rational, systematic decision making in organizational theory gave way to the exigencies of negotiation and bargaining. In 1954, as employee, student, and parent power began to appear, the theoretical question arose as to what was negotiable. By 1974 it was recognized that the definition of negotiability was associated with the power that any group had to force bargaining.

Teachers became the special, powerful group in the decision-making process because their interests involved both economic and working conditions for themselves, as well as policies related to educational functions. Having considerably upgraded their professional qualifications, teachers could now claim the same professional capability for decision making as administrators. As professionals who actually operated instructional programs within the schools, teachers demanded their right to negotiate on matters pertaining to instructional practices and policies.

American society faced new interpretations of individual rights, liberties, and privileges, reinforced by court actions. A new era of litigation arose. Any decision affecting diverse members of the public associated with the schools could become the substance of extensive and expensive litigation. Rights—of teachers, parents, students, and the public—became issues which compelled the time, attention, and effort of school administrators. Extensive legal literature had to be digested, and the school attorney became an increasingly important figure in determining policy. Another important position was established in school board deliberations in which the superintendent was subordinate.

Slowly through these two decades, sources of school support changed. Local school districts could no longer fully finance their school systems, and court decisions held that differentials of wealth among school districts of a particular state led to discrepancies in the educational opportunities afforded children. Through further state participation in the financing of schools and the provision of vast amounts of federal money for categorical aid to schools, funding bases were drastically altered. Already the school administrator had to learn how to get the dollars needed to maintain his school program from means other than the local tax levy.

In this configuration of forces the school administrator discovered that he was having to deal with different characteristics of school board members. No longer predominantly selected by blue ribbon committees or from among the associates and friends of existing school board members, new members came from special interest groups within the community and were charged with the responsibility of representing their group's interests. The superintendent's ability to survive professionally depended on how he could negotiate among the diverse interests and concerns of the members of his school board. School board members recognized their own unique interests and formed more powerful state and national organizations, which tended to work independent of their administrators.

In addition to experiencing all these other changes, the school administrator was also affected by the expansion of knowledge about administration and organizational operations. No longer could the administrator profess administrative expertise if he knew only about the content of school administration. New knowledge about administration and the complex of administrative techniques fostered by the computer revolution impelled the administrator to become expert in both the content and knowledge of operations of educational institutions and the uses of broader administrative technology.

Professional knowledge about teaching and learning also greatly expanded. These twenty years were characterized by significant progress in educational research as well as increasing criticism of the effectiveness of traditional school operations and a search for educational reform. Alternatives to the established program proliferated, and each proposal won converts not only from among members of school staffs but from patrons as well.

Such was the setting in which the administrator of 1974 practiced his profession.

Implications for the Role of Superintendent in 1974

The implications of these diverse forces affecting the superintendency in 1974 can again be grouped under four general headings.

Executive. The superintendent is still the executive officer of the school board. He stands at the head of the professional organization in relationship to the school board and community as well as to the personnel within the school system. His position now sets him apart, however, and he represents neither the local administrative spokesman for the educational profession nor the chief representative of the school board and the diverse community influences that are impressed upon it. As executive, the superintendent has been cast into a distinct role. He was formerly a recognized member of the teaching profession and became involved with prestigious and influential groups of the community. He now occupies a position between groups. His office is a focal point for all groups desiring to make impacts upon policy and program. He is now the figurehead of an agency that diverse groups seek to control or, at least, manipulate toward their own ends, and he is one of the key figures who must be manipulated.

The traditional hierarchical chart showed the superintendent at the head of the organization where he exercised his authority because of his ability to control, to interpret policies, and to allocate resources within the organization. But in 1974 his authority was curtailed and limited by new exigencies and commitments. Rather than developing recommendations for policies within the school district, he had to interpret social policy established by other agencies to which the school district had, to some extent, to conform. His ability to exercise authority and control was strictly circumscribed within the federal guidelines established for the operations of various programs within the schools; the decisions of courts on cases involving either his own or other school districts, but which, in either case, described certain imperatives or limitations for action; and by contracts which were negotiated with various groups of employees or patrons, which the school board officially adopted, and which then defined what could or could not be done in the administration of the schools.

The superintendent of schools was no longer an independent executive, exercising the authority of his position on the basis of his professional judgment, training, experience, and wisdom. He was, rather, a coordinator of influential groups and the orchestrator of diverse interests and demands made upon the schools. In the new pluralistic society, authority and control over school operations are geographically dispersed within the school organization and the community on the basis of the power that groups have to compel attention toward their concerns. The superintendent, as executive of that organization, must maintain communication with various levels of power figures representing different economic, cultural, ethnic, racial, religious, and employment sectors. His primary skills today must be the skills of political compromise, accommodation, negotiation, management of conflict, and persuasion.

As executive officer of the school district, the superintendent spends most of his time and effort in responding to social issues or conflicts that arise because the schools can now be used as a vehicle to solve social problems. In addition to meeting other demands, the superintendent today must have expertise in the techniques of eliminating segregation in the schools, in the means through which schools can help to relieve the burdens of poverty, in the relocation of schools to effect urban renewal; in instructional programs and strategies to build cultural homogeneity among minority groups, and in adult education to assume continuous employment. To the old-line superintendent, these are demands that were not inherent in the functions of educational institutions that he was prepared to administer.

Not the least of the superintendent's concerns today arises out of the fragmented perspectives on these issues held by members of his board of education. Today individual board members may demand action while others demand delay. Some may criticize the superintendent for his expressions of concern, while others may demand that he take a stand and advise them on pervasive plans. The conflicts of American society are all represented to some extent on the school board or are impressed upon the superintendent and the board through pressures from special interest groups. As executive, the superintendent has to declare himself in spite of the inevitability of his becoming the center of conflict!

Manager. As the result of his changed role as executive, the superintendent now manages by negotiation and bargaining. He is no longer the father figure dispensing largess among dependents. He is an administrator who negotiates and interprets actions and needs in terms of contractual agreements made with various groups within the organization. The superintendent has assumed a middle management position in which he has less opportunity to be self-directing and must spend more time in reactive rather than proactive activities.

Today's superintendency is affected by multiple contractual agreements, which determine policies, resource allocations, and limitations upon the exercise of authority. All of the complexities associated with these contracts and the agencies with which the school district must now interact and which have legal or assumed control over activities within the school district have produced a proliferation of positions of expertise within the school organization. Subordinate members of the administrative team can no longer be generalists like the superintendent. Most of them are now specialists whose fields of expertise are limited areas of organizational operations. Although many have developed their expertise after obtaining their educational credentials, others have come into these organizations with general business, legal, or public administrative credentials. Although technically subordinate to the superintendent of schools, in most instances subordinates have more expertise in their particular functions than the superintendent, and, consequently, he has little basis for challenging or rejecting their conclusions. Rather than judging their actions, the superintendent must adapt to them even though his own position on critical matters may be adversely determined by what they conclude.

Frequently, the superintendent cannot interpret all activities successfully, either to the board or to the public and must give his experts opportunities to become independently visible for their operations. This is particularly true with respect to negotiations for contracts in which specialized bargaining personnel must be employed, whose counsel is most frequently given directly to the board rather than through the superintendent. Today a school system of any size needs its financial expert to manage the business and financial affairs of the district. It needs its own architectural department to handle plans, contractual relationships, and supervision of new construction. No school district of any size could be without its personnel department to maintain not only the complicated personnel functions, but also the contractual and bargaining relationships with employees. Even in supportive programs, the superintendent now deals with experts who are qualified to manage their particular functions within the school organization.

Although still the manager of a legally independent governmental agency, the superintendent has closer relations and more dependency on the managers of other governmental agencies than he had twenty years ago. Closer relations with local and state agencies are necessary because of the urgency of certain problems, such as the security of buildings, maintaining order in schools, and operating various functions in accordance with laws and regulations. With the expanded social significance of school functions, coordination with other agencies is imperative.

Since the financing of school programs has become more complex, the superintendent has to spend more of his time in grantsmanship. The availability of funds for special purposes of vital concern to the school districts necessitates that efforts be made to obtain the district's fair share. Proposals are usually prepared by subordinates, but the superintendent must be active in determining sources and negotiating contracts. In the final analysis, his accountability covers proper performance under these contracts and grants as well as all the other functions of the schools.

As manager, the superintendent of schools is faced with complex problems of communication within the administrative structure. In general, the administrative structure is now more fragmented than it was in 1954, with each section having to interpret the operations of others through its own specializations. Members of specialized

sections tend to develop their own languages and systems of relationships, creating additional problems for internal or external communication throughout the administrative hierarchy.

These three factors—the proliferation of contractual relationships, the fragmentation of administrative specializations within the
hierarchy, and the magnitude of problems of communication with
the organization—constitute a further limitation on the effective use
of the power and authority of the superintendent.

Educator. As educator, the superintendent is affected by these
same forces and finds that his authority and control have eroded to
the point where he has only limited capability to direct or change the
educational program. His relationships with the professional staff are
generally controlled by contractual agreements. Although he still has
some influence over the allocation of resources, he must have new
strategies for working with particular groups of individuals if he is to
succeed in making faculty aware of needs and in mobilizing energies
to do something about them. Again, he is more a reactor than a
leader, a negotiator than a goal setter, and an expert in utilizing the
processes of leadership and group involvement than a specialist in
content. None of these dichotomies are discrete. Nevertheless, they
indicate limitations upon the freedom of action and the capabilities
for leadership of the superintendency that were never contemplated
before 1954 or even in most of the literature written about the
superintendency since that date.

With all of the new forces that limit or circumscribe the role of
the superintendency, however, the superintendent can still provide
educational leadership within the organization, and he can be held
accountable for the educational programs and the organizational
operations under his jurisdiction. This leaves the superintendent with
one opportunity, which is somewhat subject to limitation by bargaining and, therefore, makes him dependent on another type of expertise. This is the opportunity to evaluate and bring to the attention
of the staff, board, and community the effectiveness with which various segments in the school perform or fail to perform their responsibilities and achieve their objectives. Although seldom used by superintendents in a formal fashion, the power to evaluate on the basis of
educational principles can give new meaning to his role and enable
him to maintain the authority inherent in his position.

Public Relations. Since 1954 the American school superintendency, as well as other governmental positions, has been greatly

affected by the public's demand to know, and the media's assumption of responsibility for keeping them informed, about all of the business that is transacted in their behalf. In many states there are now laws requiring that all public business be conducted openly. As one administrator expressed it, the superintendent no longer has his "hole card" available. A meeting of any public body related to the schools is usually reported by television, radio, and the press, and the superintendent of schools must be prepared for the general distribution of his remarks whenever he makes any public appearance or gives any information or recommendations to any public body. Because of the availability of local television in larger communities, he is a known figure. Portions of school board meetings are even included on television news programs, and the superintendent has his office invaded by technicians who periodically set up the electronic media for recording his perspectives on lively school issues.

On the one hand, school personnel have ready access to public information systems. The school story can now be told and will probably reach a higher percentage of the concerned audience than ever before. On the other hand, even if the school district has its own public relations department for the dissemination of information, that information will not always be presented as the superintendent or his subordinates might wish. Increasingly, interpretations of points of view and recommendations are made by self-appointed individuals who have responsibilities to the media, rather than to the school district, and such interpretations may be made whether or not those individuals have the necessary background or preparation. Opportunistic reporters can readily enlarge insignificant items into mountains of controversy by giving a particular interpretation to the superintendent's utterances. Consequently, now more than ever, the superintendent has to be cautious and controlled, rather than open and flexible, in his relationships with the press. Although often lacking the resources and capability of the large-city media, the small-town media follow the examples of their urban peers and may secure even better coverage than is achieved in the urban counterparts.

Conclusion

The superintendency has indeed changed during the nearly twenty years of UCEA's existence. Always the center of some controversy, it is now at the very core of controversies affecting the schools. Established to give some independent professional thought, judgment, and action to the overall needs of the schools, the superintendency is now greatly circumscribed by forces internal and external to the schools. Designed as a position of educational leadership, it is now more significantly marked as a position of coordination and orchestration rather than one of independent leadership, although some new opportunities have yet to be fully explored or exploited. Regardless of its problems, the superintendency will persist. The opportunities for statesmanship, leadership, and executive direction, although more complex and exacting, are possibly even greater today than ever before. If there ever was a day when the position attracted the timid, that day, most certainly, is gone forever.

9. Leadership in Educational Administration by Ancillary Institutions, 1954-1974

LAURENCE D. HASKEW

Introduction

The prime institutions affecting the shape of educational administration from 1954 to 1974 were individual universities and school districts. Interacting with those prime movers, however, was another set of organizations—professional societies, private foundations, state education agencies, and the federal government. They are collectively called ancillary institutions in this discussion. Their leadership in educational administration composes the material for the present chapter.

Nature of Ancillary Institutions

When addressing education, the American polity manifests great affection for localism. It is almost equally inclined, however, to supplement localism with ancillary institutions in order to influence the performance of locals. Formation of ancillary institutions is fostered in some cases by beneficent permissiveness and in others by governmental decree. Either way, the organizations formed serve the polity as ministers to local educators. Individual universities thus joined to create a University Council for Educational Administration (UCEA) to achieve ends deemed beyond the reach of universities acting alone. The Ford Foundation is chartered under beneficent permissiveness and chooses to influence universities to equip blacks to be school administrators. State education agencies are empowered to influence local districts to employ systems approaches in educational administration. The federal government conceives and releases categorical grants to influence local educational policies. The net result is that the task environment of ancillary institutions is dominated by locals. Life processes of such institutions mirror that fact.

The life histories of ancillary organizations cannot, however, be accounted for solely by their efforts to maintain influential symbiosis with locals. Most of these organizations frequently undergo metamorphosis by themselves. Although in constant tension with the task environment composed of locals, inner circles or secretariats do form and do influence what the organization does, the goals it enunciates, the directions accorded priority, and the methodologies chosen to influence educational administration.

It is interesting that as ancillaries attain perceived potential for influencing locals, one ancillary will choose to channel its leadership efforts through another. The Danforth Foundation, for example, in 1966 chose to furnish the Southern Association of Colleges and Schools (SACS) with funds for a long-term education improvement project. As another example, the American Association of School Administrators (AASA) maintains a federal relations network as one of its major endeavors at leadership. At the other end of the spectrum, almost every ancillary at times gets into the business of leadership ordinarily undertaken by locals, such as when a state education agency operates workshops to train administrators of vocational education or a private foundation holds a colloquium on humanizing administration.

Ancillary institutions nevertheless dominantly behave as links to the current scene. Chief interpreters of that scene are locals or the individuals they employ. The needs and thrusts of ancillary institutions are preponderantly in response to signals secured from where activity is taking place. Even the programs and projects they support are already, for the most part, operating in a local setting or are being conceived by persons on the firing line. Naturally, most of the signals they get stress the continuation of what is going forward; or, in the lexicon of James Lipham, with maintenance and not with leadership defined as re-creative departures.[1] The ancillary's inner circle does interpret and select from the signals, and on rare occasions it actually invents. It frequently fabricates a "new" thrust by an ingenious combination of signals. Preponderantly, however, it manifests acute awareness of priorities and thrusts embraced by the ancillary's constituency. The federal government, for example, distributes about 90 percent of its fiscal effort for education to maintenance and about 10 percent to leadership.[2] These characteristics of ancillary institutions lie behind a declaration that the leadership existing in individual universities and school districts is present in the story of leadership among ancillary institutions from 1954 to 1974. The latter story may be fairly comprehensive in depicting a national taxonomy of direction to be taken in reshaping educational administration.

Roles of Leadership of Ancillary Institutions

To complete this foreview of ancillary institutions as operatives, we now turn to the role they assume within leadership. This necessitates defining "leadership." Paul Pigor's dictim long ago was that leadership has not transpired unless a proffered idea has been accepted and acted upon by nonprofferers.[3] This dictum does not apply in this chapter. When AASA's National Academy for School Executives (NASE) organizes and conducts seminars on planning, it is proffering changed substance for the practice of educational administration. Convincing evidence to establish that NASE's proffer has or has not been accepted and acted upon is, however, impossible to obtain. I therefore define leadership as *acts of proffering,* when that which is proffered seeks—however distantly—to change educational administration.

Roles available within proffering are numerous. Efforts by ancillaries demonstrate this. Wielding powerful sanctions, an ancillary can seek to dictate that specified change shall occur. On occasions, professional societies, at least one private foundation, a few state education agencies, and especially the federal government have been perceived by locals as essaying the role of dictator. During the two decades under review, however, few ancillary institutions adopted the role of dictator as applied to educational administration. Instead, the roles preponderantly chosen by ancillaries were of a nurturing type, in which desires to influence locals and to be in harmonious symbiosis with them produced strategies of stimulative collaboration. These roles can be described as (1) enabling, (2) formative, (3) persuasive, and (4) communicative.

In enabling roles ancillary institutions equip ideas for change with implementive resources—chiefly dollars. Professional societies and state education agencies have few dollars available other than those they get from other ancillaries, but like other ancillaries they do command other valuable resources. Among these resources may be clients who will collaborate in exploiting or testing ideas, managerial or technological know-how, prestige, command of extant knowledge, and access to pools of professional talent. It should be emphasized that an enabling role does not entail merely passive check writing. It has positive dimensions of leadership. The ancillary makes choices between seeking as resources ideas for change and ideas for maintenance. When processing ideas of leadership, ancillary institutions choose some for use as resources and others for polite rejection—thus shaping directions and objects of change. With prospective enabling roles held forth as stimuli for ideas for change in a chosen territory, ancillaries are likewise targeting efforts to bring about change. The enabling process usually opens up acts of negotiation between grantor and grantee, resulting often in grafts (of a horticultural variety) to produce fruits quite different from those the grantee originally contemplated.[4] In sum, the enabling roles of ancillaries offer opportunities for leadership that could be rather formidable if their absolute pools of resources were large enough to constitute significant sanctions. These resources do not, however, come close to being that large.

In formative roles, ancillaries seek to set influencing frameworks within which locals will operate. During the mid-1960s the New York State Education Department conducted a cooperative study of educational administration. One result was a set of criteria for (a) the practice of local educational administration, (b) local conditions that should prevail for administration to be effective, and (c) the ends that university preparation programs should achieve. The framework was made fairly firm upon the insistence of the state education agency. One variety of formative leadership is thus illustrated: locals were expected to change as they worked within a proclaimed stage setting. Although most widely used by agencies of governance, this type of formative leadership is frequently adopted by other ancillary institutions. The announcement by a private foundation of its fields of interest constitutes a formative framework. Formulation and publication of *Administrative Behavior in Education* by the National Conference of Professors of Educational Administration (NCPEA) exhibits the use of such a framework.[5] A second variety of formative leadership gives desired shape to nondirective thrusts. One facet of leadership is certainly that of providing operational means with which to carry out ideas. The Rockefeller Foundation's post-1967 design for school administrator internships furnishes a typical example. An "equal opportunity program" of the foundation became manifested, in part, by a specified vehicle, complete with specifications for who were eligible, where they were to be trained, by what means, and for what positions. A third variety of formativeness is closely akin to the second. It consists of effecting a promising methodology. In 1960 the employment of simulation as a mode of instruction for prospective and practicing school administrators was considered highly promising. UCEA made the promise exploitable over the next ten years by producing rich instrumentation for use by locals. Acting in a similar vein, several other ancillary institutions have provided, with the use of packaging, materials to develop the skills needed to perform administrative functions. To summarize formative role playing, ancillary institutions engage in setting up frameworks, establishing targets, and effecting ideas for change, thus giving them operational form. It should be emphasized, however, that locals do most of the fabrication of what emanates as proffers of leadership by ancillary institutions.

In persuasive roles, ancillary institutions incite locals to act positively toward advocated changes. One object is to encourage locals to invite changes among school districts, universities, or individuals. Another object is to help locals exploit the potential of the change. This involves instilling in practitioners persistence and a sense of pride in bringing about the change. Promotive persuasion is thus a facet of leadership. It can be coercive, as ancillary institutions with governance status have demonstrated on occasion. Persuasion can, and frequently does, ride piggyback on the outputs of the enabling and formative roles of leadership of ancillary institutions, as previously illustrated. Appearing frequently in the history of ancillary institutions from 1954 to 1974 are attempts at persuasion by demonstration—acts aimed at creating and maintaining examples of ideas for change with the hope that these examples would persuade locals to do likewise. Other frankly promotive devices include provision of awareness seminars, training seminars, invitational or wide-open institutes, and the like. The regional education laboratories (ancillary institutions) resemble private enterprise in that they merchandise their packaged innovations. Ancillary institutions, however, more commonly act as catalysts rather than merchandisers. For example, they set the stages for self-persuasion among locals—with conferences, workshops, cooperative production of reports and recommendations, school improvement councils, and university consortiums. Professional societies exhibit a fondness for annual conventions structured partially as smorgasbords of ideas in action. Judging by the sheer volume, the printed word is the catalytic medium most relied upon by ancillary institutions for performing persuasive roles of leadership. Through these and similar acts of persuasion, the collection of ancillary institutions made perhaps their strongest claim to leadership in educational administration between 1954 and 1974.

In communicative roles, ancillary institutions exhibit three types of leadership. One type is through deliberate persuasion, as just described, which patently incites change. Another type of role consists of attempting to keep locals—institutions and individuals—aware of what is transpiring in the outside world. A third involves channeling information from locals to other ancillary institutions, notably those that are governmental. Such information consists of needs, interests, feedback, petitions, and advice—as well as current undertakings by locals. These latter two types of communicative performance are predominantly concerned with maintenance. Ancillaries, however, often proffer leadership in the form of stimuli to undertake change. In order to make locals aware of what is transpiring in the outside world, ancillary institutions use scores of devices, some of which are creative in their own right. The *American School Board Journal,* a communication of the National School Boards Association, has undoubtedly had some effects upon the climates for change among local districts, and the annual conventions of that organization serve to lessen provincialism and to promote—by osmosis—changed relationships between school professionals and citizen governing boards. UCEA's *Educational Administration Quarterly* probably adds a little science to the repertoires of professors, gives some impetus to research by offering a publication outlet, and offers a framework for conceptualizations of educational administration for use or nonuse by its readers. In order to communicate information from locals as inputs to other ancillary institutions, a given ancillary institution adopts and puts resources behind advisement communications or constitutes itself as a lobby.[6] Private foundations frequently request advice from executive directors of professional societies. Almost every week, a representative of AACJC gives advice on decisions to be reached by other professional societies, the Office of Education in HEW, or the Congress of the United States. The Carnegie Foundation is especially known for its success in penetrating the inner circles of the federal government. In recent years, the Education Commission of the States has appeared as an advisor to state educational agencies, private foundations, and sundry agencies of the federal government. From almost every professional society that I examined, communiqués in the form of resolutions, reports of status studies, case-making documents, and proposal pieces have flowed to other ancillary institutions. Flowing and impinging are, of course, separate phenomena, but ancillary institutions must be given credit for their voluminous attempts to exhibit leadership by transmitting signals to each other in the period from 1954 to 1974.

By categorizing and elucidating four roles, the "institutional leadership" addressed in this chapter has now been operationally defined. It is to be hoped that these illustrations have given some concrete form to otherwise nebulous concepts. A performance exhibits qualities of leadership only when the intent of the performance is to bring about change or further change already in progress. The performances of proffering change, or of supporting endeavors that portend change, constitute leadership for purposes of this examination. Some skepticism is always present, however, that proffers correlate highly with products. Proffers consist preponderantly of gestures made toward "locals," incorporating individuals as well as institutions within the referent for locals. Gestures from ancillary to ancillary are, however, also incorporated, and some gestures are made toward the content of educational administration as a professional discipline. Whether as direct entrepreneurs or as collaborators with other entrepreneurs, ancillary institutions assume four roles. Definitions of these roles are largely created by an analyst; seldom does an ancillary institution adopt these roles as discrete entities. Instead, their outputs typically bear imprints of two or more roles. The roles, as elucidated, are (1) enabling, (2) formative, (3) persuasive, and (4) communicative.

The Field of Forces from 1954 to 1974

Roald F. Campbell's chapter in *Administrative Behavior in Education* advances the concept that administrative behavior is always, in part, a result of forces existing in the situation.[7] Enlarging that concept to a grand scale, all of educational administration can be envisioned as an anthropomorphic entity wending its way through a field of situational forces over the last twenty years, with its behaviors at various times being inevitably responsive, at least in part, to the strongest of these forces. The direction of institutional leadership during the period from 1954 to 1974 should make more sense to readers if a few prominent situational forces are identified in advance.

It seems necessary to describe first what I mean by "educational administration." Knowledge and the production of knowledge are present, as well as administrative behaviors and organizational behaviors as abstractions. Frameworks for the governance of schooling and higher education, immobile or fluctuating, are also referred to. Administrative behavior is contemplated as the practices and skills manifested by people in administrative positions. The actions of personnel associated with determining the population of administrators—who gets in and who does not—are in the picture. Looming with particular prominence is the complex of educative development for administrators and prospective administrators, including the content and methodologies that contribute to development by tutelage and experience. As nourishers of all morphologies and physiologies, research and its products complete the picture of the anthropomorphic entity. It is apparent that these diverse elements are linked interdependently in a systematic fashion. Institutional leadership consists, then, of proffering changes in one or more of these components of educational administration.

I now wish to highlight four forces that have been situational factors affecting institutional leadership during the past twenty years. These are by no means all.

In 1964 the National Society for the Study of Education (NSSE) published Part II of its yearbook, *Behavioral Science and Educational Administration*. In the opinions of many, this volume marked the emergence of a movement from adolescence into vigorous young adulthood. That movement may be labeled "The Study of Educational Administration."[8] Its beginning had been symbolized and made substantive by another book, *Administrative Behavior in Education,* published in 1957. The final chapter of Part II of the 1964 NSSE Yearbook characterizes that movement as built upon an ideational core consisting of the conscious application of intelligence and inquiry to administration as a specialized function of institutionalized education. Accompanying the core were strong supports for the method of science as *the* method of inquiry and for creation of a discipline based on theory to undergird the art or science of professional practice by administrators. The ideational core, it was said, was being transformed into a remarkably unified movement based on projects, by numerous institutionalized progeny—notably UCEA—and by a burgeoning literature, widespread experimentation with preparation programs and in-service experiences, and endeavors in research and production of materials in universities. There was also an urgent concern that certain values be used as criteria to show that educational administration no longer pursued noble obsolescence. This identifies one force that acted upon the exercise of institutional leadership during the years from 1954 to 1974.

A second force that rushed onto the perceptual scene in the early 1960s was generated by the plight of schooling caught up in the maelstrom of the inner city. Schooling was the victim of conditions not at all matching most of the assumptions previously dominating the task environment models employed in educational administration. These models had to be redone.[9] Soon, however, schools found themselves viewed not as victims but as villains with educational administration—and administrators—cast in principal roles. At the same time, however, a belief existed that educational administration—and particularly the new breed of educational administrators—could work miracles that would cure the fatal illnesses of education in urban areas. "Do something about urban school administration" therefore became and remained the outcry from 1960 to 1974.

A third force swelled to a crescendo during the period examined. Public education was being recast as an endeavor in public polity. In more down-to-earth language, the shaping of public education became everybody's concern. In protestations, of course, public schooling in America had been long recognized as a creature of

public polity. The relationship until about 1954 was, however, contractual. The polity provided benign permissiveness, support, and
neglect; public education acted as a philanthropic and largely self-
regulating contributor to the people's polity. The foregoing statement is overdrawn to emphasize the strength of the force unleashed
over the decades covered in this book. All across the country citizens
were demanding roles in making and executing decisions of governance for education;[10] even students acted as if they were citizens.
The mode of governance aspired to became participative—a traumatic
bête noire to administrators schooled in an ethos of "trusted representatives." Citizens increasingly turned to the federal government in
efforts to get public education to serve their needs—and whims. They
got results and these results impinged painfully upon traditional educational administration. Public education was seized upon to achieve
national policies; the nonlearning by black pupils in Opp, Alabama,
became a concern of the United States government. Programs to
cover not only objects of national policy but also precise methodologies for executing the policy emanated from Congress and the
executive branch. Simultaneously, the Constitution of the United
States was being propelled into the administration of school districts
and universities by the federal judiciary, on the one hand, and by
local citizen groups, on the other. To a lesser degree, but still significantly, public education was forced into closer integration with the
polity of states. One typical result of all this new placement of polity
is a woozy, but worrisome, concept called accountability and a presumably implementive technology known as systems approaches to
administration. Over the last five years, much institutional leadership
in educational administration has marched to the beats of these two
drums. This is just one example of a global situation; nearly every
component of educational administration has been affected by heavy
and mounting compulsions toward change since the mid-1960s because of signals from an aroused populism and an egregious polity.
The supernal problems that institutional leadership faces may be the
same, but the solutions demanded are certainly different.

A fourth force has been the awareness of those who profit least
from education. The most visible of these bear ethnic or other
"minority" labels, and the force has been organized around blacks,
Mexican-Americans, women, and so on. One favored advocacy of
ethnic groups is that administrators whose ethnicity is the same

as theirs can serve them better. Another advocacy is that minority employees who seldom profited in the past from career ladders in school districts should now do so as a matter of equity. Both advocacies became notable in the mid-1960s and compose a compelling force at present.

The presence of these four situational forces explains some of the roles and individual acts of institutional leadership between 1954 and 1974. They do not, however, explain all. Only the first force identified, that of the "Study of Administration" movement, was an inertial feature of the anthropomorphic entity itself. Many other inertial momenta were, of course, present within that same entity. The other three forces may be thought of as nontraditional environmental ones. But many traditional forces also continued as situational factors to which institutional leadership responded.

I would now like to turn to the roles of leadership in educational administration displayed by private foundations, professional societies, state education agencies, and the federal government, respectively.

Private Foundations

The Foundation Center's *Foundation Directory* (1971) recognizes the existence of 15,000 to 25,000 private foundations, depending upon the definition of a "foundation." It reports that 5,454 such entities each had assets of $500,000 or more and that their 1969 grants totaled 1.5 billion dollars. Only 331 foundations had assets of $10,000,000 or more. Thirty-six percent of their 1970 grants, or $281,000,000, were made to education.[11] These figures are given to stress two facts, even more important in 1977 than in 1970. First, the sheer amount of money from foundations available for education is relatively small. Second, the amounts available for influencing educational administration from 1954 to 1974 just had to be infinitesimal. In short, dollars had to be exponentially multiplied by ideas and canniness if leadership were to occur.

I used nine foundations to index the behaviors of private foundations during the period from 1954 to 1974. Although conscious that many smaller foundations were taking action in educational administration, I assumed that the direction and categorical distributions of their collective endeavors would not differ significantly from

those of the ten selected. This assumption has more than convenience to support it, but adduction at this point of justifying evidence would be diversionary.[12]

Emphases for Leadership

Upon what components of educational administration did foundations target their roles of leadership? They targeted directly upon
the production of knowledge to a very slight degree. The Spencer
Foundation, a newcomer in 1970, has targeted, by awarding seed-
grant supports to universities, a large portion of its commitments
upon the production of additional knowledge in the behavioral sciences. In 1966 the Danforth Foundation invested $1,000,000 in the
Harvard Institute for Advanced Studies in Education, and the Carnegie Corporation probably saw its $5,000,000 support for the Com-
mission on the Future of Higher Education as focused essentially
upon the production of knowledge for use by the governors and
administrators of higher education. It is almost certain, however, that
the production of knowledge was often seen by foundations as a
bonus above and beyond grants focused upon other outputs. By contributing $750,000 toward the Western State Small Schools Project
in 1965, the Ford Foundation probably foresaw the contribution of
a little new knowledge about school organization and administration
on a microscale. Six foundations contributed to the Center for Urban
Education in New York City; the production of knowledge was listed
as one justification. The Ford Foundation globalized the importance
of its program for new organizational patterns in New York City and
Pittsburgh by stressing the impact of the knowledge likely to be produced. Certainly the Danforth Foundation anticipated the side
effects of knowledge discovered through the Cooperative School
Board Project (CSBP). Whether intended or not, considerable production of knowledge ensued from grants made by private foundations to professional societies and universities; several illustrations
could be recorded. But I fear to do so would produce distortion.
During the period examined, the production of knowledge appears
more as an afterthought than as a prompting impulsion of private
foundations.

Almost completely absent during this period was any focus by
foundations upon administrative behavior or organizational behavior
as components in the construction of theory. To be sure, individuals
who received support from foundations to collect data have made

contributions to this component of educational administration, but no formative focusing by foundations themselves was unearthed.

In contrast, frameworks focusing on governance were rather common. By 1965 early interest in salvaging urban education had emerged from being a charitable contribution and had begun to manifest itself as interest in securing better frameworks for urban schooling. Several forays in this direction have already been mentioned. In the early 1960s the Carnegie Corporation supported H. Thomas James and his colleagues in a study of school boards, and it commissioned Robert Bendiner to do another study in its "crisis alertment" series.[13] In addition to granting more than $800,000 to CSBP, the Danforth Foundation chose another framework of governance—SACS—to change, and be changed by, an education improvement project. The Ford Foundation's grants to the Institute for Educational Leadership apparently intended in part to interpose new auxiliary structures for the managerial oversight of education. Several of these foundations joined in giving a start in life to the Education Commission of the States (ECS), another interposed structure. More recently, the Spencer Foundation chose ECS as the site for a permanent center for school finance studies.

At the same time a different method of focusing upon frameworks was exemplified by some foundations. Since 1959 the W. K. Kellogg Foundation has been engaged in developing a relatively new form of education—the community junior college. By 1975 junior colleges were not only vigorous components of the educative network, but they served as spawning grounds for rapidly changing notions about the end products to be sought by educational administration. The Mott Foundation's persistent investments took another pioneering start made by the Kellogg Foundation and produced the community school, now called community education, as a specialty framework in public school systems. Efforts of the Charles A. Kettering Foundation to accelerate the conversion and rebirth of the secondary school, along with its contribution to the Institute for Development of Educational Activities, provide other examples of focus upon changed ideational and valuational frameworks within schooling. Apparently similar in intent was the Danforth Foundation's 1968 grant to the National Association of Secondary School Principals (NASSP) for a project titled "Demonstration Schools for Staff and School Reorganization."

The dominant focus of private foundations during this period,

however, was upon three other components of educational administration. They were (1) recruitment, (2) educative development, and
(3) behavior on the job of administrative practitioners. It was practically impossible to distinguish one of these targets from the other
two when grants and promotive thrusts were examined. For example,
in 1968-1969, when the Rockefeller Foundation put together a field-
based internship experience for prospective urban school principals,
was it focusing upon getting blacks into principalships (recruitment),
demonstrating that internships are better than formal curricula (educative development), or producing relevant administrative behaviors
in a real-life situation? The answer is probably all three. My calculations indicate that between sixty and seventy percent of all grants
made by the sample population of foundations between 1954 and
1972 were focused on this triad of components. Fellowships or other
stipends for trainees accounted for most expenditures contemplated
in the grants. But, whether based on the grantee's choice of the
formative specifications of the grantors, educative development was a
normal accompaniment, and particular behaviors (for example, those
peculiarly required of administrators in inner-city schools) were
stated as goals or hopes. From 1963 on it was rare to find a grant not
explicitly geared to serve minorities; the majority of support for fellowships was earmarked for members of ethnic groups, and women
were also frequently given priority. Administration for inner-city
schools was almost as the prime determinant of behaviors to be
sought after 1963. Nearly twenty percent of total funding was provided for projects in which educative development was to be presided
over by school districts, without university inputs. Judging by the
university applications funded, foundations in recent years have relied heavily upon field training and student autonomy for educative
development and have had little concern for formal curricula. They
did, however, put a significant portion of their fiscal contributions
into university efforts to create new patterns for educative development of administrative leaders. One example is the Ford Foundation's allocation of $5,000,000 to the "Seven University Consortium
to Reform Graduate Programs in Educational Administration." On a
smaller scale, but highly strategic in impact, was the grant by Kellogg
of $400,000 to UCEA from 1967 to 1972 to "aid in cooperative im-
provement of training programs." A sizable portion of the same
foundation's 1973 grant to Northwestern University for a "Staff

Development Center" was used to pilot test university programs. Between 1970 and 1973 the Ford Foundation made at least $4,000,000 in grants to support university programs designated as "innovative."

Roles of Leadership Assumed

So much for the components of educational administration upon which private foundations focused from 1954 to 1974. What roles of leadership did they assume? Enabling ones in the fiscal sense, obviously. Yet the prominence and weight of these roles can be overstressed. Sixty to seventy-five million dollars is a sizable sum. When distributed over twelve years and among 100 grantees, however, its supportiveness is hardly colossal.

Formative roles were much more striking. Visibly impressed by situational forces, especially between 1964 and 1974, private foundations exhibited high degrees of purpose in their proffers. A distinctive break with tradition occurred when some either formulated on their own, or provided significant funding for, endeavors in the educative development of administrators, apart from those sponsored by universities. It is difficult to determine when foundations were setting styles and when they were following styles, but all evidence indicates they were consciously supporting what they perceived as renewal urgencies in recruitment, educative development, and behaviors on the job. In the same years, the federal government and many professional societies were playing formative roles in these same areas. Perhaps foundations were chiefly joining up with, rather than pioneering in, a movement.

Promotive roles were visible, but not numerous. In most cases foundations provided fiscal support to other promoters. Grants by Kellogg to UCEA and those by Danforth to the American Association of Community and Junior Colleges (AACJC) were examples. Several foundations made small grants to help fund promotive enterprises such as conferences, awareness workshops, and training institutes. Some foundations enjoyed strong linkages with the federal government from 1962 to 1972. They exerted influence on actions of the legislature and executive branches toward education, but only with respect to coverage under the Education Professions Development Act (EPDA) did educational administration secure mild promotive assistance from this source.

In later discussions of leadership among other types of ancillary institutions, it will become clear that private foundations during this period were primarily adding to the unique directions and methodologies that changed a small portion of educational administration. Assessing the impact of their contribution is difficult. This is because one can only speculate about the pollenization emanating from the few—and preponderantly vigorous—plants they cultivated. If they engaged in much communicative pollenization, it is not visible from their reports. But many of the individuals allied with the programs that the foundations assisted are busy bees in educational administration. They may have been responsible for considerable diffusion of changed practices.[14]

To close this section, an observation reported earlier is repeated. The foundations largely ignored the ideational core of the movement labeled "The Study of Educational Administration." If they aided it, independent actions within the locals they assisted had to generate and transmit contributions.

Professional Societies

A 1964 census of professional societies devoted primarily to educational administration yielded 264 entries; a 1974 recount showed 312. Many more were undoubtedly missed. The tally does not go below the state level nor does it fully cover higher education. Those tallied on the national and regional level included alliances of institutions (The University Council for Educational Administration and the Council of Greater City Schools are examples); alliances of individual professionals such as NCPEA, the National Association of Elementary School Principals, and Division A of the American Educational Research Association (AERA); and mixed corporate organizations (Education Commission of the States, National Organization on Legal Problems of Education, and Research for Better Schools, Inc., are examples). At the state level, state associations of school administrators and of professors of educational administration composed sixty percent of all professional societies tallied. In the total array of societies fierce individualism was occasionally discovered. The dominant impression, however, was that they comprised interdependent networks. Sampling thus appeared reasonably valid for investigative purposes. The sample consisted of seventeen professional organizations.

The sample, however, is biased. It includes UCEA, NCPEA, and AASA. Of these, I see UCEA and AASA as composing two sides of a triangle that bounds most of the leadership actually exerted by ancillary institutions. The federal government is the third side. If, however, the years from 1954 to 1964 had been the only period in view, NCPEA would have been my choice for this third side. The temptation is great to produce a biography of those three stalwart professional organizations, covering the years from 1954 to 1974. This should be done sometime at some place. This is obviously not the place, because my mission is to portray institutional leadership, not the life-styles of individual heroes. Portrayal will draw upon the total sample, with a warning that the sample is skewed.

Emphases for Leadership

Educational administration was the major concern of the professional organizations examined. One would expect them to manifest more absolute leadership in educational administration than did private foundations, state education agencies, or the federal government. They did so. The combined volume of leadership, however, was not massive; even professional societies confront the sheer realities of survival and maintenance. In the following portrayals distributions of that leadership between components of educational administration are sketched. The nonmassiveness of the leadership volume being distributed always, however, modifies the adjectives of degree.

The production of knowledge was prominent as a focus for professional organizations chiefly because UCEA was in the sample. Most products were the result of converting extant knowledge into a utilizable form rather than through production by discovery. In addition, the organizations were seldom the prime entrepreneurs for production. Individuals or teams from local agencies were the major contributors, while organizations furnished auspices. The organization was sometimes creative in setting targets and providing the stimulus for production. Since 1960 this type of initiative has been the hallmark of the inner circle of UCEA; the artifacts it produced have good reputations among professionals. More frequently, organizations served as catalysts. *Educational Futurism 1985* appropriately lists individuals as authors but also appropriately gives credit to a catalyst—NCPEA.[15] Sometimes an organization sets up a study of its own, retains a staff, and produces applied knowledge. *Educational Resources Management System,* published in 1971 by the Association of School Business Officials, is a result of that process.[16] The preceding example also illustrates two other features of the focus on producing knowledge. First, its content is based largely on conventional wisdom and pooled judgments, not upon empirical knowledge. Second, some forty to fifty percent of the production of knowledge arose from traditional areas of content—school law, school finance, budgeting, business operations, governmental structures—rather than from behavioral aspects of educational administration. Not to be overlooked, though, is the presumed stimulus afforded by some professional organizations for engagements in research by individuals. They requested research papers and commandeered or commissioned studies. Some societies offered a chance for publishing reports or for presenting papers at a national meeting. Phi Delta Kappa, NASSP, and Division A of AERA are examples, but the sterling one, of course, is the successful launching and maintenance by UCEA of *Educational Administration Quarterly* and *Educational Administration Abstracts.*

Theories to advance an understanding of organizational and administrative behaviors could have been a prominent focus for professional societies during this period. For the first decade it was. After then it apparently diminished in appeal. "The Study of Administration" was a force highly responded to in professional circles and university programs in that first decade. UCEA and, to a lesser degree, NCPEA devoted much effort to increasing that response. Even some practicing organizations began to interpret, if not spawn, products of this response; "theory X and theory Y," "idiographic and nomethetic," were on annual convention programs and in journals of organizations for school and college administrators. At least two-thirds of the pages in 1965 and 1966 volumes of *Educational Administration Quarterly* were alleged by authors to be contributions toward a theory of educational organization or administrative behavior. By 1968 the resources invested by professional societies, including UCEA and NCPEA, in forays toward the building of theory declined. In NCPEA in 1974, for example, there was only one small interest group devoted to organizational theory. One reason, perhaps, for the apparent decline in interest was a combination of disillusionment and a feeling that this field of interest was obsolete. A more likely explanation was the fact that an increasing proportion of resources from all professional societies was being devoted to educative development. I developed an additional explanation which says that the efforts of UCEA plus those of individual scholars had been so successful by 1963 that promotion of the quest for theory was transferred into the open market. Here, textbooks, monographs, and recognition by individual universities were now incentives for scholarly inquiry, with grants or university salaries available as supportive resources. Whatever the reason, it appears that in 1974 building and applying theory were seldom targets among the sample of organizations viewed.

Recruitment in educational administration constitutes a focus the history of which, from 1954 to 1974, closely parallels that of the production and utilization of theory. Recruitment aims at determining whether people are fit to occupy and continue in administrative positions. In *Administrative Behavior in Education*, published at the beginning of this period, Roy Hall and Kenneth McIntyre viewed as imperative the co-optation of highly talented individuals to pursue careers as school administrators.[17] Ten years later in Part II of the 1964 *NSSE Yearbook*, Jack Culbertson enunciated the same urgency.[18] During the interim years NCPEA and UCEA pointed to this problem over and over through conferences, sessions devoted to analyzing the problem, and publications, as did other societies in the sample, to a lesser degree. Few professional organizations, however, manifested leadership in solving the problem, with a few ad hoc exceptions. In the second decade these organizations paid almost no attention to elitist selection. Among journals published in 1973 I did find three plaintive notes to the effect that three to four times as many candidates for positions in educational administration were being prepared as the demand justified, implying that the time had come to be more selective. But situational forces other than elitism were at work after 1965. Even then, professional societies proffered little leadership in giving members of ethnic groups or women a better chance at being administrators. Some did indeed offer examples in their own selection of interns, and several opened their assembly programs to contributions from minorities. A few issued publications on how to cope with equal employment opportunity or affirmative action. But, all in all, professional organizations between 1954 and 1974 ceded leadership in recruitment of personnel to locals and to other ancillary institutions. As always, however, some significant footnotes exist. In their own enterprises for educative development,

four members of the sample tended to restrict patronage to people
with extraordinary qualifications. Most of the NASE seminars fit this
category, as do UCEA's career development seminars. UCEA was
constantly producing and promoting content for university-prepara-
tion programs which had selective side effects. Also, several decisions
by private foundations and the federal government to escalate preparation and placement of individuals from minorities received suggestions from secretariats of professional organizations. My generalization that they "ceded" appears, however, to be valid.

The structural aspects of programs for the preparation of school
administrators offered another focus. Such aspects had to do with
externally constraining the preparation required for the approval of
individuals, as well as the university programs offered. The basic idea
was to raise quality by sanctions such as licensure, accreditation, or
standards connected with prestige. The idea of quality, as opposed to
quantity, was prominent in 1954 and was still being stressed in 1964.
AASA's Committee for the Advancement of School Administration
(CASA) devoted major effort to establishing quality by setting certain standards. One dramatic outcome was AASA's adoption in 1959
of a required two-year graduate specialization for membership after
1964.[19] This sanction galvanized a widespread "reform" of state and
national standards for licensure and institutional standards of accreditation, with strong promotive leadership from many other professional organizations. After a few years AASA withdrew this sanction
but tried another tack. It created and operated the National Academy for School Executives, one intent of which was to produce a live
criterion for better quality in continuing education for administrators. Even "standards" for professors received little play from
NCPEA and from UCEA, which in 1964 produced a volume dealing
with framework, *The Professorship in Educational Administration.*[20]
When UCEA was first organized in 1957, invitations to participate
went only to universities considered by some people to be outstanding. For several years thereafter some members were advocating an
exclusive role for the organization. Seven other organizations in the
sample manifested significant involvements in the game of setting
standards. As is generally known, however, the tide of prolixity and
tokenism in certificating administrators and accrediting institutions
rolled on inexorably during the period. By 1970, it appears, most
professional organizations had given up on leadership by external

constraints. A slight flurry did occur when Nova University and the National Program for Educational Leadership appeared on the scene. Another flurry is currently arising from university quarters. Their fiefdom of advanced and continuing preparation is being invaded by private enterprise and by external organizations (such as the American Management Association and the Educational Testing Service), as well as by their brethren—school districts and organizations of professionals. Mutterings about imposition of standards can be heard, but no action is yet visible.

Beyond a doubt, the brightest light in the firmament of professional societies between 1954 and 1974 was educative development. In the first decade, UCEA and NCPEA were the prime focusers. Reference has been made earlier to UCEA's yeomanly forays toward developing educative content, providing instrumentation for delivering that content (such as the Monroe City Simulation), and disseminating adoption of that instrumentation. In addition, during those years, UCEA was proffering constant leadership in developing definitive models for the whole complex of educative development. *Preparing School Administrators: New Perspectives* (1962) and *The Internship in Administrative Preparation* (with CASA in 1963) are typical artifacts emerging from UCEA's formative pooling of intellectual insights.[21] The interdisciplinary nature of content was a central force for advocates of "The Study of Educational Administration." UCEA picked up this thrust and tried to get it implemented. UCEA was characterized recently as "a ubiquitous discoverer of new horizons." This propensity was evident in the first decade and continued from 1964 to 1974. Credit can probably be given to NCPEA for discovering the international horizon of endeavor to enlighten and propagate the study of educational administration, but UCEA was the instigator in what became the Commonwealth Council for Educational Administration in the early 1960s. In the late 1960s UCEA pointed to the necessity for establishing a common cause between categorical and general preparation programs. It started a push in this direction with a project joining special education with UCEA in a search for common and specialized learning.[22]

NCPEA, undoubtedly the examplar of the use of nonorganization as organizational strategy, made its follow-up on *Administrative Behavior in Education* largely ad hoc. It apparently reasoned that professors would create ideas and would then influence each other in their implementation. In the first decade this worked fairly well. Professors did share ideas and gimmicks for educating administrators. Continuing interest groups came into being and some interest was keen enough to result in actual products. For a time the annual meetings resembled a swap-shop for methodologies of preparation; what happened after the meetings is impossible to trace. One interest group formed around competency based preparation programs and became quite a producer and disseminator. When futurism came along and a chairman built an annual program largely around it, NCPEA followed through with a committee that finally wrote a book.[23] NCPEA also gave its blessings to the production of other documents, but as an organization it left production up to whoever wanted to participate. To date, it has not even been able to get the annual Walter D. Cocking Lectures into print. It would appear that in 1974 NCPEA was not too concerned with proffering strong leadership in meeting the criteria of content and methodology it supported in 1954. Instead, it concentrated once a year on maintaining a communicative clearinghouse for less than ten percent of the full-time professors of educational administration in the United States.

Since 1960 there has been a phenomenal rush by societies of practitioners into the operation of enterprises dealing with educative development. In 1974 they operated almost every vehicle ever invented for the educative development of professionals. They laid claim, justifiably, to having "practicalized" the content for the educative development of administrators. Some interpret their forays into content as a backlash spawned by products of the forces of "The Study of Educational Administration," but many of the professional contributors to their enterprises have "The Study" as a heritage. Professional organizations have, however, been involved to only a mild degree in the design of curriculum. Typically, they do attempt some kind of an identification of needs, usually rather superficial, deduce titles for tutelary enterprises, and select individuals to bring "the word." This is known as the design of curriculum; the actual curriculum depends chiefly upon those who bring and dispense the word. Nor can they be credited with much focus upon proffering leadership in establishing changed methodologies for educative development. A few have certainly tried protocol films, analysis clinics, simulation exercises, and similar innovations. The usual case, however, is for experts to offer very quick expositions, with a short time devoted to questions. On the other hand, UCEA and some professional organizations have been recently exploring prospects for finding interfaces among curriculum and content. One small pilot project was conducted by NASE-UCEA in 1975. But, even if professional organizations view qualitative focuses as minor in the development of professionals, the sheer quantity of educative development for which they are obligating themselves gives magnitude in 1974 to what was unheard of in 1954.

Roles of Leadership Assumed

In proffering leadership from 1954 to 1974, professional societies assumed each of the types of roles identified earlier. Illustrations used for emphasis, it is assumed, sufficiently convey the nature of their performances so it is necessary to examine only a few striking features here. One of these features is the overweening confidence displayed in print. This was to be expected in the case of Phi Delta Kappa and most of the leagues of practitioners, but even UCEA chose tomes and periodicals as the major way to produce widespread change. "Publishing" and "leadership" appear to be synonyms among professional organizations. A second feature is the nature of enabling roles. Seldom did one professional organization support the ideas of another. Enabling activity was almost exclusively an inter-organizational, rather than an intraorganizational phenomenon. To procure resources, professional societies occasionally, but not often, went to private foundations or the federal government. They depended mainly on dues or contributions of manpower from members. Applying so much dues money to leadership was weighed against benefits for the membership, an achievement that should not escape attention. Nor should the successes in co-opting brainpower from locals be ignored. A third noteworthy feature was the assumption of roles by AASA and its correspondents in establishing frameworks at the state level. What is noteworthy is not the success but the bravery displayed in choosing to be reconstructive. The more sophisticated forays of UCEA into establishing intellectual frameworks may have had a more lasting effect, but AASA actually became involved.

There is yet a fourth feature prominently displayed by just one organization. UCEA very early adopted the instrumentive variety of formative leadership. It is true that the genius of its long-time executive director for scanning horizons and identifying promising future directions awes most professionals. The major role of UCEA has, however, been to invent and develop practical ways to progress toward recognized goals. Cadres of professors are still trying to improve upon the mousetraps they produced at UCEA's instigation. A fifth feature, the last one covered here, was the scarcity of promotive roles—at least in the sense of valiant, political or persuasive efforts to overcome local opposition and secure, in actual practice or as an influence in planning and preparation, what was proffered.

State Education Agencies

This section addresses only those agencies with jurisdiction over elementary and secondary schools. State agencies for higher education were not examined. Ancillary institutions with state governance charters, the fifty state education agencies, are presumably provincial in prime orientation. They do not, however, behave that way. The leadership they exhibited from 1954 to 1974, though varied, was remarkably similar in direction. This similarity is partially due to the nongovernmental ancillary institutions their offers have created—the Association of State School Governing Boards, the National Council of Chief State School Officers, and numerous progeny allied with that council. Also accounting in part for this similarity was a somewhat uneasy but burgeoning enmeshment with agencies of the federal government. Several other influences also worked to spawn similar efforts at leadership. Content of this section is derived almost exclusively from across-states phenomena. A reminder may be appropriate, however. "Leadership" as used here does not connote roles of the state agency in improving all aspects of education. Instead, "leadership" entails educational administration only and is the phenomenon operationally defined earlier. Finally it should be noted that "leadership" refers to change, not maintenance.

Emphases for Leadership

Knowledge, the production of knowledge, and the production and utilization of theory did not emerge as areas for emphasis by state education agencies, even after a sample examination of Title I and Title III of ESEA project reports was conducted.

In contrast, administrators and the development of their skills received strong emphasis from these agencies after 1965. No reference is made here to the amazing array of enterprises involving staff development made available to state agency personnel. Some of these were inventive, some were stellar, but most were imitative. In such engagements, the agency served as a local. Acting as ancillaries, however, every state agency engaged in helping local administrators to develop "new" skills such as planning, managing by objectives, becoming agents of change, defining needs, budgeting programs, using management information systems, and others. Gaining affective and cognitive empathy with minority groups, presiding over community participation, conducting collective negotiations, and acting as a defendant in a federal court suit—these were only a few examples that focused on personal development. The influence of the federal government is obvious among such listings; requirements for skills came largely out of new federal rules for the game of administering. In order to deliver such equipment to administrators, a few state agencies had assistance from regional education service centers, others contracted with universities or private enterprises for instruction, most relied upon their own employees, and some mounted major cooperative projects such as "Kansas 76."[24] How much personal and administrative development occurred is unknown, but much promotive leadership existed.

Closely akin was another form of impulsion. When systems definitions of "modern administration" emerged in the 1960s, many entities became involved in developing and installing management information systems.[25] The records examined indicate state education agencies were among the first to adopt and disseminate these systems. For example, in 1969 thirty agencies reported they were developing or had installed statewide management information systems. In fact, by 1970 some type of systems approach was being used in communication between local districts and state agencies in a decided majority of states, including all the populous ones. Thus, by establishing sanctioned expectations state education agencies were adding additional content to the practice of educational administration. By the same actions, they were pushing administrators to establish changed organizational behaviors. A somewhat different, and even traumatic, employment of settings to effect change occurred in Colorado. The state education agency was persuaded by advisors from local districts and the legislature to place accreditation of school districts on a product-audit basis. Less regulatory, but very much attended to, was the setting created by the New York State study of administration, mentioned earlier. In summary, by manufacturing and proclaiming settings the state education agencies focused rather profusely on redefining school administration between 1964 and 1974.

After 1958 licensure for administrators was predominantly a ministerial function delegated—with relatively few prescriptions—by state legislatures to state education agencies. This regulatory tool could be used to emphasize recruitment in educational administration. By 1960 the majority of state education agencies had linked licensure to another ministerial function delegated to them—that of accrediting the preparation programs of colleges and universities. Program accreditation is a means for focusing upon educative development in educational administration. Adoption of the "approved program" by state education agencies placed considerable emphasis on both components—recruitment and educative development. During this period every state made what it called "upgrading changes" in establishing criteria for licensure and for approval of preparation programs. In some states candidates for accreditation and accompanying preparation programs multiplied—superintendents, chief business officers, assistant superintendents, special education directors, and so on. In others, stipulations of content for preparation programs and for duration of programs became almost routine. Twenty-two states established required internships. Many required the university as a whole to formulate and evaluate preparation programs for administrators, in contrast to allowing departments of educational administration to oversee them. In 1974, responding to well-known problems, fifteen state education agencies had some sort of mandate for involving nearly everybody as arbiters of, and participants in, the operation of accreditation and preparation programs. Four or five had mandated, and several more were developing, what they called competency based criteria.[26] I personally feel that these efforts did very little to change either the professional caliber of administrators or the educative development they received. It is obvious, however, that state education agencies were focusing heavily on recruitment and educative development during this period. Singled out for particular admiration were seven state education agencies who supported, by approving programs and granting licensure, many experimental, off-beat forays that universities proposed.

Roles of Leadership Assumed

It is clear that state education agencies assume roles within two categories—establishing formative frameworks and assuming sanctioned promotiveness. This summation tends, however, to obscure some interesting features of their performances. These are singled out for comment.

In one sense, state education agencies performed as communicators par excellence. Title V of ESEA did far more than grease squeaky wheels.[27] Among other things, it bought airplane tickets. Staff members of these agencies were not only in Washington but also all over the map—participating in development projects, attending conferences, hearing the latest word, visiting innovative centers, and so on. On some occasions at least, what they received as "waves of the future" bore upon educational administration. They returned home with reams of materials and faced even more constantly pouring in from external sources. Assuming that most agencies formed only the receiving side of the communication triangle as a result of all this action, some agencies did outstanding jobs in completing the triangle. They acted upon the signals acquired and disseminated these signals to locals.

Contrary to the stereotypical views held by some professors, most enunciations and promulgations from state education agencies are not bureaucratic brainstorms. They are composites of judgments and advice by locals. The outputs may still be stupid or wrongly based, but they are usually the least common denominators of what twelve, or thirty, or one hundred professionals on the firing line think are appropriate. In 1972 when the commissioner of education in Texas recommended, and the state board of education adopted, a new competency based framework for approved preparation programs for administrators in universities, they in fact acted upon a formulation made by twenty-seven professors and school district administrators after studies and conferences enlisting more than 200 other people.[28] An important feature of leadership in state education agencies is typified by the foregoing illustration. By organizing and conducting cooperative studies and composite formulations, these agencies actually proffered behavior modification and educative development to individuals. Returning to the Texas illustration, participants from universities and school districts probably learned more from each other about the possibilities in preparation programs for administrators than most had ever before perceived, and they encountered challenges to their long held tenets never before experienced. Many states exhibited this variety of enabling leadership. The impression received, however, was that most agencies using this participative device did not know what they were doing.

One more performing role deserves special attention. Promotive in nature, it involves technical consultation. In this role, a state education agency uses individualized, in-depth consultation to help a local effect change. Examples of such performance appeared in many states as district pilot projects (in "comprehensive planning" or in "educational assessment," for example). This type of performance was the exception not the rule, however. The net result was that any serious attempts to redefine administrative excellence were all too often lost. Retreating to secondary and tertiary impulsions—training sessions, awareness conferences, stipulations on forms for reporting, regulations, and printed matter—state education agencies were seldom able to get beyond tokenism in executing systems approaches, for example. Because of certain constraints, state education agencies were unable to avail themselves of consultation in their nurturing efforts. The agencies are not being held up as culprits. Instead, this particular feature is pointed out for a loftier purpose. It demonstrates the fact that potentials for leadership in ancillary institutions can be easily overrated, especially when they are instruments of governance.[29]

The Federal Government

This discussion omits any portrayal of the "Feds-in-Education" syndrome so prominent on the educational scene during most of the period from 1954 to 1974. Prior to reporting on its institutional leadership in educational administration, however, I would like to offer an interpretation of "the federal government" which so often appears on succeeding pages. I do not use that name to designate some omnipotent presence lurking in the heavens. Instead, I use it to designate a visible and sizable puppet whose strings are pulled by political and other signaling processes. In the case of educational administration, most of the strings are pulled by ordinary people. The puppet dances in response to the strings pulled. We are dealing, however, not with inanimate puppets but with human beings with wills. These people do impose personal wills on some gyrations, but very often the puppet says to us, "please pull me." In short, we are the federal government.[30]

Relative to its total engagements with education from 1954 to 1974, address by the federal government to educational administration was very small. An exception must be noted. If "address" includes ricochets from national policies toward education, educational administration received a lion's share. Desegregation, equity toward the disadvantaged, the Fourteenth Amendment over and over again, civil rights, and the federal courts as governors of school districts are only a few of the documentations that indicate transformations in the task of school administration were major objects of the federal government. If "address" is measured as proportionate distributions of fiscal support, however, the share for educational administration was extremely small. No accurate tracing of the absolute sum for educational administration is available; I documented approximately $92,000,000 in supports of leadership, committed between 1954 and 1974. If that figure is at all accurate, it totals more than the combined supports for leadership granted by private foundations, professional societies, and state education agencies (from state revenues). Still, even if the programmatic attachments accompanying these funds had been brilliant strategies, the sum is certainly not stupendous.

Emphases for Leadership

Every component listed earlier for the anthropomorphic entity of educational administration was focused upon by the federal government.

Focus upon research and development deserves primary attention, because the other ancillary institutions concentrated so little attention upon that component. With passage of the Cooperative Research Act (CRA) in 1959, the Congress and the United States Office of Education (USOE) embarked upon a tortuous endeavor. A history of that endeavor has been published under the authorship of Richard A. Dershimer, and I make no effort to summarize it here. From my bibliographic files I extracted fifteen published studies I deemed most significant for the period from 1954 to 1974. Twelve of the fifteen bore the standard acknowledgment of support by a grant from USOE. The majority of formal research in this period was probably supported by federal funds. These were not, of course, always from funds provided under the CRA. Those who pull the strings have ways of getting the puppet to put earmarked money in numerous pockets, many of which have incongruous labels. Fellowship funds, for example, were often used to support research. Most professors are rather skeptical of the research emanating from the networks of regional laboratories and research and development centers financed by federal funds, but some of their products must be counted as useful artifacts for educational administration. Around the ERIC Clearinghouse for Educational Management at the University of Oregon a potent research endeavor in educational administration has grown, again largely supported by federal funding. The RFPs for research sent out by USOE—and other federal agencies —have sometimes been in areas of educational administration and have often been stimulants to researchers, even when they haven't gotten a contract. The opinion can be held—as is the case with some members of Congress—that little research that is useful to posterity has resulted from federal support for educational research, but it must be admitted that even the little done in educational administration constituted a worthwhile focus for the federal government.

Focuses upon recruitment in educational administration were arrived at slowly by the federal government. Those who pulled the strings for categorical programs (such as vocational education, the sundry titles of NDEA, education for the handicapped, and the Emergency School Assistance Act) were interested in recruitment, to be sure. Few, however, were interested in providing personnel for the pursuit of administration of even a categorical variety. Title IV of NDEA, for example, was enacted in 1953 to provide graduate fellowships for prospective university professors; not until 1968 did "educational administration" get listed in USOE's guidelines as a field of study. Much recruitment was authorized under Title I of ESEA, but before 1969 no signals from the federal government labeled administrators as likely recipients. In 1967, however, the puppet danced and produced EPDA; USOE danced and produced a strategy called "leverage" for implementing discretionary portions of the act; more strings were pulled and administrators became leverage personnel. Stipends for administrative trainees were authorized and, because of the programmatic bent of the Bureau of Education Personnel Development (BEPD), the award of these stipends was geared to highly selective recruitment of trainees. That leverage, hence leadership, had been generated was testified to by the flood of applications and proposals from universities. The next step was to reduce that flood, pursuant to the urgent advice of those who pulled the strings, preselecting those institutions most likely to succeed. The latter gimmick later evoked punitive reprisals, but in the meantime consciousness of leverage by administrators spread widely through categorical programs not supported by EPDA. Those who knew how to pull strings secured funds earmarked for training stipends, as well as program costs, in nearly all categorical enactments by Congress or HEW. Naturally, as a puppet on strings, the federal government has directed its recent recruitment toward ethnic groups, women, the inner cities, and societal change. Altogether, its focus on recruitment reached notable levels by 1970.

The federal government's focus on educative development displayed an analogous life-style. I was a member of a group that made yeomanly efforts in 1959 and 1960 to get the federal government to step in where the Kellogg Foundation very justifiably left off in the "preparation program" of "The Study of Educational Administration." The puppet did not dance. Later, a few steps emerged from the Bureau for Vocational Education and, still later, from other categorical sources. In 1968, a year after authorization from EPDA, an examiner would have been forced to report almost no focus by the federal government on educative development for personnel in educational administration. This slow start makes the very restricted—and very hard won—engagements with preparation programs under EPDA especially striking. Seldom has so little dancing produced so much commotion. The dancing was named the "Educational Leadership Program," but that does not mean that there was consistency in rhythms or steps. The program was linked to an approach prevailing in 1968 and 1969—one based largely on stipends. But for fiscal 1971 it was described as "a program designed to support projects which engage the system of education across all its operating levels—schools working along with institutions which train administrators, in concert with community facilitating and influencing agencies."[31] According to the prospectus, by engaging in such projects for improvements, administrators would be trained, training programs would be changed, and organizational effectiveness would be increased. In the fiscal years 1971 through 1974, some $15,000,000 was awarded to twenty-eight projects and an estimated 4,000 trainees were served. Included, however, were two large projects, members of which were dancing under the same label but in quite different postures—the Major Cities Consortium of six universities and the National Program of Educational Leadership (NPEL), involving eight institutions. As is well known, NPEL was testing possibilities for crossovers in careers as well as unorthodox preparations. The other consortium essentially combined six universities in urban districts working individually. How innovative or comprehensive all the projects were is a matter for minor debate. Apparently, only NPEL aroused enough interest on the parts of outside professors to become controversial and even that controversy was muted in 1975. Judging by fiscal reports, some two-thirds of expenditures for the Educational Leadership Program went into stipends for students; proving that, with money, a wide variety of students could be procured. Other than that, changes made by these preparation programs is now virtually lost among the folklore used by those involved with programs. Nor is it apparent that anything analogous to *Administrative Behavior in Education* is forthcoming.

The federal government has so many people pulling strings, resulting in so many subordinate projects, that logical categorizations are almost impossible. This discussion has made no reference to these projects. A few deserve recognition. From 1972 to 1974 under Title V of ESEA, some funding was provided for the Ohio State University *State Governance Project*.[32] It produced significant new knowledge in that field and bears the imprint of Roald Campbell. Earlier, the "Designing Education for the Future Project" and its successor, "Improving State Leadership for Education Project," left residues that cannot be ignored when accounting for the shaping of educational administration in the preceding decade. Several projects conducted with funding provided under Title III of ESEA made methodological, if not substantive, contributions to the practice of educational administration. The report of the study that launched AASA's National Academy for School Executives bears the standard acknowledgment to the Bureau of Research, USOE. The same is true for all volumes issuing from the National Educational Finance Project, and who could teach a modern course in school finance without these? This truncated listing will have served its purpose if it causes readers to perceive that the focus of the federal government may not have been exactly revolutionizing, but for the last decade no one can fault its prolixity.

Roles of Leadership Assumed

On the surface, the federal government plays, always relatively, an enabling role. Employing the analogy of the puppet once more, this becomes "supporting the people who pull the strings, namely us." But this support usually has programmatic attachments. Acts of Congress are parables of such support: four or five lines to authorize enabling funds, perhaps twenty percent of the content devoted to logistics for distribution of funds, most of the remainder specifying the programs to be conducted with money, and then a few lines telling HEW to add more programmatic stipulations and judgmental calls. It could thus be said that enabling roles are simply formative roles in different costumes. This is caricature, however.

Formative leadership was very much present but was still strongly modifiable by the formative ingenuity and forcefulness of those who received grants. A Roald Campbell or an Edgar L. Morphet can be bothered, but apparently not appreciably shaped, by formative leadership of the federal government. As a matter of fact, a close study of agencies in the executive branch reveals more instances of formative leadership through finding ways to support compelling ideas presented by outsiders, then instances where the reverse occurred. Professionals in agencies of the executive branch, however, are constantly negotiating with applicants for grants and are sometimes adding or subtracting certain features of projects. The impact of regulations largely formulated by these professionals is well known, but checks are exercised by the *Federal Register* and, recently, by Congress. In the past, commissioners and bureau chiefs did develop brave programs of leadership internally, but Congress has now rather effectively put a stop to such programs. In short, in the last decade the formative roles of the federal government have probably been the strongest ones exhibited by any ancillary institution. The puppet, however, has hardly become a dictator.

Promotive roles also characterize the federal government, especially agencies of its executive branch. The syndrome of delivery and diffusion for programs and dollars is strongly compulsive in these agencies. I found little manifestation, however, of promotive roles in educational administration. A three-person team in BEPD was insufficient to do much promotion within, much less outside, USOE, and UCEA with NCPEA and a diversified AASA did not exert much pressure to enlarge that team.

A rather low-key performance of *communicative* roles was exhibited. A few grants supported ancillary institutions or universities in providing communication. Conferences conceived and initiated by USOE were contracted for; only five focused primarily on educational administration. Federal funding of ERIC was, of course, a major contribution to communication. Three or four regional laboratories conducted enterprises in communication targeted upon administration. Miniscule amounts were provided through grants to publish project reports; the amounts available to only a few projects were enough to make widespread distribution possible. And not to be minimized is the communication transpiring through advisory councils, external auditing teams, review panels, and individual external consultants. Nevertheless, when these efforts were compared with average efforts of the federal government to communicate about all of its educational interests the subject of educational administration received little attention.

In Conclusion

I have attempted to describe the leadership exhibited by ancillary institutions in the period from 1954 to 1974. I would now like to offer two thematic derivations.

One derivation is a strong suspicion that the roles described appear as much more reconstructive than the anthropomorphic form of educational administration in 1974 appears as reconstructed. This suspicion is not an evaluation in any sense. The most perdurable social force known is that of maintaining the status quo. Proffers of leadership are always trying to steer, with small prods, a mastodon. We will have not found many ways to get those prods through tough hides into the nervous system. Until we do, post hoc examiners will view most activity intended for leadership as busywork by dedicated hobbyists. As purposeful as they may be, perhaps—only perhaps— these hobbyists (or faddists) should ask more pointedly just what actual chances their prods have of penetrating through to the behavioral system of the anthropomorphic entity.

The second derivation smacks of interpreting history. Referring largely to the force labeled "The Study of Educational Administration" at the outset, a colleague later labeled the two-decade saga "From Birth to Puberty."[33] I hope he is correct. The history encountered in executing the present assignment, however, tends to indicate that another title, "From Center to Upstage," is more fitting. After 1965 the activist was cast as the leading protagonist. Movements, not substance, were the major concerns. "Get trainees heretofore neglected, get special 'quickie' programs going, the field is the best training ground, everybody get into the act of preparing and retraining a new breed of administrators" were the plot lines. Cohorts crowded downstage, most crying "me, too" and a few shouting "up with my gimmick." Long-needed quickie actions were encouraged by activists. Chroniclers in 1994 may point to this period as one of explosive fermentation, of almost frenetic renewals by trial and error. Others may see it as a wasteful hiatus because it left no residue that educational administration could ingest for its benefit. Its cohorts reduced, by defection, the protagonist for intellectualism—and the resulting administrative behaviors—moved upstage as the script seemed to dictate. Discussions were progressing, considerable business was transpiring, subgroups of cohorts were forming, intelligence agents were often downstage, and sundry activities indicated new strategies might be forming. When the curtain fell in 1974, however, the Study of Educational Administration was still upstage. Was it preparing to resume the leading role or retiring to obscurity?

Notes

1. James M. Lipham, "Leadership and Administration" in *Behavioral Science and Educational Administration,* Sixty-third Yearbook of the National Society for the Study of Education, Part II, Daniel E. Griffiths (ed.) (Chicago: University of Chicago Press, 1964), 119-126.

2. Charles L. Schultze, Edward R. Fried, Alice M. Rivlin, and Nancy H. Teeters, *Setting National Priorities: The 1973 Budget* (Washington, D.C.: The Brookings Institution, 1972), 318-321. The distribution of percentage stated is, however, my calculation based upon analysis of funds committed in FY 1972, 1973, and 1974.

3. Paul J. Pigors, *Leadership or Domination* (Boston: Houghton Mifflin, 1935).

4. Unwitting testimony, perhaps, to the foregoing proclivities appears in Howard Hillman and Karin Abarbanel, *The Art of Winning Foundation Grants* (New York: Vanguard Press, 1975).

5. Roald F. Campbell and Russell T. Gregg (eds.), *Administrative Behavior in Education* (New York: Harper and Brothers, 1957).

6. Stephen K. Bailey, *Education Interest Groups in the Nation's Capital* (Washington, D.C.: American Council on Education, 1975).

7. *Ibid.*, 228-268.

8. Griffiths (ed.), *Behavioral Science and Educational Administration*. See especially chapters 2 and 15 by Hollis A. Moore and Lawrence D. Haskew, respectively.

9. Improving State Leadership in Education Project, *Revitalizing Education in the Big Cities* (Denver: The Project, 1972), 1-26.

10. Dimensions of that demand are set forth by Allan C. Ornstein, *Metropolitan Schools* (Metuchen, N.J.: Scarecrow Press, 1974).

11. Marianna G. Lewis (ed.), *The Foundation Directory*, Volume 4 (New York: Foundation Center, 1971). Volume 5 was issued in 1975, changing only slightly the figures reported.

12. Data were secured primarily from annual reports or similar compilations for 1960 to 1973 of the following private foundations: Danforth, Ford, Kellogg, Rockefeller, Carnegie, Mott, Charles A. Kettering, Spencer, and Lilly. Most illustrations are likewise drawn from these sources but are supplemented by observations I was privileged to make through involvements with sundry projects.

13. Robert Bendiner, *The Politics of Schools: A Crisis in Self-Government* (New York: Harper and Row, 1969).

14. A more positive view of influence by foundations appears in *Decade of Experiment: The Fund for the Advancement of Education, 1951-1961* (New York: The Fund, 1961).

15. Walter G. Hack *et al.*, *Educational Futurism 1985* (Berkeley, Calif.: McCutchan, 1971).

16. William H. Curtis, *Educational Resources Management System* (Chicago: Research Corporation of the Association of School Business Officials, 1971).

17. *Ibid.*, 393-424.

18. *Ibid.*, 303-330.

19. American Association of School Administrators, *Your AASA in 1958-59* (Washington, D.C.: AASA, 1959), 9. See also AASA's *Something to Steer By* (Washington, D.C.: AASA, 1958).

20. Donald A. Willower and Jack C. Culbertson (eds.), *The Professorship in Educational Administration* (Columbus, Ohio: University Council for Educational Administration, 1964).

21. The persistent and prolix efforts of UCEA to influence preparation programs for school administrators by studies and materials cannot be chronicled here. *The Preparation and Certification of Educational Administrators: A UCEA Commission Report* (Columbus, Ohio: UCEA, 1973) cites examples and makes pertinent recommendations. Issues of the *UCEA Newsletter*, 1970 to 1974, report upon scores of endeavors and opinions.

22. Charles Meisgeier and Robert Sloat (eds.), *Common and Specialized*

Learnings for Special Education Administrators (Austin: Department of Educational Administration, University of Texas, 1970).

23. Hack, *Educational Futurism 1985.*

24. Joseph A. Sarthory, *Educational Leadership as Organization Renewal: Kansas 76* (Topeka: Kansas State Department of Education, 1971).

25. Charles W. Nix, *Internal Planmaking in State Education Agencies* (Denver: Improving State Leadership in Education Project, 1971).

26. *The Preparation and Certification of Educational Administrators: A UCEA Commission Report and Summary* (Columbus, Ohio: UCEA, 1973), and T. M. Stinnett, *A Manual on Standards Affecting School Personnel in the United States,* 1974 edition (Washington, D.C.: National Education Association Division of Instruction and Professional Development, 1974), with supplementation by telephone interviews between state certification officers and me.

27. Jerome T. Murphy, "Title V of ESEA: The Impact of Discretionary Funds on State Education Bureaucracies," *Harvard Educational Review* 43 (August 1973), 362-385.

28. Gary Branson, *State Policy Making for the Public Schools of Texas* (Columbus, Ohio: Educational Governance Project, Ohio State University, 1974), 45-53.

29. The generalizations presented are derived by me from close consultations with several state education agencies. Considerable literature tends, however, to document such conclusions. For examples: Mike M. Milstein, *State Education Agency Planning and Federally Funded Programs* (Denver: Improving State Leadership in Education Project, 1971), and Burton D. Friedman and Laird J. Dunbar, *Grants Management in Education: Federal Impact on State Agencies* (Chicago: Public Administration Service, 1971).

30. The "puppet" metaphor is the way I refer to the depictions in analytic masterworks such as: Stephen K. Bailey and Edith K. Mosher, *ESEA: The Office of Education Administers a Law* (Syracuse, N.Y.: Syracuse University Press, 1968); Harry L. Summerfield et al., *Power and Process: The Formulation and Limits of Federal Educational Policy* (Berkeley, Calif.: McCutchan, 1974); Norman C. Thomas, *Education in National Politics* (New York: David McKay, 1975).

31. An intra-bureau memorandum, mimeographed.

32. A terse description appears in Roald F. Campbell and Tim L. Mazzoni, Jr. (eds.), *State Policy Making for the Public Schools* (Berkeley, Calif.: McCutchan, 1976).

33. Memorandum to me from Professor E. Wailand Bessent.

10. The Nature of Leadership

EDWIN M. BRIDGES

Montaigne stated his position succinctly: "All I say is by way of discourse, and nothing by way of advice. I should not speak so boldly if it were my due to be believed." The present comments about leadership need to be viewed in light of this same caveat. It is obvious that a host of singular contributions has been made to our understanding of leadership during the past two decades; indeed, these contributions have been competently summarized and evaluated elsewhere.[1] Yet, without disparaging the inestimable value of a retrospective analysis, it is no less appropriate that we consider fresh perspectives for future efforts in the training and education of administrators.

Abstract knowledge about leadership, no matter how elegant it may be conceptually, will not suffice for a practicing administrator, especially when the effects of the spillover from the organization's "culture" can have a drastic and unanticipated impact upon the organization itself and the lives of all of its inhabitants. The persistent lack of a positive relationship between formal preparation and administrative effectiveness, is not fictional, nor are the complaints about training that tumble from the lips of practitioners.[2] Both the informal appraisals and the formal evidence suggest a pithy, albeit disconcerting, question, "To what extent, and in what precise ways, do our graduate leadership training programs prepare individuals to deal with the realities of leadership?" Does formal preparation help the student contend with the demands for leadership placed on him when he becomes an administrator? Or, do our preparatory programs present points of view and provide experiences that are indeed dysfunctional for those who aspire to be leaders in formal organizations? Do these would-be leaders, to paraphrase Kenneth Burke, become unfit by being fit for an unfit fitness?[3] If so, how does this trained incapacity become an unintended consequence of our well-intentioned efforts? To explore these questions, let us first examine the attitudinal socialization of leaders, and then, in due course, their socio-technical socialization. The combined impact of these two forms of socialization is naturally synergistic in character.

Attitudinal Socialization of Leaders

Leaders, as well as nonleaders, harbor a strong desire to know how well they are doing in the world of work,[4] for occupational success has important economic, social, and psychological meanings for them.[5] The leader's desire for knowledge of results is not easily satisfied, however, because few school systems evaluate the performance of their leaders on a regular and continuing basis. Since systematic efforts to inform educational leaders of the quality of their contributions are rare, relatively few leaders routinely receive organizationally prescribed feedback that they can use to judge their success or failure. Confronted simultaneously with the urge to be successful, with the desire to have dependable knowledge of results, and with the problematic character of gauging his success within the organization, the leader understandably seeks ways to reduce the uncertainty about his success.

One of the ways in which leaders deal with the lack of evaluative feedback is to impose expectations, and, consequently, evaluations, upon themselves.[6] The "ego ideal"[7] represents such a set of internalized standards and shapes part of the leader's reflexive role expectations, i.e., those expectations that the occupant of a role holds for himself concerning his behavior.[8] A major component of the leader's ego ideal is a heroic one. The leader believes that he should be the originator of actions for others; in other words, he should have a special sense of direction for the organization and should be able to secure the commitments and efforts of others in service of this mission. How this overly ambitious definition of roles evolved and what the dysfunctional consequences are likely to be for the unwary holder of such a grandiose conception will be examined in the balance of this discussion.

The leader whom the trainee regularly encounters in the literature in educational administration exhibits heroic qualities. Leadership is described in lofty rhetoric; the anguish, perils, and difficulties of being a leader are generally obscured by the extended portrayals of its pleasure-giving possibilities.[9] The leader is viewed as a potent force for good in the organization; his task is to use the influence of his office to bind the wills of his subordinates in accomplishing purposes beyond their own self-serving ends. The following excerpts exemplify the conceptions of leadership that pervade the literature:

> There is no greater test of leadership on the part of a principal than his positive influence on the professional growth of his teachers. . . . He is responsible for contributing definitely to the professional improvement of his teachers and he will probably not succeed unless he becomes to them a stimulating professional leader.[10]
>
> The elementary school principal holds a key position in the improvement of the professional staff. . . . Whether the school becomes a challenging educational enterprise or a dull and dreary place for children depends not so much upon what is there at the outset of his effort as upon the quality of leadership he provides for the staff.[11]
>
> We may begin by noting that administration mainly is concerned with eliciting human behavior in the service of some goal. Whether we are concerned with manufacturing motor cars or with teaching children, it is human behavior which accomplishes the tasks that need to be done. The science of administration may thus be viewed as a science of managing behavior. . . . The unique task of the administrator can now be understood as that of mediating between these two sets of behavior-eliciting forces, that is the nomothetic and the idiographic, so as to produce *behavior which is at once organizationally useful as well as individually satisfying.* Action which will lead to such behavior on the part of personnel is the highest expression of the administrator's art.[12]

It is clear that the bias of the administrator as the initiator of action and the chief determiner of individual and organizational consequences is evident in both the conceptually complex and the simplistic treatments of administration.

The strength and exalted character of leadership are also evident

in the research questions that are formulated in educational administration. When hypotheses are framed that explore the relationship
between administration and such factors as morale, turnover, and
productivity, the administrator invariably is treated as the independent variable.[13] If a statistically significant relationship is found
and the investigator ventures a causal inference, the effect is attributed to the formal leader. On those rare occasions when attention is
paid to the influence of subordinates and the influence of superordinates is considered to be problematic, results show that leaders are
not the masters of their own destinies.[14] Furthermore, recent experiments raise serious doubt about the legitimacy of directional inferences reached from correlational data. Managerial styles appear to be
shaped by the performance of subordinates; productivity determines
the level of the leader's initiating structure and consideration rather
than the reverse.[15] Although these investigations were designed to
assess the validity of the conventional wisdom in the literature on
administration, their impact is likely to be negligible. The longevity
of strongly held preconceptions is not to be underestimated; the scientific community,[16] as well as the military,[17] clings steadfastly to its
myths. Under such circumstances, the would-be leader will continue
to be subjected to a process of socialization that assumes that the
leader is the independent variable. Research, therefore, cannot be
depended upon to temper the fantasies of leadership stimulated elsewhere.

   Distinctions between leadership and administration that are
commonly drawn in the literature on educational administration further kindle exaggerated conceptions of the potency of leadership.
The administrator is depicted as a colorless organizational custodian
who maintains established structures, procedures, and goals, while
the leader is pictured as a kind of enlightened maverick who disrupts
the status quo.[18] Both the leader and the administrator are presumed
to be capable of realizing their divergent purposes through some art-
ful combination of delegated status and achieved prestige. Influence
is acknowledged to be the energizing force by which the leader and
the administrator fulfill the definitions of their roles; scant attention
is paid, however, to the factors that enhance or impair a person's
ability to influence the flow of events within an organizational setting. By diverting attention from the problematic character of influence to the issue of stability versus change, the academic community

is apt to intensify, rather than moderate, the leadership fantasies of its audience. Since Americans are inclined to equate change with progress and stability with stagnation, trainees can be expected to identify with a progressive leader rather than an unimaginative administrator who remains in a steady state. In either event, the trainee's understanding of the limits of influence is likely to be limited.

Because of the implicit and explicit way in which leadership is treated in formal preparation, the leader tends to judge his performance in office by the extent to which his presence affects the nature and function of the organization. Adopting this noble, albeit unrealistic, yardstick for estimating his efficiency, the leader may expect several dysfunctional consequences. He is faced with an agonizing dilemma in enacting his role. He aspires to perform glorious deeds; yet his power is limited and his preparation has not equipped him to function under conditions in which he has little power. In addition, the leader is predisposed to seek out those settings that offer him the opportunity to create something that expresses his fondest ideas and dreams; these dreams often become nightmares, as new settings are one of the most complicated obstacle courses devised by God.[19] Finally, the leader's overly ambitious conception of his role inevitably leads to disappointment,[20] and his preparation does not equip him to manage this disappointment. Let us examine each of these dysfunctional consequences in greater detail before shifting from an analysis of the attitudinal socialization of leaders to one dealing with socio-technical socialization.

An Agonizing Dilemma

As has been suggested, the leader of an educational organization is likely to overestimate his potential for influence; his powers are more limited than he anticipates. Many formal leaders lack the authority to veto the appointment of new teachers; decisions on selection are made at higher levels in the organizational pyramid with no significant input from first-line supervisors.[21] Nor do administrators have the unfettered right to transfer unacceptable subordinates. School boards have bargained away the right to make decisions on transfers; such decisions are governed in large part by seniority and by the preferences of teachers. Salaries and fringe benefits are fixed through collective bargaining. Level of training and years of experi-

ence rather than the assessments of performance made by a superordinate determine the financial rewards that an individual receives.
The ultimate power—dismissal—virtually disappears as a source of
formal influence when the teacher reaches tenure; even during the
probationary period, the power to dismiss is checked by an elaborate
system of safeguards built into agreements reached between boards
of education and teachers' associations. The power to make work
assignments is also curtailed by these agreements. Constraints on the
power of formal leaders to develop work schedules encompass teaching assignments, as well as noninstructional duties, and grievance
machinery exists to insure that these constraints are not disregarded.
This loss of administrative discretion and power to make decisions
has been so excessive that it has stimulated a counteroffensive in
some districts; parent unions have formed and initiated legal action
to restore the formal powers of boards and administrators.[22] But
until the courts rule on these cases, the restrictions on the leader's
ability to exercise formal power remain in effect.

Even if the courts were to reinstate some of the formal powers
of the educational leader, however, his ability to influence and to
manage effectively would still be undermined by the fact that his
competence does not match the expertise of his subordinates. An
optimal distance between manager and subordinate simply does not
exist in most educational organizations.[23] When the capacity of subordinates equals or exceeds the capacity of their managers, the formal leader cannot effectively judge his subordinates. As a consequence the leader is weak in selection, lacks proficiency in matching
talents and tasks, experiences intense anxiety about determining the
relative rewards of his subordinates, and hesitates to transfer them.
At the same time, those subordinates who know more about their
work than their superiors are able to question the administrator's
plans, actions, and claims to superiority.

When the formal leader eventually recognizes that his capacity
to influence is limited, his prior socialization experiences are likely to
produce a crippling effect. On the one hand, the leader finds it difficult to abandon the power fantasies that have been nurtured and
reinforced during the preparatory phase of his career. On the other
hand, the leader has little sense of how he can effectively expand the
scope of his influence in a setting that is not conducive to leadership.
As long as the leader clings to an unrealistic ego ideal and is unable to

devise ways of satisfying it, he subjects himself to intense feelings of self-doubt and inadequacy. The longer these sentiments persist, the greater is the likelihood that they will impair the physical and psychological well-being of the leader.[24]

If preparatory programs are to assist the leader in coping with this dilemma of leadership, trainees must be encouraged to examine the constraints upon exerting influence within educational organizations, to explore the implications of these constraints for setting realistic, reflexive role expectations, and to consider ways in which leaders may extend their influence. Although the literature on these issues is meager, a few pockets of insight can be found. March's analysis of leadership in organized anarchies provides some intriguing notions about how leaders might cope with a condition of powerlessness. His eight tactical rules include such prescriptions as "facilitate opposition participation" and "manage unobtrusively."[25] March maintains that the direct involvement of dissident groups is a relatively effective depressant of exaggerated aspirations, while unobtrusive management[26] can be used to affect many parts of a system with a minimum expenditure of attention and energy once the process has been activated. By way of illustration, the leader may change the procedure for reporting faculty teaching loads from listing the number of courses taught to listing the number of student credit hours taught; as long as this accounting procedure remains in effect, its impact is apt to be pervasive and substantial. The discussion of self-forcing (for excellence) and self-enforcing (for control) organizational designs by Sayles and Chandler[27] also suggests ways in which leaders with a relatively low amount of formal influence can indirectly induce higher levels of performance within an organization. Analyses of these two types offer constructive leads for those who are interested in helping future leaders to deal with the harsh realities of leadership in educational organizations.

An Encounter with "Craziness"

The person whose soul is driven by omnipotent fantasies stalks the organizational landscape for opportunities to achieve membership in the leadership hall of fame. He yearns to create a Camelot or a New Jerusalem, to mold a setting that bears his personal imprint. The chance to conceive a bold new mission, to sculpt a novel organizational structure, and to handpick a staff that is committed to reaching the promised land is irresistible. The leader's pursuit of the Alternative of Grandeur[28] gives meaning to his life; unbeknownst to him, however, his quest is also apt to be the harbinger of personal and organizational misfortune.

If the leader stumbles upon an opportunity to create an organizational utopia and opts to meet the challenge, he is likely to encounter more perils than possibilities. The creation of new settings is a formidable intellectual undertaking; there is little evidence that most leaders have mastered the complexities inherent in these ventures.[29] The probability of failure remains relatively high because our understanding of how to implement educational innovations faithful to their original intent is overshadowed by our ignorance. The leader who is unable to control the impulse to act out his fantasies of leadership is therefore on a collision course with "craziness, i.e., inadequate, self-defeating, self-limiting, and other destroying behavior."[30]

"Craziness" manifests itself at the very outset of his venture. In an effort to assemble a group of like-minded people, the change-oriented leader seeks individuals whose fervor and risk taking rival his own. This emphasis on zeal and a penchant for the unprecedented attracts the true believers, as well as the agents of responsible change, and it is difficult to distinguish between the two.[31] Consequently, the leader is apt to find himself with a few individuals who will distort his ideas into something monstrous;[32] the results are disastrous for the undertaking.

Wooing rituals during the recruitment period also evidence craziness. Intent on coaxing the best crew to board his S. S. *Immortality,* the leader transforms all of the shortcomings of the setting into exhilarating challenges. Majestic expectations are created, more is promised than can be delivered, and individuals are hired who have utopian views of the future. A bit of self-deception soothes the leader's conscience; he is convinced that the difficulties already apparent will be overcome if the right individuals can only be persuaded to contribute their time, energies, and talents. However, since the difficulties are not likely to be surmounted and the inflated expectations are not likely to be met, the stage is set for profound disillusionment.

The craziness continues with the launching of the S. S. *Immortality.* Its captain, like the commander of its sistership, the *Titanic,* underestimates the hazards of the voyage and fails to program ways of dealing with adversity. For example, his initial enthusiasm for his crew blinds him to the ubiquitous emotional problems of human organizations. Since he does not recognize any need to forge a structure for resolving the conflicts that are likely to arise between him and his subordinates, interpersonal conflicts are suppressed and impede progress. The leader's fondness for his own conceptual vision is similarly destructive. He is unable to see the innovation in its proper symbolic form; it is a slogan system that contains persuasive but ambiguous rhetoric. Unaware that he is attempting to steer the ship with an unanalyzable abstraction,[33] the leader fails to initiate the procedures needed to clarify the operational meaning of the slogan. Because the participants never agree upon a standard interpretation of the innovation, they are unable to develop a coherent blueprint for action. The ship understandably flounders.

Finally, craziness ensues when the leader overestimates one of the most precious resources of his organization—time. Even the best conceived innovations encounter unanticipated problems that compete for the time and the attention of staff members.[34] As a result, the staff is apt to be overwhelmed by the need to cope continuously with the unanticipated consequences of change while it concurrently attempts to wrestle with the fuzziness of the leader's formal doctrine and seeks to solve the ever present human problems of organizational life. If this analysis is reasonably accurate, the leader is saddled with a classic case of Catch-22; he faces almost certain craziness if he acts out his fantasy of leadership and a sense of deprivation if he does not.

A Vulnerability to Disappointment

Despite the profession's emphasis on success and its corresponding neglect of failure, the leader is destined to experience disappointment in the course of his career. He is, in fact, more vulnerable to personal loss than a less ambitious person would be. Furthermore, his preparation and identification with faulty leadership images diminish his capacity to manage this disappointment.

There is an enormous gap between what the leader wants to accomplish and what is feasible within the realities of his formal power base. In addition, the leader lacks the understanding required to implement the audacious ventures he spawns. Since his desire to perform miracles exceeds his power and intellectual resources, there is a great potential for personal loss and disappointment.

Less obvious is the distress that accompanies success. The leader who positively answers his personal challenge also robs his role of its power to stimulate and excite him; consequently, his wages for success are boredom, as well as fame and fortune. Since his fantasy of leadership demands a steady diet of challenge, the leader now confronts a new task: how to put meaning and novelty back into his life.[35] The task is likely to exact huge psychic costs from the leader because underemployment of his resources is as stressful for him as overemployment.[36] The longer he takes to restore the challenge to his role and the more prolonged and intense his psychological stress, the greater is the probability that he will suffer temporary or permanent physical impairment.

The anguishing aspects of leadership are also apparent in the vicissitudes of institutional life. Educational organizations, as is known, have abruptly shifted from an expanding to a declining state.[37] This totally unexpected transition poses new threats of disappointment for educational leaders. In a period of expansion, opportunities to act out one's fantasies of leadership were ample; however, as enrollments and economic resources have now declined, such opportunities have shrunk dramatically. There are significant numbers of fully credentialed administrators who seek but do not find, positions of leadership.[38] Unless universities begin to follow more restrictive admission policies, this flow of unplaced—and perhaps unplaceable—leaders will increase. Flooding our educational institutions with occupationally immobile individuals will have unhealthy consequences for both the individual and the organization.[39]

The declining state of education has produced other occasions for disappointment. Financially pressed school districts are unable to satisfy the salary demands of teachers; these teachers then vent their wrath against their administrators. The teachers act out their own frustrations by devaluing the contributions of administrators and by insisting that their number should be substantially reduced. The leader is bluntly told that his services are unwanted and unnecessary. He encounters abuse rather than admiration, rejection rather than acceptance; the contradiction between his personal fantasies and the institutional realities becomes painfully clear.

Financial pressures and declines in enrollment further increase the likelihood of disappointment through the demotion, if not the outright dismissal, of the leader. The number of reassignment notices has jumped in recent years; although exact figures are not available, demotions probably occur with greater frequency now than at any time since the greatest depression. We know woefully little about the nature and consequences of "skidding" for the individual and the organization. Perhaps we have ignored studying this topic because it is unpleasant, and we are not inclined to look at the distasteful side of leadership.

The career cycle is also a breeding ground for disappointment. During middle-age, many leaders face a career crisis.[40] Their career jet begins to run out of fuel, and they enter a glide path that leads to occupational oblivion. The leader recognizes that he has achieved his maximum, and his hopes for the future are no longer sources of comfort in a time of despair. Rather, he sees the future as a source of fresh disappointments, a grim reminder of defeat and unfulfilled hopes and dreams. Retirement is another event within the normal career cycle that may produce an emotional ordeal for the leader.[41] The period of disengagement signifies the leader's loss of identity and his primary source of self-justification. The more successful he has been, the more significant will be his separation from the world of work.

The leader's ability to manage his disappointments depends partially on the availability of social support and the extent to which significant others tolerate signs of emotional disturbance.[42] His own definition of his role, which has been shaped in part by his prior socialization, inhibits him from expressing feelings of dependence and from seeking help from others, including members of his own family. Leaders are loath to express dependence because they believe such sentiments will be identified with weakness, a characteristic that is incompatible with the image of a leader. In seeking help, the leader must abandon, for the moment, any pretension of superiority; he fears that this temporary admission of impotence will be costly. He does not drop his defenses nor let other people know the depth of his needs lest these individuals fail to satisfy these needs and lose respect for him.[43] The leader thus denies himself the very social support that might enable him to adjust to his disappointment.

The Socio-Technical Socialization of Leaders

The dysfunctional consequences of the leader's formal preparation are not limited to the internalization of faulty role expectations.

Besides acquiring an unrealistic ego ideal, the aspiring leader receives training that is of questionable value to him in fulfilling the technical and social demands of his role. To reveal some of the deleterious effects of formal preparation, the work of the student and the actual leader will be compared. For purposes of analysis, the polarities in the work of the student and that of the manager will be underscored; the variations in work within each of these two roles will be ignored. The dysfunctional character of formal preparation is likely to be most pronounced when the work of the student and the work of the manager diverge to the extent described in each of the following sections—the rhythm and hierarchical nature of work, the character of communications related to work, and the role of emotions in work.

Rhythm of the Work

One way of assessing the relationship between student and managerial work is in terms of its rhythm or tempo. Managerial work is characterized by brevity, variety, and fragmentation.[44] The manager's workday is hectic, unpredictable, and riddled with fifty to one hundred different occasions for decision.[45] The pressure of the leader's agenda forces him to spend minuscule amounts of time on most of his activities. More than half of the leader's activities are completed in less than ten minutes, many last less than two minutes, few consume as much as an hour. His work pace, therefore, is more like that of a doer than a thinker.

The work that the leader performs during these relatively brief episodes is varied. In the course of his workday, the leader engages in several different types of activities; he reads his mail, answers his correspondence, attends to his phone calls, holds numerous scheduled and unscheduled meetings, and tours his organization. The roles that he plays during these activities are also diverse in character. On one occasion the leader may act as the symbolic head of the organization, while on other occasions he may function as the institution's disturbance handler, resource allocator, or negotiator.[46] He alternates erratically between the significant and the trivial.

The lack of a pattern in the leader's work indicates fragmentation as well as variety. Few administrators are able to devote more than thirty uninterrupted minutes once or twice a week to a single task, regardless of its importance to themselves or to their organization.[47] Interruptions and emergencies are commonplace; undisturbed time alone is a rarity. As a consequence, leaders must become proficient at superficiality, and they must be able to shift their thoughts and their moods quickly and frequently.

The tempo of the student's work is quite different. A student spends most of his workday in essentially two types of activities— desk work and class attendance. Daily events are rather predictable. He attends Cloud 9-I from 9:00 to 10:30 three days per week, Cloud 9-II from 1:00 to 3:30, and Cloud 9-III from 4:00 to 5:00. When class is not in session, the student basks in the quietude of the library. He mostly reads and contemplates; occasionally he writes. In comparison with the work pace of the manager, the student's tempo is snail-like. There are few surprises and much time alone.

The modes of thought to which the student is exposed during his workday further groove him for a decelerated work pace. In order to navigate the university maze successfully, the student must avoid superficiality because it is equated with incompetence. He is pressured to attain a state of mind that is deliberate, thorough, precise, systematic, and occasionally creative. Even on those rare occasions when the student is expected to demonstrate his capacity to cope with the realities of practice, reflection is singularly more important than action. The student is judged primarily by the thoroughness of his analysis rather than by the feasibility of his actions. Rationality is king, and the student is his dutiful subject.

The fledgling leader is thus ill prepared to handle the accelerated tempo of the managerial role. The volume of work that confronts the leader forces him to be superficial; he lacks the time to be consistently thorough. Yet his prior socialization has taught him the skills and the importance of painstaking analysis prior to action. Inevitably a conflict arises between the external need to act and the internal need to understand; the result is analysis paralysis. The leader is simply unable to make judgments unless they are preceded by a protracted period of analysis. His capacity for logical analysis has been developed at the expense of his intuitive skills, the kinds of skills that may have previously enabled him to cope effectively with the brevity, variety, and fragmentation inherent in his work.

The leader's formal preparation may have at least one other unwanted side-effect. As a leader, his workday is crammed with scores of demands for his time and attention. Situations flash before him at a significantly greater rate than they did when he was a student; what is routine for the leader may therefore be a rat race for the student.

If the student turned leader is unable to adjust his durational expectancies, i.e., his expectations about how long events last or should last,[48] he will be overwhelmed by the constant need to shift his emotional and mental gears. The more serene the work situation of the student and the longer he is exposed to it, the more difficult his adjustment will be to the hectic work pace of the practitioner.

The Hierarchical Nature of the Work

Positional rank in the organizational pyramid provides a second way to examine the degree of correspondence between the work of a student and the work of a leader. The use of this dimension further highlights the lack of symmetry between student and managerial work; the student occupies a subordinate role, whereas the leader is primarily a superordinate. This discrepancy in hierarchical rank may be nonfunctional in several respects.

Conflict resolution is a major responsibility of the formal leader. When disagreements develop within the organization, he is expected to handle the conflict. He may attempt to resolve it in one of several different ways. He may use forcing behavior and win-lose arguing (competition); he may confront the disagreements and engage in problem solving to find solutions (collaboration); he may withdraw, pass the buck, or fail to take a position (avoidance); he may attempt to soothe the parties and seek harmony (accommodation); or he may split the difference by dividing gains and concessions between the parties in conflict (compromise). Whether the aftermath of the conflict is constructive or destructive depends in part upon which of these methods the leader uses. If he chooses collaboration, the leader is more likely to create productive relationships with his subordinates,[49] to integrate the efforts of people within the organization, and to enhance the relative performance of his organization.[50]

The leader's previous work experiences as a student, however, predispose him to use avoidance rather than collaboration to resolve conflict. Studies of the modes used by students to deal with disagreements that they have with their classroom teachers reveal a heavy reliance upon avoidance. Collaboration is one of the means least used for resolving conflict. This pattern is consistent across three different levels of education: high school, undergraduate, and graduate.[51] Given the amount of time that students spend in classrooms and the frequency with which conflict between teachers and students is reported, it is reasonable to expect that most students will acquire a passive orientation toward the resolution of conflict. The more veridical this picture of the process of socialization in the classroom is, the more likely leaders are to use avoidance as opposed to collaboration in handling conflicts with their superordinates and subordinates.[52]

In addition to their responsibility for resolving interpersonal conflict, formal leaders play a central role in the organization's system of evaluation. They are expected to provide periodic evaluations of school personnel, to weed out the incompetents based on these assessments, and to use these evaluations as occasions for fostering professional growth. In performing these evaluative functions, administrators are inclined to be lenient; they seldom rate their subordinates' performance as fair or unsatisfactory.[53] The positive skew of personnel efficiency ratings stems in part from the contradictions between the legitimate power and the expert power of the administrator; he is expected to evaluate the performance of professionals who may possess competencies that are markedly different from his own.[54] Administrators are also inclined to be lenient in performing their roles as evaluators, because leniency is a potentially potent strategy for increasing the willingness of subordinates to comply with managerial initiatives.[55]

The leader's academic preparation is a third factor that may contribute to the soft character of his personnel evaluations. He withholds negative information from his subordinates because he is unable to cope with the kinds of emotional demands that are imposed by the evaluation process. As a leader, he must evaluate others under conditions of public disclosure; he is required to provide the person being evaluated with a copy of the rating, to indicate what the person must do in order to attain a satisfactory evaluation, and to defend the rating before an impartial third party if the person being evaluated disagrees with the assessment of his performance.

As a student, however, the future leader makes evaluations under conditions of nondisclosure. The institution erects elaborate safeguards to protect the anonymity of the student when he evaluates the performance of his professors. The student does not have to defend his judgment, he is not held publicly accountable for it, and he is not faced with the need to confront the professor with negative information in a face-to-face encounter. In short, the student is spared the ordeal inherent in public evaluations. There is no potential loss of face, there are no threats to his career, and there is no taste of the unpleasantness that accompanies the giving of negative judgments in social encounters. If the university fails to arrange some type of experience that corresponds more closely to the conditions under which the leader will be expected to evaluate others, lenient assessments of personnel by leaders will probably continue.

Advancement from a subordinate to a superordinate role involves one other responsibility for which the leader's work experiences as a student appear to be dysfunctional. An essential characteristic of managerial work is getting work done through employed subordinates for whose work he is held accountable.[56] Outcomes of the formal leader are therefore partially dependent upon the efforts and activities of his subordinates. Any limitations these subordinates have are apt to be costly for the leader. Outcomes of the student, on the other hand, are primarily determined by his own efforts and abilities; since his work is largely individualistic and competitive, the deficiencies of his fellow "employees" enhance rather than diminish his standing in the workplace. Accustomed to having his rewards flow directly from his own efforts, the student is likely to experience severe difficulties in adjusting to work that makes him vulnerable to the shortcomings of others. For example, the leader may suffer from quantitative role overload because he is unwilling to become dependent on others by delegating work and responsibilities. The more individualistic and competitive the university is and the more successful the student is in this competitive struggle, the greater will be his frustration in adjusting to the dependent character of the leader's role.

The Character of Work-Related Communications

A third dimension that can be used to assay the agreement between student work and managerial work is communication, the process by which stimuli are transmitted in order to modify the behavior of other individuals.[57] In order to facilitate the examination of the continuities and discontinuities in the communicative activities of students and managers, communication will be analyzed in several ways—the role of the communicator (sending versus receiving); the medium of communication (oral, written, and nonverbal);

and the directional flow of the communication (one-way versus two-way). This analysis suggests additional reasons for questioning the appropriateness of formal preparation for administrative work.

Perhaps the most striking feature of the manager's communicative activity is its social character; managers spend a great deal of their workday engaged in interactions with others. Studies of managers in different types of organizations and hierarchical roles consistently show that administrators rely chiefly on two-way, oral communications in carrying out their work.[58] Approximately seventy percent of the manager's time involves face-to-face communications with others. Moreover, in these conversations managers seem to distribute their time somewhat equally between sending and receiving roles. Written communications in the form of routine reports, periodicals, and letters are processed quickly and cursorily.

Furthermore, studies of executives at work show that nonverbal behavior is a significant medium of communication.[59] Formal leaders, like others, apparently have interpersonal reflexes,[60] i.e., spontaneous, automatic, and stable ways of relating to others that are often independent of, or at variance with, the verbal content of their communications. The not-so-muffled behavioral messages of an executive communicate a sense of the kind of person he is, the kind of person you are, and the kind of response he expects from you, the other person. These nonverbal messages are not limited to the body language expressed in interpersonal settings; they are also evident in the ways in which administrators allocate their time, structure the physical environment of their workplace, and present themselves physically to others.[61]

The work-related communications of students contrast sharply with those of managers. Administrators seem to spend roughly equivalent amounts of time in sending and receiving roles; students, on the other hand, are more likely to be receivers than senders. The size of classroom groups shapes the frequency with which students can enact sending roles; since the size of the group is negatively related to the distribution of participation within the group,[62] the larger the size of the student's classroom or "work group," the more restricted are his opportunities to be a sender. The instructional methods of the teacher, as well as the size of the group, set limits on the possibilities of students to play sending roles. Professors who rely heavily on lectures and recitations obviously restrict the occasions for students to be senders rather than receivers. The conceptions of the professor as expert and the student as learner further increase the probability that the professor, not the student, will serve in the sending role.

Unlike administrators, students function in a workplace that deifies the written word. The student typically spends more time in reading and writing activities, the equivalent of desk work for administrators, than in work-related personal interactions. As a result, the student's chief mode of communication in both his sending and receiving roles is written language; moreover, his fate in the university workplace depends almost entirely on how well he is able to express himself in writing, using the impersonal language and the detached style of the academician. To minimize the impact of nonverbal cues, universities often conceal the identities of students at the time their written papers are being evaluated. If the student is enrolled in a degree program that requires a dissertation, his experiences with the written word will be even more pronounced. There is clearly a major discrepancy in the modes of communication that are most relevant to the work of students and that of managers.

The directional flow of communications for students and administrators is also different. While the direction of communications in administrative work is characteristically two-way, the student is more typically involved in one-way communications. The forces that shape the direction of the communication flow are not unlike the ones that account for the differences between students and managers with respect to their communicative modes and roles. The administrator frequently works in small face-to-face interpersonal settings that are conducive to the exchange of information, ideas, opinions, and feelings. The student, on the other hand, often enacts his role in isolation. Since he reads the written efforts of individuals with whom he is unlikely to interact, the dialogue he carries on is essentially with himself. In the classroom the student has relatively few exchanges with others. Besides the constraints on two-way communications imposed by group size and the professor's instructional methods, there is something in the nature of a university that discourages the expression of puzzlement or ignorance. Even if the student feels the need to reveal his lack of understanding, he is likely to remain silent for fear of being judged incompetent. All of these forces combine to produce a one-way flow of communication in the student's work.

These disparities in the work-related communications of students and managers may be the source of several dysfunctional consequences. Problems of communication pervade organizations; the literature is filled with studies that provide insight into the character of these difficulties.[63] Diagnoses of troubles in sending and receiving messages within organizations are varied and numerous, while efforts to remedy these problems have enjoyed only limited success. One possible explanation for the pervasive nature of communicative difficulties and the apparent lack of success in alleviating these problems is to be found in the prior socialization of both superordinates and subordinates.

Organizational participants, irrespective of hierarchical rank, have spent from sixteen to twenty years in student work, work that affords restricted opportunities to enact different types of communicative roles, to communicate through different media, and to engage in two-way communications. An occasional experience in a sensitivity training group, the reading of a few studies about processes of communication, and participation in a relatively brief, though concentrated, workshop on communication are unlikely to overcome the effects of a lengthy "work" experience. The more extended the exposure to student work and the more this work ignores both the need to provide a balanced set of experiences in work-related communications and the need to use these experiences as occasions for developing competence in communication, the greater the incidence of communicative problems will be.

Thus far, this analysis of work-related communications has dealt with the probable baneful consequences of the university's imbalanced treatment of communications; sins of omissions, rather than commission, have been underscored. Preparatory programs may also be guilty of providing experiences that directly undermine the effectiveness of administrators in communicating with others through written language. Term papers, theses, and dissertations are the stock-in-trade of the student. He is urged to write in an impersonal, inert, passive, and often dull style; his audience is the academic community, a group that equates impersonality with objectivity. The audience of the manager, on the other hand, is comprised of subordinates, clients, and the organization's various publics; they are apt to equate impersonality with stiffness and insensitivity. Therefore, the more it succeeds in developing competencies in writing that are functional for the academic world, the more the university inclines the administrator to suffocate feelings of warmth toward other human beings "under a pile of bureaucratic cant."[64]

The Role of Emotions in Work

A fourth way to analyze work is in terms of the significance that is attached to emotions or feelings. A student works in a setting that stresses the virtue of rationality. When he enters the House of Intellect the student pays a hidden tuition; he renounces the right of emotional expression. Ideas, not feelings, are the currency of the realm. As a result, the student is unlikely to find himself in work situations that encourage him to express how he feels; his feelings are institutionally irrelevant as well as individually bothersome. How he manages his emotions is a private rather than a public matter. There are few occasions when he is expected to assist others in clarifying their feelings, nor is he given opportunities to exercise or test his competence in interpreting the feelings of others. Rarely is the student forced to cope with the emotions of others or to witness situations where people constructively and openly work through their emotional difficulties. Affective neutrality is the dominant expressive state, as it is congruent with the contemplative and scientific character of academic work.

The emotional tone of the administrator's interpersonal environment is more varied and jagged. Periods of emotional tranquility are punctuated by episodes of emotional turbulence. As the central figure in the organization's system of authority, the manager is at times the target of emotional outbursts; feelings, not ideas, are the weapons used to influence the actions he takes on behalf of the institution. On other occasions, the administrator serves as the organization's "ire extinguisher"; when tempers flare, he is expected to subdue the emotional flames. At other times the administrator acts as the organization's chaplain; people need his authentic support. Yet how does he offer his support without exposing himself to exploitation?[65] The emotional problems of living with people are numerous;[66] unlike the student, the administrator is likely to encounter them in his work and to suffer important, negative consequences unless he is unable to deal effectively with them.

If the discontinuities on the emotional side of student and managerial work are as pronounced as the preceding analysis suggests, the experiences a student encounters in his work are not apt to develop the competencies he needs to manage the emotional demands placed upon him as an administrator. There is, moreover, the possibility that formal preparation may even have crippling effects. In the past twenty years institutions of higher education have increasingly emphasized the contributions of the social sciences and quantitative research in preparing educational administrators. The modes of thought and analysis that students encounter in the social science literature encourage them to adopt outer rather than inner perspectives when viewing events.[67] A student is schooled to comprehend situations in terms of conceptual categories and frameworks that are products of the academic community. These concepts and paradigms incline the user to understand people solely in the light of theoretical principles; the concept of man as scientist generally disregards the need to understand others from their own frame of reference. If the individual does rely exclusively on external perspectives and ignores the inner perspectives of those being observed, emotional blindness[68] may occur. Should the student's insight be offset by losses in affective empathy, has this formal preparation been functional or dysfunctional?

The placidly emotional work environment of the student may also contribute to the trained incapacity of the leader; it ill equips him to handle the most powerful of human emotions—anger. Mired in its code of rationality, the university regards rage as antithetical to rule by reason. Disputes are to be settled through cool debate rather than by physical or emotional aggression. Since reason is the only legitimate means of resolving conflict and anger is viewed as the natural enemy of rationality, members of the university community are nurtured in an emotional environment designed to insulate them from the ravages of rage. In consequence, the student turned administrator becomes easy prey for militant individuals and groups. They use anger to intimidate him, and he capitulates to escape the discomfort that their wrath engenders.[69] If the militants are social activists, administrators are all the more easily victimized. If administrators return the anger of social protesters with anger of their own, then they feel guilty, as if they had betrayed their own "liberal" credo.

A third feature of preparation that may inhibit the development of the student's emotional competence is the university's indifference towards the biological bases of human performance and functioning. Schools of administration have not developed training programs that seek to unify body, mind, and behavior just as Western societies have not evolved institutions for total medicine. The neglect of the life sciences persists despite their implications for regulating a person's emotional and intellectual life.

By way of illustration, the study of biological clocks or bio-rhythms reveals some interesting and potentially useful knowledge about cycles in the temporal architecture of human beings. According to one branch of biorhythm theory, all human lives fluctuate predictably in three separate cycles: a physical cycle of twenty-three days, an emotional cycle of twenty-eight days, and an intellectual cycle of thirty-three days.[70] In each cycle, half of the days are minus and half are plus; for example, on the fourteen plus days of one's emotional cycle one is cheerful positive, and optimistic while on the fourteen minus days one is moody and pessimistic. The most critical period for the individual, however, in on those days when he is moving from a plus state to a minus state or the reverse. It is during switchover days that he is most vulnerable.

Despite the absence of compelling scientific proof for bio-rhythm theory, industries and companies throughout the world are acting on its possibilities.[71] In Japan a transportation company warns its drivers when they are entering a critical period and urges them to drive carefully that day. In the first year the system was tried, the accident rate dropped fifty percent; the accident rate has declined every year since. Similar results might conceivably be achieved with emotional cycles; the incidence of human problems could perhaps be reduced substantially by letting people know when they may be especially vulnerable to interpersonal mishaps.[72]

Summary

Several questions were posed at the beginning of this chapter, among which were the following: Has formal preparation for leadership been dysfunctional? If so, how does this trained incapacity become an unintended consequence of our well-intentioned efforts? To stimulate an examination of these questions, the socio-technical and attitudinal socialization of administrators was analyzed in light of what is known about the realities of leadership.

In discussing the attitudinal socialization of leaders, I contended that the administrator thirsts for knowledge of results; he is unlikely,

however, to receive any formal feedback from his fellow function-
aries. The leader seeks to reduce the uncertainty surrounding his success by judging his performance in terms of his ego ideal. The leader's
formal preparation through its implicit and explicit treatment of
leadership inclines him to adopt a grandiose ego ideal; this heroic
conception has several dysfunctional consequences for its unwary
holder.

First, the leader is impaled on the horns of an agonizing dilemma. On the one hand, he earnestly aspires to lead his subordinates to
what he considers the promised land; on the other hand, the organizational realities are not conducive to the fulfillment of this leadership fantasy. Second, the omnipotent component of his ego ideal
predisposes the leader to seek situations that apparently offer him
the maximum opportunity to act out his leadership fantasies. Since
these situations are perilous undertakings, the leader is snared in a
Catch-22. He faces "craziness" if he succumbs to his leadership fantasy and a sense of loss if he does not. Third, the excessively ambitious ego ideal of the leader makes him especially vulnerable to disappointment; this same heroic conception, however, deters him from
seeking the socioemotional support he needs to deal constructively
with his disappointment.

To assess the impact of the leader's socio-technical socialization,
I examined the relationship between the work of the student and the
work of the manager along four dimensions—the rhythm and the
hierarchical nature of work, the character of work-related communications, and the role of emotions in work. Each of these four dimensions revealed major disparities between student and managerial
work; furthermore, the analysis highlighted numerous dysfunctional
consequences.

Both the rhythm of the student's work and the modes of
thought to which he is exposed during his training prepare him for a
slow work pace. The tempo of the manager's work, however, is hectic and fragmented. The student's formal preparation makes it difficult, therefore, for him to exercise discretion within the abbreviated
time frame of the practitioner. He is apt moreover to be overwhelmed by the constant need to shift his mental and emotional
gears.

When the hierarchical nature of student and managerial work is
analyzed, the difference in positional rank suggests several additional

sources of the leader's trained incapacity. The student acquires a passive orientation to the resolution of conflicts; this type of orientation prompts the leader to use techniques that are dysfunctional for the organization he heads. The subordinate nature of student work also fosters the continuation of lenient assessments of personnel and promotes a reluctance to delegate.

Discontinuities in the work-related communications of students and managers supply further grounds on which to question the appropriateness of leadership training. Administrators spend roughly equivalent amounts of time in sending and receiving roles; students, on the other hand, are far more likely to be receivers than senders. The spoken word is the major medium of communication for administrators, while the written word is the chief medium of communication for students. Nonverbal communication plays a significant role in the work of the administrator and is relatively unimportant in the work of the student. The direction of communications in administrative work is characteristically two-way, whereas the student is more typically involved in one-way communications. These disparities are a principal source of the administrator's communicative difficulties.

With respect to the role of emotions in work, the substantive content of the student's formal preparation and the placid emotional environment in which he works undermine his capacity for affective empathy, his ability to cope with anger, and his competence to manage his own inner emotional life. The more extended his training, the more likely he is to become an emotional cripple.

Since the preceding analysis is a mixture of logic, speculation, and empirically derived facts, few remedies have been proposed. It is conceivable that the answers to the questions that originated this discussion will not be so disquieting when the gap between fact and fancy is narrowed. In the meantime, however, the hypothesis of trained incapacity stains all of our houses.

Notes

1. Neal Gross and Robert E. Herriott, *Staff Leadership in Public Schools: A Sociological Inquiry* (New York: John Wiley, 1965); Donald A. Erickson, "Essay Review: Some Misgivings Concerning a Study of Leadership," *Educational Administration Quarterly*, 1, 3 (Autumn 1965), 52-59; Fred E. Fiedler, *A Theory of Leadership Effectiveness* (New York: McGraw-Hill, 1967); Samuel C.

Shiflett, "The Contingency Model of Leadership Effectiveness: Some Implications of Its Statistical and Methodological Properties," *Behavioral Science*, 18, 6 (November 1973), 429-440; Jacob W. Getzels, James M. Lipham, and Roald F. Campbell, *Educational Administration as a Social Process* (New York: Harper and Row, 1968); Andrew W. Halpin, *The Leadership Behavior of School Superintendents* (Chicago: Midwest Administration Center, University of Chicago, reprinted 1959); W. W. Charters, Jr., *Teacher Perceptions of Administrator Behavior* (St. Louis, Missouri: Washington University, Cooperative Research Project Number 929, 1964); Cecil A. Gibb, "Leadership" in *Handbook of Social Psychology*, Vol. IX (Reading, Mass.: Addison-Wesley, 1969), 205-282; and J. Timothy McMahon, "The Contingency Theory: Logic and Method Revisited," *Personnel Psychology*, Vol. 25 (1972), 697-710.

2. For a summary of this research see Edwin M. Bridges and Melany E. Baehr, "The Future of Administrator Selection Procedures," *Administrator's Notebook*, XIX, 5 (January 1971) and Edwin M. Bridges, "The Urban Principalship" in Donald A. Erickson and Theodore Reller (eds.), *The Urban Principalship* (1976).

3. Kenneth Burke, *Permanence and Change* (New York: New Republic, 1935).

4. A more extended discussion of this topic is to be found in Edwin M. Bridges, "Personal Success as a Determinant of Managerial Style" in Kenneth McIntyre (ed.), *The Principalship in the 1970's* (Austin: University of Texas Press, 1971), 13-24.

5. Harry Levinson, *The Exceptional Executive: A Psychological Conception* (Cambridge, Mass.: Harvard University Press, 1968).

6. Bridges, "Personal Success as a Determinant of Managerial Style."

7. Levinson, *The Exceptional Executive.*

8. Robert L. Kahn and Robert P. Quinn, "Role Stress: A Framework for Analysis" in Alan McLean (ed.), *Mental Health and Work Organizations* (Chicago: Rand McNally, 1970), 50-115.

9. Seymour B. Sarason, *The Creation of Settings and the Future Societies* (San Francisco: Jossey-Bass, 1972), 181-215. There are a few exceptions, however; see Edwin M. Bridges, "Administrative Man: Origin or Pawn in Decision Making?", *Educational Administration Quarterly*, 6, 1 (Winter 1970), 7-25; Donald A. Erickson, "Moral Dilemmas of Administrative Powerlessness," *Administrator's Notebook*, XX, 8 (April 1972); and Michael D. Cohen and James G. March, *Leadership and Ambiguity: The American College President* (New York: McGraw-Hill, 1974).

10. William C. Reavis, *et al., Administering the Elementary School* (New York: Prentice-Hall, 1953), 303.

11. Charles R. Spain, Harold D. Drummond, and John I. Goodlad, *Educational Leadership and the Elementary School Principal* (New York: Rinehart and Company, 1956), 69-70.

12. Egon G. Guba, "Research in Internal Administration—What Do We Know?" in Roald F. Campbell and James Lipham (eds.), *Administrative Theory as a Guide to Action* (Chicago: Midwest Administration Center, University of Chicago, 1960), 120-121. Italics in original.

13. For example, in the first nine volumes of the *Educational Administration Quarterly* only two studies were reported that treated the administrator as the dependent variable.

14. For example, see Aaron Lowin and James R. Craig, "The Influence of Level of Performance on Managerial Style: An Experimental Object-Lesson in the Ambiguity of Correlational Data," *Organizational Behavior and Human Performance*, 3 (1968), 440-458, and Bruce J. Crowe, Stephen Bochner, and Alfred W. Clark, "The Effects of Subordinates' Behaviour on Managerial Style," *Human Relations*, 25, 3, 215-237.

15. Lowin and Craig, "Influence of Level of Performance."

16. Thomas S. Kuhn, *The Structure of Scientific Revolutions*, second edition (Chicago: University of Chicago Press, 1970).

17. See the case of strategic bombing in Harold L. Wilensky, *Organizational Intelligence* (New York: Basic Books, 1967).

18. James M. Lipham, "Leadership and Administration" in *Behavioral Science and Educational Administration*, The Sixty-third Yearbook of the National Society for the Study of Education, Part II, Daniel E. Griffiths (ed.) (Chicago: University of Chicago Press, 1964), 119-141.

19. Sarason, *Creation of Settings and the Future Societies.*

20. For an interesting discussion of this problem, see Abraham Zaleznik, "Management of Disappointment," *Harvard Business Review*, 45, 6 (November-December 1967), 59-70.

21. See study by Department of Elementary School Principals, *The Elementary School Principalship in 1968* (Washington, D.C.: Department of Elementary School Principals, National Education Association, 1968).

22. *Parents Union for Public Schools in Philadelphia and Jacquelyn Gayle Viale and John Ritter Fernandez* v. *Board of Education of the School District of Philadelphia*, Court of Common Pleas of Philadelphia County, January Term, 1975.

23. Elliott Jaques, *Work, Creativity, and Social Justice* (New York: International Universities Press, 1970), 140-143.

24. Hans Selye, "On Stress and the Executive," *Executive Health*, IX, 4 (1973), 1-4.

25. Michael D. Cohen and James G. March, *Leadership and Ambiguity, the American College President* (New York: McGraw-Hill, 1974), 207-215.

26. *Ibid.*

27. Leonard R. Sayles and Margaret K. Chandler, *Managing Large Systems, Organizations for the Future* (New York: Harper & Row, 1971).

28. See Louis M. Smith and Pat M. Keith, *Anatomy of Educational Innovation: An Organizational Analysis of an Elementary School* (New York: John Wiley, 1971).

29. See Neal Gross, Joseph B. Giacquinta, and Marilyn Bernstein, *Implementing Organizational Innovations: A Sociological Analysis of Planned Educational Change* (New York: Basic Books, 1971); W. W. Charters, Jr. and Roland J. Pellegrin, "Barriers to the Innovation Process: Four Case Studies of Differentiated Staffing," *Educational Administration Quarterly*, 9, 1 (Winter 1973), 3-14; Smith and Keith, *Anatomy of Educational Innovation*; and Sarason, *Creation of Settings.*

30. Seymour B. Sarason, "The Creation of Settings" in S. B. Sarason and F. Kaplan (eds.), *The Yale Psycho-Educational Clinic: Collected Papers and Studies* (Boston: Massachusetts State Department of Mental Health, 1969).

31. Warren G. Bennis, "The Sociology of Institutions or Who Sank the Yellow Submarine?", *Psychology Today*, 6, 6 (November 1972), 112-120.

32. *Ibid.*

33. For a discussion of the term see Seymour B. Sarason, *The Culture of School and the Problem of Change* (Boston: Allyn and Bacon, 1971), 24-28.

34. Smith and Keith, *Anatomy of Educational Innovation*, 140-148.

35. Sarason, *Creation of Settings and the Future Societies*, 228-237.

36. Joseph E. McGrath (ed.), *Social and Psychological Factors in Stress* (New York: Holt, Rinehart and Winston, 1970).

37. James G. March, "Analytical Skills and the University Training of Educational Administrators," *Journal of Educational Administration*, XII, 1 (May 1974), 17-44.

38. Gerald E. Sroufe, "Nova's Ed.D. Program for Educational Leaders: Looking Backward, Looking Forward," *Phi Delta Kappan*, LVI, 6 (February 1975), 402-405.

39. For an insightful look into this issue, see Thomas E. Powers, "Administrative Behavior and Upward-Mobility," *Administrator's Notebook*, XV, 1 (1966). Also, see Douglas M. More, "Demotion," *Social Problems*, 9 (Winter 1962), 213-21, and Fred H. Goldner, "Demotion in Industrial Management," *American Sociological Review*, 30 (1965), 714-724.

40. Harry Levinson, "On Being a Middle-Aged Manager," *Harvard Business Review* (July-August 1969), 51-60.

41. Edward Gross, "Work, Organization and Stress" in Sol Levine and Norman A. Scotch (eds.), *Social Stress* (Chicago: Aldine, 1970), 57-110.

42. Barbara Snell Dohrenwend and Bruce P. Dohrenwend, "Class and Race as Status Related to Sources of Stress" in Levine and Scotch (eds.), *Social Stress*, 111-140.

43. Fernando Bartolome, "Executives as Human Beings," *Harvard Business Review*, 50, 6 (November-December 1972), 62-69.

44. Henry Mintzberg, *The Nature of Managerial Work* (New York: Harper & Row, 1974).

45. Ray Cross, "The Principal as a Counterpuncher," *National Elementary Principal*, II, 2 (October 1971), 26-29.

46. Mintzberg, *Nature of Managerial Work*, 54-99.

47. See Mintzberg, *Nature of Managerial Work*, 31-35.

48. Alvin Toffler, *Future Shock* (New York: Random House, 1970), 40-42.

49. R. J. Burke, "Methods of Resolving Superior-Subordinate Conflict: The Constructive Use of Subordinate Differences and Disagreements," *Organizational Behavior and Human Performance*, 5 (1970), 393-411.

50. Paul R. Lawrence and Jay W. Lorsch, *Organization and Environment, Managing Differentiation and Integration* (Homewood, Ill.: Richard D. Irwin, 1969).

51. David W. Jamieson and Kenneth W. Thomas, "Power and Conflict in the Student-Teacher Relationship," *Journal of Applied Behavior Science*, 10, 3 (1974), 321-335.

52. The research literature on the conflict-resolution modes used by administrators is scant and does not seem to be entirely consistent with this view; see Donald L. Sayan and W. W. Charters, Jr., "A Replication among School Principals of the Gross Study of Role Conflict Resolution," *Educational Administration Quarterly*, VI, 2 (Spring 1970), 36-45. It should be noted, however, that the Jamieson-Thomas study examined how a subordinate handles conflict with a superordinate, whereas Sayan-Charters looked primarily at how a superordinate handles a conflict between a subordinate and an organizational "outsider." The conflict-resolution modes used by administrators when they are in conflict with a superordinate or a subordinate differ, perhaps, from the techniques they use when attempting to resolve conflicts between two other parties.

53. The "leniency hypothesis" is discussed more fully in Edwin M. Bridges, "Faculty Evaluation—A Critique and a Proposal," *Administrator's Notebook*, XXII, 6 (1974).

54. Anne E. Trask, "Principals, Teachers, and Supervision: Dilemmas and Solutions," *Administrator's Notebook*, XIII, 4 (December 1964).

55. Peter M. Blau, *Bureaucracy in Modern Society* (New York: Random House, 1956), 70-79.

56. For a provocative discussion of this conception of a manager, see Jaques, *Work, Creativity, and Social Justice*, 130-145.

57. Donald A. Erickson and K. George Pedersen, "Major Communication Problems in the Schools," *Administrator's Notebook*, XIV, 7 (March 1966).

58. Mintzberg, *The Nature of Managerial Work*, 38-44, and Harry F. Wolcott, *The Man in the Principal's Office* (New York: Holt, Rinehart and Winston, 1973).

59. Richard C. Hodgson, Daniel J. Levinson, and Abraham Zaleznik, *The Executive Role Constellation* (Boston: Harvard University, Division of Research, Graduate School of Business Administration, 1965); and James M. Lipham and Donald C. Francke, "Non-Verbal Behavior of Administrators," *Educational Administration Quarterly*, II, 2 (Spring 1966), 101-109.

60. Timothy F. Leary, *Interpersonal Diagnosis of Personality* (New York: Ronald Press, 1957).

61. Andrew H. Halpin, "The Eloquence of Behavior" in *Theory and Research in Administration* (New York: Macmillan, 1966), 253-279; and Lipham and Francke, "Non-Verbal Behavior of Administrators."

62. Edwin J. Thomas and Clinton F. Fink, "Effects of Group Size," *Psychological Bulletin*, 60, 4 (1963), 371-384.

63. See Peter M. Blau and W. Richard Scott, *Formal Organizations* (San Francisco: Chandler, 1962), 116-139; Erickson and Pedersen, "Major Communication Problems in the Schools"; Wilensky, *Organizational Intelligence*; and Harold Guetzkow, "Communications in Organizations" in James G. March (ed.), *Handbook of Organizations* (Chicago: Rand McNally, 1965), 534-573.

64. Halpin, "Eloquence of Behavior," 267.

65. John C. Glidewell, *Choice Points: Essays on the Emotional Problems of Living with People* (Cambridge, Mass.: MIT Press, 1970), 49-102.

66. *Ibid.*

67. For an insightful discussion of this issue, see Severyn T. Bruyn, *The Human Perspective in Sociology* (Englewood Cliffs, N.J.: Prentice-Hall, 1966), 23-70.

68. Term borrowed from J. Sterling Livingston, "Myth of the Well-Educated Manager," *Harvard Business Review*, 49, 1 (January-February 1971), 79-89. His view of the potential impact of training on empathy differs somewhat from the one expressed in this chapter.

69. Harry Levinson, *Executive Stress* (New York: Harper & Row, 1970), 56-67. The significance of anger for leaders is also discussed in Allison Davis, "Black Leadership and Anger," *School Review*, 81, 9 (May 1973), 451-459.

70. Jean Mackenzie, "How Bio-Rhythms Affect Your Life," *Science Digest*, 74, 2 (August 1973), 18-22.

71. *Ibid.*

72. Another school of thought among the biorhythm theorists underscores the importance of circadian or daily rhythms of the body. These "minicyclists" are interested in the relationship between daily body time and such phenomena as vulnerability to illness, ability to endure physical pain and emotional trauma, and the effects of drugs. Despite the fact that the research is based primarily on animals and not on human beings, the findings are provocative. For example, researchers have administered the same dosage of drugs to animals at different times during the day. The time of day at which the drug was administered determined the observed effects; these effects ranged from the desired therapeutic outcomes to unwanted lethal consequences. Similarly, animals have been exposed to harmful bacteria; time of exposure again proved crucial. Animals died or escaped harm in relation to the time of day when they were injected. Still other studies show that emotional trauma and very tense or frustrating tasks do not have the same impact at all times of the day. These investigations suggest that individuals who listen to their inner whisperings and schedule their activities in light of their own circadian rhythms may be able to minimize the potentially devastating effects of emotional ordeals. For example, an administrator may schedule a tough bargaining session to coincide with the time when his body is most able to cope with a hostile emotional environment. The implications of biorhythm theories may seem a bit ridiculous; yet major leaps in our understanding of the individual's ability to cope may well depend upon the willingness of a venturesome few to experiment with paradigms not presently legitimated by the profession. See Guy Gaer Luce, *Body Time* (New York: Pantheon, 1971).

Part IV

THE CHANGING NATURE
OF ADMINISTRATIVE STUDY

The three preceding parts of this book deal with the context of administrative inquiry and practice and the changing nature of the practice of educational administration over the period from 1954 to 1974. Part IV assesses the changing nature of administrative study.

The initial chapter by Alan K. Gaynor considers change in educational organizations. In his review of the literature Gaynor observes change as a complex systems problem. Complexity increases exponentially—relationships are not linear; they are mutually and collectively interactive. Conventional concepts of change in schools have tended to be individually oriented and have thus ignored organizational constraints; they have tended to emphasize adoption and have paid little attention to implementation.

Gaynor concludes that the field of educational administration must consider the explicit relationships between psychological and political-economic variables as well as the study of the complex process of implementation of change. He calls for scholars to synthesize and reconceptualize research in the field and urges the development of strategies for implementation based on political, economic, environmental, and structural considerations.

A hallmark often attributed to the period from 1954 to 1974 in the study of educational administration concerns the rise of theory. In the second chapter in this section Andrew W. Halpin and Andrew E. Hayes trace the role of theory in the study of educational administration. The function of theory in the conduct of research in educational administration was first enunciated at the 1954 meeting of the National Conference of Professors of Educational Administration. Halpin maintains that the substance of the theory movement was composed of:

1. Recognizing the role of theory in research, more especially, the use of hypothetic-deductive approaches;

2. Regarding administration as a proper subject for research and study;

3. Recognizing that educational administration draws heavily from the behavioral sciences.

The movement was well accepted and expanded through the first decade. By 1964, however, decline and shifting of attention to specific responses for national crises appears to have aborted the movement.

Four factors that contributed to the decline after 1964 are identified: the idea of administrative theory was oversold, the twin facets of theory—use of theory as a basis for research and administrative theory as a guide to action—were not differentiated; the relative immaturity of the movement could not withstand the shock waves of the 1960s, with subsequent federal intervention; and the necessary critical mass of talent and research findings was not built and stabilized to withstand the assault of the 1960s.

Halpin and Hayes see the future of theory in educational administration as more bleak than uncertain. The forces of opposition to growth and development are still present, and no significant new impetus is apparent. It appears that the only hope lies in a few scholars who, without much support from either institutions or the "masses" in the profession itself, dedicate themselves to rigorous research and scholarship to keep the flickering flame alive.

Another view of research and inquiry over the period from 1954 to 1974 is described by Immegart. In his examination of the volume, focus, and method of research in the field, it appears that changes have been largely modest and incremental rather than dramatic and revolutionary. The volume of research has expanded, largely due to the increase in numbers of doctoral dissertations. The focus of research has shifted slightly as most work continues to be oriented toward task areas, with a small proportion oriented toward problems derived from the impact of social forces. Methodology similarly remains much the same but with somewhat more rigorous analysis of more sharply defined status studies.

In general, research in educational administration continues to be practical and reflective of immediate concerns. There is little agreement on central concepts, theories, or models, and, ironically, research has had little impact on the practice of educational administration in the schools.

In the fourth chapter of Part IV Robin Farquhar examines preparation programs for administrators. Three major evolutionary periods are identified, with 1954, 1964, and 1974 as midpoints in major periods. Farquhar describes preparation programs in each decade in terms of characteristics of the thrusts of students, courses, faculty, and programs.

The preparation program of the decade surrounding 1954 was oriented toward practitioners. The decade surrounding 1964 saw the breakthrough of the "theory movement." The third, and current, decade in the evolution of preparation programs is characterized as one of "adversity and diversity."

Farquhar suggests that not only were there three discrete periods of preparation programs for educational administrators over the two decades, but that fundamental movements were observable as well. The pendulum has swung from practice to theory and back to practice. In addition, there has been a tendency to move from emphasis on control toward more freedom and an increased concern for congruence between requirements for an administrative job and the content of preparation programs. Farquhar's discussion suggests that the inherent strength of preparation programs in educational administration is their ability to change; thus a cautiously optimistic view of the future might be assumed.

11. The Study of Change in Educational Organizations:
A Review of the Literature

ALAN K. GAYNOR

We trained hard . . . but it seemed every time we were beginning to form up into teams we were reorganized. I was to learn later in life that we tend to meet any situation by reorganizing, and a wonderful method it can be for creating the illusion of progress while producing confusion, inefficiency, and demoralization.

Gaius Petronius
Roman author, 66 A.D.

The Problem

Over and over again in *The Culture of the School and the Problem of Change,* Sarason[1] plays upon the theme that the more things change the more they stay the same. In one sense this theme is a lament; it struck me that way as I struggled along with Sarason in his efforts to come to grips with the problem of change, or the lack of it, in schools. In another sense, though, it represents a hypothesis, open to empirical study. To consider the lament as a hypothesis forces us to define our terms, something the singer of sad songs doesn't have to do.

In this case there are two terms that require definition: things and change. They are, of course, related. What things define the

234

change in such a way that when we observe the things we know the change has occurred and, even more important, that it has not occurred? There is no clear way for accurate judgments to be made about the effects of an innovation unless accurate information is available about the extent to which the innovation has actually been implemented.[2] It also does not make any sense under the same conditions to talk about the causes of the innovation or the success or failure of the diffusion effort. As Pincus has noted: "The responses of schools to opportunities for innovation appear therefore to be complex; and between adoption and the implementation, innovations routinely disappear or suffer sea-changes."[3]

The foregoing serves to point out that change is a complex systems problem, the dynamics of which have proven to be largely counterintuitive.[4] The total system of change almost always operates on many levels, from the intrapsychic to the interinstitutional,[5] and in a political environment[6] which may be only randomly or latently connected with any planned change effort. It is evident that the complexity of the change process increases in direct proportion to the number of levels of the system affected and the number of elements contained within levels; it should be equally evident and even more significant that this complexity increases exponentially because relationships among these levels and elements are not simply linear; rather they are mutually and collectively interactive.

Considering planned change, then, as an exceedingly complex event—much more complex than even the most sophisticated of change activists may realize[7]—what do we know about the process that can be summarized at this time and to what extent does this knowledge represent an increment over the last twenty years? I believe the following generalizations, which are both useful and supportable, can be made. The remainder of this chapter is devoted to their explication.

1. The study of change has had multiple, sometimes conflicting, roots; even today, there is little work that broadly synthesizes the traditional domains of conceptualization and research on change.

2. One of the most heated distinctions among theoreticians has been that drawn between those perspectives emphasizing the stability of social systems and those emphasizing their essentially conflictual nature; there has been little emphasis upon the mutuality of continuity and change in social systems.

3. There has been a relative neglect in the literature on planned change of the political and organizational aspects of the change process.

4. Until very recently there has been virtually no literature dealing with the *implementation* of innovations in complex organizations.

5. Knowledge about planned change grew dramatically between 1954 and 1974 but not without fragmentation and distortion.

6. Some of the potentially most fruitful work on change has been done in recent years by evaluators, researchers, and sociologists employing multiple methods of data collection, especially in longitudinal studies of implementation in schools.

7. The current level of fragmentation and distortion in the knowledge base with respect to planned organizational change suggests both redirections in research and synthesis and some important caveats for knowledge users.

The Study of Change: Trends and Roots

There is clear and simple evidence that the study of change in education has accelerated over the past twenty years. There was no heading for "Educational Innovation" in the *Readers' Guide to Periodical Literature* in 1955. The heading first appeared in Volume 29, March 1969-February 1970, with eight listings under that heading. Listings increased with each volume; Volume 33, March 1973-February 1974, had twenty-four listings. The heading "Innovations in Education" first appeared in *Education Index* in Volume 16, July 1965-June 1966. Listings under that heading rose to a high of fifty-nine in the next volume, but by Volume 19, July 1968-June 1969, they had dropped to twenty-three. This happened primarily because certain types of articles previously listed under this heading were now being listed under more specific headings such as "Technological Innovations."

More important to this study of change has been the publication of several major annotated bibliographies, collectively based upon reviews of thousands of individual entries.[8]

Sociological Roots of the Study of Change

The study of change—or, more accurately, the study of stability and change—has been a major domain of interest for sociologists and their predecessors since the 19th century.[9] The emphasis in theoretical sociology has been upon societal (i.e., macrostructural) change, primarily that which occurs through natural diffusion.[10] Interest among educators has been at a more applied level, focusing upon more manageable subinstitutional units and emphasizing planned rather than natural change.[11] Despite these differences in emphasis among theoretical sociologists and more applied researchers, it seems to me that emphasis upon the differences at this point is not what is practical and useful. The differences, while real and heuristic for analytical purposes, are also many faces of the same thing. It seems important for us to concentrate upon similarities as well as differences.

I think that scholars and practitioners oriented toward applications have much to learn from the classic debates among sociologists. Their subject matter is not as different from ours as we may think it is. Their seemingly abstract conceptualizations and international studies provide for us broad handles with which to grasp our more limited subject matter and wide lenses with which to see the larger relationships among our microtheories, planning tools, and specific strategies for bringing about change in organizational settings.[12]

Evolutionary Theory

For 100 years one of the major lines of conceptualization among theoretical sociologists has been evolutionary theory, deriving its initial impetus, of course, from the work in biology of Darwin,[13] although his work was significantly influenced by the earlier socio-economic concepts of Malthus. Early twentieth century empirical findings tended to undermine evolutionary theory in its unilinear form, and neoevolutionists have since developed multilinear, as well as general and specific, theories of social evolution. Appelbaum summarizes the recent history of the movement this way: "Evolutionary theories in the social sciences, at least those which call themselves such, have recently enjoyed a revival. . . . [A number of writers] have attempted to come to grips with the great cultural diversity noted by sociologists and anthropologists in the years following Spencer's works on evolution, a diversity which had long discredited evolutionary theories *qua* evolutionary theories."[14]

A number of important organizational theorists, particularly those whose work is characterized by a dominant ideology based on human or organizational development, are, in my view, modern day descendants of the evolutionary theorists.[15] The theory is indeed an appealing one in that it provides us with a sense of meaning in our lives and hope for better days to come in the "Model II, System 4, Theory Y, self-actualized" world beyond bureaucracy. Social evolutionists, however, have had considerable difficulty demonstrating empirically the validity of their theoretical position. Argyris, in a recent and compelling analysis of the failure of several alternative schools to implement successfully their espoused values of collegial collaboration among students and teachers, suggests in conclusion that it is the essential status quo, not an evolutionary future, that is programmed into the organization as organism, or at least into the people who comprise it.[16]

I am trying here to make three points about the implications of evolutionary theory for our understanding of change in organizations: that it is relevant in that the questions it has evoked historically are still valid for neoevolutionary theory, that its oversimplicity heightens our appreciation of the actual complexity of the change process, and that modern multilinear theories of social evolution have been developed in feeble and tardy recognition of that appreciation.

Functional versus Conflict Theories

Perhaps the most heated debate among theoretical sociologists over the last forty years has been between those espousing functional and those espousing conflict theories of social systems. This macrotheoretical issue among sociologists may also be the most important one for those of us whose primary interest is in understanding the process of change at the subinstitutional level of society. I believe that it is. I also believe, however, as I indicated earlier, that our best interest is not to be served by taking sides in the debate but by recognizing that, in a meaningful sense, it is a spurious debate.

For example, Dahrendorf, a leading conflict theoretician, is credited by the Etzionis with the following position: "Structural-functional theory, he feels, explores the factors that hold social units together, the forces of integration, but is not adequate to handle the forces of disruption and change."[17] Dahrendorf, in a discussion of the basic postulates of the functionalist and conflict models, argues the distinction between, as well as the complementarity of, the two theoretical positions: "[I]t seems meaningful to say that both models are in a certain sense valid and analytically fruitful. Stability and change, integration and conflict, function and 'dysfunction,' consensus and constraint are, it would seem, two equally valid aspects of every imaginable society. They are dialectically separated and are exhaustive *only in combination* as a description of the social problems."[18] In organizations as in societies, change has no meaning without some concept of stability, stability no meaning without some sense of the possibility of change.

It seems important before moving on to emphasize that the fundamental conceptual integration of stability and change is not simply an abstract idea but a very practical one. For example, it is not by chance that Sarason, in his concern for *change* in schools, elaborates at length about their existing programmatic and behavioral *regularities*.[19] It strikes me that this close-knit relationship between seeming opposites is at the heart of Miles's reflections upon the prospects for change given the historical characteristics of schools: "It seems that many aspects of schools as organizations, and the value orientations of their inhabitants, are founded on history and constitute what feel like genotypical properties. These are important to the schools; they help maintain continuity and balance in the face of the school's ambiguous mission and its vulnerability to external pressures from parents and others. Therefore, it is likely that, while rapid shifts in specific school practices are relatively more possible, changes touching on the central core of assumptions and structures will be far more difficult to achieve."[20] Willower, too, underlines the importance of both elements: "Processes and structures basic to institutional stability *and* change should be explored intensively."[21]

Given the important implications of the functionalist and the conflict models for understanding the stability and change of educational organizations, what are the essential elements of these models? According to Dahrendorf, they are as follows:

The Functionalist Model. (1) Every society is a relatively persisting configuration of elements; (2) Every society is a well-integrated configuration of elements; (3) Every element in a society contributes to its functioning; (4) Every society rests on the consensus of its members.

The Conflict Model. (1) Every society is subjected at every moment to change; social change is ubiquitous; (2) Every society experiences at every moment social conflict; social conflict is ubiquitous; (3) Every element in a society contributes to its change; (4)

Every society rests on constraint of some of its members by others.[22]

It should be pointed out that there is a fundamental difference of view between the two competing schools about the extent to which the functionalist model can accommodate within its assumptions the dynamics of change. Parsons speaks to this issue from the perspective of the functionalist:

Contrasted then with stability or equilibrating processes are those processes which operate to bring about structural change. That such processes exist and that they are of fundamental scientific importance is nowhere in question. . . . As I see it now, the distinction between the two pairs of concepts is one of level of system reference. The structure of a system and of its environment must be distinguished from process *within* the system and in *interchange* between the system and its environment. But processes which maintain the stability of a system, internally through both structure and process, and in interchange with its environment, i.e., states of its equilibrium, must be distinguished from processes by which this balance between structure and more "elementary" process is altered in such a way as to lead to a new and different "state" of the system, a state which must be described in terms of an alteration of its previous structure.[23]

It seems to make sense to me to close this section on the sociological roots of the study of change with one further citation from the work of Parsons, one which not only enlivens the state of the debate illustrated above but which also has ties with the point made earlier about the need for accurate information about the extent to which change has actually been implemented: "Since the basis of generalization in science is always the demonstration of relatedness in process of variation (in one sense change), there must always somewhere be a distinction between the features of the phenomena under observation which do and which do not change under the relevant limitations of time and scope and in the respects which are defined as important for the purposes in hand. The specificities of significant change could not even be identified if there were no *relative* background of nonchange to relate them to."[24]

The Current State of Knowledge About Planned Change: Major Lines of Development

There are a variety of ways in which the literature on change has been organized by scholars in the field and it is obvious that there are many other ways in which it could be organized by other interested reviewers. As indicated earlier, Havelock organizes his massive synthesis of the literature essentially within a communicative framework.[25] That is, he looks at innovations as flows emanating from outside the system, perhaps several systems removed, and conceptualizes inter- and intrasystem flows through channels with capacities that can be enhanced by favorable circumstances—some of which may be under partial control of a "change agent"—and that can also be blocked as the result of unfavorable circumstances—some of which may be partially due to poor planning or incompetent execution by the person attempting to implement the change. In my judgment, this work represents the most important synthesis of empirical and conceptual material on planned change available to us. While monumental, it is not, however, complete.

A second significant attempt to map the literature on change was made by Baldridge. Far less elaborated than Havelock's and a topical outline rather than a theoretical synthesis, it does, however, take a point of view somewhat neglected by Havelock. Baldridge's perspective is essentially much more political than sociopsychological, and for this reason his commentary tends to complement rather than duplicate Havelock's in any significant way. Although Baldridge pays some heed to the perspective of human relations, he focuses much more upon "authorities," "partisan groups," and "organizational conflict" as agents and promoters of change. In my view his is the more balanced, though certainly not the more exhaustive, of the two works.[26]

My own approach is more eclectic than either Havelock's or Baldridge's. My purpose is not to repeat what they have already said; rather it is to provide some material from the literature in support of the generalizations made earlier. Those generalizations deal not with the production of knowledge[27] per se, but with the process of change in educational organizations, including the *utilization* of knowledge as part of that process.

The Individual as the Agent or Unit of Change

As I see it, from the perspective of the educator interested in planned change, the major weakness is the predominant emphasis in the literature upon the individual as the agent, and especially as the adopting unit of change. Gross *et al.* argue this point effectively:

There have been a number of major reviews of diffusion and adoption studies in the past few years (Katz *et al.*, 1963; Lionberger, 1964; Rogers, 1962). Rogers reviewed 506 studies in anthropology, rural sociology, educational and medical sociology.... After his extensive review of adoption and diffusion studies Rogers proposes a model to explain why individuals do or do not adopt innovations.... We believe, however, that this model has little use in explaining the success or failure of the implementation of innovations in schools or other types of organizations. Its lack of utility is due to certain of its assumptions which are not applicable to the implementation of *organizational* innovations.[28]

People operating as members of organizations are simply not as free as independent entrepreneurs (e.g., farmers and physicians) to *implement* significant innovations entirely on their own initiative. They are freer to propose innovations than they are to implement them, although even proposing innovations may be affected by the structural characteristics of the organization and its environment[29] as well as the personal characteristics and social relationships of the individual.[30]

It seems clear from the work of a number of researchers that the implementation of an innovation is typically subject to *organizational* constraints that transcend individual motivations.[31] Organizational constraints occur under several types of conditions that are common to schools. Such conditions are found, for example, where the proposed innovation requires a change in the relational patterns between the system and its environment, among units within the system, or among individuals within units or a significant reallocation of resources among units at any level of the system.

The following description by Bentzen of the effects of typical system constraints upon members of the League of Cooperating Schools communicates a practical feeling of what may otherwise be viewed as an abstract concept:

The concept of self-renewing schools conjures up an image of each school doing its own thing with resources ready at hand, but the truth of the matter seemed to be that a school was hard put to get the resources it needed to stay on a path of its own. District offices allocated services to all their schools from a central pool, according to schemes which usually allowed little flexibility for the school staffs who used them. Districts, furthermore, typically offered few appropriate resources for a school that might be toying with ideas outside of the current district pattern of schooling. Thus, even though League schools had been formally granted the freedom to deviate from district norms, the organization of district resources tended, in general, to conserve the status quo so that League schools could find little district assistance in making their freedom a reality.[32]

The work of theoreticians[33] describing the characteristics of schools and analyzing the implications of those characteristics for stability and change simply reinforces the challenging observations of scholarly practitioners like Bentzen and Sarason.

In reporting a comparative case study of four schools attempting to implement differentiated staffing, Charters and Pellegrin make the following observation—an observation that seems, again, to re-emphasize the organizational nature of the innovative process, in this case from the perspective of the relationship of roles among individuals within units: "The translation of general values and objectives into specific, concrete new behaviors for staff members is infinitely more complex and difficult than the participants had anticipated. Such a translation nonetheless appears absolutely essential to the success of any innovation."[34]

Emphasis upon Adoption Instead of Implementation

Consistent with their emphasis upon the individual as adopter, most researchers have assumed, at least implicitly, that adoption is tantamount to implementation. There is evidence, however, that especially for organizational innovations this assumption is not a valid one. Pincus has noted, for example: "Perhaps the most common complaint of the R & D community about adoptions is that the innovations are not actually implemented as prescribed. . . . For the schools' purposes, verbal adoption of innovations may be entirely sufficient, and a preference for the verbiage of magnificent vistas has been noted by various observers."[35] Goodlad and Klein have pointed out that, despite years of discussion and professional support leading to widespread adoption of such innovations as ungraded classes and team teaching, these innovations are rarely implemented. A school district will adopt ungraded classes and then implement them by teaching an essentially graded curriculum in the "ungraded" classes.[36]

Consistent with the observations of Goodlad and Klein, Carlson, in writing about a case study of a school where the superintendent had reported the successful adoption of programmed instruction, concluded: "Teachers invented ways which permitted them to recapture some aspect of this role (their old role as director of learning). It would appear, therefore, that if the logic of programmed instruction is to have its way in schools, then a new definition of what teaching consists of must be instilled in the teachers."[37]

In the last five years there has been a growing interest in and some important work has been done on case research on the implementation of complex innovations in schools.[38] Sarason's description of the history of the Yale Psycho-Educational Clinic[39] is another example of this kind of work—not in a school but in an educationally related field. The total research of this kind across the country seems, however, far below the level of what is needed. In a sense it seems only to accentuate the urgency of Bennis's observation made almost ten years ago: "What we know least about—and what continually vexes those of us who are vitally concerned with the effective utilization of knowledge—is *implementation*."[40]

Sociopsychological Study and Normative-Reeducative Strategies of Change

The roots of most of the approaches to the study and practice of planned change really lie in rural sociology[41] and in the human relations movement.[42] Rural sociologists have contributed several basic kinds of knowledge about the process of change. Employing a methodology based on trend analysis similar to that used in technological forecasting,[43] rural sociologists were able to describe both the rate and the staging of the diffusion process. On the basis of their research they were also able to describe the modal characteristics of people active at each stage of innovation.[44] The exact names given to the stages vary somewhat among writers, but they are generally familiar to readers of that literature. Rogers, for example, identifies five: awareness, interest, evaluation, trial, and adoption.[45]

The investigations of rural sociologists focused primarily, of course, upon the agricultural extension model of research, development, and diffusion; one of their major concerns, therefore, was the relationship between the stages of diffusion and the work of the "change agent." Associated with the curve of diffusion and the stages of innovation was a typology of individuals. Rogers's titles are reflective of the conceptualization common to this line of research: innovators, early adopters, early majority, and laggards.[46]

It is out of this research milieu that the concept of the "resister" derives, the defender of the status quo, unfortunately with a generally negative connotation. Consistent with what I perceive to be the importance of stability in institutions as well as openness to change, I find myself in strong and essential agreement with Klein about the positive value of the defender role. I think the following statement is representative of Klein's position: "The difficulties which arise stem from the very magnitude of the changes being projected, from the rapidity with which changes can occur, and from the troubling realization that changes often are irreversible as well as far-reaching, ensuring the prolongation of error as well as accuracy. However, the most important generator of defense would appear to be the frequent alienation of the planners of change from the world of those for whom they are planning."[47]

What is being discussed here is not the toleration of dissent (in this case the dissent of the defender of the status quo), but our very gratitude for the presence of the dissenters in our midst. "[A]s change agents we must be concerned with the opposition's values and recognize that, to a great extent, their values are ours as well. Moreover, it would help if we could grant that, in upholding these values, the defenders—however wrong we believe they are in the stands they take and the votes they cast—are raising questions which are important in our society and which we must answer with them."[48] In a sense what we are talking about is the corollary to Pogo's famous observation: We have found our sister and she is *them*.

While the human relations movement has its roots in the Hawthorne plant,[49] it flowered through the National Training Laboratory and its descendants. The movement has made a significant contribution in its application of knowledge from the social sciences to personal and organizational development, especially knowledge about group dynamics and the interrelationships among individuals, groups, and larger systems. The literature is replete with writings on human relations.[50] Work of applied social scientists in using and studying the use of survey feedback and the laboratory method in altering attitudes and in reshaping organizational behavior (e.g., leader behavior, role behavior in groups, and interpersonal behavior) has added profoundly to the understandings and strategies available to those who wish to effect change.

Despite their enormous contributions to our understanding of the change process, laboratory-oriented researchers and practitioners have tended to overemphasize the attitudinal components of stability and change and to underemphasize the macrostructural, especially the political aspects of systems life. Baldridge argues this point simply and cogently: "Finally, a major weakness of the human relations approach is that it almost entirely ignores *external factors*. The external world impinges on organizations at dozens of points, and change is often the result of interaction between the organization and its environment. The human relations school has largely ignored this fact, and in so doing has ignored a significant impetus for organizational change."[51]

Baldridge identifies other omissions and distortions associated with the human relations perspective: (1) The small-scale, individualistic changes produced by human relations strategies are inadequate to improve an organization's activities significantly or to affect major processes of the system such as administration, evaluation, and coordination; (2) the human relations perspective tends to define conflict as illegitimate and symptomatic of a sickness in interpersonal relationships, overlooking the fact that many conflicts are not caused by blocks in communication or failures of interpersonal relations but stem from scarce resources, divergent values, and multiple goals; (3) the human relations school does not seriously consider the problems of formal systems and formal bureaucracies; (4) the cost of applying the human relations strategy to an organization is extremely high; and (5) there is reason to believe that the link between high morale and productivity is not as simple as most human relations analysts suggest.[52]

The Lack of Emphasis upon Political and Other Environmental Variables

Easton defines politics as the authoritative allocation of values through the binding decisions of authorities.[53] Conflict theorists from Marx to Dahrendorf (and Baldridge) have well understood the root relationship between conflict and change in institutional life. The conflict of values to be allocated is as great in American society today as it ever has been; it is perhaps more intense than it has been at any time in our nation's history.[54] The impact of powerful forces upon schools, the so-called politicization of education, is well established. Illustrative of this state of affairs is the following statement by Guthrie and Skene: "Three major trends in America today are combining to escalate educational policy decisions to the state level. The first is the growing politicization of education generally. The second is the increasing erosion of lay control at the local school district level. The third is the likelihood of a centralized system of school finance resulting from equal protection suits such as *Serrano* and *Rodriguez*."[55] In reviewing the literature on the changing nature of political research in education, Kirst and Mosher described the opening up of American educational politics and its effect upon research:

In the past research was retarded by practicing educators who posited that public education should be a unique nonpolitical function with a separate and independent governmental structure. This isolationist stance led researchers studying school operations to ignore their political environments. In the past decade social forces affecting the schools have changed this situation and created a more open system of educational politics. Researchers are now examining both the interchanges between the government of education and its environment, and the intra-system networks for influence. Most of the research has concentrated on the allocative consequences of political interactions—who gets what, when and how.[56]

What I find disturbing, as I read the main body of literature on change in education, is the overwhelming emphasis upon writings that reflect almost exclusively the influence of rural sociology and the human relations school. What is missing, it seems to me, can best be illustrated by reference to several of the topics used by Baldridge in synthesizing his review of the literature on organizational change processes.[57] These topics suggest what has not been emphasized in most of the change literature: "Deliberate Action by Authorities and Partisans," "Organizational Conflict as a Promoter of Change," and "Partisan Groups as Agents of Organizational Change."

Even political conceptualizations, at least to the extent that the term politics is construed narrowly (traditionally), may not be rich enough for our current needs. I am encouraged, of course, by the emergence of a specialized political literature in education over the past decade, especially that describing research in this field which provides new insights for our understanding of change in educational systems.[58]

Beyond politics itself, however, I think there is a need to conceptualize the organizational environment of schools in a more sophisticated way than I have observed in most of the literature to date. Available to us, for example, is Evan's conceptualization of "the organization-set" as well as the seminal work of Emery and Trist transferring the concept of the causal texture of the environment from the psychological literature to the organizational literature. Another important contribution to our thinking about the relationship between organizational and environmental variables is Terreberry's elaboration upon the ideas of Emery and Trist.[59]

These recent conceptualizations of the organizational environment are exciting in that, first of all, they seem to provide a good fit for the empirical reality of schools. Second, they seem to provide precisely some of the kinds of descriptions of the change process that have been most neglected in the literature. As Terreberry points out, and as I have pointed out earlier: "Many social psychologists . . . study change in individuals and groups *within* organizations, but with no reference to variables of organizational level."[60]

It seems to me to be a reasonable hypothesis, one worthy of systematic consideration, that many school organizations, especially many urban school organizations, have or are moving from a "placid-clustered" environment to a "turbulent field" environment. Terreberry describes the nature of this evolution:

The evolution of organizational environments is characterized by a change in the important constituents of the environment. The earliest formal organizations to appear in the United States (e.g., in agriculture, retail trade, construction, mining) operated largely under placid-clustered conditions. Important inputs, such as natural resources and labor, as well as consumers, comprised an environment in which strategies of optimal location and distinctive competence were critical organizational responses. Two important attributes of placid-clustered environments are: (1) the environment is itself *not* formally organized; and (2) transactions are largely initiated and controlled by the organization. (Italics in original.)

Later developments, such as transport technology and derivative overlap in loss of strength gradients, and communication and automation technologies that increased economies of scale, gave rise to disturbed reactive (oligopolistic) conditions in which similar formal organizations become the important actors in an organization's field. They are responsive to its acts . . . *and* it must be responsive to theirs. . . . The critical organizational response now involves complex operations, requiring sequential choices based on the calculated actions of others, and counteractions. (Italics in original.)

When the environment becomes turbulent, however, its constituents are a multitude of other formal organizations. *Increasingly, an organization's markets consist of other organizations; suppliers of material, labor, and capital are increasingly organized, and regulatory groups are more numerous and powerful.* (Italics added.)[61]

I have quoted at some length from Terreberry in the belief that some readers may not be very familiar with the concepts and the concepts have powerful implications for change in educational systems. It may be, for example, that in those cases in which school systems find themselves in turbulent environments, that rational planning models of the synoptic type may be less strategic: "Since uncertainty is the dominant characteristic of turbulent fields, it is not surprising that emphasis in recent literature is away from algorithmic and toward heuristic problem-solving models; that optimizing models are giving way to satisficing models; and that rational decision making is replaced by 'disjointed incrementalism.' "[62]

For several years some students of change have held to the thesis that organizational change is generally externally motivated.[63] This hypothesis becomes even more compelling when one considers the extent to which environments are evolving toward the turbulent field state: "A major corollary is that the evolution of environments is characterized by an increase in the ratio of externally induced change over internally induced change in a system's transactional interdependencies. . . ."[64]

Terreberry also suggests that environmental evolution may make an external system (that subsystem, the primary responsibility of which is external relations) more significant to the organization. Specifically, information from outside its borders may, through environmental evolution, become increasingly important to the organization. Such an event would almost certainly enhance the relative importance of its boundary spanning personnel. This proposition makes sense to me. I can think of some school principals, for example, who have used their boundary spanning position under conditions of high turbulence to build a much more significant power base for themselves than would ever have been possible in a more homogeneous and stable environment.

Technology as an Element in Change

Technology is another variable associated with change which has been given only relatively passing attention in the literature. Current research is equivocal; there is evidence, however, to support technology as a major variable affecting organizations. Aldrich's conclusions reflect this lack of certainty about the relationship between technology and organizational structure: "[W]ith regard to the importance of organizational technology, the findings of this study should serve to keep alive the theorist's interest in the role of technology in organizations. . . . [I]f the assumptions of this article are accepted, then the Aston group's rejection of technology as an important variable has been shown to be ill-advised and premature."[65] Hage and Aiken, in a study of social welfare and health organizations, found a positive relationship between the amount of routine work and such structural variables as centralization and formalization.[66] Findings by Hickson *et al.* are particularly interesting in that they suggest a kind of contingency relationship with respect to the impact of technology on the organization: "Operations technology is shown to affect only those structural variables immediately impinged on by the workflow. Thus the smaller the organization the more completely its structure is pervaded by the immediate effects of this technology; the larger the organization the more these effects are confined to variables such as the proportions employed in activities that are specifically linked with workflow, and technology is not related to the wider administrative and hierarchical structure."[67]

None of these findings is from the literature dealing specifically with organizational change; their implications for the impact of changes in technology upon other organizational variables seem clear, however.

Systems Planning as an Element in Change

An area of conceptualization relevant to change, which has been elaborately developed in the last twenty years, is that related to systems planning and management. Development in this area has some of its roots in the military (e.g., the use of PERT techniques in the development of radar during World War II) and was tied closely to the rapid emergence of computer technology in the decade of the 1960s. While systems approaches to planning and development have been used at all levels from world dynamics[68] to project management,[69] application of these approaches is relevant to the maintenance of stability as well as to the implementation of change. The literature tends not to distinguish between these two types of applications but rather to discuss systems techniques as general management tools.[70]

Most of the literature on management systems focuses upon *operational procedures* such as network analysis, program budgeting, and operations research. The intent of these procedures is simply to maintain and improve the effectiveness of a system. It can thus be argued that systems analysts and systems theorists focus exclusively upon methodologies and concepts which simply "reinforce a going system of distributive inequities."[71] To the extent that this charge is valid, it follows implicitly that a discussion of systems approaches has no place in a review of the literature on change. Why then, in this chapter, do I call your attention to the literature on systems?

The answer, as I argued earlier, is that I believe that stability and change are but two faces of the same state of being. I believe that systems theories,[72] and even systems techniques, contain within them elements of change as well as elements of continuity. It seems self-evident that given a changing environment, which is the basic assumption of open systems theory, stability has no practical meaning except in terms of adaptation—that is, change. The argument then boils down *not* to whether adaptation is essentially a way of maintaining the system (which some, like Wolin, would argue is bad) but rather to the unanswerable and, in fact, meaningless questions of "How much change is change?" and "How much adaptation does it take before the system is not the system anymore?"

Coming down from what may appear to be a high level of abstraction to a level of concrete specificity, let me say that I believe that even a concrete operational technique such as program budgeting contains within it *potential* elements of change. I emphasize the word "potential" because in many cases the environment of the system may be so hostile or inert that significant changes never come to pass; the logic of the potential seems clear, however: program budgeting systems produce new information; information is power; new information is new power—power to do new things, power to change.

I believe the same kind of reasoning could be applied to any of the new systems tools. Together they represent a significant technology, and we can think of a contingency model of technology in the same way that we have already begun to think of contingency models of leadership[73] and contingency models of organizations.[74] The contingency model is simple: it simply states that the relationship between two things is *dependent*; in this case the relationship between systems technologies and institutional change is dependent. It is dependent, of course, upon a whole complex of other relationships, some of which we know something about and most of which remain the focus for continuing conceptualization and research. The same can be said, however, of theories of conflict, human relations, or whatever. Each conceptual framework is analytically separable, but they are all part of the same whole, and we don't alter elements central to one without impacting elements central to the others.

Recapitulation

I end where I began, with a set of generalizations which I believe validly describe, at least from one perspective, the current state of knowledge about planned change. I think we know more about diffusion and adoption of innovations among individuals than we know about implementation and institutionalization of innovations in complex organizations (and we should remember that even an elementary school is a complex organization). I think that research on planned change has a history of fragmentation and distortion. Research has been fragmented in a number of directions: between the theoretical and applied sociologists; among the rural sociologists, the human relationists, the political scientists, and, to a new and limited extent, the organizational ecologists; between those focusing on individuals as agents and adopters of change and those focusing on organizations; between those focusing on the internal and those focusing on the external subsystems of organizations; and, finally, between those focusing on institutions as adaptive, stable systems and those primarily concerned with the conflict dynamic of change. The distortion lies in the overemphasis in the literature on research and theory dealing with individuals and human relations and the underemphasis on research and theory dealing with organizations and their complex and changing environments. The literature on management systems reflects predominantly operational concerns with little consideration given to the implications of operations planning and management information systems for the relative stability and change of the organizations that implement them.

Implications

This assessment, if it is an accurate one, has clear, practical implications for those of us whose expressed interest is in the study of planned change in educational organizations—including both researchers and funding agencies. It states that we know a great deal about the conditions under which change does and does not occur; but it also suggests that our conceptual map is systematically distorted and that we need to shift our focus as researchers and underwriters.

It seems evident that we need to study more carefully the relationship between sociopsychological and political-economic variables (that is, in a sense, between the internal and external subsystems of schools and school systems). We also need to understand more precisely the nature of educational environments and their relationship to changing patterns and policies within educational organizations.[75]

In addition to a more powerful understanding of the political-economic aspects of change, we also need to acquire more intensive knowledge of the complex, usually fatal, process of implementation. Fortunately, we have begun to focus on this important and previously neglected phase of organizational change, especially in the last seven years. Organized efforts, often under federal auspices or with the assistance of private foundations, have begun to build a base of new knowledge in this area.[76]

It is important that the study of implementation of innovations be expanded through the use of multiple methods of data collection (especially through repeated interviews and observations), and through the design and support of long-term investigations—investigations not simply of efforts in development and dissemination, but of those involving organizational dynamics and consequences of implementation. Unfortunately, even recently, major funding agencies, public and private, have been unwilling or unable to make the long-term commitments necessary to sustain these kinds of intensive, longitudinal pieces of research and evaluation.

There is a need for more empirical research of the types noted. There is also a powerful, continuous need for scholars to synthesize and reconceptualize research findings across disciplines and specialties in order to develop an increasingly generalizable and useful theoretical base to guide practical efforts at change and further research and development. It is hoped that interest among scholars and support among institutions can be maintained toward this end.

Finally, the findings noted here suggest some areas of thought and direction for those whose working interest lies primarily in the practical reform of educational institutions. An important implication for these users of knowledge is, it seems to me, a kind of caveat: Don't trust the first thing you read or the first expert on change who crosses your path. The written material is probably incomplete and the expert is probably incapacitated, at least in part, by the biases of his own training and scholarly predilections.

The change process is as complex as the target organization and there are many variables one should think about. This is not to advocate paralysis by analysis, but recent evidence suggests that the more carefully planned and the more complex (!) an innovation is, the more likely it is to succeed.[77] Strategies for implementation should be based upon political, economic, environmental, and structural considerations[78] as well as normative-reeducative ones. Experts should be used only in carefully structured ways, planning should consciously and systematically draw upon diverse perspectives, and ultimate responsibility for the change should always reside inside the target organization, not with outside experts. The evidence throughout the literature seems clear on this, especially recent case studies of implementation.[79]

In conclusion, I believe we have more knowledge than we think we have—and much more than we had in 1954—despite the fact that much more understanding is required. It is hoped that in the next twenty years we can get beyond the description of the current state of affairs iterated so often during the last twenty years and recently reiterated by a Rand Corporation evaluator: "American education has not been dramatically transformed by efforts at planned change. In fact, despite the diligent and often ingenious efforts of the last years, relatively few things have worked at all!"[80]

It is clear, however, that the culture of the school is formidable and the forces of continuity are strong. The onus of proof always lies with those who would have things different. Perhaps we should have to prove the value of the status quo, but the fact of the matter is that generally we don't. Perhaps life would simply be too difficult for most of us if we had to.

Notes

1. Seymour B. Sarason, *The Culture of the School and the Problem of Change* (Boston: Allyn and Bacon, 1972).
2. The terms "change" and "innovation" are used interchangeably here, except that innovation connotes the idea of a product with definable characteristics whereas change focuses not upon the characteristics of the innovation, per se, but upon the differences between the characteristics of the innovation as implemented (or as proposed) and the relevant characteristics of the system prior to the implementation of the innovation. See Herbert Hyman, Charles Wright, and Terence Hopkins, *Applications of Methods of Evaluation: Four Studies of the Encampment for Citizenship* (Berkeley: University of California Press, 1962).

3. John Pincus, "Incentives for Innovation in the Public Schools," *Review of Educational Research* 44 (Winter 1974), 113-144.

4. Jay W. Forrester, *World Dynamics* (Cambridge, Mass.: Wright-Allen Press, 1971).

5. Ronald Havelock, Janet Huber, and Shaindel Zimmerman, *Major Works on Change in Education: An Annotated Bibliography* (Ann Arbor, Mich.: Institute for Social Research, University of Michigan, 1969).

6. J. Victor Baldridge, "Organizational Change: The Human Relations Perspective versus the Political Systems Perspective," *Educational Researcher* 1 (February 1972), 440; David Easton, *A Systems Analysis of Political Life* (New York: Wiley, 1965).

7. Seymour B. Sarason, *The Creation of Settings and the Future Societies* (San Francisco: Jossey-Bass, 1972).

8. J. Victor Baldridge, *Organizational Change Processes: A Bibliography and Commentary* (Stanford, Calif.: Stanford Center for Research and Development in Teaching, Stanford University, 1970); Havelock *et al., Major Works on Change in Education*; Louis Maguire, Sanford Temkin, and Peter Cummings, *An Annotated Bibliography on Administering for Change* (Philadelphia: Research for Better Schools, 1971).

9. Auguste Comte, *System of Positive Polity* (London: Longmans, Green, 1877); Emile Durkheim, *Suicide* (New York: Free Press, 1951); Karl Marx, *Capital* (New York: International Publishers, 1967); Herbert Spencer, *Sociology* (New York: Appleton, 1892).

10. Richard Appelbaum, *Theories of Social Change* (Chicago: Markham, 1970); Amatai Etzioni and Eva Etzioni (eds.), *Social Change* (New York: Basic Books, 1964); Wilbert E. Moore, *Order and Change* (New York: Wiley, 1967).

11. Havelock *et al., Major Works on Change in Education*; Warren Bennis, Kenneth Benne, and Robert Chin, *The Planning of Change* (New York: Holt, Rinehart, and Winston, 1969).

12. Gerald Zaltman (ed.), *Processes and Phenomena of Social Change* (New York: Wiley-Interscience, 1973).

13. Charles Darwin, *Origin of Species* (New York: Appleton, 1859).

14. Appelbaum, *Theories of Social Change*.

15. Chris Argyris and Donald Schön, *Theory in Practice: Increasing Professional Effectiveness* (San Francisco: Jossey-Bass, 1974); Warren Bennis and Philip Slater, *The Temporary Society* (New York: Harper and Row, 1968); Rensis Likert, *Human Organization: Its Management and Value* (New York: McGraw-Hill, 1967); Abraham Maslow, *Motivation and Personality* (New York: Harper and Row, 1954); Douglas McGregor, *The Human Side of Paradise* (New York: McGraw-Hill, 1960).

16. Chris Argyris, "Alternative Schools: A Behavioral Analysis," *Teachers College Record* 75 (May 1974), 429-452. See also Chris Argyris, "Single-Loop and Double-Loop Models in Research on Decision Making," *Administrative Science Quarterly* 21 (September 1976), 363, and especially the reply to Argyris in the same issue, 376-377.

17. Amatai Etzioni and Eva Etzioni (eds.), *Social Change*, 78.

18. Ralf Dahrendorf, "Toward a Theory of Social Conflict," *ibid.*, 103-104. Italics added.

19. Sarason, *Culture of the School and the Problem of Change.*

20. Matthew Miles, "Some Properties of Schools as Social Systems," in Goodwin Watson (ed.), *Change in School Systems* (Washington, D.C.: National Training Laboratories, 1967), 20.

21. Donald Willower, "Schools, Values and Educational Inquiry," *Educational Administration Quarterly* 9 (Spring 1973), 13. Italics added.

22. Dahrendorf, "Toward a Theory of Social Conflict."

23. Talcott Parsons, "Some Considerations on the Theory of Social Change," *ibid.*, 219-239. Italics in original.

24. *Ibid.* Italics in original.

25. Havelock *et al.*, *Major Works on Change in Education*; compare Thomas S. Robertson, *Innovative Behavior and Communication* (New York: Holt, Rinehart, and Winston, 1971).

26. See also J. Victor Baldridge and Terrence Deal (eds.), *Managing Change in Educational Organizations* (Berkeley: McCutchan, 1975) as an example of a recently edited work which includes material on organizational change for unusually diverse perspectives on planned change.

27. Fritz Machlup, *The Production and Distribution of Knowledge in the United States* (Princeton: Princeton University Press, 1962); Edmund Short, "Knowledge Production and Utilization in Curriculum: A Special Case of the General Phenomenon," *Review of Educational Research* 43 (Summer 1973), 237-302.

28. Neal Gross, Joseph Giacquinta, and Marilyn Bernstein, *Implementing Organizational Innovations* (New York: Basic Books, 1971), 20-21. Italics in original.

29. James Q. Wilson, "Innovation in Organization: Notes toward a Theory," in James D. Thompson (ed.), *Approaches to Organizational Design* (Pittsburgh: University of Pittsburgh Press, 1966); compare Ray Jurkovich, "A Core Typology of Organizational Environments," *Administrative Science Quarterly* 19 (September 1974), 380-394; Paul R. Lawrence and Jay Lorsch, *Organization and Environment* (Homewood, Ill.: Richard D. Irwin, 1969).

30. Richard O. Carlson, *Adoption for Educational Innovations* (Eugene, Ore.: Center for the Advanced Study of Educational Administration, University of Oregon, 1965); Everett M. Rogers, *Diffusion of Innovations* (New York: Free Press, 1962).

31. Mary M. Bentzen, *Changing Schools: The Magic Feather Principle* (New York: McGraw-Hill, 1974); Gross *et al.*, *Implementing Organizational Innovations*; Sarason, *Culture of the School*; Sarason, *Creation of Settings*.

32. Bentzen, *Changing Schools*, 42.

33. Rachel Elboim-Dior, "Organizational Characteristics of the Educational System," *Journal of Educational Administration* 9 (May 1973), 3-21; Miles, "Properties of Schools"; Donald J. Willower, "Educational Change and Functional Equivalents," *Education and Urban Society* 2 (August 1970); Wilson, "Innovation in Organization."

34. W. W. Charters and Roland Pellegrin, "Barriers to the Innovation Process: Four Case Studies of Differential Staffing," *Educational Administration Quarterly* 9 (Winter 1972), 14.

35. Pincus, "Incentives for Innovation," 125.

36. *Ibid.*

37. Carlson, *Adoption for Educational Innovations*, 84.

38. Abt Associates, "A Multidisciplinary Study of Planned Educational Change," paper delivered at the annual meeting of the American Educational Research Association (Washington, D.C.: April 1, 1975); Bentzen, *Changing Schools*; W. W. Charters *et al.*, *Contrasts in the Process of Planned Change of the School's Instructional Organization* (Eugene: Center for the Advanced Study of Educational Administration, University of Oregon, 1973); Charters and Pellegrin, "Barriers to the Innovation Process"; Malcolm Levin and Roger Simon, "The Creation of Settings: A Developmental Perspective" (mimeo), (Toronto: Ontario Institute for Studies in Education, 1973); Rand Corporation, "The Field Evaluation of Programs for Educational Change," paper delivered at the annual meeting of the American Educational Research Association (Washington, D.C.: March 31, 1975); Roland Pellegrin, *Some Organizational Characteristics of Multiunit Schools* (Eugene: Center for the Advanced Study of Educational Administration, University of Oregon, 1970); Richard Schmuck and Philip Runkel, *Organizational Training for a School Faculty* (Eugene: Center for the Advanced Study of Educational Administration, University of Oregon, 1970).

39. Sarason, *Creation of Settings*.

40. Warren Bennis, *Changing Organizations* (New York: McGraw-Hill, 1966). Italics in original.

41. Rogers, *Diffusion of Innovations*; Havelock *et al.*, *Major Works on Change in Education*, Chapter 10.

42. Warren Bennis, *Organizational Development: Its Nature, Origins, and Prospects* (Reading, Mass.: Addison-Wesley, 1969); Leland Bradford, J. Gibb, and Kenneth Benne, *T-Group Therapy and Laboratory Method* (New York: Wiley, 1964); Robert Blake and Jane Mouton, *Building a Dynamic Corporation through Grid Organization Development* (Reading, Mass.: Addison-Wesley, 1969); Robert Chin and Kenneth Benne, "General Strategies for Effecting Changes in Human Systems," in Bennis *et al.*, *Planning of Change*; Robert Golembiewski and Arthur Blumberg (eds.), *Sensitivity Training and the Laboratory Approach: Readings about Concepts and Applications* (Itasca, Ill.: F. E. Peacock, 1973); F. J. Roethlisberger and William J. Dickson, *Management and the Worker* (Cambridge, Mass.: Harvard University Press, 1942); Edgar Schein, *Process Consultation: Its Role in Organizational Development* (Reading, Mass.: Addison-Wesley, 1969); Schmuck and Runkel, *Organizational Training*.

43. James R. Bright, *A Brief Introduction to Technology Forecasting: Concepts and Exercises* (Austin, Tex.: Pemaquid Press, 1972); Joseph P. Martino, *Technological Forecasting for Decisionmaking* (New York: American Elsevier, 1972).

44. Rogers, *Diffusion of Innovations*.

45. *Ibid.*

46. *Ibid.*

47. Donald Klein, "Some Notes on the Dynamics of Resistance to Change: The Defender Role," in Goodwin Watson (ed.), *Concepts for Social Change* (Washington, D.C.: National Training Laboratories, 1967), 28-29.

48. *Ibid.*, 32.

49. Roethlisberger and Dickson, *Management and the Worker.*

50. Baldridge, *Organizational Change Processes.*

51. Baldridge, "Organizational Change," 7. Italics in original.

52. *Ibid.*

53. Easton, *A Systems Analysis of Political Life.*

54. James W. Guthrie and Edward Wynne (eds.), *New Models for American Education* (Englewood Cliffs, N.J.: Prentice-Hall, 1971).

55. James W. Guthrie and Paula H. Skene, "The Escalation of Pedagogical Politics," *Phi Delta Kappan* 54, 6 (February 1973), 386-389.

56. Michael W. Kirst and Edith K. Mosher, "Politics of Education," *Review of Educational Research* 39, 5 (December 1969), 623-639.

57. Baldridge, *Organizational Change Processes.*

58. Laurence Iannaccone, *Politics in Education* (New York: Center for Applied Research in Education, 1967); Ralph B. Kimbrough, *Political Power and Educational Decision-Making* (Chicago: Rand-McNally, 1964); Michael Kirst (ed.), *State, School, and Politics: Research Directions* (Lexington, Mass.: D.C. Heath, 1972); Nicholas Masters *et al., State Politics and the Public Schools: An Exploratory Analysis* (New York: Knopf, 1964); Jay D. Scribner, "The Politics of Educational Reform: Analyses of Political Demand," *Urban Education* 4 (January 1970), 348-374; Harry L. Summerfield, *Power and Process: The Formulation and Limits of Federal Educational Policy* (Berkeley: McCutchan, 1974); F. M. Wirt and M. W. Kirst, *The Political Web of American Schools* (Boston: Little, Brown, 1972).

59. William M. Evan, "The Organization-Set: Toward a Theory of Interorganizational Relations," in James D. Thompson (ed.), *Approaches to Organizational Design*; F. E. Emery and E. L. Trist, "The Causal Texture of Organizational Environments," *Human Relations* 18 (1965), 21-31; Edward Tolman and Egon Brunswick, "The Organism and the Causal Texture of the Environment," *Psychological Review* 42 (January 1935), 43-72; Shirley Terreberry, "The Evolution of Organizational Environments," *Administrative Science Quarterly* 12 (March 1968), 590-613.

60. Terreberry, "Evolution of Organizational Environments," 611. Italics in original.

61. *Ibid.*, 600.

62. *Ibid.*, 598.

63. Carlson, *Adoption for Educational Innovations*; Daniel E. Griffiths, "Administrative Theory and Change in Organizations," in Matthew B. Miles (ed.), *Innovation in Education* (New York: Horace Mann-Lincoln Institute of School Experimentation, Columbia University, 1964).

64. Terreberry, "Evolution of Organizational Environments," 599.

65. Howard E. Aldrich, "Technology and Organizational Structure: A

Reexamination of the Findings of the Aston Group," *Administrative Science Quarterly* 17 (March 1972), 40.

66. Jerald Hage and Michael Aiken, "Routine Technology, Social Structure, and Organizational Goals," *Administrative Science Quarterly* 14 (September 1969), 366-377.

67. David J. Hickson and D. S. Pugh, "Operations Technology and Organizational Structure: An Empirical Reappraisal," *Administrative Science Quarterly* 14 (September 1969), 378-397.

68. Jay W. Forrester, "Counterintuitive Behavior of Social Systems," *Technology Review* 73 (January 1971), 52-68; D. H. Meadows *et al.*, *The Limits to Growth* (New York: Universe Books, 1972).

69. Desmond L. Cook, *Educational Project Management* (Columbus, Ohio: Merrill, 1971).

70. Frank W. Banghart, *Educational Systems Analysis* (London: Macmillan, 1969); Cook, *Educational Project Management*; Harry J. Hartley, *Educational Planning-Programming-Budgeting: A Systems Approach* (Englewood Cliffs, N.J.: Prentice-Hall, 1968); Roger A. Kaufman, *Educational System Planning* (Englewood Cliffs, N.J.: Prentice-Hall, 1972); Daniel Stufflebeam *et al.*, *Educational Evaluation and Decision Making* (Itasca, Ill.: F. E. Peacock, 1971); Ralph A. Van Dusseldorp *et al.*, *Educational Decision-Making through Operations Research* (Boston: Allyn and Bacon, 1971).

71. Samuel G. Christie, Review of *The Political Web of American Schools* by F. M. Wirt and M. W. Kirst, *Educational Administration Quarterly* 9 (Winter 1972), 77-81.

72. Forrester, *World Dynamics*; Easton, *A Systems Analysis of Political Life*.

73. Fred E. Fiedler, *A Theory of Leadership Effectiveness* (New York: McGraw-Hill, 1967); Paul Hersey and Kenneth Blanchard, *Management of Organizational Behavior* (Englewood Cliffs, N.J.: Prentice-Hall, 1972).

74. Lawrence and Lorsch, *Organization and Environment*.

75. With respect to the latter, I think we need to develop an adequate construct of organizational environment fitted to schools and school systems; we need to explicate operational measures of that construct; and we need to make predictions and test the validity of our construct on both historical and current data. Ultimately we want both to be able to place schools and school systems empirically according to the measurable characteristics of their environments and to relate those characteristics to significant organizational variables (e.g., the relative power of boundary spanning personnel in the school system and community).

76. For example, Project Rural, Abt Associates, Cambridge, Mass.; Programs 20 and 30, among others, The Center for the Advanced Study of Educational Administration, The University of Oregon; The League of Cooperating Schools, I/D/E/A, The Kettering Foundation; and The Field Study of Programs for Educational Change, The Rand Corporation, Santa Monica, California.

77. Dale Mann, "The Politics of Staff Development," in Rand Corp., *The Field Evaluation of Programs for Educational Change*, 10.

78. Harry L. Summerfield, "Structural Analysis in Policy Formulation in the Example of Federal Educational Policy," paper delivered at the annual meeting of the American Educational Research Association, April 1975.

79. Bentzen, *Changing Schools*; Rand Corp., *Field Evaluation of Programs*. I suspect, in fact, that one key to successful innovation is the presence *in the organization*, especially at upper- and middle-management levels, of what might be called cosmopolitan-locals. Contrary to the traditional conception of cosmopolitan-localism as a unidimensional bipolar construct, the brief here is for a construct of two independent dimensions where the high local-high cosmopolitan is hypothesized as the most likely and most effective change agent and linker.

80. Dale Mann, "An Introduction to the Rand Corporation's Study of the Change Agent Programs Sponsored by the U.S. Office of Education," in Rand Corp., *Field Evaluation of Programs*, 2.

12. The Broken Ikon,
Or, What Ever Happened to Theory?

ANDREW W. HALPIN AND ANDREW E. HAYES

During the past twenty years the attitudes taken by many professors of educational administration toward the role of theory in research on administration have reflected a strange historical course —it has been a yo-yo kind of affair, marked first by infatuation, and then later by disenchantment. Both the upswings and the downswings have been exaggerated, for the swing in neither direction has been justified by the reality of "the facts."

How, then, did the emphasis upon the role of theory begin? The function of theory in research on administration was first enunciated to a national representation of professors of educational administration at the 1954 National Conference of Professors of Educational Administration (NCPEA) meeting in Denver.[1] The decision to produce the Campbell and Gregg book, *Administrative Behavior in Education*[2] was also made at that same meeting. That book appeared in 1957; it was the first text in educational administration to contain a few chapters that dealt with the role of theory in research. Meanwhile, Coladarci and Getzels had published their monograph on the use of theory in educational administration,[3] and in November 1957 the first UCEA seminar was held at the University of Chicago; the topic was "Administrative Theory."[4] In 1959 two monographs by

Griffiths dealt respectively with administrative theory and the need for higher standards of research in educational administration.[5] By 1960 graduate courses in educational administration in several major universities had been modified to stress the role of theory in research, and a few courses entitled, "Administrative Theory"—or some variant thereof—had begun to appear in the curriculum.

Hollis Moore has described the "Ferment in School Administration" during the period between 1947 and 1963; he traced the contributions of the Kellogg Foundation, the American Association of School Administrators (AASA), the Cooperative Program in Educational Administration (CPEA, a program funded by the Kellogg Foundation), NCPEA, and the University Council for Educational Administration (UCEA) to the changes in the character of graduate training in school administration. As Moore notes: "Early publications, either inspired or sponsored by NCPEA, stressed 'democratic administration' concepts. By the mid-1950's the stress shifted to the contribution of the several social-science disciplines. The high-water mark of the later development was the 1954 conference at Denver, where representatives from the social sciences attended the conference for the first time. As the 1960's began, the third major shift in emphasis occurred: This time it was 'administrative theory' which occupied the center of the stage."[6]

Although "administrative theory" did indeed occupy the center of the stage as the 1960s began, by 1964—the very year in which Moore's chapter had been published—"the new movement" had already begun to run down. In his 1965 review of the 1964 *National Society for the Study of Education Yearbook,* Halpin noted that progress during the decade from 1954 to 1964 had been only modest[7]; even then he suggested a few reasons why the theory movement had already started to wane. Ironically enough, the same "maiden" issue of *The Educational Administration Quarterly* that presented Halpin's review also published Hills's cogent and prophetic article, "Educational Administration, A Field in Transition?"[8] Hills showed that actually very little of the new movement was "taking," and that few of the leaders of the movement—busy as they were, talking only with each other—realized how very thin the progress was, and how very shallow the few roots of that progress were. Indeed, several of the major findings of Campbell and Newell's recent study of the professorship in educational administration[9] vividly reaffirm the trends and the observations that Hills had noted almost a decade earlier.

In sum, as we look back over the past twenty years, we find that the theory movement had a "pretty good run" for the first decade, but that it then suddenly went into a decline during the second decade. And now far less serious attention is granted to the topic of "Administrative Theory"; furthermore, the crops of dissertations in educational administration that have come forth during the past decade most flagrantly violate the major principles of theory-oriented research. Indeed, many professors today have relegated the avant-garde work in the period from 1954 to 1964 to a few respectful footnotes, and they indulgently regard the efforts of that period as quaint but, of course, misdirected and highly impractical.

Accordingly, the theory movement was a popular ikon for a decade, and it did invoke certain set ceremonial responses from many professors and students, especially at the major universities and from those younger and brighter professors at less prestigious universities who were, themselves, upwardly mobile. But now today, "theory" is treated as if it were a broken ikon to be stored in a cobwebbed attic, along with a few scraps of late-Victorian furniture. And one could be easily persuaded to believe that theory has no relevance for our current concerns for research and application in educational administration. Nor can one deny that the emphasis on theory is certainly not compatible with the frenetic demands of the social activists among us.

Yet any professor who adopts too cavalier an attitude toward the place of theory in our field cannot help but be nagged by the fact that many of the concepts that were developed or delineated during the halcyon decade of the theory movement are even now part of the very language in which he thinks and speaks about administration. This language is more than a mere residue of jargon that remains stuck on our tongues. It stays with us because it has proven useful, and because it allows us to phrase our questions for inquiry with greater precision than had been possible, say, prior to 1954. Specifically, the language of social systems theory is now "with" both the professor and the practitioner alike. Furthermore, we now have a subfield: the politics of education, which just did not exist a decade and a half ago. And the thrust given by the theory movement has had a spill-over effect also in shifting the emphasis from educational finance to the economics of education.

One must admit to the apostate—or to those professors who never "believed" in the first instance—that in truth the expectations of leaders of the theory movement have never been even remotely realized, and the quality of most studies and dissertations produced with the pretension of representing theory-oriented research is indeed underwhelming.[10] Yet the apostate finds himself still stuck with a disturbing residue of "something" (or some things) left from the theory movement that just does not wipe out. The ikon may be broken, yet we hesitate to throw it into the junk heap. We store it in the attic, for, who knows, we may sometime have to take it back down into the living room—maybe even put it in the picture window —if only to impress "the right company."[11]

The ambivalence that so many of us feel toward the theory movement and what it stood for cannot be glibly "explained" with any simple pat answer. Iannaccone has made an excellent effort to explain what happened[12]; his observations are illuminating, extremely perceptive, witty, and, naturally, slightly biased. Yet he touches only a part of the story. Halpin, in his two papers presented in 1967,[13] also attempted to "explain" what had gone wrong. It is obvious that he too caught only part of the picture, and his views reflect his own heavy bias. Nor can the present chapter escape the traps that both Iannaccone and Halpin stumbled into earlier; "A Foggy View from Olympus" and "The Smoggy View from the Valley" have much in common. Nevertheless, given this caveat, we shall proceed—foolhardily perhaps, as did our predecessors—in a fresh effort to tackle the question, "What ever happened to theory?"

In commenting about the apparent demise of the "theory movement" we must do better than Hamlet at the graveside. The "Alas, poor Yorick" routine, although dramatic, can teach us nothing unless we can see beyond the particular set of events and can also delineate how this sequence of events is related both to changes in "The American Scene" during the past decade *and* to specifiable and perseverative characteristics of educational administration as a profession.

Our present comments on "What ever happened to theory?" are therefore made in an effort to analyze the professoriate in educational administration as a profession and educational administration itself as an academic discipline within the university. This approach, in turn, forces us to look at a few of the social, political, and ideological factors in American education, and in our society itself, that so inexorably shape the attitudes and beliefs of professors of educational administration and that hence determine the form, the content, and the objectives of our present doctoral training programs in this field. These observations are closely related to those found in the following five sources: the Iannaccone paper, Campbell and Newell's study, Campbell's 1971 review, Walker's observations, and Halpin's two 1967 presentations.[14]

The New Movement and Administrative Theory

To establish the required perspective for our discussion we must begin with the 1954 NCPEA meeting. The eight CPEA centers were represented at this meeting, and their individual center programs by then had been in operation for either three or four years; it was time for an exchange of ideas and for some tentative evaluation of their efforts in research. And for the first time three behavioral scientists —not members of the in-group of professors of educational administration—had been invited to participate in the meeting: Coladarci, Getzels, and Halpin. Here let it be noted that Getzels, as early as 1952, had published what was probably the first paper in which an attempt was made to provide a theoretical framework for the study of educational administration.[15]

These three psychologists sharply criticized the shortcomings in research methodology that were rampant in the then current CPEA endeavors. In particular they criticized the use of naive, shotgun empiricism and urged their colleagues to make a greater use of explicit theory, as a basis from which testable hypotheses could be generated. They noted that only research with an explicit theoretical basis could permit a generalizability of findings and only such research could encourage both the accumulation of systematic knowledge and the generation of further empirically testable hypotheses. The research orientation of most professors of educational administration at that meeting was so rudimentary that these three behavioral scientists had great difficulty in explaining to the group even the meaning of "an operational definition." Moreover, much of the early research within the CPEA had relied mainly on descriptive rather than inferential statistics. Griffiths was chairman of the subgroup with which these three men had spent the most time. He quickly saw the significance of what they were saying, absorbed it, and, soon afterwards, acted upon it.[16]

Then in 1957 the Campbell and Gregg book was published,

Campbell and Halpin joined the faculty at the University of Chicago, where Getzels and Guba had already affirmed an emphasis upon theory-oriented research, and the UCEA seminar on "Administrative Theory" was held. That title was something of a catch phrase.

It is obvious that every new movement—whether in politics, in religion, or in education—needs a new flag, a new banner, or, at a minimum, a new pennant. It needs a slogan, a new drumroll that will rally the troops to action. For reasons far more adventitious than many of us would like to admit, the slogan for the "New Movement" became "Administrative Theory." This slogan was concise, and it did not, indeed, violate the truth of the intentions of the leaders of the New Movement. Yet, in due time, the slogan itself led us astray.

The New Movement did indeed kindle a kind of intellectual excitement that previously had been conspicuously missing in the field of educational administration. And what did it emphasize? Essentially, and in bare bones, only three major points:

1. That the role of theory in research be recognized and that "nakedly empirical research" be rejected in favor of hypothetico-deductive research rooted in theory;

2. That educational administration not be viewed parochially, and that certainly it not be construed as distinct from other kinds of administration. That administration, without adjectival qualifiers—i.e., business administration, public administration, educational administration, etc.—be indeed regarded as a proper subject for study and research;

3. That, because education (and the schools as institutions) can be construed most usefully as "A Social System"—in the Parsonian sense—educational administration must, perforce, draw heavily upon insights furnished by the behavioral sciences.

In retrospect these recommendations seem scarcely momentous, yet the very fact that these three objectives needed to be declared explicitly speaks eloquently about what had been "the state of the art" in the training of graduate students in educational administration prior to 1954.

The Midwest Administration Center at the University of Chicago contributed immensely to the thrust of the theory movement. In order to understand why this impetus was not easily transplanted to other universities, one must first understand a few salient characteristics of the University of Chicago at that time. For the stretch of years between 1957 and 1965, the center, with Roald Campbell as its director, entered its most dynamic period; its professors and graduates had great influence in shaping the course of graduate training in administration both in this country and abroad. Five characteristics of that program made this influence possible.

1. The University of Chicago was a privately endowed university; it was not encumbered by "service station" demands for field services, and the operation of its program was constrained by few political considerations at either the local, state, or federal level.

2. The choice of doctoral students was highly selective; "walk-in" customers were not necessarily repudiated but they certainly were not avidly embraced.

3. There was a minimal reliance upon external funds from federal sources. Ample monies were received from private foundations, but these came essentially "without strings." When federal money was used, it came principally from the Cooperative Research Program of the Office of Education. At that time this program permitted the research investigator to define the problem in terms of the knowledge about education he sought, rather than in terms of "educational" or "political" desiderata stipulated by the sponsoring agency. External funds were accepted only when there was clear evidence that the thrust of the program to be funded was concordant with the philosophy of the center and with the educational objectives of the graduate program at Chicago.

4. Among the faculty of the Department of Education there was consensus about the nature of graduate education, about the necessity for a continuing *study* of education, and about the standards to be maintained. There was no schism such as is found in many departments today between, on the one hand, a large group of practitioners stressing "the nuts and bolts" of administration while also dutifully rendering services in the field and, on the other hand, a minority group of "token" scholars who were expected to provide a patina of respectability to research studies that were pedestrian at best, if not downright shoddy.[17]

5. A sufficient number of professors oriented toward research were gathered under a single roof to permit the formation of "a critical mass" of men and their knowledge.

Given this intellectual climate that prevailed at Chicago, it is no accident that the emphasis in educational administration upon empirical research well grounded in theory found support and encouragement there. But, to set the record straight, one critical point needs to be made clear. Getzels, Guba, and Halpin, inter alia, were concerned with improving the quality of research in educational administration; they never had any illusions about devising either *a* global theory of administration, or worse yet, of creating *the* theory of administration. Their aspirations were far more modest; their efforts were directed primarily against the naked empiricism that had prevailed in the research at that time. Indeed Halpin, in the opening paper for the 1957 conference, was scrupulous in referring to "The Development of Theory *in* Educational Administration,"[18] a far cry from announcing a search for *a* theory of administration.

Many of us today are beset by doubts about the usefulness of theory, and we have become both frustrated and disenchanted on this score. It may be helpful to remember that in any domain, whether professional, political, or religious, one should avoid responding too quickly to frustration by seeking conversion to a new faith. One should, instead, examine the roots of his own beliefs more closely to discover where and how he went wrong in his encounter with the brick wall of reality. It is regrettable that "The True Believers" among us are prone to seek fresh conversions, but only because such believers seldom really understand the basis for their belief in the first instance.

The self-corrective principle in the scientific method is still available to use: we need only be wise enough to use it. However, apart from the assumptions and principles that guided the behavioral scientists who had participated in the early phase of the theory movement, what are the substantive achievements that can be identified with the movement during the decade from 1954 to 1964?

By substantive achievements we mean major research contributions, contributions which, for the most part, have opened new conceptual vistas and generated fresh testable hypotheses. As examples we will cite, inter alia, five studies and will present them in order of their publication. The first is Halpin's study in which he used the Leadership Behavior Description Questionnaire (LBDQ) developed by members of the Personnel Research Board at The Ohio State University in earlier studies of the leadership behavior of aircraft commanders.[19] By factorial methods, two dimensions of leadership behavior had been identified: consideration and initiating structure-in-interaction.

Halpin noted that "democratic administration" was not an especially useful concept, that this concept did more to muddy our thinking and our acting about leadership than to clarify it. School administrators tended to perceive consideration and initiating structure as antithetical behaviors, and what they believed to be "democratic administration" turned out to be behavior high in consideration but low in initiating structure, behavior which the empirical evidence shows to be associated with *ineffective* leadership. The empirical findings of this study and of related studies were less important than their effect in opening the path for a fresh conceptualization of leadership behavior, especially in respect to the consideration and initiating structure dimensions of behavior. But even more than this, he exposed the poverty of the trait approach to leadership.

The second study, by Getzels and Guba, used role theory to develop a model of administration as a social process and posited two major dimensions of behavior in this respect: the nomothetic dimension and the ideographic dimension.[20] The major strength of this model is that it interlocks both psychological and sociological constructs into a schema from which fruitful, testable hypotheses have been derived. (A latter elaboration of Getzels's approach appears in the book, *Educational Administration as a Social Process* by Getzels, Lipham, and Campbell.[21])

The third study is perhaps the most monumental single study ever conducted within the field of educational administration. *Administrative Performance and Personality*, by Hemphill, Griffiths, and Fredericksen, is an intensive study of the personality characteristics and administrative performance of a sample of elementary school principals.[22] These principals were subjected to a highly sophisticated and realistic set of simulated experiences in which they performed tasks demanded of principals in their day-to-day job. One very practical outcome of the study was that the simulation technique, used originally for research purposes, was later modified for use as a powerful device for the pre-service and in-service training of elementary school principals. At both the theoretical and the practical levels, one other finding and observation stands out clearly: the principals' scores on their simulation experiences provide a useful and meaningful set of criteria for judging the administrative performance of these principals.

The fourth study, by Carlson, studies a sample of recently appointed school superintendents and compares those who had been appointed from within the school system with those who had been appointed from outside the particular system.[23] In short, this is a comparison between "the locals" and "the cosmopolitans," between those superintendents who are place bound (i.e., geographically) and those who are career bound—that is, oriented to their profession rather than to a geographic location. Carlson then shows "how and why" the career bound executives are in a better position than the place bound executives to effect organizational change. Carlson's participation in our field at that time is noteworthy. Because his training was essentially sociological rather than psychological he was able to give us a point of view different from those offered by such men as Charters, Getzels, Halpin, and Hemphill. Indeed, perhaps one shortcoming of the early period of the theory movement was that it was perhaps too heavily influenced by psychologists. Yet we cannot rewrite history in retrospect; in the mid-1950s it was indeed the psychologists who were the first "outsiders" lured into the area of educational administration.

In the fifth study Halpin and Croft report on the Organizational Climate Description Questionnaire (OCDQ) which they administered to the teachers and principals of seventy-one elementary schools.[24] By factorial methods they identified six organizational climates. The six climates were posited along a *rough* continuum running from the "open" climate at one end to the "closed" climate at the other. One important contribution of this study is that it provides a way for conceptualizing the organizational climate of a school multidimensionally rather than in accord with the simplistic, unidimensional concept of "morale." Later, in 1966, Halpin made a few observations about the relationship between "change" and "organizational climate."[25]

Here, then, are five types of studies that characterize research within the "New Movement." There were other studies, of course, but many of them were derivative. But these five, none of which is derivative, represent the temper of research in educational administration during the period from 1954 to 1964. Three of these five studies—those done by Halpin, by Hemphill and his colleagues, and by Halpin and Croft—raised serious questions about the uncritical use of current criteria for recruiting, selecting, and training school administrators.

In short, during the first decade the products of the theory movement, although not staggering, were also certainly not inauspicious. Yet one further admission must be granted; the major initial research contributions were made by a very small cadre of investigators, and the thrust of the movement was clearly evident at only a few universities.

What Went Wrong with the Movement?

What, then, went wrong? Why did the movement run down?

One reason is because the *idea* of administrative theory was, in the first instance, oversold. Because many of us had expected too much, too quickly, and too easily, we foredoomed ourselves to disappointment. We became the victims of our own "extravagant expectations," a phenomenon that the eminent historian, Boorstin, has beautifully described.[26]

Halpin had been aware of the risk that the emphasis on theory might become distorted and that the "movement" could degenerate into just another passing fad. We quote here his remarks on this score, made in November 1957.

In the world of everyday affairs we are all barraged by appeals to change to something new, appeals often bolstered by the argument that the new is more scientific. This applies to detergents, automobiles, and movements in education. For example, there is a tendency in education to latch onto new movements not so much because of their intrinsic soundness, but simply because they are new. "Progressive" education, the look-and-say method of teaching reading, and group dynamics have all been embraced with greater enthusiasm than understanding. Fads and styles in education, like the length of women's skirts, have had their ups and downs and have been pursued accordingly. We would like to hope that our pursuit of theory in educational administration is based upon appeals of less transitory revelation. Our task deserves a stronger commitment than this.

Some of us will need to examine our motives rather carefully. Are we seeking a better *understanding* of theory, or are we trying to *promote* the idea of theory? These motives are starkly different. In seeking a better understanding of theory, and through patient application to the development of better theory, we shall gain greater acceptance for this approach. But this acceptance will come about through the merit of what we actually accomplish, not through claims of what we intend to accomplish. Neither a particular theory nor the *idea of theory* are things to be sold, to be marketed as an advertiser might market a new breakfast cereal.

Most administrators develop skillful techniques to secure support for the programs they initiate; this often is necessary in education, and for this reason some promotional ability on the part of the administrator is useful. But because these promotional skills have proven effective in other areas, a few of us may be tempted to apply them to the present endeavor. This would be a mistake, would reflect motives alien to our purpose. Our gains must be measured by the integrity of the ideas we generate, not by the number of supporters we enlist.[27]

We are not comforted by the fact that Halpin's prophecy was so accurate. The sad fact is that the idea of theory was indeed promoted and oversold; it became a victim of extravagant expectations.

A second reason why the movement ran down was because it possessed from the very outset two facets, each of which had not been properly differentiated from the other. One facet was the emphasis upon the use of theory (i.e., theoretical models in the strictly scientific sense of the term) as the basis for empirical research on administration. It was not necessary that such models pertain directly, and certainly not exclusively, to the field of educational administration. Thus, for example, the Getzels model had its genesis in Parsonian theory; its actors were leaders or administrators, strictly in their role of group leader. (Halpin, in the "paradigm," had concurrently delineated the difference between the behavior of an administrator as a group leader and his behavior as a decision maker,[28] and the Hemphill, Griffiths, Fredericksen study later gave ample empirical verification to this distinction.[29]) Likewise Hemphill's theory of leadership had been derived from a context apart from education.[30] Neither Getzels nor Hemphill was presumed to be developing a theory of administration. The proper title for what was being done by the behavioral scientists was: "The use of theory in designing and conducting empirical research on the behavior of *actors* within an organizational (or administrative) context."

Yet the second facet of the movement referred to the term "administrative theory" in a different way. Here, the term "administration" was used in an overarching sense; its meaning was tinged by concepts that had been developed during the period before 1950 in the study of administration; these concepts were essentially prescriptive in character rather than explanatory in the scientifically analytical sense. Furthermore, these concepts referred to the process of administration but provided few linkages between the behavior of the actors engaged in this process and the dynamics of the process itself. The process, as delineated, was analytical in its own way, yet was posited as a rather free-floating albeit rational entity, which operated apart from the interplay among the actors and the unique characteristics of the social system of the specific organization.

This heritage of work in administration, much of which had come from the field of public administration, spoke in the language of what ought to have been in behavior, rather than what was. And it was altogether too easy for this use of language to seep into the discussions about administrative theory, thus causing many workers to seek the Holy Grail of THE theory of administration. Accordingly, the initial response to the theory movement was dictated by which of these two facets the respondent chose to perceive as representing the essence of the movement. The language and mode of thinking of behavioral scientists were, however, new, strange, and confusing to most professors of educational administration during the decade from 1954 to 1964, whereas the language before 1954 was highly familiar. It was therefore only natural that most professors of administration chose to respond to the second facet of the movement, and to deal with it, not in its own terms and language—as these were intended—but in accord with the concepts and language that they already knew. Consequently, the behavioral scientists who had given the theory movement its initial thrust saw the movement as meaning one thing, while most professors of administration saw it as meaning quite another.[31] This lack of consensus contributed to the movement's premature decline.

A third reason why the movement ran down was that it had not matured sufficiently by 1964 to withstand the shock waves of "The Violent 1960s." Let one example suffice. Behavioral scientists during the period from 1954 to 1964 had concentrated upon variables *within* the organization with little concern for the external variables impinging upon the organization from the outside world. This should not be surprising when one considers the calm temper of the 1950s. This was before Selma, The Great Society, and Vietnam, before the rapid politicization of public education and "the politics of confrontation."

In the 1950s few of us had thought about spill-over effects; this concept was alien to us because our schools were still relatively insulated from the external society. Yet a host of these effects drastically exposed the innocence of the theoretical models that behavioral scientists had designed. In short, these scientists had been caught off guard; they had failed to anticipate the turmoil of the 1960s and its impact upon the schools. (At the same time, our politicians, our statesmen, and our economists were no less caught off guard.) These scientists had not plugged into their equations (or into their models) the necessary and pertinent array of external variables. But please note that this does not mean that the *method* they had advocated had thereby been invalidated. Not at all. For indeed, from the outset the method—even as scientific method in the biological and physical sciences—had possessed a built-in provision for self-correction.

Even today, the variables can still be revised and the models corrected. Let us illustrate with a simple example. Hayes has found that, in response to the OCDQ, schools where teachers are unionized show a marked homogeneity of response on many items.[32] Indeed, a new constellation, or factor, emerges from such data with sufficient strength to permit one to differentiate between unionized and non-unionized schools on the basis of OCDQ responses. Could Halpin and Croft have been able to anticipate this finding in 1962? Of course not, simply because there were few unionized schools at that time. Does this finding suggest the possibility that other measures of attitudes that we still use with innocent confidence may indeed be distorted by confounding elements that we have not yet identified? Of course. In sum, the behavioral sciences are contending with a society in a state of rapid flux, and for this reason the theoretical models of one decade ordinarily need to be modified so as to take into account new social forces and attitudes that previously could not have been even imagined, let alone identified. This limitation applies across the gamut of the behavioral sciences and is not confined to models that pertain to theory in administration.

The fourth reason why the movement faltered is that a sufficient "critical mass" of research talent and research findings (i.e., findings based upon theoretically oriented research, not on unsophisticated surveys) had not been built before the 1960s struck. Simply put, we did not have at hand sufficient talent in depth. Nor is this surprising, for—prior to 1964—only a handful of universities were producing doctoral graduates in educational administration who were well trained in research methodology. In sum, the good intentions of the first decade of the theory movement had failed to be turned into actuality by the time the violent 1960s began to overwhelm all of us.

At this juncture, let us summarize the four primary reasons why the theory movement stalled:

1. It was overpromoted.

2. The two-faceted nature of its original thrust produced dissension about its meaning and intention.

3. The theoretical models available had not matured sufficiently to withstand the spill-over effects of the 1960s. Specifically, not enough attention had been given to external variables and to the impact of a terrifying pace of change in the larger society.

4. A sufficient critical mass of research talent and research findings had not been developed *in time.*

Impact of the 1960s

This, then, is where things stood as we crossed the threshold into the period of Lyndon Johnson's "Great Society." Before 1965 and 1974 the impact of the frenetic 1960s hit all of us. Federal intervention in the educational enterprise produced drastic changes in the social order. And, as education became increasingly politicized, our schools and colleges were also shaken by a myriad of spill-over effects from the external environment and from the larger society.

Iannaccone and Campbell[33] have elsewhere discussed the broad social upheaval that occurred during the 1960s. Note that the changes of that period not only contributed to the decline of the theory movement, they also changed the character of public education and the nature of the training of professional educators in several pervasive and dramatic ways. Here the present writers will review only a few events of that period.

Specifically, the federal government and, more particularly, the United States Office of Education (USOE), took a new and active stance in its relationship to both public and private schools. The first great breakthrough in federal aid occurred in the Elementary and Secondary Education Act of 1965; it involved a series of programmatic and innovative imperatives which plunged the federal government smack into the middle of the total educational enterprise. These activities included grants for research and development and provision for a set of regional educational laboratories and research and development (R and D) centers. The series of programs and priorities that were mandated entailed a massive shift in the locus of policy-making power in American education. The research that was sanctioned was focused and oriented toward action; in many

instances the programs developed had not only educational implications, but profound social and political implications as well. We witnessed the case of the dream of Rousseau revisited[34]—with a ven-
geance, and with "The Planners" exuding confidence and cockiness
as they emptied bulging pockets of money into each new educational
venture.

One cannot create competent research investigators by fiat.
Even in the best of times, our country has never had an abundance of
talent in this area. The regional laboratories and the R and D centers
started as a crash program and with much promotional hoopla and
the usual extravagant promises and expectations. At that time no
great research talent was available, and there certainly were not
enough *trained* men and women ready to staff the public schools, the
colleges of education, *and* the new federal parasystem of education.
Here, too, not only the expanding USOE program required staffing;
the Office of Economic Opportunity programs and projects that had
been generated by Title IV of the Civil Rights Act also demanded
staffing. Professional educators were suddenly showered with instant
wealth and funding. In our public schools and universities the new
fairhaired boys became those men who developed skill in writing proposals and in getting more and more of "the long green." It was a
frenetic period during which promoters and entrepreneurs moved
into the ascendancy. The day of the "goodie bundles" had arrived.
Elsewhere Halpin has discussed the psychological dynamics of participants in "The Funded Life."[35] And Iannaccone has stated the
problem effectively:

Money makes the mare go round. Changing funding patterns determine research
and other work activities for all of us some of the time and some of us all of the
time. In educational administration the latter is the larger number. External
funding for university research is not an unmixed blessing for any of the parties
to the transaction. As noted earlier, the frequent complaint of funding agencies
heard in the sixties that the research they bought did not make a difference reflected their own poor purchase. *No other field better illustrates the fact that
when you buy researchers, you get researchers who can be bought.* The sensa-
tional, seductive, shifting, sixties saw more such sales and purchases than educational administrative history had ever seen before. The wonder is that anything
was produced. . . . *Is it any wonder then that as granting agencies moved toward
educational crisis management, research professors in educational administration
replaced the search for concepts with social concerns and focused on producing
solutions instead of understanding problems.*[36]

In some universities the traditional standards for tenure and promotion were modified so that promoters and entrepreneurs could be rewarded for the external funds they got rather than for the substantive services they produced or the contribution they made to knowledge. The impact of such external funding upon the American university has been soberly analyzed in two recent books.[37]

It is doubtful whether profound scholarship can ever flourish in a frenetic climate, especially in one that has become highly politicized. Scholarship requires conditions that permit reflectiveness, time to read and absorb, time to engage in divergent as well as convergent thinking. But these are precisely the things that were not encouraged within the educational establishment during the years from 1965 to 1974. The word was action, action, action; airport professors proliferated, and within the colleges of education private little empires appeared. Each "emperor" was able to buy his quota of "slave labor," i.e., well paid graduate students to do his donkey work for him. The quid pro quo often turned out to be an assurance for the student that his emperor would manage to get the slave's dissertation approved. To achieve this end the emperor was forced to devise ways to circumvent any professor who was knowledgeable about research methodology and who also insisted upon maintaining high academic standards.

And the more money that was poured into action programs, the less other money was made available for basic research. Hence, the *basic* research investigator had few funds with which to support worthy students. And, quite naturally, students gravitated toward "the operators" and the entrepreneurs. Willie Sutton, the great Boston bank robber, was once asked, "Willie, why do you rob banks?" Unhesitatingly, he replied, "Because that's where the money is."

But, on the broader scene, the period from 1965 to 1974 saw an increase in violence, a rash of skyjacking, waves of political terrorism, and the emergence of a new phenomenon—the politics of confrontation. Schools became a prime arena for many confrontations that were a direct outcome of the spill-over effects from the external surroundings. A new term, "crisis management," became a throbbing part of the school administrator's vocabulary. Furthermore, a series of court decisions imposed fresh constraints upon the degrees of freedom that an administrator had available in making even day-to-day decisions. Within a milieu such as this, we can understand why such new subfields as the politics of education and the economics of education became so important. Our entire society had become increasingly politicized, and our schools could not escape the shock of this trend; indeed, the schools in particular found themselves in an especially vulnerable position.

And during this chaotic period the formal leaders of large organizations of all kinds—whether school administrators, university presidents, mayors, governors, or even the President of the United States—were forced most reluctantly to recognize the impotence of their own leadership. In short, how does one lead in a situation where the society itself, as well as the major formal institutions within it, are riven with dissent? Within a climate of this kind much of what we in educational administration have been teaching and have assumed to be almost axiomatic suddenly appears to be glaringly unreal and irrelevant. What, then, can we as professors of educational administration say? It is regrettable that one reaction to this embarrassment is for educators, themselves, to criticize sharply graduate training programs in educational administration—certainly not on the grounds that they fail to provide enough useful information drawn from the research literature and from an understanding of theory, but rather on the grounds that such training is not sufficiently practical and down-to-earth.

Thus, for example, in a report of a conference on the big city superintendency the statement is made that "there was general agreement among participants that graduate programs for developing school administrators were not of much value."[38] And here let it be noted that one of the participants in that conference was a U.S. Commissioner of Education. Likewise, in a recent meeting of leaders from the professoriate of educational administration and superintendents, an attempt was made to gain the group's support in securing funds for a training program for administrators of urban schools. The primary rationale for the program was that "we [the professors] don't know where it's at." Such expressions are perhaps but noises made by those people seeking goodie bundles, or by those who do not have training in either the basic disciplines or administrative theory but who have, nonetheless, discovered some "new knowledge" from their own experience.

In this instance, the willingness of professors to yield to the "superior" knowledge of practitioners and, in this case as well as others, the unabashedness with which these same professors announce the poverty and uselessness of training programs they, themselves, direct, should certainly give us pause.

Campbell and Newell, in their recent study of professors of educational administration, throw some light on this problem; they note that "it seems fair to say that the professors were not very concerned about problems facing the academic field of educational administration, and *some had difficulty in differentiating their role from practitioners in the field*." Further, they report that "professors of educational administration engage in many activities, but they appear to have little time or inclination toward research. Unlike some of their colleagues in the traditional disciplines, professors of educational administration not only teach and advise students, but they also spend considerable amounts of time doing field studies. We have no way of knowing precisely what these field studies were about. We suspect, however, that many of them dealt with problems specific to one situation and thus their power for generalization was limited."

Campbell and Newell note, also, the "professors devoted an unusual amount of their time to field services—often much of it for private remuneration. While they worked out of the university and enjoyed the benefits of its prestige, they did not appear to be at home there. The practice-oriented professors tended to be younger than the average, but they often enjoyed higher rank and higher consulting income than average." Campbell and Newell estimated about 20 percent of the population were clearly in that category. Their conclusion was that "an entrepreneurial spirit exists in some quarters which places too high a premium on opportunities to consult for private gain."[39]

The paired observations that the professors had some difficulty in differentiating their role from that of practitioners in the field "and that the professors worked out of the University—but did not appear to be at home there" succinctly reveal the story.[40] The primary identification of these men and women is "with the field," not with the university. With respect to the research aspirations of professors of educational administration, Campbell and Newell have reported that "a research commitment of as much as 50 percent of [their] time was desired by only 6 percent of the entire group."[41]

Campbell and Newell's conclusion is a classic understatement, "It seems doubtful that a professional field can be appropriately developed with so little energy going into its study."

Research in Educational Administration

Make no mistake about it, the findings of the Campbell and Newell study are utterly damning to the profession. And given these findings, is there any wonder that the theory movement failed to flourish? Bluntly, the professoriate in educational administration is just not interested in research or in the *study* of administration.

Furthermore, even when research is conducted in educational administration, little information is produced. Most of these research efforts are independent of other research work and, for numerous reasons, usually are not developed beyond the initial stage; each fresh effort seems to start, and also stop, at "square one." Griffiths has noted that "significant bits of research, theory, and theorizing are not being followed up. Much research which opens an area gets no further because no one picks it up."[42] Furthermore, much of the activity that has been conducted under the name of research has been worthless at best and, hopefully, not harmful. Iannaccone has described the condition well: "We have produced studies which are methodologically bad, theoretically useless, and which are focused on trivial problems."[43]

Haller has noted, however, "that earlier [dissertation] research consisted overwhelmingly of status studies of one sort or another, in which the students' findings consisted of reporting of marginals derived from questionnaires. Currently [1971], dissertations are more likely to concern relationships among constructs, and are much more likely to be explanatory in nature."[44] At first glance, the statements made by Haller and Iannaccone seem to be in conflict; several outcomes of the theory movement can, however, account for the findings by Haller and yet support Iannaccone's ideas about the state of research in administration.

Associated with the theory movement was a "language" of organizations and organizational phenomena. This language had its basis in sociology and psychology, for the most part, and was expanded to include some components (terms) that are unique to the educational organization. Researchers in the basic disciplines had long known the importance of operational definitions for research. Accordingly, the originators of the theory movement, that is, the men who were most influential at the outset, worked to establish operational definitions for constructs which had been used, or were being used, to describe relationships within and among educational organizations. These definitions often were associated with procedures for measuring the presence of the construct. Consequently, the efforts of early researchers and others through the period from 1954 to 1974 have produced numerous questionnaires, tests, scales, and other measurement procedures. To cite a few examples: Halpin and Croft developed the OCDQ to measure the organizational climate of elementary schools; researchers at the Personnel Research Board developed the Leader Behavior Description Questionnaire (LBDQ), the 16 Personality Factors Test was developed by Cattell and others to measure personality characteristics; Fiedler developed the Least Preferred Coworker questionnaire (LPC) to measure personality; Willower developed the Pupil Control Ideology Scale (PCI) to measure the pupil control ideology of teachers; Smith *et al.*, developed the Job Description Index (JDI) to measure the job satisfaction of personnel;[45] etc. etc.

Yet the impact on subsequent research of these efforts to develop the operational definitions and the resulting measurement procedures should have been predictable. Those graduate students and professors who had previously been busily engaged in the construction and administration of questionnaires for descriptive studies no longer had to construct such questionnaires. They now simply seized upon the language that was being applied to educational organizations and merrily "lionized" a few instruments,[46] and *voilà*, a research question—perhaps even stated in the form of a null hypothesis to assure the absence of bias on the part of the researcher. Instead of letting the problem determine the instrument, here we find study after study in which the instrument dictates the problem. Furthermore, the choice of dependent and independent variables too often appears to be adventitious, and seldom does one find a cogent a priori case made on theoretical grounds alone for *why* any relationship should be expected between X and Y in the first instance. It would indeed be salutary if a few more doctoral candidates—and, perhaps, even their chairmen—would read and heed the cogent remarks made by Guba and Getzels in their classic study of personality and teacher effectiveness.[47] Moreover, there is a stark difference between the work of the original developers and that of those who seized upon their work in the degree of tentativeness of the claims that are made about the usefulness of results.[48]

Certain consequences of these research efforts were also not anticipated by either developers of the measurement procedures or users of these procedures. These consequences are not, however, unfamiliar to experts in the field of measurement and research methods. For example, most of the tests, questionnaires, and procedures that are used in administrative research were developed independent of each other. The objective of most developers was to devise instruments that contained "items" indicating the degree of presence of some trait. This is a different purpose than one developing a procedure which contains "items" that not only indicate the degree of presence of a trait but that also define the trait operationally. This distinction does not become critical until the validity of the measurement device is questioned or until the devices are used in research to measure traits that the investigator hypothesizes to be related to each other. In such cases the responsibility then rests heavily upon the researcher to demonstrate the validity as well as the independence of the procedures he has used.

If, for example, a researcher seeks to determine the relationship between the leadership behavior of the principal and the morale of teachers, he may define "morale" operationally as the traits measured by the Purdue Teacher Opinionnaire (PTO) and "leadership behavior" operationally as the traits measured by the LBDQ. Correlational techniques probably would be employed to provide input to the question about the relationship between morale and leader behavior. So, what is the problem?

The items that compose the LBDQ are examples of "leader behaviors." On the other hand, some items of the PTO are simply *presumed* to be indicators of the presence of morale. For example, one subtest is named "Rapport with Principal." Indeed, the research question in the example above pertains to the nature of that relationship and to demonstrating just what relationship obtains between "Rapport with Principal" and "Morale"—a relationship that cannot be taken as a "given" but that must be construed as an empirical question yet to be answered. But, more specifically, the items in the "Rapport with Principal" subtest are almost identical to some of those found in the LBDQ. Accordingly, the only way for the relationship under investigation not to be found to "exist" would be for the items of the respective questionnaires to possess reliabilities so low that significant interinstrument correlations would be thereby precluded.

Examples of methodological weaknesses such as the one just cited can be found in almost any issue of publications that report research on administrator behavior. Accordingly, whatever the reported findings and the resulting inferred conclusions, research of this kind can serve no useful purpose unless such methodological shortcomings are first eliminated.

One other methodological problem is significantly related to the utility of research findings in the area of educational administration. Once tests, questionnaires, and measurement procedures have been developed and have achieved a reputation of sorts, they then tend to be used uncritically. We must remember, however, that every measurement procedure is composed of a set of "indicators." These indicators are selected by the developers according to some criteria for selection and a rationale is presented for their selection. But these indicators of a construct usually possess only circumscribed usefulness—i.e., they apply only within a given type of organization, social system, time-frame, geographical location, etc. (In some cases these indicators will be found to apply to situations beyond the setting in which they were originally derived, yet this extended application must be established empirically and cannot merely be gratuitously assumed.) Thus an "item" may be a useful indicator of a trait at a given point in time or within a given social setting, but, when significant changes occur in that setting, the item may no longer be a useful indicator of the trait. For example, during the early 1950s, owning a television set may have been a useful indicator of economic position, whereas today this item would not discriminate among economic groups.

A further example of the effect of the times and spillover from the social system into the schools was noted recently. A male photographer had made a photograph of a beaming junior high school girl who had just removed her first cake from the oven. The photographer saw the situation as an example of the girl's satisfaction with accomplishing a task. A young woman teacher, however, declared that the photographer was a male chauvinist because he was implying that the place for a woman was in the home. As research investigators, we need to learn not to impute our own perceptions of events to other perceivers. We simply cannot take for granted how another perceiver will view any given test item; homogeneity of perception is a question the answer to which must be determined empirically.

More than a decade has passed since many of the currently popular questionnaires were developed; indeed many of them were developed before our encounter with 1960s. Accordingly, perforce of questionable value are recent studies with instruments that have not taken into due account the question of whether the original indicators today reflect the same behavior or attitude initially indicated.

Because of limitations in methods such as those cited (and others could have been mentioned) the "information base" that is specific to educational administration is extremely weak. Furthermore, even with the amount of activity that has been pursued in the name of research, the study of educational administration has not kept pace with the study of administration in either political science or sociology. The "science of administration" as a discipline did not emerge in education to the point of developing or sustaining a critical mass of researchers within the domain of educational administration. Consequently, the science of administration still remains lodged within the general social sciences.

It is unfortunate, however, that professors of educational administration do not maintain close ties with the basic disciplines. Campbell and Newell report the relationships. "These figures suggest that training in one or more of the basic areas, even at the master's level, is still relatively uncommon among professors of educational administration. For the most part, the development of the professional field of educational administration, initiated by such institutions as Teachers College and Stanford during the early decades of this century, appears to have been emulated by many universities, both public and private, across this continent. These programs, designed originally for practitioners have, often with little modification, also been used for the preparation of professors. The notion that any professional field must make extensive use of the concepts found in the basic disciplines does not have as firm a place in the professoriate in educational administration as we believe it should."[49]

But even in the basic disciplines all is not well. For example, Churchman indicates that "at the present time we understand very little about managerial behavior, because in all studies of behavior we concentrate our attention on what the observer sees the manager doing." He continues by saying that "science is incapable as yet of generating an adequate science of management simply because it has no basis or technique by which it can adequately judge the difference between good and bad, or healthy and unhealthy types of managerial behavior."[50]

Furthermore, Campbell has said that "we had unrealistic expectations about the potential contributions of the disciplines. We failed to realize that the disciplines themselves are in a process of development."[51]

On this score, note a recent critique by Gibson and Teasley of research based upon the humanist model of organizational motivation. They conclude:

In view of the lack of empirical evidence to support the humanistic model, one wonders how it maintains support. There does indeed seem to be an almost metaphysical attraction to the Maslow hierarchy and to the various spin-off theories that comprise the humanistic model. The impact of the model is discernible in practically every form of organization from complex bureaucracies to small intimate groups such as the family. And those who support the thesis may well be right. But our review indicates that for now faith rather than empirical evidence must be used to support the concept.[52]

By failing to recognize limits on the development of other disciplines, educational researchers became too enthusiastic about the basic disciplines and their potential contribution to educational administration. Disappointment soon followed because there were no miracles waiting for us. Campbell has suggested that we not seek such miracles but that we approach the disciplines more realistically.[53]

One consequence of the disillusionment with the social sciences was a renewed interest in the humanities as a basis for "truth" in educational administration. Programs were offered in several universities that were based upon such an approach, and other departments of educational administration encouraged students to venture into the humanities. Harkin, in his recent analysis of educational administration and the humanities, offers an alternative:

Without impugning the value of the humanities as a means of developing sensitivity and insight that can serve as basis for social action, one can point out that these ends do not demand the use of the humanities. On the contrary, the behavioral sciences can serve equally well, and from the standpoint of economy, much better. The theoretical formulation, research outputs, and inquiry modes of those disciplines, whose dress and speech were borrowed (by educational administration) a decade or more ago, could have provided a means to those same ends if they had been honestly adopted and rigorously applied to the educational organization. The fact that an idea such as: "Schools are not independent agencies but are an integral part of the total socio-cultural system" can be classed in 1970 as a "dawning recognition" is suggestive of the superficial attention given the substance of that earlier enthusiasm.[54]

In addition to the humanities other areas have been given special attention by researchers in educational administration during the past decade. Funding patterns which emerged from political and social forces developed interests in the creation of new specializations. These funded specializations (some examples are listed below) provided financial support for doctoral students and professors to develop courses and programs in the particular areas of specialization. Unfortunately (or, fortunately, as the case may be), the language was available to describe and promote the specialization, but the information bases simply had not been developed enough to support its development. Moreover, these "specialists" were often astonishingly unaware of the marginal utility of their efforts for understanding the relationships within the field of educational administration. Because the assumptions of a particular specialization and what was indeed known about the use of theory in research in administration conflicted, "cover stories" were devised to promote the role of each particular specialization. Usually a slogan was selected as the banner for the specialization. "Organizational Development," "Management by Objectives," "Group Process," "Operations Research," "Management Information System," "Minority Relations," and "Collective Bargaining" are just a few. It is clear that in most cases educational administration was being *used* as a means for promoting the social or political goals of the funding agencies even before an adequate base of knowledge had been assembled to predict the consequences of such actions.

Furthermore, the social and political goals were often presented only as vague statements of intentions, and insufficient time was allowed before beginning activities to convert such statements into operational terms around which information could be gathered. The reinforcement systems (e.g., funding, promotions, etc.) had little or no relationship to the presence or absence of a substantive base for development of the discipline. For example, little attention was given to the substantive base for equal educational opportunity before action was begun in that domain.

Iannaccone's summary seems to describe the situation:

The field of research in educational administration has qualities I think of as inverted Protean and late Athenian. Inverted Protean because just as it begins to grasp something it changes its form. Late Athenian because, like the men St. Paul saw gathered around the unknown God, seeking "some new thing," it is all too superstitious, anxious to choose some new doctrine, with new demi-gods every two years. One manifestation of this quality, I would hypothesize, may be found in testing the proposition that each year of research in educational administration is better predicted by a content analysis of the *Saturday Review* or some other widely distributed periodical than any set of academic journals. Ironically, this irreverance for scholarship has led educational administration research into being truly irrelevant. Many of its research proposals are what could be called late contemporary. Its findings produce that slight sense of embarrassment we feel wearing last season's fashions. When the significance of proposed research is defined as its timeliness for contemporary crisis in public policies rather than as the concepts and explanation it offers, then not only must its findings be published concurrent with, if not before, crisis, but public policy makers must at best be guided by mere findings rather than by understanding. Under these conditions, theory guided research and research based theory can contribute to understanding episodic crisis. However, it cannot grow beyond them if it remains enslaved by them.[55]

But, enough!

Summing Up the Theory Movement

On the basis of the present brief review of the rise and fall of the theory movement during the past two decades, what are the salient observations that we have made? Let us summarize eleven points:

1. A "language" of administrative theory and techniques for empirical research was introduced to educational administration by the "movement," and this language has now become a part of "the conventional wisdom" of our field—totally apart from the question of whether this language is being used appropriately or not. There-

fore, future efforts to develop more competent skills in research will require only a better and more accurate understanding of the present concepts, but not the new learning of a fresh set of concepts. The pivotal concepts are already at hand; we need only learn how to understand and appreciate them and how to develop skill in using them. It is regrettable, however, that today much of what passes as "understanding" even among many professors of educational administration is an understanding that is only "word deep." The ability to match the names of investigators with names of the specific concepts with which they are associated is not enough; it would be helpful if one also *understood* the concepts themselves.[56]

2. Within the field of educational administration a modest *information base* has already been built. Granted that only a start has been made in this direction and that progress has been slow, yet there is enough of a base to permit the generation of useful hypotheses and to encourage us to refine our procedures further.

3. The information base in the related basic disciplines is not completely solid or perfect but, nonetheless, sociology, psychology, and political science research have indeed developed propositions that seem applicable to educational organizations. These propositions, and the research efforts to date within these areas of the behavioral sciences, do indeed provide educational administration with a good start for identifying viable research questions and for devising appropriate research procedures.

4. Procedures of organizational analysis have been developed that can be applied not only in practical administration but also in planning research and generating research questions. The procedures recommended by Perrow, Seiler, Tannenbaum[57] and others deserve careful attention.

5. The development of "specializations" has provided education with a few useful procedures that have been developed within disciplines other than education. Here we refer to: methodologies of organizational development, management procedures (especially those associated with "management by objectives," and management information systems), operations research methods, and techniques devised within the area of economics that pertain directly to planning, labor relations, and collective bargaining.

6. Statistical procedures have been improved to such an extent that multivariate relationships can be investigated quite easily.

(Marked improvements in computer technology have contributed to this progress.) At present few people in the field of educational administration have mastered these procedures, but there is a small cadre of training investigators who can offer us hope in applying these procedures to administrative research.

7. Research methods that have been used in the past have been criticized by a few observers for being either inadequate, inappropriate, or both. But there is scant justification for this criticism. The primary problem with much of the earlier research in educational administration is that not enough attention has been paid to the development and specification of appropriate research questions. For example, if a research question can be formulated accurately and if the problem can be identified, then research procedures such as the case-study method, participant observation,[58] and delphi techniques can be used to generate specific hypotheses. However, other methods that make generalization possible must then be used in further research designed to test the specific hypotheses that have been generated.

At present, in addition to classical research methods, we can use "newer methods" such as: simulation techniques, sample-free calibration procedures[59] and an impressive array of multivariate statistical techniques.

8. Values, or "oughts," cannot serve as a basis for decision making. Churchman has stated the issue well: "Agreement always has its opposite side and often becomes disagreement in the next generation, especially in healthy societies where social change is bound to occur. A rational mind will want a far better basis for the judgment of excellence."[60]

9. The distractions of the past decade have been devastating to the theory movement. We can foresee no end to these distractions at the present time, especially in the face of the recession-inflationary character of the 1970s and the fact that in certain respects education is a declining industry. During the past two decades research in educational administration has not enjoyed stable financial support. Unless a deliberate and substantial effort is made to provide this support in the decade ahead, we will witness a further decline in, and repudiation of, the theory movement. We think such support for research will be brushed aside by events associated with the rapid emergence of fresh social problems, swift changes brought about as a

result of new legal precedents, and continuing wide-spread politicization of education.

10. The labor organization movement in our schools has had a
sharp impact upon the behavior of administrators. Yet little research
has appeared that takes this impact into account, nor have our extant
research procedures shown much sophistication in dealing with ways
in which the labor organization movement vitiates the meaning and
significance of many of our testing procedures.

11. The decline of the theory movement can be attributed, at
least in part, to the resistance (or, perhaps, even the ignorance) of the
practice-oriented professors. Accordingly, if any effort is to be made
to revitalize the movement, then this effort will need to be accompanied by a parallel "development" movement in which information
that has been secured from research is translated into information
that is meaningful and useful to practicing administrators. On this
score, Campbell and Newell's comment is pertinent: "Any profession
must take its cues from two sources: the conditions which exist in
the field of practice and the state of knowledge in the supporting
disciplines. Frequently in educational administration we have vacil-
lated between the two positions, at one time emphasizing basic
knowledge and theory development and another time the problems
confronting the practitioner in the field of practice. We can not settle
for one or the other; there must be a continued interaction between
the two. Our concern is that professors generally seem somewhat
complacent about both of these mainsprings to the profession."[61]

In summarizing these eleven salient points, we have tried to be
just in describing how we believe the theory movement *could* be
revitalized. But we have also been wistful, hopeful, and Pollyannish;
indeed, we find ourselves reminded of a wise observation made by
the Irish novelist, Lawrence Durrell, "Where nothing is real, everything is plausible."[62] Likewise, if the present authors should deny
"the reality" of most of the events of the past two decades in the
field of educational administration, then we, too, could insist that
the projections and the recommendations that we have made are
indeed plausible. But this plausibility is indeed specious.[63] Yet it is
altogether too easy for all of us to become beguiled by our own
rhetoric and the pompous pieties we write—especially when these
pieties express what both our readers and we, ourselves, would like
to believe.[64]

So, what can we conclude? Twenty years later, the theory movement has little to show for its efforts. Indeed, the situation may be much worse today because so much shoddy work in the name of research was ground out by men whose understanding of the role of theory in research was shallow. Certainly the ideas behind the theory movement have never received acceptance at the grass roots within the professoriate. Indeed, it has never been a popular movement at all. So, let the movement die. Those professors and younger students who intend to do research of respectable quality will, on their own, find and use the pertinent research and discussions that appeared during the period from 1954 to 1974; others will neither find it nor want it. There is no point in trying to promote a set of ideas that have so little popular, or broad, appeal. The promotional approach is not suited to our purpose; it has failed during the past twenty years, and it will continue to fail because the means for "promoting" inevitably corrupt the ends. Why should we have believed in the first instance that an emphasis upon research in educational administration and the wise use of theory to undergird such research was a venture for the masses within our ranks? The experience of the past twenty years certainly suggests that it was not. So, where does that leave us now? Perhaps we may need to change our sights and revise our approaches and our expectations. Perhaps we may need to remember lines taken from a totally different context:

Strait is the gate, and narrow is the way . . . and few there be that find it. (Matthew 7:14)

So be it!

Notes

1. Principally by Arthur P. Coladarci, Jacob W. Getzels, and Andrew W. Halpin.

2. Roald F. Campbell and Russell T. Gregg (eds.), *Administrative Behavior in Education* (New York: Harper and Brothers, 1957).

3. Arthur P. Coladarci and Jacob W. Getzels, *The Use of Theory in Educational Administration* (Stanford, Calif.: Stanford University, School of Education, 1955).

4. Andrew W. Halpin (ed.), *Administrative Theory in Education* (Chicago: Midwest Administrative Center, University of Chicago, 1958; republished by Macmillan, New York, 1967).

5. Daniel E. Griffiths, *Administrative Theory* (New York: Appleton-Century-Crofts, 1959); *Research in Educational Administration* (New York: Bureau of Publications, Teachers College, Columbia University, 1959).

6. Hollis A. Moore, Jr., "The Ferment in School Administration," in Daniel E. Griffiths (ed.), *Behavioral Science and Educational Administration*, Sixty-third Yearbook of the National Society for the Study of Education, Part II (Chicago: University of Chicago Press, 1964), 11-32, esp. 24.

7. Andrew W. Halpin, "Essay Review of *Behavioral Science and Educational Administration*," *Educational Administration Quarterly* 1 (Winter 1965), 49-53.

8. Jean Hills, "Educational Administration: A Field in Transition?" *Educational Administration Quarterly* 1 (Winter 1965), 58-66.

9. Roald F. Campbell and L. Jackson Newell, *A Study of Professors of Educational Administration* (Columbus, Ohio: University Council for Educational Administration, 1973). An abridged version by the same authors and with the same title appears in *Educational Administration Quarterly* 9 (Autumn 1973), 3-29.

10. For example, more than 300 studies and dissertations based upon the Halpin-Croft Organizational Climate Description Questionnaire (OCDQ) have been reported in the literature. But most of these studies are trivial; they suggest that many authors certainly never read the original monograph with care. Two 1976 doctoral dissertations at the University of Georgia provide a critical review of these OCDQ studies. The first, by James W. Mullins, is "Analysis and Synthesis of Research Utilizing the Organizational Climate Description Questionnaire: Organizations Other than Elementary Schools; 1963-1972"; the second, by Charles Green, analyzes and synthesizes the research for elementary schools.

11. One never knows; theory may turn out to be as valuable and prestigious as a Tiffany lamp, or as some other objet d'art of the Art Nouveau period.

12. Laurence Iannaccone, "Interdisciplinary Theory Guided Research in Educational Administration: A Smoggy View from the Valley," *Teachers College Record* 75 (September 1973), 55-66.

13. Andrew W. Halpin, "A Foggy View from Olympus," *Journal of Educational Administration* (May 1969), 3-18; republished in William G. Walker, A. R. Crane, and A. Ross Thomas (eds.), *Explorations in Educational Administration* (St. Lucia: University of Queensland Press, 1973), 377-390; "Administrative Theory: The Fumbled Torch," in Arthur M. Kroll, *Issues in American Education* (New York: Oxford University Press, 1970), 156-183. Although both these papers were presented in 1967, they experienced a "publication lag."

14. Iannaccone, "Interdisciplinary Theory Guided Research"; Campbell and Newell, *Study of Professors*; Roald F. Campbell, "Educational Administration—A Twenty-Five Year Perspective," *Educational Administration Quarterly* 8 (Spring 1972), 1-15; William S. Walker, "Theory and Practice in Educational Administration: 1973," *Studies in Educational Administration* 1, Commonwealth Council for Educational Administration, a paper presented on August 27, 1973, at a regional conference of the Administration held at Suva, Fiji; Halpin, "Foggy View from Olympus"; "Administrative Theory: The Fumbled Torch."

15. Jacob W. Getzels, "A Psycho-Sociological Framework for the Study of Educational Administration," *Harvard Educational Review* 22 (Fall 1952), 235-246.

16. Griffiths, *Administrative Theory*. Furthermore, soon afterward Griffiths collaborated with John K. Hemphill and Norman Fredericksen in producing one of the more outstanding research studies in the field of educational administration, *Administrative Performance and Personality* (New York: Bureau of Publications, Teachers College, Columbia University, 1962).

17. At Catatonic State University, for instance, the colleagues of "the token scholar," when they seek assistance for one of their doctoral students in preparing his dissertation, seldom invite the scholar in at the take-off of the flight but always during the crash landing. Typically, the student gaily gathers his data first and then later presents them to the "consultant" as "a basket case" and queries, "What should I do with them now?" The consultant must at this juncture show great restraint in not replying with a succinct but vulgar suggestion.

18. Andrew W. Halpin, "The Development of Theory in Educational Administration," in Halpin (ed.), *Administrative Theory in Education*, 1-19. This same chapter also appears as Chapter 1 in Andrew W. Halpin, *Theory and Research in Administration* (New York: Macmillan, 1966).

19. Andrew W. Halpin, *The Leadership Behavior of School Superintendents* (Columbus, Ohio: Ohio State University, 1956); republished by the Midwest Administration Center, University of Chicago, 1959.

20. Jacob W. Getzels and Egon G. Guba, "Social Behavior and the Administrative Process," *School Review* 45 (Winter 1957), 423-441.

21. Jacob W. Getzels, James W. Lipham, and Roald F. Campbell, *Educational Administration as a Social Process* (New York: Harper and Row, 1968).

22. John K. Hemphill, Daniel E. Griffiths, and Norman Fredericksen, *Administrative Performance and Personality* (New York: Bureau of Publications, Teachers College, Columbia University, 1962).

23. Richard O. Carlson, *Executive Succession and Organizational Change* (Chicago: Midwest Administration Center, University of Chicago, 1962).

24. Andrew W. Halpin and Don B. Croft, *The Organizational Climate of Schools* (Chicago: Midwest Administration Center, University of Chicago, 1963); the original monograph is out of print, but an only slightly abridged version of this report appears as Chapter IV in Andrew W. Halpin, *Theory and Research in Administration* (New York: Macmillan, 1966).

25. Andrew W. Halpin, "Change and Organizational Climate," *Ontario Journal of Educational Research* 8 (Spring 1966), 229-248; republished in *Journal of Educational Administration* 5 (May 1967), 5-25.

26. Daniel J. Boorstin, *The Image: A Guide to Pseudo-Events in America* (New York: Atheneum, 1971). This book was originally published in 1962 under the title, *The Image*, or *What Happened to the American Dream?*

27. Halpin (ed.), *Administrative Theory in Education*, 13-15.

28. Andrew W. Halpin, "A Paradigm for Research on Administrator Behavior," in Roald F. Campbell and Russell T. Gregg (eds.), *Administrative Behavior in Education* (New York: Harper and Brothers, 1957), 155-199. This

same chapter is republished as Chapter II in Halpin, *Theory and Research in Administration*, 22-77.

29. Hemphill, Griffiths, and Fredericksen, *Administrative Performance*.

30. John K. Hemphill, "Administration as Problem Solving," in Halpin (ed.), *Administrative Theory*, 89-118.

31. It is worth noting that the titles of Griffiths's two 1959 monographs refer respectively to the two facets that we have discussed here.

32. Andrew E. Hayes, "A Reappraisal of the Halpin-Croft Model of the Organizational Climate of Schools," an unpublished paper that was presented during the annual meeting of the American Educational Research Association, New Orleans, 1973. In that paper, Hayes demonstrates a pattern of responses by teachers in unionized schools that is markedly different from those of teachers in nonunionized schools.

33. Iannaccone, "Interdisciplinary Theory Guided Research"; Campbell, "Educational Administration—A Twenty-Five Year Perspective."

34. Robert Nisbet, "Rousseau and Equality," *Encounter* 43 (September 1974), 40-51. This is an especially cogent analysis, with particular pertinence for education in the U.S. today.

35. Andrew W. Halpin, "Change: The Mythology," *Theory into Practice* 8 (February 1969), 3-10; republished in William G. Monahan (ed.), *Theoretical Dimensions of Educational Administration* (New York: Macmillan, 1975), 459-472.

36. Iannaccone, "Interdisciplinary Theory Guided Research," 61, italics added.

37. Robert Nisbet, *The Degradation of the Academic Dogma: The University in America, 1945-1970* (New York: Basic Books, 1971); Adam Ulam, *The Fall of the American University* (LaSalle, Ill.: Library Press, 1973).

38. Richard I. Miller, *The Seat of the Heat: The Big City Superintendency* (Dayton, Ohio: Mead Corp, 1970), 38. This is a report of a conference held in Jamaica in October 1969 and sponsored by the Mead Educational Services Division of the Mead Corporation.

39. Campbell and Newell, *Study of Professors*, 49, 133, 140.

40. Especially at this present time of inflation and budget cuts in our universities, this failure to differentiate roles is likely to become increasingly costly to professors of educational administration in the development of their careers. For example, as university tenure and promotion policies become tighter, the locus of decision on such matters is being steadily shifted to the top echelon of university administration and to committees throughout the university appointed by the top administrators. The "rules of the game" among such administrators and senior professors from other than professional colleges are startlingly different from the rules as wistfully perceived by those professors of education who have difficulty in differentiating their own role from that of practitioners in the field. In the experience of one of the present authors, who worked for several years with the provost and with committees throughout the campus, one of the more scathing comments about professors of education heard over and over again was, "He doesn't understand the meaning of a university." And it is regret-

table that in most instances the victim was incapable of understanding the meaning of this indictment.

41. Campbell and Newell, *Study of Professors*, 140.

42. Daniel E. Griffiths, "Theory in Educational Administration: 1966," in George Baron, Dan H. Cooper, and William G. Walker (eds.), *Educational Administrations: International Perspectives* (Chicago: Rand McNally, 1969), 154-166.

43. Iannaccone, "Interdisciplinary Theory Guided Research," 65.

44. Emil Haller, letter to Roald F. Campbell, quoted in Campbell, "Educational Administration," 10.

45. Ralph M. Stogdill and Alvin E. Coons (eds.), *Leader Behavior: Its Description and Measurement* (Columbus, Ohio: Bureau of Business Research, Ohio State University, 1957); Raymond B. Cattell, *Personality and Motivation: Structure and Measurement* (Yonkers, New York: World Book Co., 1957); Fred E. Fiedler, *A Theory of Leadership Effectiveness* (New York: McGraw-Hill, 1967); Donald J. Willower and R. G. Jones, "When Pupil Control Becomes an Institutional Theme," *Phi Delta Kappan* (November 1963); P. C. Smith, L. M. Kendall, and C. L. Hulin, *The Measurement of Satisfaction in Work and Retirement* (Chicago: Rand McNally, 1969).

46. Alan F. Brown and John H. House, "The Organizational Component in Education," *Review of Educational Research* 37 (October 1967), 399-416. Note especially the remarks on p. 401.

47. Egon G. Guba and Jacob W. Getzels, "Personality and Teacher Effectiveness," *Journal of Educational Psychology* 46 (April 1955), 330-343.

48. For example, few users of the OCDQ bothered to pick up any of the suggestions that Halpin had made in respect to future research in this area. See Halpin, *Theory and Research in Education*. Compare especially pp. 227-232.

49. Campbell and Newell, *Study of Professors*, 138.

50. C. West Churchman, *Challenge to Reason* (New York: McGraw-Hill, 1968), 26, 29.

51. Campbell, "Educational Administration: A Twenty-Five Year Perspective," 11.

52. Frank K. Gibson and Clyde E. Teasley, "The Humanistic Model of Organizational Motivation: A Review of Research Support," *Public Administration Review* 32 (January and February 1973), 89-96.

53. Campbell, "Educational Administration: A Twenty-Five Year Perspective," 11.

54. Roy E. Harkin, "Educational Administration and the Humanities," *High School Journal* 55 (January 1972), 139-150, esp. 146.

55. Iannaccone, "Interdisciplinary Theory Guided Research," 58.

56. Indeed, it is this very point that accounts for the difference between the optimistic view about the impact of "the theory movement" expressed by Getzels in chapter 1 of the present book and the rather pessimistic view of that impact that has been offered by the present authors. Getzels is correct in stating that the number of references to theory, and to particular research concepts, that appear in current textbooks far exceeds the number of such references in

the textbooks of only a decade ago. The critical question is whether this increase in the number of references reflects much more than a form of "professional name-dropping." The authors of textbooks, often with a little nudging from their publishers, tend to go along with the "in thing"—in this case, paying obeisance to "theory"—in much the same fashion as the Leonard Bernsteins, and others among the beautiful people, tend to go along with whatever is perceived as the radical chic of the moment.

57. Charles Perrow, *Organizational Analysis: A Sociological View* (Belmont, Calif.: Brooks/Cole, 1970); John Seiler, *Systems Analysis in Organizational Behavior* (Homewood, Illinois: Irwin, 1967); Arnold S. Tannenbaum, *Social Psychology of the Work Organization* (Monterey, Calif.: Brooks/Cole, 1966).

58. Iannaccone, "Interdisciplinary Theory Guided Research," has described the products of the early phase of the theory movement as pseudo-theory and maintains that our field is not yet ready for analytical theory. Moreover, he urges us to make greater use of the case method, and the participant observation method in our research. One may grant that these methods can be useful in generating fresh hypotheses, but the methods, by themselves, cannot provide a dependable way of testing empirically the tenability of these same hypotheses. In short, information secured through these two methods cannot be dependably generalized. Indeed this was the rock on which the research efforts of the Harvard Business School foundered. The contributions of Elton Mayo, L. J. Roethlisberger, and their colleagues were exciting and creative, but the greater part of their contributions remained as hypotheses not as generalizations whose dependability has been demonstrated. The Harvard School of Education picked up the case-study method that had been emphasized by the Harvard School of Business. But the pursuit of the case-study method by the School of Education led this group further and further away from a strong research thrust that would permit the empirical verification of the various hypotheses that had been promulgated. The path that followed resembled that taken by Freudian psychoanalysts who persistently refused to let their hypotheses be tested in the crucible of empirical verification. The "human relations" approach so popular at Harvard and the Freudian approach have one feature in common; they both rely heavily upon faith. (See Gibson and Teasley, "Humanistic Model.") Accordingly, the present authors view Iannaccone's suggestion as another Lorelei song—seductive, but also inviting shipwreck. If we should choose to follow this path we will waste precious years in another diversion.

59. Georg Rasch, *Probabilistic Models for Some Intelligence and Attainment Tests* (Copenhagen: Danish Institute for Educational Research, 1960).

60. Churchman, *Challenge to Reason*, 28.

61. Campbell and Newell, *Study of Professors*, 147.

62. Here we are also reminded of a popular maxim among Spaniards. "Spain is a country where everything is possible but nothing probable."

63. How many times must we persist in the expression of hopeless hope. Campbell and Newell (*Study of Professors*, 149) suggest that at least half the institutions of higher education ought to discontinue their meager programs in

educational administration "and that the remaining institutions should not only continue their work in this field but most of them should strengthen their programs, often very substantially." They continue: "Educational Administration needs what the Flexner report provided for medicine in 1910." This is, of course, true, but one of the present authors can remember when both Roald F. Campbell and he had made the identical observation twenty years ago. Nor were we alone. Yet who listened? Likewise, the pleas for higher standards in graduate programs in educational administration also went unheeded. And so, when any of us make similar entreaties today, even as the present authors have just outlined eleven ways in which the theory movement could be revitalized, we must appraise with cold objectivity the likelihood that anyone will listen, and, what is more, will act upon such suggestions.

64. A forceful, recent example can be found in the way that Americans were beguiled for several years by Mr. Nixon's and Dr. Kissinger's assessment of the U.S. "success" in Vietnam and Cambodia; we believed because we *wanted* to believe. For a related discussion, see Andrew W. Halpin, "Change: The Mythology," *Theory into Practice* 8 (February 1969), 6-10.

13. The Study of Educational Administration, 1954-1974

GLENN L. IMMEGART

Research or inquiry in educational administration has been the subject of a number of assessments since the benchmark events that substantially redirected the activities of professors in this field in the early and middle 1950s.[1] The purpose of this investigation into research activity is to build upon existing assessments of inquiry in educational administration; to extend, update, and refine what we know about research in educational administration; and to attempt to ascertain differences in the state of scholarship and inquiry in 1974 as compared to 1954, as well as trends over this period. Finally, prospects for the future are derived in the light of the analysis of the past twenty years.

Research is defined for purposes of this assessment as any systematic process of investigation engaged in for the purpose of generating knowledge.[2] Scholarship is defined as the broad, effective, and convincing use of evidence or research in *published* writings, and is used in the basic sense of "extensive knowledge" and the use of it as opposed to conjecture or the use of hearsay or opinion. Educational administration is defined as the organization, direction, control, and management of all matters pertaining to the operation of education or an educational organization. The "study of educational administration" is defined by the linking of this definition and the definition of research; it includes inquiry and research by those in the field and by others from other professions or disciplines. It does *not* mean, however, all inquiry that focuses on educational administrators or uses them as subjects or all inquiry conducted by professors of, or graduate students in, this professional field.

The primary intent of this investigation into inquiry and scholarship in educational administration is not to assess the research in an evaluative or qualitative manner or to assess the adequacy of such research.[3] Rather, data were sought in order to ascertain what was being done and what has happened in the field with respect to research in a quantitative and trend sense over the period from 1954 to 1974. The focus is on the field as a whole and not on its subspecializations as such. It must be pointed out, then, that what is true for the field as a whole may not be so for some of the subspecializations of the field.

The assessment involves analyses of scholarship and research activity as revealed in published research reports, journals, and textbooks during the period from 1954 to 1974. In addition, research activity in educational administration is assessed by means of analyzing such miscellaneous sources as association programs and conferences; reports of centers, groups, and agencies; and from other source books in education and educational administration.

Published Research

The first and basic aspect of this assessment of research activity in educational administration is the analysis of published studies. In this section, findings about research for the period from 1954 to 1974 are presented, with quantity of studies, the focus of inquiry, methodologies used, the state of research in 1954 and 1974, and trends over the period considered in that order. The analysis deals with dissertation research and published studies of professors and researchers in, and external to, educational administration.[4]

Quantity of Studies

Three sources (the 1950 *Encyclopedia of Educational Research,* which predates the period but which was certainly a basic research reference in 1954; Hollis Moore's report of the output of the

Cooperative Program in Educational Administration (CPEA) centers;[5] and issues of the *Review of Educational Research*) give some indication of the volume of published research in educational administration at the outset of the period from 1954 to 1974. However, these sources all involve cumulative collections of studies (do not reflect research volume for a given year), overlap (that is, some studies are reported more than once in or across the sources), and include citations that are not research as operationally defined above. With that in mind, the 1950 *Encyclopedia* included 1,256 citations on topics related to educational administration, of which 288 (or 22 percent) were studies. Moore's report on CPEA center activity listed 239 publications of which forty-seven (or 20 percent) were research. The 1955 issues of the *Review of Educational Research* on the topics of "teacher personnel administration" and "educational organization, administration, and finance" included 971 citations of which 277 (or 28 percent) were studies. Realizing that the 612 studies identified represent a cumulative listing (some dating back to the 1930s or before), that some studies are mentioned more than once in the sources, and that some dissertations are included in listings, it can be estimated that the volume of published (nondissertation) research per year at the outset of the period from 1954 to 1974 was approximately sixty (give or take five) studies per year.

With regard to dissertation research, estimation was easier but still not precise. Using *Dissertation Abstracts* and the Phi Delta Kappa (PDK) *Research Studies in Education* (which overlap and neither of which includes everything), the volume of dissertations in educational administration for 1954 was probably in excess of 250 studies. *Dissertation Abstracts* revealed 236 studies from fifty-two institutions and the other source listed 248 studies. On this basis it can be estimated that over 250 dissertations were completed in educational administration during this year.

In total, taking the yearly rate of dissertations of 250(+) and the published study yearly rate of sixty (±five), the volume of research in educational administration at this time (1954) was approximately 310 studies per year.

For the middle of the period (1964), analysis reveals that, of the 1,537 citations on topics related to educational administration in the 1959 *Encyclopedia*, 455 (or 29 percent) were research. The relevant issues of the *Review of Educational Research* included 781 citations of which 221 (or 28 percent) were studies. It must again be remembered that these are cumulative listings, have some overlap, and include dissertations. Further, the Cooperative Research Program (CRP) of the U.S. Office of Education supported 11 studies in educational administration in 1964 (a total of forty-seven over the period 1957 through 1964)[6] and the new Center for the Advanced Study of Educational Administration (CASEA) at the University of Oregon had published one study. Other studies were, however, being published more frequently in journals and in monograph or book form.[7] Taking all of this into account, the yearly rate of published (non-dissertation) research midway between 1954 and 1974 was probably in the order of seventy (±five) studies per year.

Dissertations completed in 1964 numbered 456 from seventy-nine institutions according to *Dissertation Abstracts,* and only 288 were listed in the PDK *Research Studies in Education.* (The latter figure is obviously "low" and can be explained only by the policies or procedures of that collection at the time.) Robbins and Williams[8] reported that 488 dissertations were completed during the 1963-1964 academic year. This latter figure appears to be an accurate estimate since *Dissertation Abstracts* does not list studies from all universities.

In sum, the yearly rate of output from research at mid-period (1964) was approximately 558 (488 + seventy±five) studies per year. This represents an 80 percent increase in output over the first ten years of the period from 1954 to 1974, mostly attributable to an increased quantity of dissertations.

It is unfortunate that the study was made too close to 1974 to have the best data for all purposes of analysis; hence, where 1974 data were not available, the most recent available data were used. With regard to published (nondissertation) research, the 1969 *Encyclopedia* revealed 2,057 citations on topics related to educational administration, of which 728 (or 35 percent) were studies. Because the *Review of Educational Research* stopped its topical review policy in 1967 and because of the advent of *Educational Administration Abstracts* from the University Council for Educational Administration (UCEA), the latter was used for the end of the period. The *Abstracts* represent a better source of data in that it is not internally duplicative and provides a broader, interdisciplinary coverage of journals and reported research. Over the period from 1967 to 1974 the

Abstracts listed 5,456 abstracts of which 1,596 (or 29 percent) were of studies or research as defined above. Analysis revealed an uneven proportion of research in the *Abstracts* over its nine years of existence, and hence taking the fraction, one-ninth of 1,596, is probably a more accurate estimate of recent yearly output than the 1974 figures per se. Thus, for the current rate of research, 177 studies would appear to be a justifiable yearly rate based on the research abstracted in this source. In addition, other studies were variously reported, including fifteen studies published over the period from 1965 to 1974 by CASEA at the University of Oregon. Considering necessary adjustments as in all of the above calculations, the current rate of output of published (nondissertation) studies is approximately 198(±) studies per year.

Dissertations completed in 1972 (latest available data), according to analysis of *Dissertation Abstracts*, numbered 796 from 101 universities. PDK *Research Studies in Education* for 1970 listed 970 studies. And, it must be noted, opinion differs on the current volume of dissertations. Knezevich's analysis[9] indicated a continually growing number of dissertations in educational administration into the 1970s. Haller,[10] on the basis of his work, projected a downward trend in numbers of dissertations from the approximate peak of 1,041 as reported by Campbell and Newell[11] for 1969-1970. Analysis supported the latter view and, when adjusted, the current yearly rate of output is estimated to be between 800 and 850 per year.

Thus, the yearly rate of research at the end of the 1954-1974 period was in the range of 998 to 1,048 researches per year. The 1974 output represents an increase of 79 percent over the 1964 output and an increase of 222 percent over the output at the beginning of the 1954-1974 period.

It should be noted that these conclusions on research output are conservative in comparison with other estimations.[12] However, given the data on professorial time commitment to research and scholarly writing as revealed by Hills and the Campbell and Newell study,[13] these totals seem more realistic than do earlier estimates and other projections. There has been an increase in numbers of studies, but analysis indicated neither the volume, nor its increase, was of the magnitude commonly thought. These data further support Griffiths's early contention that most of the research on educational administration is done by graduate students and, to a lesser extent, those from other fields and disciplines.[14] Professors of educational administration appear to contribute but a minor amount to the total number of studies on a yearly basis or cumulatively.

Focus of Inquiry

In analyzing studies which resulted in the above findings on volume or quantity, research focus was also determined according to a classification scheme based on that used in *Educational Administration Abstracts*. From this analysis it was concluded that dissertation and professorial research in 1954 was primarily concerned with a focus upon "task areas." Most popular with dissertation researchers were studies on curriculum or instruction, pupil personnel, staff personnel, finance, legal responsibilities, and "general administration." For professors and other researchers, studies on finance, pupil personnel, staff personnel, school plant and services, school-community relations, supervision and evaluation, and educational organization were most popular, with studies on communication, morale or climate, and administrative positions or behavior beginning to emerge.

In 1964 the dissertations classified were spread more evenly over the scheme of classification, with studies focused on tasks still being most frequent and with very few attempts to focus inquiry on matters related to societal influences. Dissertation researchers at this time continued to concern themselves with the task areas of finance, pupil personnel, staff relations, and "general administration" but, in addition, emphasized educational organization; administrative role, behavior, position, and effectiveness; supervising and evaluating; and decision making. Dissertation researchers also began to show some concern for morale or climate and educational policy. At this time professorial research continued to focus primarily on task areas, with finance and staff personnel as the most emphasized areas of content. Professorial research began to give more attention to societal factors (most particularly social class structure and mobility), negotiating, legal responsibilities, and administrative behavior and position or role. Although professorial research was still clearly heaviest in task areas in general at this time, studies were somewhat evenly distributed within this category and through the classification scheme (in general) with the exception of the emphases noted above.

At the end of the 1954-1974 period, dissertations continued most often to focus on task areas but revealed a growing concern for societal factors, particularly minority group relations. Most popular at this time with dissertation researchers were administrative behavior, role, position, and effectiveness; staff personnel; educational organization; and morale or climate. Less interest was exhibited for finance and pupil personnel; and change, negotiations, decision making, political aspects of administration, and school boards or governance received increased attention. Professorial research continued to maintain a basic focus on task areas, with most emphasis in this regard on staff and pupil personnel. Administrative behavior remained an important area, and interest increased with respect to societal factors (most particularly minority group relations and social class structure and mobility) and functions of administration (most notably morale or climate, decision making, supervising and evaluating, organizing, changing, and communicating).

In conclusion, from all of the analysis, research in educational administration has maintained a "practical" emphasis, and throughout the 1954-1974 period (although less so at the end of the period) a focus on task areas predominated. There was evidence that focus for dissertations took its cues for changes in direction from shifts in professorial research, and that both (professorial and dissertation research) shifted emphasis in terms of social concerns or problems and presses in the field (e.g., negotiations or minority group relations). Overall, the matters of staff personnel and "general administration" have received considerable attention, with administrative position and behavior, finance, pupil personnel, and educational organization receiving a bit less attention. Interest in curriculum or research oriented toward instruction in an administrative sense has waned over the period, and studies focused on administrative functions (negotiating, decision making, building morale or climate, and changing) are increasing.

Methodology

Analysis of the methodology of studies in educational administration for the period from 1954 to 1974 was necessarily restricted. In this regard, the type of analysis used to ascertain the quantity and focus of studies was not adequate for assessing methodology. For an assessment of methodology one cannot work with titles, and most abstracts are inadequate for even a general scrutiny of research methodology. Hence, one must deal with studies as such, or at least abstracts adequate for ascertaining methodology. The approach used in order to assess methodology was, therefore, to obtain a general feeling for methods of inquiry for the period from analyses directed toward other purposes, drawing on other studies of methodology, and analyzing the studies reported in *Educational Administration Quarterly* and *Journal of Educational Administration.*

Methodology at the outset of the period (1954) was readily established. The researches of Bretsch and Haller[15] were most helpful relative to dissertation research. The former provided data on the methodology of dissertations at the beginning of the period, and the latter provided data for the period from 1960 to 1966. The published studies analyzed from the two journals covered the period from 1963 to 1974 and because of the source may well be more "selective" than representative. In any event, the evidence on methodology of studies was selective and at best indicative, particularly with respect to the latter years of the period.

At the outset of the 1954-1974 period, research meant one of two things: either the search activity that went into developing a textbook or an elemental analysis of data. In the former sense, it involved searching out and reporting opinion, ideas, and practices as well as extant demographic or statistical data on schools, schooling, or the education profession in textbook form. In the second sense, research meant searching out or generating data and descriptively analyzing these data. Thus, research or investigation in this sense was typically of two types: the status study and the survey (or descriptive study). With the status study, the researcher utilized documents or existing data, but he also did some analysis and associating (or correlation) of data. In the survey (or descriptive study), the researcher typically queried respondents via questionnaire, or less frequently by interview, and then collated and analyzed the responses. Given the state of the field in 1954 these were legitimate research or investigative activities. Nonetheless, discontent with the prevailing concepts of inquiry was being voiced, and the need for more rigorous research methodology was beginning to be suggested. The success stories and reports of exemplary experiences or ideas (no matter how analytically done) referred to by some at the time as "research" are not justifiable as inquiry, although many school surveys (used for practical purposes) and case studies (used largely for instructional purposes) employing sound investigative procedures were developed at this time. In fact, right after 1954, one of the first additions to the repertoire of the researcher in educational administration was use of the case study as a research methodology.

Dissertation research at the outset of the 1954-1974 period was studied by Bretsch and, although his investigation included studies done only at four universities, there is little reason or evidence to suspect that his data or findings were atypical. Bretsch[16] found that dissertations were limited in general significance and were directed toward the solution of practical problems. He found that, with few exceptions, the studies were of the descriptive type and most did not test hypotheses. None of the studies were experimental, and most of the studies of relationship were "those in which associational relationships were established." Few studies extended earlier research or attempted to test or validate previous inquiry. Some were identified which "pioneered" new areas or new approaches and were of "high" quality. Interestingly, the more rigorous dissertation researchers were most "cautious" in setting forth their conclusions.

In his study of dissertations, Haller[17] found that for the 1960-1966 period most dissertations (an estimated 80 percent) were still based primarily on survey data. The modal data generation procedure was clearly the questionnaire or checklist prepared by students. Only a modest but increasing number of dissertations were experimental (0 to 4.3 percent) and a modest but decreasing number used observations (4.1 to 0 percent) over the period. Further, Haller found that from 85 to 90 percent of the studies sampled were cross-sectional ("snapshots") in terms of time perspective, and the remainder were roughly divided between longitudinal and historical time perspectives. In terms of types of analyses of data in dissertations, he found dissertations shifting from a descriptive (66.7 percent) mode in 1960 to an explanatory (71.2 percent) mode in 1966. Of the explanatory studies in 1966, 78 percent of these used bivariate (two variable) analyses and 22 percent employed multivariate (multiple variable) analyses. The latter increased from 0 in 1960 to over 22 percent (or 15.6 percent for the total number of studies) for each of the last two years of the period. Finally, Haller found that between 85 and 90 percent of the studies in his sample made no attempt to control experimentally or statistically for the effects of variables that might affect results. Thus, by 1966, the typical dissertation employed survey data, was cross-sectional in time perspective, used an explanatory analysis, and had no controls.

In the analysis of the research reported in the *Quarterly* (1955-1974) and the *Journal* (1963-1974) much the same picture was revealed.[18] Studies were preponderantly descriptive or correlational in design (82 percent), used survey data (82 percent), were cross-sectional in time perspective (88 percent), and employed few controls beyond selection of subjects (7 percent) or in statistical analysis (5 percent). Research in the *Quarterly* used explanatory analyses (58 percent) more than descriptive ones (42 percent), and bivariate and multivariate analyses were about equally utilized; in the *Journal* explanatory analyses were used mostly in those studies reported since 1970, with descriptive analyses used mostly prior to 1970, and bivariate and multivariate analyses about equally employed since that time. Research in the *Journal* was, with four exceptions, "nonfunded" while two-fifths of the nondissertation studies reported in the *Quarterly* were funded.

These findings, though indicative and incomplete, do reveal that the concept of research in educational administration has changed since 1954 but not so dramatically or pervasively as is commonly thought. From the data examined and analyzed it can be concluded that instrumentation has been refined (or, we are getting better survey data) and that more rigorous analyses (bi- and multivariate correlational approaches) are being employed. However, study designs, data generation, time perspective, and lack of controls limit investigative effort and research quality. At least the status study in a nonanalytical sense appears to have dropped away and textbook writing is no longer construed as a major aspect of "research" activity as was the case in 1954. Nevertheless, preoccupation with instrumentation or procedures of analysis has a limited potential for substantively improving inquiry, and it is also quite possible that sophisticated procedures of analysis are being improperly employed. Thrusts for rigor and sophistication in inquiry have, in fact, been limited over the period from 1954 to 1974, and their effects need to be assessed in a qualitative sense. Movement toward "science" or rigor in the methodology of inquiry more broadly conceived has, therefore, been modest as might be expected with the prevailing professorial commitment to research.[19] Rather, the period from 1954 to

1974 was a time of testing and of limited refinement for research methodology.

The State of Inquiry in 1954 and 1974

In 1954 the state of the study of educational administration was at a pre- or early-scientific level. Research in the field consisted of either writing a textbook or doing a status study (usually non-analytical) or descriptive survey. Professorial activity was devoted to all of these aspects of "research" and dissertation investigators were limited to status studies or surveys. Output of researches for the 1954 year was 310 studies of which 250 (±five) were doctoral dissertations. Studies typically sought to ascertain "states of affairs," to assess "new or emerging practices," or to link or associate (in a non-statistical sense) variables such as school size and personnel practices. Analysis in studies was restricted, and researchers were more interested in description than in explanation. Concern was basically in terms of task areas and the practice of educational administration.

The state of the study of educational administration in 1974 revealed a number of changes. First, research was now defined, if not always operationalized, as it was for purposes of this investigation. Research output had increased to approximately 998 to 1,048 studies per year of which 800 to 850 were dissertations. Researchers from other fields and disciplines were increasingly researching in the field, and researchers (dissertation and professorial) in educational administration had borrowed methodologies, procedures, and concepts from other arenas to facilitate investigation in the field. Studies in 1974 focused on a broad range of topics, although task areas were still popular, and certain areas such as school finance, administrative behavior, politics of education, and administrative functions had become well defined and reasonably productive areas of inquiry. Researchers were employing a variety of methodological approaches at the end of the 1954-1974 period, but most significant was the increase in sophistication in using instruments (for data collection) and a shift to explanatory (bivariate and multivariate) as opposed to purely descriptive analyses. The "typical" study was hard to identify at this time, but following a modest shift at mid-period toward empirical or "pure" research, concern in inquiry remained for "practical relevance" or empirical validation.

Trends Over the Period

From this analysis of inquiry in educational administration from 1954 to 1974, the following trends have been identified:

1. There was a shift in the field's conception of "scholarship" toward that of increasing use of the products of empirical investigation and activity.

2. The volume of studies in educational administration (in terms of yearly output) increased.

3. The period witnessed increased efforts to publish and disseminate research.

4. The doctoral dissertation was "discovered" and was increasingly viewed as an important element in inquiry in the field.

5. There was mounting interest in the study of educational administration by those from other fields and disciplines but "interdisciplinary" activity was limited to particular areas or was realized in selected and isolated subspecializations.

6. Studies of educational administration over the period from 1954 to 1974 reveal both an increasing testing of a variety of methodologies and exploration of a broader range of topics or concerns as well as bias toward methodology and content (or study focus).

7. Inquiry in the field evidenced a preoccupation on the part of researchers with the refinement of instruments for collecting data and procedures for analyzing data.

8. Despite a brief tendency at mid-period for some researchers to shift to a modest concern for "pure" or empirical research, researchers in the field have maintained a basic concern for practical relevancy and empirical validation.

Journals, Textbooks, and Association Efforts

The assessment of the use of research and scholarship in the journal literature was selective because of the volume of material covered over a twenty-year period by any particular journal and because of the extensive periodical literature with relevance for educational administration. Leads for journal selection (in terms of what professors read) were taken from the Campbell and Newell study,[20] but the selection of journals was, in the end, arbitrary. Analysis of the use of research and scholarship in journals involved three basic kinds of publications: journals in educational administration, general education journals, and journals from related fields and disciplines.[21]

Beginning with the institutionalized journals or organs in educational administration as such, *The Administrator's Notebook* was, from its inception, devoted to interpreting significant research for the practicing administrator. From 1952-1953 through 1972-1973 the *Notebook* contained 190 articles of which 43 percent were research reports. Of the 190 articles, some 40 percent over the period were concerned with task areas emphasizing matters of school-community relations, staff personnel, curriculum and instruction, and pupil personnel. From analysis and classification, it was determined that general topics were next most frequent (24 percent) and included writings focused on general administration, school boards, teachers, policy, and educational organization. Early in the 1954-1974 period administrative position, effectiveness, and behavior received some emphasis, while later in the period administrative functions (supervising and evaluating, decision making, and goal setting or planning) represented growing concerns. Only minimal direct treatment over the years was given to articles on societal factors as such. Most of the studies reported were doctoral dissertations done at the University of Chicago's Midwest Administration Center.

Toward the middle of the 1954-1974 period, two scholarly journals were begun (the *Journal of Educational Administration* in 1963, the *Educational Administration Quarterly* in 1965). Prior to this time the periodical literature in educational administration was limited to "practitioner" publications, and these typically devoted little space to research or scholarly writing as defined here. Both of these scholarly journals publish a small number of articles per year, usually ranging from eight to sixteen plus reviews, although in 1973 the *Journal* expanded to twenty-four articles. Because of this, topical coverage as revealed by classification was restricted, had many gaps, and was limited by "themes" and some degree of author-subject bias in both of the periodicals. Over the period of its existence the *Journal* has tended to emphasize general topics such as "general administration" and administrative functions such as supervising or evaluating, goal setting or planning, and initiating change. Some emphasis on preparation programs for administrators and a growing importance of research were noted with the *Journal*. Over the period some 40 percent of the articles were research reports and over one-half of all studies reported in the *Journal* appeared in the 1970 issues and those that followed. The *Quarterly,* with a relatively uniform yearly quantity of articles (thirteen to sixteen per year), tended to give more emphasis to finance, staff personnel, decision making, educational organization, general administration, preparation programs for educational administrators, and the politics of education. Approximately 50 percent of the articles in the *Quarterly* were studies, and the 1973 issues contained over 80 percent research reports. In only two years less than one-third of the articles in the *Quarterly* were reports of studies. The methodology of the research reported in these two sources was discussed above.

Scholarship (as operationally defined here) was revealed in the three educational administration journals examined as was a continual and growing concern for inquiry in the field. Because of the limited volume of articles and research reports in these three organs, coverage of the field as revealed through classification scheme analysis was spotty, and selectivity and a degree of provincialism were characteristics of all of the publications. Analysis also revealed that these journals were somewhat devoid of scholarly criticism or critical dialogue.

In turning to the general education journals, which, according to the Campbell and Newell study, professors of educational administration tend to read (and use?) most, the picture of scholarship changes. The four sources analyzed here gave varying degrees of coverage to the content of educational administration, to educational administration as such, and much less emphasis to studies or research in educational administration. Also, these representative general education journals were "less" scholarly than the educational administration journals in terms of the reporting of research, and all gave emphasis to materials focusing on task areas or "general administration." They were neither sources that reveal much inquiry about educational administration nor sources that, in terms of content, adequately cover the field or deal with new focuses.

Analysis of the selected standard journals from other disciplines and professional fields was assumed to be the best test of whether interdisciplinary activity was taking place and whether inquiry in educational administration was accorded status by those in other disciplines or fields. All of the disciplinary journals analyzed were more scholarly than the general education or educational administration journals in terms of quantity and proportion of research reported. However, none of the issues of these journals sampled contained entries that were "studies in educational administration." This leads to the tentative conclusions that interest in educational administration by other disciplines is at best limited, that inquiry in educational administration is not accorded the status of efforts related to disciplines, and that those from other disciplines who study educational administration tend to report their work in educational administration or "interdisciplinary" journals rather than their standard ones.[22] The issues of the *Public Administration Review* sampled in this analysis revealed only two items (one in 1971 and one in 1972) on educational administration. One of these was a study. This journal, however, was not research oriented (contained only a few studies per year) and appeared to have only recently discovered "educational administration." The *Administrative Science Quarterly*, recognized throughout the 1956-1974 period as the scholarly journal on administration, has included only eighteen articles on educational administration of which eight were reports of studies. Thus, only about 4 percent of the *Administrative Science Quarterly* articles dealt with educational administration.

Although overall journal quality and journal *article* quality[23] and scholarship are uneven, making generalization difficult, it can be concluded that scholarship in educational administration as revealed through the analysis of journals improved during the period from 1954 to 1974. Most helpful has been the establishment and institutionalization of the *Journal* and the *Quarterly* along with the *Administrator's Notebook*. Even though limited in size (number of articles) and in scope, these are more scholarly than the practitioner-oriented periodicals in educational administration or the general education journals.

Analysis of scholarship and the use of research in textbooks for the period from 1954 to 1974 involved an arbitrary sample of twenty-six textbooks.[24] Included in the sample were textbooks of an introductory or general nature and those dealing with the elementary and secondary principalship. Specifically, the following trends were indicated by the analysis of the texts examined:

1. Textbooks revealed a greater variety of thrusts, focuses, "slicings of the pie," degrees of specificity, amount of content, and rela-

tively more reliance on research in 1974 than was true in 1954. Books of readings, reference books, and theme or concept focused sources increased as have books of research and compendiums of research.

2. There was less of a lag in the use of content or knowledge in 1974 (with the exception of books of readings which tend to compound the knowledge usage lag).

3. Many textbook writers shifted from drawing upon other education sources such as texts, reports, and association publications for content in 1954 to drawing more broadly on the literature from a variety of professional fields and disciplines.

4. Most writers shifted from drawing upon opinions, experience, and institutional or status research from districts, associations, state departments, and the U.S.O.E. for content and evidence in 1954 to using concepts and findings from empirical studies of researchers (including dissertation researchers) for content and evidence in 1974.

5. Many writers moved from the almost exclusive use of research from education and psychology for findings in 1954 to the use of research findings from other professional fields and disciplines in 1974.

6. Most writers changed from using basically secondary sources such as library reference books, collections, or compendiums for information in 1954 to the use of primary or original sources of information in 1974.

7. Textbook writers tended to move from a broader citing of sources geographically within education and educational administration in 1954 to a more restricted and selective citing of authors by location and of authors' theses or thrusts across disciplines and fields in 1974.

8. In 1954 some writers shifted from an explicit thrust emphasizing action and practical aspects (problems, lists, "how to") to an empirical, conceptual, theoretical, and/or open-ended perspective linked to applications or field problems and issues in 1974.

9. There was a movement away from practitioner writers and association publication in 1954 to scholar-researcher writers and the private sector publication of texts in 1974.

10. Many texts in 1974 revealed a higher level of sophistication in conceptualization or abstract analysis with respect to the use of models, theory, and research, and in linking the conceptual realm with practice or problems of the real world than was true earlier.

11. There was less agreement in texts in 1974 (than in 1954) on central concepts or on what the content of administration is or ought to be. In this regard, regionalism and specialization were apparent; few authors made efforts to collate or pull things together; scholarship varied internally within the field of educational administration; and subareas or groups tended to function separately with little open debate or dialogue or concern for the total field as such. This appeared to result from differing focuses, disciplinary backgrounds, and values or allegiances of textbook writers.

A number of association or collective efforts had an effect on the study of educational administration over the 1954-1974 period. These will be treated only briefly here since the chapter by Haskew deals with this topic in more detail. What has not happened with respect to association or collective activity is, however, probably as important as what has happened.

From the early impetus for inquiry fostered by the National Conference of Professors of Educational Administration (NCPEA),[25] the American Association of School Administrators (AASA), and the Kellogg Foundation through more structured and formalized group efforts that followed, collective activity has had varying effects on the study of educational administration. The eight CPEA centers provided a base on which to build.[26] In addition, associations like UCEA —through seminars, studies,[27] publications,[28] the *Quarterly,* and the *Abstracts*—or the American Educational Research Association (AERA)—through special interest groups, the *Encyclopedia,* and the *Review of Educational Research,* 1952-1967—have played important roles. Later in the period from 1954 to 1974, CASEA at Oregon through studies, publications, and ERIC efforts[29] and the National Conferences on School Finance contributed positively to inquiry. And, beyond such formal efforts, collective activities of (1) professors with similar interests, (2) the researcher-disciple model, (3) institutional centering on topics or concepts, and (4) sequential studies were all evidenced in the study of educational administration.

Such efforts have the potential for both positive and negative outcomes (and both were observed in educational administration). Not only have such efforts stimulated inquiry, but they have also led to specialization and segmentation.

What has not happened through collective activity should be considered as well. It is unfortunate that analysis did not reveal effort which could truly be viewed as programmatic research; few instances of collating, synthesizing, and analyzing empirical evidence were noted;[30] little in terms of truly interdisciplinary inquiry was observed; and little collective activity was devoted to research in comparison to other concerns in educational administration such as preparation programs or developmental activities. All in all, association and collective activity was revealed as a mixed blessing, but institutionalized mechanisms like the UCEA *Quarterly* or the AERA *Encyclopedia* appear to have had the greatest positive effects.

Conclusions (General Assessment)

The major conclusions of this investigation and assessment of the study of educational administration from 1954 to 1974 are as follows:

1. A twenty-year period of history is indeed a short span of time, particularly for expecting dramatic progress in terms of improvement in the quality of scholarship or inquiry in an emerging field that is basically a field of practice.

2. It is clear that the definition of what comprises educational administration is changing; the conception is broadening and there is less agreement today in this respect than was the case in 1954.

3. The concept of research (as used in educational administration) has changed to a more rigorous and scientific one.

4. Research in educational administration has increased quantitatively, although not so dramatically as many think, and most of this growth was due to increased numbers of researchers (more dissertations completed, increasing outside interest in the field, and more researchers involved in inquiry) as opposed to improved productivity on the part of the researchers.

5. Research in educational administration has improved qualitatively, but again not to the degree hoped for, and this was due to the efforts of a small number of researchers and some of those who entered the professorship during the 1954-1974 period. Some—but not enough—have done exemplary work in inquiry. The field is still far from being research oriented.[31]

6. Scholarship (as operationally defined herein) improved in journals[32] and textbooks over the 1954-1974 period, although generalization in this regard is difficult and misleading. Some writers have

significantly extended scholarship through their research and writings. The literature in the field remains uneven, with many examples of poor scholarship in both the journal and textbook literature.

7. Interest in scientific research appeared to reach a peak at the middle of the period in terms of the kind of studies done and the use of studies in the literature. The early and mid-1960s were when the greatest support of research in terms of funding took place and when most of the important researches were conducted. Volume has increased since then, but the developmental shift in emphasis in funding and activity (a shift to applied empirical evaluation and a desire for payoff) has had an effect on inquiry.[33]

8. The focus or subject of research is expanding in educational administration with more topics, aspects, dynamics, and variables being studied. Nevertheless, a preoccupation with task areas and concern for "practical relevance" prevails in the field. Content is more diverse in textbooks in the field, and there is less agreement on what the content ought to be or how it should be ordered. Other fields and disciplines have had an effect on both the focus of studies and the content in textbooks.

9. Methodological improvements have occurred in inquiry in educational administration, but these have been restricted by bias in terms of concepts, instrumentation, and analysis. A great range of methodologies has been tried from case studies to experiments (even the "novel" approach), but advances in sophistication are most notable in terms of instruments for gathering data and procedures or approaches for analyzing data. More broadly conceived in terms of study design, problem development, time perspective, and "controls," methodological improvement has been less obvious.

10. There is, in fact, little agreement in the field of educational administration with regard to central concepts, theory, or models to guide investigative efforts. Research tends to follow "hot" topics, social concerns, popular concepts, or "practical presses of the time." Gibson has noted the limited use of theory in the field and Brown has focused on the "softness" of theory in scholarly writings (including research) in educational administration.[34] Taking all of the evidence into account, it seems that concepts or ideas that guide research in educational administration are at best derivatives from prior studies (not logical constructs) or from other arenas, when they are employed at all.

11. There are really no significant programmatic efforts in the study of educational administration. Collective activity has assisted inquiry in this field, but it has fallen short relative to important kinds of collective efforts in research such as collation, synthesizing, analyzing, and cumulatively building knowledge or attacking related problems.

12. Substantive dialogue and interaction are conspicuously absent in the published literature on educational administration.

13. The relationship between research and practice was little improved from 1954 to 1974; some evidence indicates the relationship may have deteriorated. Analysis yielded little evidence that research and inquiry have had any substantial impact on practice. Practitioners, and even many professors, do not use the scholarly literature or seek out studies let alone put the findings of investigations to work. Rather, in 1974 there appeared to be two bodies of literature in educational administration—the "scholarly" and the "practical." This could be expected, however, when research follows "presses" in the field and, further, when dissertation research (the volume aspect) takes its topical cues from professorial interests. Evidence or findings may well tend to be after the fact.

14. There has been a growing and pervasive "specialization" and segmentation taking place in the field of educational administration. As the professoriate has grown larger and subgroups have developed strong ties to other fields or disciplines, communication in the field as a whole has become more difficult, and overall identification has weakened. Factional dialogue and special interests have replaced total field dialogue. Few are left to pull together or collate diverse interests. Colleagueship, methodology, and problems all appear to be fragmented by specialization. Dialogue and differences of opinion are conspicuously absent, especially as they take place in the field of educational administration at large.

15. Analysis underscored the fact that support of research activity was critical in getting significant studies done. Organization and focus helped, but resources were essential. The costs of research in terms of man hours or dollars is high in terms of yield when compared with other kinds of activities. Support in this respect includes not only the commitment and efforts of professors and researchers but also institutional arrangements and policy facilitative to inquiry in universities as well as funding from government and foundations.

Beyond these conclusions there arises an important question and at least two needs for further investigation. The question is, simply, to what degree has the universities' push for research and publication caused professorial researchers to carve out delimited specializations and explore easy (and irrelevant) problems in "quick and dirty" ways? Or, put another way, what are the rewards for engaging in rigorous inquiry in educational administration? In addition, it is apparent that a need exists to assess studies in educational administration qualitatively in order to ascertain the adequacy of this body of research.[35] Too much dismay is continually voiced based on impressions; it is time to look at the evidence. Another need is to study the researchers in educational administration. Who are they? What do they do? How were they trained? What facilitates their inquiry? Answers to such questions are obviously related to any effort to maximize research in the field.

In addition to the above conclusions about the study of educational administration from 1954 to 1974 and the questions raised, a number of paradoxes were revealed by the analysis. These are important in any consideration of the present state of inquiry in the field and can be set forth as follows:

1. It is commonly stated that one of the most important characteristics of educational administration after 1954 has been an emphasis on research, yet this was not evidenced either in the analysis of scholarship in the literature or in the research activities of the professoriate. Research is being used more in the writings on educational administration, but even the most scholarly publications in the field do not compare favorably with those from the disciplines in terms of the extent to which research is used. Furthermore, much research is not reported, and the use of research is restricted by provincialism and regional or conceptual biases. Scholars should be more concerned with omissions and the selective use of empirical evidence than they should be impressed with the adequate and effective coverage of relevant inquiry. Early in the period Griffiths pointed out that there was a dearth of researchers in this field and that most research in the field was done by graduate students or outsiders. At the middle of the period Hills found that the "much discussed emphasis on research, at least in terms of professorial research, is more myth than reality."[36] Most recently the Campbell and Newell study[37] revealed that, by the professors' own admission, the mean investment of time

in research *and* scholarly writing is only about 10 percent of a professor's total commitment of time. About one-fifth of the professors of educational administration do no research, and only 8 percent of them spend 30 (or more) percent of their time on research and scholarly writing. Although, according to the Campbell and Newell study, UCEA professors tend on the average to spend close to 20 percent of their time on research and scholarly writing, this finding must be tempered in terms of a research emphasis by the phrase "*and* scholarly writing." There was more research and it was used more in 1974, but whether there was more than a professed emphasis on research can be questioned. At best there was increasing attention to research and a modest reliance on inquiry in writings.

2. We know a great deal more than we did about educational administration, yet we still do not know much about it. From the very volume of research activity in this field between 1954 and 1974 it is clear more is known now than was then. However, given the suspect quality of much research in education and educational administration, the "hit and miss" nature of investigative efforts, and the effect of such research on the literature and practice, it seems that, while we know more, we still do not know very much.

3. Research is important to educational administration, yet no one is willing to support research in this field. Everyone—from practicing administrators to graduate students, professors, and university administrators—extols the value of research in this field. Nevertheless, practitioners make little use of research, tend not to read scholarly publications, and even inhibit researchers wanting to collect data in the field. Graduate students do doctoral studies but seldom attempt other investigations. Professors spend little time on scholarly writing or research, and, according to the Campbell and Newell study, tend not to value the more scholarly publications nor desire to do more research.[38] University administrators use research and scholarly activity as a criterion for academic advancement but, for the most part, do little more than funding agencies or foundations do in fiscally supporting basic research in educational administration. Current indications are blatant that funding prospects for research in this field have all but dried up.

4. Educational administration is a field of study, yet it is only a "field studied." The conclusions here are supported by Boyan's observation that educational administration is more a *site for* inquiry

than a *field of* inquiry.[39] One would expect in a field of study at least some limited ordering of concepts (taxonomy), agreement on the meaning of terms, and concerted and cumulative investigative activity. Given the prevailing lack of agreement on the ordering of knowledge, the absence of programmatic research, the preoccupation with the same problem areas, and the professorial investment of time in research in educational administration, the field at best is one of professional practice and not (yet) a field of study. (Only the work of a few dedicated researchers lends support to the notion that it is a field of study.)

5. Educational administration *is* and *is not* a special field. Despite some valiant efforts to merge the "administrative sciences," there is little to indicate that this has been achieved beyond the confines of a very few university training programs or isolated groups of professors. From this analysis, educational administration journals are devoid of research and scholarship in public or business administration, and the reverse is also the case. Further, within the broad field of education, educational administration is a distinct entity and for all practical purposes "school" and higher education administration remain relatively separate.

6. A more extensive knowledge base is needed in educational administration, yet no one is doing much about it. Professorial interest in research has already been indicated. Association activity and publications have had a mixed effect on empirical activity in the field. In addition, more effort and resources in the 1970s (as opposed to the 1960s) are devoted to the dissemination and use of knowledge than to the production of knowledge or to the improvement of the knowledge base (such as through collation, synthesis, or critical analysis) in educational administration.

Finally, some significant problems that can inhibit progress in the future or that can limit the efforts of researchers in the field were revealed by this analysis. Most of the problems with respect to research in the field noted by Griffiths in his 1959 and 1965 analyses[40] are still with us today. Some have intensified or compounded; few have gone away. These and the problems noted by others[41] need not be restated here. Instead, the list of problems generated in the course of this analysis, which included consideration of the problems noted by others, will be set forth.

1. There is an acute problem in the availability of research in

the field of educational administration. The problem goes beyond dissemination as such, and includes all aspects of recording, publishing, listing, and making available researches. For the most part, only a small proportion of the research in the field is readily available to users, and much of the identifiable research is difficult, if not impossible, to obtain.

2. There is a problem of mounting proportions in terms of judging the quality or adequacy of studies and lines of research. Impressions are rampant, but, as compared to ten or twenty years ago, there are extant procedures for evaluating research reports.[42] Taking current volume into account (even these more conservative estimates), it is time to gauge the quality of studies in educational administration and to identify those studies and lines of inquiry that are indeed suspect.

3. There is a distinct problem in the support of research in educational administration. Researchers and nonresearchers in the field, associations, institutions, and funding sources all must give support to inquiry. Support must be realized in its broadest sense. Most distressing is the decrease in external funding for research in educational administration.

4. It is clear that professors themselves pose problems for inquiry in educational administration. Their training, interests, dispositions, and desires as well as related matters of teaching or entrepreneurial work load, use of time, and rewards are all directly related to improving the study of educational administration.

5. Regionalism, provincialism, and specialization singly and collectively are important problems relative to research activity in educational administration. From this analysis, at least, these matters are intensifying not decreasing.

6. The lack of collation, analysis, and synthesis of studies and findings (with only a few exceptions) makes efficiency in investigation and building on past efforts virtually impossible.

7. Scholarly dialogue and critiquing are glaringly absent from the literature in educational administration. Substantive debate, encounter, and interchange are, however, basic to the pursuit of truth in all areas of the social and behavioral sciences.

8. The obvious lack of agreement on content, theory or constructs, and taxonomy in educational administration was apparent throughout this analysis and will continue to plague researchers. If

the theory movement has indeed fizzled,[43] inquiry will suffer most; taxonomy, or content and content ordering activities, though often viewed as mundane, is no less important.

9. Finally, inquiry or research activity itself presents problems. It is a time-consuming endeavor, is demanding, and seldom offers a neat, tidy, and comfortable arena. The researcher, typically, must thrive on uncertainty and the problems that abound. Not all professors of educational administration can, or should, be researchers, but, for those who are committed to inquiry, ways must be found to direct and support their energies in this activity for the good of the field.

The Future

Prospects for the study of educational administration over the next ten to twenty years, based on this and other analyses, involve at best an "iffy" situation. It appears that empirical activity cannot be "forced" beyond a certain degree. Improvement and sophistication in inquiry may well be a function of natural maturation in a field and, as such, can simply be either fostered or impeded. Such maturation and development may, further, be characteristically uneven—that is, growth may occur in some respects and not in others at a given time, or periods of change may be followed by periods of synthesis and stability.

There is, of course, a need to extend our analysis of inquiry in the field of educational administration. As noted earlier there is too much conjecture in this regard. Investigations such as this one provide certain kinds of evidence as well as the preliminary "counting and definitional" work that precedes more rigorous analysis. More rigorous analyses, comparative studies, and the assessment of studies and lines of research in terms of adequacy, as well as further scrutiny of researchers and the use of research in this professional field, are all needed. Strategies and activity along these lines must foster gains already realized and focus energy and resources toward critical impediments and facilitators of inquiry.

Central to any effort to increase the sophistication and effects of research in educational administration are the matters of funding, professor-researchers, and institutions or institutional settings where the professor-researchers function. In the first respect, fiscal resources are absolutely necessary to do research. Professors, graduate students, and researchers from other areas cannot be expected to engage in significant research on "nickels or dimes" or by "boot-legging" studies on developmental or other projects. If the history of scientific inquiry has collectively revealed anything, it is that research is a costly endeavor and that payoff *is* both delayed and limited especially until the value of inquiry is established. What must be determined is whether a better lobby, more and more competent researchers, time to establish the worth of informed practice, or something else is needed to increase the funding of research in educational administration.

Professor-researchers are also critical in improving inquiry in educational administration. This is not to say that all professors should, or ought to, be researchers. Nevertheless, the field must recognize the limitations of drawing on dissertation research and investigations of those outside the field as basic sources of inquiry for building knowledge about educational administration. Researchers in the professoriate must assume even more responsibility for inquiry in the field than they have in the past. The skills of researchers must also be updated and improved. There is some (but not definitive) indication from the above analysis of research methodology that sophistication in professorial research tends to follow similar advances in sophistication in dissertation research (even though dissertation researchers take "topical" cues from professors). This suggests that as dissertation researchers move into the professorship they bring with them improved skills of inquiry. Better research training programs (preservice and in-service) need to be developed in educational administration in order to improve and update the research skills of professors. And, further, role differentiation[44] in terms of more time and freedom for professor-researchers (less time doing "other" things), beyond the notion of the "funded project," ought to be explored, along with ways to stimulate collegial activity.[45]

Attention must also be given to institutions or the institutional settings[46] in which professors of educational administration work. How much the current institution of higher education inhibits research should be assessed. With declining external support, even modest institutional commitments to inquiry (money for collecting data, computer time, or released time from teaching) are essential, if not for the long term, at least to get over the hump. (Associations and school districts should likewise develop greater commitment in this regard.)

Furthermore, institutions ought to look critically at two other matters: the push for (and way in which professors are asked to seek) funding and the prevailing "publish or perish" syndrome. With the former, not only are professors expected to attract funding for their research externally, but sufficient "overhead" to support the university must also be included. How many studies are not funded because of mounting overhead charges? With the latter, given the tendency to lengthen the time for decisions on tenure in many universities, some might profitably consider tempering the frantic press on young professors to conduct research and publish. Research and scholarship cannot be programmed and perhaps cannot always be fostered under conditions of stress or forced activity. In any event, how much "poor," or less than significant, research results from the pressure to do studies (volume) for purposes of promotion? Do professors under such circumstances select easily handled topics and do "any kind" of research in order to satisfy reward systems at the expense of more important lines of inquiry or scholarship?

Beyond this, other institutional variables and dynamics require scrutiny. What kind of institutional arrangements and staffing patterns facilitate professorial research? What kinds of institutional policy and internal mechanisms of resource allocation are conducive to inquiry? What kinds of support and rewards sustain research and scholarly efforts? What kinds of colleagueship are needed by researchers? Investigative efforts are beginning to be made into these kinds of concerns.[47] But, it is imperative that a better understanding of research activity in the university setting, as well as of the effects of institutional variables on researchers, be achieved.

Regardless of how this investigation or its conclusions are taken, those in educational administration should continually take an interest in, and engage in dialogue about, inquiry in this field. Stocktaking is necessary to increase the effects of research activity, and the lessons of 1954 to 1974 ought to provide a good base on which to build.

Notes

1. Hollis A. Moore, *Studies in School Administration* (Washington, D.C.: American Association of School Administrators, 1957); Daniel E. Griffiths,

Research in Educational Administration (New York: Bureau of Publications, Teachers College, Columbia University, 1959); Daniel E. Griffiths, "Research and Theory in Educational Administration," in W. W. Charters, Jr., *et al.*, *Perspectives on Educational Administration and the Behavioral Sciences* (Eugene, Oregon: Center for the Advanced Study of Educational Administration, 1965), 25-48; Andrew W. Halpin, *Theory and Research in Administration* (New York: Macmillan, 1966); Andrew W. Halpin, "A Foggy View from Olympus," *Journal of Educational Administration* 7:1 (May 1969), 3-18; Emil J. Haller, "The Questionnaire Perspective in Educational Administration," paper presented at the American Educational Research Association Meeting, March 1970; R. Jean Hills, "Educational Administration: A Field in Transition," *Educational Administration Quarterly* 1:1 (Winter 1965), 58-64; John W. Brubacher and H. Gerard Rowe, Jr., "Professors of Educational Administration: Researchers, Teachers, or ...?" mimeographed report, University of Connecticut, December 1969; Melvin P. Robbins and Traver Williams, "The Doctoral Dissertation and the Discipline of Educational Administration," paper presented at the American Educational Research Association Meeting, March 1970; Donald J. Willower, "Some Inquiries in Educational Administration," *The Researcher of the Northeastern Research Association* 9:1 (February 1971), 38-45; Roald F. Campbell, "Educational Administration—A Twenty-Five Year Perspective," *Educational Administration Quarterly* 8:2 (Spring 1972), 1-15; Parker A. Moore, "Towards a Programmatic Knowledge Production System in Educational Administration: The Professors' View," paper presented at the American Educational Research Association Meeting, February 1973; R. Oliver Gibson, "Trends in Educational Administration Research in the United States," paper presented at the international Intervisitation Program, 1974; and Daniel J. Brown, "The Poverty of Educational Administration: A Case for Mathematical Modeling," *Planning and Changing* 5:3 (Fall 1973), 131-137. See also Kenneth E. McIntyre, "The Gordian Nots of Writing," *Educational Administration Quarterly* 5:1 (Winter 1969), 2-5; Ralph B. Kimbrough, "Toward Professional Development," *Educational Administration Quarterly* 6:1 (Winter 1970), 2-6; Andrew W. Halpin, "Administrative Theory: The Fumbled Torch," in *Issues in American Education* (New York: Oxford University Press, 1970); Norman J. Boyan, "Problems and Issues of Knowledge Production and Utilization," in Terry L. Eidell and Joanne M. Kitchel (eds.), *Knowledge Production and Utilization in Educational Administration* (Eugene, Oregon: University of Oregon Press, 1968), 21-36; Jack A. Culbertson, "Trends and Issues in the Development of a Science of Administration," in W. W. Charters, Jr., *et al.*, *Perspectives on Educational Administration and the Behavioral Sciences* (Eugene, Oregon: Center for the Advanced Study of Educational Administration, 1965), 3-22; and Roald F. Campbell and L. Jackson Newell, *A Study of Professors of Educational Administration* (Columbus, Ohio: University Council for Educational Administration, 1973).

2. Glenn L. Immegart, "Suggestions for Leadership Research," in Luvern L. Cunningham and William J. Gephart (eds.), *Leadership: The Science and the Art Today* (Itasca, Illinois: F. E. Peacock, 1973), 220.

3. Such as Benjamin S. Bloom, "Twenty-Five Years of Educational Research," *American Educational Research Journal* 3 (1966), 211-221; Daniel E.

Griffiths, "The Ten Most Significant Educational Research Findings in the Past Ten Years," *Action* 6:10 (May 1967), 1-10; or Mark R. Shibles, "Significant Educational Research During the Past Ten Years," seminar presentation at the American Educational Research Association Meeting, February 26, 1973.

4. The basic sources of data used in this analysis were *Dissertation Abstracts* (1954, 1964, and 1972); Phi Delta Kappa's *Research Studies in Education* (1954, 1964, and 1970); issues of the *Review of Educational Research* (1952-1967); *Educational Administration Abstracts* (1966-1974); *The Encyclopedia of Educational Research* (1950, 1960, and 1969); and the following research reports: Moore, *Studies in School Administration*; Howard S. Bretsch, "An Evaluation of Doctoral Dissertations in Educational Administration in California," *California Journal of Educational Research* 8:2 (March 1957), 51-58; Haller, "The Questionnaire Perspective"; and Robbins and Williams, "The Doctoral Dissertation."

5. Moore, *Studies in School Administration*.

6. Griffiths, "Research and Theory in Educational Administration," 29.

7. For example, Ralph B. Kimbrough, *Political Power and Educational Decision Making* (Chicago: Rand McNally, 1964); Andrew W. Halpin and Don B. Croft, *The Organizational Climate of Schools* (Chicago: Midwest Administration Center, 1963); and Richard O. Carlson, "Succession and Performance among School Superintendents," *Administrative Science Quarterly* 6 (1961), 210-227.

8. Robbins and Williams, "The Doctoral Dissertation."

9. Stephen J. Knezevich, *Doctorate Needs in Educational Administration During the 1970's and 1980's: A Preliminary Analysis* (Columbus, Ohio: University Council for Educational Administration, undated).

10. Based on a discussion with Professor Emil J. Haller (at Cornell University) in June 1974.

11. Campbell and Newell, *Study of Professors*, 1.

12. For example, Griffiths, "Research and Theory in Educational Administration"; Knezevich, *Doctorate Needs in Educational Administration*; or as can be estimated from some of the analyses of data in Campbell and Newell, *Study of Professors*, 54-55.

13. Hills, "Educational Administration"; Campbell and Newell, *Study of Professors*, 56-60.

14. Griffiths, *Research in Educational Administration*, 8-9.

15. Bretsch, "Evaluation of Doctoral Dissertations"; Haller, "Questionnaire Perspective."

16. Bretsch, "Evaluation of Doctoral Dissertations," 53-54.

17. Haller, "Questionnaire Perspective."

18. For another perspective on inquiry in educational administration as revealed in the *Quarterly* and *Administrator's Notebook*, see Brown, "The Poverty of Educational Administration."

19. As revealed by Hills, "Educational Administration"; and Campbell and Newell, *Study of Professors*.

20. Campbell and Newell, *Study of Professors*, 76-77.

21. These were: *Educational Administration Quarterly* (1965-1974), *The*

Journal of Educational Administration (1963-1974), *Administrator's Notebook* (1952-1973), *The Phi Delta Kappan* (1957-1958, 1963-1965, and 1972-1974), *School Review* (1953-1954, 1955-1956, 1963-1965, 1968-1971, and 1972-1973), *Harvard Educational Review* (1954-1972), *Educational Leadership* (1954-1959, 1963-1965, and 1970-1972), *Administrative Science Quarterly* (1956-1973), *Public Administration Review* (1954-1955, 1964-1965, and 1971-1972), *American Sociological Review* (1954, 1964, and 1972), *The Journal of Personality and Social Psychology* (1965-1966 and 1972), *The Journal of Applied Psychology* (1954-1956, 1965, 1967, and 1970-1972), *American Political Science Review* (1954, 1964, and 1972), and *The American Economic Review* (1954, 1964, and 1972).

22. It was, for example, pointed out by my colleague, Professor Walter I. Garms (University of Rochester), that although the *American Economic Review* devotes little attention to educational administration, the more interdisciplinary *Journal of Human Resources* has contained thirty-one studies on educational administration since 1966.

23. See also McIntyre, "Gordian Nots of Writing."

24. These texts are not herein identified since identification seems irrelevant for purposes of this assessment.

25. The writer is indebted to Professor Wayne Hoy (Rutgers University), who made historical materials of NCPEA available for analysis.

26. Moore, *Studies in Educational Administration.*

27. See, for example, John K. Hamphill, Daniel E. Griffiths, and Norman Frederiksen, *Administrative Performance and Personality* (New York: Bureau of Publications, Teachers College, Columbia University, 1962); Campbell and Newell, *Study of Professors*; and Daniel E. Griffiths (ed.), *Developing Taxonomies of Organizational Behavior in Educational Administration* (Chicago: Rand McNally, 1969).

28. Jack A. Culbertson and Stephen P. Hencley (eds.), *Educational Research: New Perspectives* (Danville, Illinois: Interstate, 1963).

29. The writer is indebted to Dr. Philip Piele (University of Oregon) for making CASEA Center materials available for analysis.

30. A notable exception is Roald F. Campbell, Jacob W. Getzels, and James M. Lipham, *Educational Administration as a Social Process* (New York: Harper, 1968).

31. See also Kimbrough, "Toward Professional Development," 3.

32. See also McIntyre, "Gordian Nots of Writing," 3.

33. See also Halpin, "Foggy View from Olympus."

34. Gibson, "Trends in Educational Administration Research"; Brown, "Poverty of Educational Administration."

35. See William J. Gephart and Bruce B. Bartos, "Profiling Instructional Package," Occasional Paper #7, Phi Delta Kappa Research Service Center, August 1969.

36. Griffiths, *Research in Educational Administration,* 7-9; Hills, "Educational Administration," 61.

37. Campbell and Newell, *Study of Professors,* 56-57.

38. *Ibid.*, 57, 72, and 76.

39. Boyan, "Problems and Issues," 29.

40. Griffiths, *Research in Educational Administration*; and Griffiths, "Research and Theory."

41. Those listed in note 1 (above).

42. Gephart and Bartos, "Profiling Instructional Package."

43. Halpin, "Administrative Theory."

44. Fremont A. Shull, Jr., "Professorial Stress as a Variable in Structuring Faculty Roles," *Educational Administration Quarterly* 8:3 (Autumn 1972), 49-66.

45. See Ronald G. Corwin, "Beyond Bureaucracy in Educational Research Management," mimeographed paper, Department of Sociology, Ohio State University, May 1974.

46. James D. Thompson, Robert W. Hawkes, and Robert W. Avery, "Truth Strategies and University Organization," *Educational Administration Quarterly* 5:2 (Spring 1969), 4-25.

47. See, for example, William E. Glueck and Cary D. Thorp, "The Role of the Academic Administrator in Research Professors' Satisfaction and Productivity," *Educational Administration Quarterly* 10:1 (Winter 1974), 72-90.

14. Preparatory Programs in Educational Administration, 1954-1974

ROBIN H. FARQUHAR

The most vexing problem I encountered in preparing this chapter was with the arithmetic implicit in the topic I was given. The title of this volume, in fact, suggests that 1954 and 1974 were somehow watershed years in the development of educational administration. While this is undoubtedly true for some of the topics included in this book, it is not the case with preparatory programs.

The development of educational administration as a self-conscious field of professional preparation is a relatively recent phenomenon. I assume that it is this phenomenon with which I am expected to deal here. A sweeping scan of preparatory programs leads me to believe that their development can be most fruitfully discussed in terms of three major periods, each approximately one decade in duration, none of which either begins with 1954 or ends with 1974. Rather, I think the first period extends from the late 1940s to the late 1950s, the second from the late 1950s to the late 1960s, and the third from the late 1960s at least to the mid-1970s (and I feel we can project it with some confidence a few more years toward the end of the decade).

This perspective left me in somewhat of a quandary, given the specific dates to be covered in my assignment. I think, however, I found a way out of it. The years 1954 and 1974 (and I hope I may be permitted the liberty of introducing the year 1964) fall more or less in the middle of the decades with which I'm concerned. Thus, if I treat those years as central years within major periods rather than as watersheds between major periods, then I can use them as launching pads to examine the developmental periods I wish to focus on, thereby both satisfying myself and remaining faithful to the title I've been given.

This, then, is what I propose to do. I'll begin with a descriptive analysis in which I'll sketch briefly a preparatory program which a "typical" doctoral student in educational administration might have followed in 1954, and I'll relate this to the main trends taking place in the development of administrative preparation during the ten-year period surrounding 1954; I'll do the same thing for programs in and around 1964 and 1974. Secondly, I'll attempt a short interpretive analysis of trends in administrative preparation over the past quarter-century, as they appear to have developed according to my earlier description. Finally, I'll indulge in a modest projective analysis of what the short-range future seems to hold for the development of preparatory programs deriving from my preceding interpretation.

Description

In trying to sketch administrative preparation programs which typical doctoral students might have followed in 1954, 1964, and 1974, one has three main options. One can take a single university and describe the program it offered in each of the three years; or one can describe one university's 1954 program, another university's 1964 program, and a third university's 1974 program; or one can survey a number of universities and inductively generate a typical university program for each of the three years. The first approach has the advantage of institutional consistency, but its generalizability depends on how representative the selected university is; the second option, while having variety, has no more generalizability than the first and it lacks the advantage of institutional consistency; the third choice has obvious generalizability, but it lacks the realism inherent in the description of a particular university's actual program.

The procedure to be followed here will combine the first and third options in an effort to satisfy the criteria of realism, institutional consistency, and generalizability. Thus, for each of the three periods involved, I shall first sketch the program offered by a particular university—the same one in each case, one which I feel is generally representative of member institutions in the University Council for Educational Administration (UCEA) (a medium-sized, primarily public university located in a mid-eastern American city which has been in UCEA since the Council's beginning); and I shall then discuss the general trends in preparatory programs which emerge from a survey of developments in a variety of institutions during the period concerned. (I'll focus particularly on programs at the doctoral level.) My data base for this analysis derives from a fairly thorough review of relevant literature, from my own experience as a UCEA central staffer for five years and subsequently as a university department chairman and professor of educational administration, and from pertinent information I solicited in 1974 from several UCEA plenary session representatives.

The 1954 Program and Developments during the Surrounding Period

The typical educational administration student following a doctoral program at "University X" during 1954 was probably a white male in his mid- to late-thirties and was admitted on the basis of his previous academic record and his performance on normed tests of cognitive ability. He was an established educational administrator and continued as such throughout the program, because no study beyond the master's level was required for administrative certification in his state, graduate assistantships and fellowships were extremely rare, and full-time residency was unnecessary for doctoral study. He and most of his fellow students thus held administrative positions within school systems in and around the city where the university was located, and they took most of their courses in the late afternoons and evenings, on weekends, and during the summer months.

The student's program consisted of at least seventy credit hours (comprised largely of numerous two-credit courses) plus a dissertation, so the teaching demands placed upon the two full-time faculty members in educational administration were extremely heavy. Both of these professors had been successful school administrators themselves, and they retained their contacts with practitioners through active participation in state administrators' associations and the school study council based at the university; but they had little time left for research.

About a third of the student's program consisted of courses in his major area of study—educational administration. These included a required core of four credit hours in "Current Practices in School Administration" (which emphasized school law, school system organization, the administration of personnel and the instructional program, school finance, pupil accounting, public relations, and building construction and maintenance) plus a variety of courses in which he could study more intensively the specialized task areas to which he was introduced in the core offerings. About a quarter of his program was devoted to courses in a minor field of study—normally either elementary or secondary education. He was also required to take about one-sixth of his courses in the "foundations" field of educational history, philosophy, and psychology. The remaining quarter of his program was divided almost equally between courses in statistics and research methods and electives in areas outside of his minor field (including a couple of courses in disciplines other than education). In addition, he could gain limited credit for participation in a school survey, and he completed a dissertation on a problem concerning staff supervision, pupil accounting, educational finance, or school facilities.

This student was involved in the early stages of what Hollis Moore has referred to as "the ferment in school administration."[1] In 1954 program designers at "University X" were in the midst of a decade during which educational administration was discovering itself as a field of academic specialization, and consciously striving to find a "handle" by which it could become a distinctly recognized "discipline." Prior to this period, near the end of World War II, programs in educational administration consisted of "largely folklore, experiences recounted by professors to students in summer sessions, with little research into the process or theory of administration."[2] But the juices of disciplinary consciousness were stirring during the establishment of the National Conference of Professors of Educational Administration (NCPEA) at Endicott in 1947, and they began to flow in response to the stimulation of funds provided by the W. K. Kellogg Foundation to inaugurate the Cooperative Program in Educational Administration (CPEA) at five universities recognized as regional or national leaders in 1950 and three more in 1951. These events demonstrated a growing awareness of educational administration as a specialized field of professional endeavor, a concern with the need to promote its development through scholarly inquiry and rigorous preparation, and a recognition that leading universities were an appropriate setting for the advancement of such study. This "movement" was further enhanced when a few social scientists first attended the 1954 NCPEA meeting in Denver and when, a year later, the Committee for the Advancement of School Administration (CASA) was founded with CPEA and the American Association of School Administrators (AASA) as primary partners. The decade was climaxed with the conception, in 1956, of UCEA on the campus of Columbia University.

Most of the major developments in preparatory programs during the period surrounding 1954 occurred at the CPEA centers. Thus, many of that decade's achievements were not then evident at "University X" which, like most institutions, was not a CPEA center. It remained for UCEA, during the next period, to create a nationwide communication and participation network for sharing information, ideas, materials, and program developments among CPEA centers and between them and other universities. But much of the most significant progress in the past quarter-century was initiated during the 1947-1956 period, thanks to the Kellogg money in the CPEA centers. New staff were employed, which permitted some degree of specialization among faculty (while the typical department seldom had more than five professors, it did permit the growth of expertise in terms of administrative roles, levels, or task areas), and this in turn led to greater depth and concentration in both course offerings and research activities. Student assistantships and fellowships were awarded, and this led to improved student recruitment efforts, to less geographic parochialism, and to more full-time resident study. A body of literature began to emerge with the publication of case studies and texts focusing upon important human and conceptual skills in educational administration. The social sciences were "discovered" as a source of theories and concepts that have some relationship to administrative behavior in organizational settings such as schools and school systems. At about the same time, the internship was introduced as a period of apprenticeship during which the student could learn on the job under the joint supervision of an accomplished practitioner and a university professor. Finally, the growing self-consciousness of educational administration as a field of academic specialization was evident in the efforts of some institutions to prepare future professors of educational administration.

The 1964 Program and Developments during the Surrounding Period

The growing impact of these developments was apparent in the program offered by "University X" in 1964. The typical student enrolled at that time was, like his predecessor a decade earlier, a white male—but he was about five years younger. While he, too, was admitted on the basis of his academic record, his motivation for applying had not been strictly intrinsic: the state now required that he complete a doctorate or seventy hours of graduate study before he could become a superintendent. He had been a school principal, but he gave up this post to pursue graduate study because the university required that he spend at least two consecutive trimesters in full-time residence; fortunately, he had obtained an assistantship which helped supplement his wife's salary while he studied. Being on campus all day, he learned a great deal from informal interactions with his fellow students—a relatively large group which included some from outside his own state (there was even one foreigner from Canada) and a few blacks. (Unlike himself, several of his fellow students decided, as the program progressed, that they would forsake the "firing line" for careers in the professorship after graduation.) The full-time residency also made it possible (in fact, it was expected) for him to become familiar with the university's library, to learn his way around the computer center, to discover the strengths and weaknesses of all five full-time professors in the department of educational administration (one of whom had never been a school administrator, but was an ardent researcher), and to spot the "good" courses offered in other departments "across campus."

The basic organization of his program was similar to that of his predecessor ten years earlier, but there were some differences in its content. There were fewer offerings now because the department had consolidated a number of discrete courses into integrated seminars which facilitated specialization in one or two task or process areas; this had become possible because of the recognition that certain basic concepts and theories were common to administrative behavior in different settings, and because the full-time residency requirement made it feasible to program offerings in larger blocks of time. The introductory core now included a course on "Foundations in Educational Administration" which dealt with the sociological and economic base of educational administration, its philosophical content, and interrelationships with other governmental units. The two courses previously available in the form of field studies and school surveys had been reduced to a single offering, the first half of which was an on-campus seminar in the theory and methodology of educational planning. Besides these changes, there were some recent additions to the program—an independent study option, an advanced research seminar in educational administration, two new courses in supervisory behavior, and a foreign language requirement. Perhaps the lower age and more limited administrative experience of many students accounted for the increased popularity of the internship as an elective. And for the noneducation options there was considerable pressure to take a few graduate courses offered by social science departments "across campus." This proved helpful at the dissertation stage because it was becoming fashionable to do theses that involved the generation of hypotheses from social science theory and the empirical testing of these hypotheses in educational settings.

This student was being prepared as an "applied social scientist," and he was a participant in what may be referred to as the "golden age" of educational administration. While "University X" was not at the forefront of innovators during the period of unprecedented change that took place between the late 1950s and the late 1960s, there is evidence in its program that it was affected by these developments, due in large part to its active membership in UCEA. It was a period of high excitement, deep commitment, and shared goals—a period of expansion centered around efforts to build a discipline and achieve full academic acceptability. The period was ushered in with the publication under NCPEA auspices of Campbell and Gregg's *Administrative Behavior in Education* in 1957, followed one year later by the landmark seminar at the University of Chicago recorded in Halpin's *Administrative Theory in Education* and, a year thereafter, by Griffiths's seminal volume on *Administrative Theory*.[3] Thus, the "theory movement" in educational administration was born; it was nurtured throughout this period by leading scholars too numerous to mention here and was aggressively facilitated by UCEA which, under Jack Culbertson's inspirational leadership, grew in size, prestige, and influence throughout this decade. The "movement" was founded on the belief that educational administration is an applied social science and that, as such, it can be investigated empirically through the application of concepts and modes of inquiry from social science disciplines in an effort to generate a body of knowledge and theory that will help to explain the nature of educational organizations and the behavior of leaders within them. The ramifications of this belief for research, training, and practice in educational administration were immense, and they were feverishly pursued during a decade of UCEA-sponsored seminars, task forces, and interest groups which resulted in numerous publications, research projects, program innovations, and new instructional materials—aided by two five-year operating grants from Kellogg.

The enthusiasm of this period was not limited to universities that were members of UCEA (although they were heavily represented among the authors of the publication which reflects the height of the "movement"—the sixty-third yearbook of the National Society for the Study of Education[4]). It caught on in the developed Commonwealth countries, emanating in the first International Intervisitation Program in 1966. And it caught on among leading agencies in "the field" at all levels—as illustrated by the introduction by the National Council for the Accreditation of Teacher Education (NCATE) (with CASA assistance) of accreditation standards for administrative preparation in 1959, AASA's decision in the same year to require two years of graduate study in an NCATE-accredited program for admission to active membership in the Association, the initiation of federally funded scholarship programs in educational administration through the National Defense Education Act (NDEA) and the National Institute for Mental Health (NIMH), and countless other examples.

The impact of this "movement" on preparatory programs has been documented elsewhere.[5] Its highlights included the following developments. Research became substantially more sophisticated, new knowledge was generated, and theory related to educational administration was refined. Heavy doses of social science were incorporated into preparatory programs, especially through courses taken "across campus" (notably in sociology, social psychology, and economics, and—latterly—in political science and anthropology). A few universities established graduate schools of administration to provide common learning experiences for prospective business, educational, and public administrators, and recruitment pools were expanded to encourage the enrollment of younger students and minority group members. "Lecture-and-textbook" courses began to be replaced by seminars and workshops relying heavily on the use of reality-oriented multimedia instructional materials and methods (including extensive work with cases, simulations, games, laboratory training exercises, computer aided instruction, sensitivity training, tapes, films, etc.), and increased emphasis was placed on field-related experiences artic-ulated with on-campus learnings through internships, field station assignments, and other clinical activities. Finally, in departments of educational administration young faculty members were added, many of whom had little if any administrative experience but sub-stantial training in the social sciences (during this period, faculty spe-cializations shifted from a focus on educational levels or task areas to expertise in academic subdisciplines or bodies of theory). All of these developments were facilitated by the almost universal requirement of at least one academic year of full-time residency in doctoral pro-grams.

It was clearly an era of expansion (the typical department of educational administration numbered from five to ten full-time fac-ulty members—an increase of about 100 percent over the previous decade—and student enrollment increased proportionately), an era of change and of high expectations. The excitement of discovery led program designers beyond the social sciences into other sources of potentially relevant content as well—the humanities, the sophisti-cated management and planning technologies developed in govern-ment and industry, the schools of business and public administration, and the human relations laboratories. Everywhere one looked, there seemed to be something promising that could be incorporated into our preparatory programs.

It is not possible, however, to sustain a "movement" forever on the basis of anticipatory excitement. Sooner or later, the "promised land" must be found, or the thrust will lose force and direction. This is inevitable in such developmental activities as program design, for there is no "promised land"; the societal context for which we are preparing educational administrators is changing constantly and, accordingly, our efforts to improve our preparatory programs must continue indefinitely. Because some of us were not prepared to accept this verity, we experienced some disillusionment when we began to sense that the "movement" to which we had committed so much faith, hope, and effort was not going to lead us to a universally perceived "promised land." This sensation was emerging toward the end of the period when it became apparent: (1) that we had not succeeded in developing a unique and coherent "science" or "discipline" of educational administration, (2) that the graduates of our programs were unable to solve quickly some of the most pressing problems in American education, and (3) that the potential for theoretical integrity in our programs was receding as we continued to discover new sources of apparently relevant content.

So as this period drew to a close in the late 1960s, we entered a stage of initial disappointment, followed by a reassessment of progress and a search for new directions. Nevertheless, the experience was worth having, and we shall probably never have another one quite so significant and exciting again. We grew immensely as a field of study during that period, and we gained much that we shall never lose—we discovered some content that will always be relevant, we achieved some visibility and respect in several areas where we were previously unheard of, and we built a lasting sense of shared commitment that is essential to the survival of any field of study.

The 1974 Program and Developments during the Surrounding Period

The searching expansion and resultant variety that followed the more coherent "theory movement" in educational administration were evident in the programs available at "University X" in 1974. The "typical" student, like his predecessor ten years earlier, was a male in his early thirties; but, unlike his predecessor, he was black and he aspired to a senior administrative post in a major urban school system. He was pleased to be a part of the large group of students who enrolled with him, because he had not been very optimistic about his chances of getting into this extensive seventy-two-hour program which was necessary for his administrative certification and which required an academic year of full-time residence. He was also pleasantly surprised to note that fully a third of his fellow students were black and nearly a quarter of them were women. His pleasure was somewhat tempered, however, by his realization that "University X" had established an affirmative action policy which gave preference to black males, black females, and white females—in that order —and by his recognition that he had benefitted from an open admissions policy which permitted a large number of students to pursue an introductory core program following which they had to "survive" an intensive diagnosis before being admitted to full doctoral candidacy —a diagnosis that placed heavy emphasis on personal values and commitments toward open educational climates, skill in interpersonal relations, and knowledge of the society and culture, rather than depending exclusively on the traditional measures of cognitive ability.

He and many of his fellow students had been awarded graduate assistantships or teaching fellowships which enabled them to participate directly in the instructional and research activities of the fourteen faculty members in the department (two of whom were black). His feeling of involvement continued to deepen when he found that he was expected to contribute actively in efforts throughout the department to review and revise thoroughly the numerous policies and offerings comprising the various programs in educational administration.

The department permitted him a great deal of flexibility in determining those elements that would constitute his doctoral program. But like all students, he first had to complete the required core —an integrated twelve-credit sequence drawing heavily on the social sciences and taught by a team of professors of educational administration, each of whom produced specific content packages along with test items to evaluate student competency in the areas concerned. The main components of the core included a comprehensive overview of educational organization and governance, an introduction to the theory and conceptual systems underlying "administrative science," a counseling experience intended to help the student define his career goals and design a doctoral program that would be maximally relevant to him, and a practicum involving laboratory experiences in administrative behavior through the use of a simulated urban school system. Following completion of the core and prior to embarking upon the remainder of his doctoral program, he was required to pass a general diagnostic assessment (an objective examination of knowledge in educational history, philosophy, statistics, research, and psychology) and to receive a favorable faculty evaluation of his profile (which was developed and maintained as he progressed through the core with input by both himself and faculty members). He was then free to select from a wide variety of courses, seminars, workshops, and several independent study options (including a paid internship, which could be taken in any of numerous agencies related to education, and which required concurrent participation in seminars on campus and related assignments) in order to round out his training; the only stipulations were that he had to complete approximately thirty-four credits in his major field (including an area of administrative specialization) and that he had to take some courses in the humanities and social sciences.

Following completion of his course work, the student was required to demonstrate competency in educational administration (normally through passing a comprehensive written and oral examination and satisfactorily fulfilling the requirements of an internship or providing other evidence of successful administrative performance) and competency in tools of research (through presenting and defending a proposal for his doctoral thesis). Finally, he undertook the dissertation, typically a rigorous exercise in applied research which, it was hoped, would really "make a difference" in the world of education. While completing the thesis he was required to enroll in the department's doctoral dissertation seminar.

This student was experiencing the effects of what might be referred to as "the age of diversity and adversity" in educational administration—a period extending from the late 1960s to the mid-1970s and which will probably continue through the latter half of the decade. There appear to have been three major phenomena that generated the "shape" of this period. One, a legacy from the 1960s, was the phenomenon of growth—both in the level of sophistication of preparatory programs and in the variety of content and activities comprising them. A second was the phenomenon of relevance—concern with the application and utilization, rather than merely the production and dissemination, of knowledge, concern with assessment and accountability, and concern with performance and competence. The third basic phenomenon was that of democratization, reflected in efforts to open up access to preparation programs, to involve students in departmental decision making, and to increase flexibility and individualization in program determination. These three phenomena of growth, relevance, and democratization are clearly evident in the program of "University X" described above. The diversity inherent in them is well signaled in the two five-year plans prepared by UCEA for the 1969-1979 period—plans which are remarkable for their wide variety of objectives and activities and for their thematic emphasis upon the use of knowledge in very broad terms. The adversity inherent in the phenomena is hinted at in such events as the decline in UCEA membership since the late 1960s, the repeal in the early 1970s of AASA's requirement that its active members must have completed two years of graduate study in a university accredited by NCATE, and efforts during the mid-1970s in several states to impose competency-based criteria for administrative certification.

Numerous developments in preparatory programs during this period illustrate the influence of the growth, relevance, and democratization phenomena. Program content continued to expand, with forays into futurism, values clarification, organization development, and sophisticated quantitative analysis, to name but a few. Theory generated from the social sciences came to be viewed with some skepticism as efforts were made to identify and apply discriminating criteria for determining those concepts and modes of inquiry that are most directly pertinent to the analysis and administration of educational organizations; similarly, program designers became increasingly concerned with establishing relationships between the preparation they offered and the required competencies and performance criteria of the roles for which their students were being trained. The expansion of content and the concerns with competence contributed to increased differentiation and specialization in preparation; basically, the emphasis shifted from discipline-oriented program design to career-oriented program design—thus, we find components introduced to facilitate specialization by role (e.g., for prospective administrators of special education, career education, higher education), specialization by function (e.g., for educational planners, operations researchers, change managers), and specialization by context (e.g., for inner-city educational administration, administration of Indian schools, educational administration for international development). The renewal and refinement of specializations oriented toward careers required the introduction of much more flexibility and individualization than was characteristic of most programs in the 1960s; students in many institutions became free to "build" or "negotiate" almost their entire programs by selecting components from a wide variety of alternatives—including prepackaged multimedia modules, courses offered by any departments on campus, unstructured "independent study" options, or miniactivities developed especially to serve individuals or small groups of students—all in an effort to maximize the appropriateness of the preparation experience to the unique needs and aspirations of particular students. The growing student orientation in program design was also apparent in the emergence of nationwide, nonresident operations such as those offered by Nova and Walden Universities and England's Open University.

In support of these developments in program content and structure it was necessary to devise new methods and materials to facilitate student learning. The technologies of audio cassettes, video tapes, and computer systems were harnessed to permit the generation of much more sophisticated approaches to instruction through laboratory training, simulation, gaming, and other role-playing devices. And field-related experiences became more common and more carefully designed, monitored, and evaluated than they were a decade earlier. The educational administration clinic, the field laboratory, and the rotating internship were developments through which practical experiences could be consciously articulated with program components on campus, individually tailored to particular students' interests, and rendered productive in terms of problem resolution in the host systems. One other approach worth noting is an interest that emerged on the part of a few institutions in serving as continuing resources to their students after graduation. Traditionally, contact by an educational administration graduate with his alma mater had been limited to annual alumni fund requests, periodic questionnaires seeking his retrospective assessment of the value of his preparatory program, and an occasional missive from the university's placement office. Some program designers began to recognize, however, that their responsibilities to their students do not end with the awarding of degrees, that the needs of educational administrators for assistance in analyzing and solving problems and for personal and professional counsel are immense, and that resources exist on university campuses that can and should be addressed to helping meet those needs. These institutions therefore started initiating arrangements whereby their resources could be quickly and easily tapped via phone, telelecture, and other direct access interactive mechanisms.

The personnel involved in preparatory programs also changed during this period. The typical department of educational administration now housed more than ten full-time faculty, an increase of at least 50 percent since the mid-1960s. There was no longer any way to identify a single rubric by which their specializations could be categorized: a few retained the specializations oriented toward tasks and levels that predominated in the 1950s; many still espoused the subdiscipline- and theory-oriented specializations that emerged during the 1960s; but several of the newly appointed professors were specialists in particular administrative problems, functions, settings, or other bases of expertise that are represented in the immense diversity of preparatory programs in the mid-1970s. There was, as a result, some lack of cohesion and integration—or even mutual understanding —among faculty in the larger departments of educational administration, just as there was within the programs they offered. This was not viewed as necessarily undesirable—it was a natural concomitant of the diversity and flexibility that characterized the programs—but it differed from the relationships that pertained a decade earlier. And many of the students were also different. Open admissions policies, affirmative action programs, and the increasing emphasis in selection on affective and performance criteria (rather than previous academic achievement) resulted in much more reform-mindedness and better racial and sexual balance among students of educational administration than were characteristic of their predecessors a decade earlier. (There were even a few among them who had never been professional educators.) They played an increasingly significant role in changing preparation programs, and one sensed that their chances of "making a difference" in education after graduation were relatively good.

Summary of Trends in Preparatory Programs

It is obvious from the foregoing description that preparatory programs in educational administration have undergone substantial change during the past quarter-century, both quantitatively and qualitatively. In terms of sheer growth the record is impressive, as documented in reports by UCEA and by Knezevich.[6] In 1940 about forty universities offered PhD programs and about thirty offered EdD programs in educational administration; in the mid-1970s about eighty offered the PhD, and close to one hundred offered the EdD. So the number of doctoral programs in educational administration more than doubled in the US alone during the period covered in this chapter (with the most rapid growth occurring in the 1960s); in addition, about a dozen doctoral programs in educational administration were inaugurated in other countries during this period, most of them in Canada.

The figures on degrees awarded also attest to this growth as well as to the amount of production relative to other fields. More doctorates are produced in education than in any other field, and the proportion is increasing; in 1969-1970 about one-fifth of all doctorates awarded were in the field of education. (There are more nonuniversity employers of those who hold doctorates in education than in any other field.) Further, among the areas of doctoral specialization within the field of education, there are more doctorates awarded in educational administration than in any other; this proportion has been declining—in fact, it was virtually halved from over 30 percent to about 15 percent during the past decade—because of the increasing number of specialized areas within education in which doctorates are awarded. Nevertheless, the absolute number of doctoral degrees awarded in educational administration continues to grow; it doubled from the mid-1950s to the mid-1960s, doubled again from the mid-1960s to the mid-1970s (increasing by over 70 percent between 1965 and 1970 alone), and is projected to double once more between 1974 and 1984 (although the rate of growth will likely decline over this period). In 1970-1971, the number of doctorates awarded in educational administration exceeded 1,000 per year for the first time.

Subject to some debate is whether or not the demand of employers for those who hold doctorates in educational administration can accommodate continuing increases (albeit at a declining rate) in the supply from universities. The UCEA report suggests that it cannot, for the number of people in the US holding administrative certificates already grossly exceeds the number of available positions requiring such certification. The Knezevich report, on the other hand, does not predict a glut because the number of positions in educational administration projected to become open over the next decade substantially exceeds the number of doctorates in educational administration likely to be awarded during that period. The basic distinction between these two conflicting conclusions is, of course, in the significance for employment accorded to administrative certification per se. Knezevich believes that, while there are and will continue to be many more people holding certificates than administrative jobs available for them, employment preference will be given to those among them who have doctorates in educational administration. Whether or not he is correct, it is probable that most universities will act as if he is, and that the growth of doctoral production in educational administration will continue, at least through the remainder of this decade.

Quantitative issues aside, it is clear that preparatory programs in educational administration have undergone substantial development of a qualitative nature during the period with which this chapter is concerned. In terms of broad generalizations, a number of trends may be identified. The underlying purposes of the programs seem to have shifted from a focus on imparting information about administrative tasks and processes to those being trained to perform them, through a focus on preparing individuals who will contribute to the development and implementation of educational administration as an applied behavioral science, to a focus on providing students with opportunities to learn and demonstrate the competencies necessary to deal with major problems that will confront them as educational leaders. Concurrently, the content of preparatory programs has changed, with the earlier emphasis on the accumulated wisdom of professionals being supplemented (and in some cases supplanted) by the theoretical insights of social scientists and, subsequently, by material drawn together from a wide variety of sources and organized into units related to problems or modules oriented toward competency. And the structure of programs has undergone both a consolidation and rationalization of earlier components and a proliferation of more recently generated options for specialization.

Changes in instructional approaches have been characterized by significant sophistication and diversification over the past quarter-century. The erstwhile "lecture-and-textbook" format has been largely replaced by seminars, workshops, and independent study; these have been facilitated by the use of new reality-oriented instructional methods (e.g., simulations, case analysis, gaming, laboratory training) and materials (e.g., tapes, films, in-baskets, computer programs); and they have been supplemented by a growing variety of relatively sophisticated experiences based in the field.

Students are increasingly influencing what and how they will learn in our preparatory programs, and they themselves have changed. The pools from which they are recruited have been expanded (to promote greater representation from racial minorities and women, in particular), the criteria by which they are selected have been broadened (to incorporate affective and performance factors rather than only cognitive measures), and their motivations to enroll have shifted (in that, added to the early aspiration "to get ahead in the system," was the desire to qualify for the professoriate and, more recently, the hope of learning how to change the system).

Finally, as both a cause and a result of these trends, the staffing of departments of educational administration has altered over the years. The professoriate has become younger, better educated (at least in a formal sense), more liberal, less experienced (in terms of administrative practice), more diverse (in regard to race, sex, and substantive specialization), and better accepted by academic colleagues "across campus"; and, while the functions of professors have always been variable, one may perceive a basic shift in the primary orientation of their roles during the past quarter-century from that of the paternal instructor, through that of the teaching scholar, to that of the learning facilitator.

Interpretation

The foregoing section describes the "what" and "when" of changes in preparatory programs in educational administration since the late 1940s. It is the purpose of this section to interpret the "why" and "how" of these developments. There are many ways in which such an analysis could be approached, and only two will be attempted here: in the first, program trends will be viewed from the perspective of major thematic dichotomies that help to explain their directions; in the second, they will be examined in terms of certain causes and effects that can be associated with them.

Thematic Dichotomies

An analysis of the changes in preparatory programs described above suggests that they developed (or may be interpreted) in relation to two basic thematic dichotomies. One is the "theory-practice" issue. (I recognize that theoreticians, in particular, do not accept this as a legitimate dichotomy. ["There is nothing so practical as a good theory!"] Nevertheless, the issue, whether misnamed or not, is a real one and is popularly referred to in this way. Accordingly, for want of a better term, I shall use the "theory-practice" designation.) On this issue, the pendulum in administrative preparation has swung from one extreme toward the other and has started swinging back again. In the 1950s preparatory programs were highly "practical": the content was drawn largely from the administrative experiences of professors and others and was organized according to task areas based on the divisions of labor then common in school systems; the students were typically practicing educational administrators hoping to become more senior educational administrators; and many of the faculty were formerly successful practitioners. But they were having difficulty achieving academic acceptability.

It is fortunate that some social scientists "discovered" educational administration (and vice versa), and the pendulum swung quite drastically toward the "theory" side of the issue: courses became infused with concepts from the social sciences, and reading lists were peppered with books and articles by scholars in those disciplines; modes of inquiry from the social sciences were followed in research in educational administration, and many students were encouraged to pursue careers in the professoriate so that they might continue to build the theoretical knowledge base of educational administration; young professors were employed who had had no administrative experience but who were willing and able to contribute to the development of an administrative "science" or "discipline" within the field of education; an effort was made to retain some connection with "the field" through occasional internships, but these experiences were seldom well articulated with what was learned in the university courses (especially those taken "across campus" in social science departments). The use of cases and simulations offered one of the few potentially effective bridges between theory and practice, but they were not sufficient to silence the cries of "irrelevance" which were increasingly heard from practitioners.

Gradually it was concluded that educational administration was an essentially professional, rather than an academic, discipline and that the hope of achieving a value-free "science" in this field was rather futile. Nevertheless, much of importance had been learned from the social sciences, and so forays were made into areas less theoretically based to tap their potential for further helpful insights. Educational administration had discovered its mind, and efforts were launched both to expand its mind and to rediscover its heart. The pendulum thus began to swing back in an attempt to find an appropriate balance between theory and practice: the potential of reality-oriented instructional methods and materials was further exploited;

the internship was supplemented with other experiences related to the field, and conscious articulation was sought between them and activities based at the university; courses incorporated new content from the humanities and from other fields of professional endeavor; students were sent "across campus" less often, and resources from there were incorporated more frequently into the offerings of departments of educational administration; and the organizational rubric of programs shifted from a theoretical and subdisciplinary base to a competency and problem base—a shift that was reflected both in the expertise of newly hired professors and in the options for specialization and differentiation offered to students.

The second dichotomy concerns the "freedom-control" issue. Here, the pendulum has made only one major swing during the period concerned. Until the late 1960s it was close to the "control" side of the issue: programs contained large segments of required experiences, most of which were gained in prescribed courses dominated by professors; departmental policies and program changes were determined by the faculty; professors were rewarded largely in accordance with traditional academic standards; students were generally "batch-processed" through their programs, their progress being recorded in the form of checklists and letter grades; and on-campus residency became a virtually universal requirement.

Then the winds of reform which had been blowing across our campuses finally seeped into departments of educational administration, and the pendulum swung toward the "freedom" side of the issue. Some universities adopted open admissions procedures, several invoked affirmative action policies, and many liberalized their selection criteria to permit admission of students on grounds other than strength of academic background—in essence, access to programs was opened up. The programs themselves became much more flexible, available options were increased, and students were encouraged to put together their own programs in accordance with their unique needs and aspirations. The predominance of fully structured formal courses diminished, and multimedia modules, specially tailored minicourses, and independent study options emerged as alternatives from which programs could be built. The variety of available instructional approaches, field experiences, and dissertation formats increased markedly. Students were actively involved in the departments in reviewing and revising their programs and policies, and their progress began to be assessed in terms of performance-related competencies rather than formal examination grades received. Different faculty members were recognized as having (and needing) different strengths, and were judged accordingly, and some nationwide programs were inaugurated without any residence requirements whatsoever.

This analysis of trends in administrative preparation according to two thematic dichotomies has obviously been overdrawn and oversimplified. The changes have been neither as dramatic nor as universal as has been suggested. Nevertheless, a retrospective overview suggests that program developments have moved in the general directions indicated (i.e., from a practical orientation to a theoretical orientation and back toward a more balanced position, and from a syndrome of control toward a syndrome of freedom). By emphasizing these flows it has been possible to establish them as helpful perspectives for the analysis of trends in program over the past quarter-century.

Causes and Effects

Another basis for interpreting changes in programs is in terms of their causes and effects. Regarding the former, three main kinds of contextual factors seem to have contributed heavily to program developments. One involves substantive and technological advances. Research and development in educational administration and related fields, particularly since our "discovery" of the social sciences, have added extensively to our body of knowledge, and the content, structure, and staffing of our programs have been adjusted accordingly: additional subjects have been introduced, others have been discarded or consolidated, wider choices have been offered, new specializations have emerged, and longer periods of full-time study have been encouraged. Further, the nature of education and the problems confronting administrators have changed, with the result that the knowledge, skills, and competencies required by our graduates have shifted over the years; we have responded (normally in reaction rather than anticipation) with relevant content components, restructured learning formats, and new instructional materials in an effort to address these needs. And technological innovations have enabled us to tap the potential of a variety of audiovisual and electronic media, particularly in our efforts to provide learning experiences that simulate reality in a "laboratory" environment.

A second kind of contextual factor influencing our programs involves cultural and social pressures. Societal values have shifted markedly in the direction of egalitarianism, humanitarianism, and participative democracy in recent years. In reacting to the pressures generated by these shifts, we have changed our procedures for recruitment and selection (e.g., affirmative action, open admissions, noncognitive criteria), revised our content (e.g., humanities, organization development, social anthropology), adapted our structures (e.g., flexibility, individualization), and actively involved students in the review and revision of our programs and policies, in establishing their learning objectives, and in determining the components of their own administrative preparation. Together, these innovations represent a response on our part to culturally and socially rooted demands for more openness, authenticity, and relevance in our programs.

Third, our programs have been affected by economic and political forces. Throughout most of the 1960s education was treated as a "favored child" in public policy. It was viewed economically as an investment with a high yield and politically as a function with high priority, for it was widely believed that education could effect social mobility, national productivity, civil obedience, and even ecological balance. Foolishly, although understandably, educators encouraged these public expectations, and we were rewarded with unprecedented support which enabled us to grow and innovate at a furious pace. This syndrome of growth and innovation was evident in our preparatory programs as well as in the nation's school systems. We borrowed liberally from other fields of study, added (sometimes indiscriminately) to our offerings, experimented with numerous technological tools, produced far more administrators with certification than there were administrative positions for them, seldom evaluated our output in any systematically valid way, and usually forgot about our graduates once they had left campus. Then the bottom fell out. Someone discovered that there remained too many disadvantaged groups and illiterate individuals, that crime and disease still abounded, that environmental problems were worsening, and that educators had in general failed to meet the public's unrealistic expectations for them. The yield from education's investment was questioned, and its political priority declined. Moral and financial support diminished. We were asked to defend our actions and were expected to account for our stewardship. The reactionism and retrenchment that hit the school systems also affected our preparatory programs. Many of us became obsessed with concern for relevance and accountability. We produced competency-based modules by the dozens (often in response to state directives), we pruned departmental budgets to the bare essentials (always in response to university directives), we strove to relate our program components to performance criteria (partially in response to Equal Employment Opportunities Commission directives), and we paid more attention to the fate of our graduates and to our continuing responsibility to help them cope. Although it would be an exaggeration to state that we "ran scared," we certainly became more vigilant.

It is much easier to comment on the causes of developments in our preparatory programs than to discuss their effects. While there may have been some improvement in the nation's quality of life over the past couple of decades, it is difficult to credit any such improvement directly to education. While there may have been some improvement in American education during these years, it is difficult to credit any such improvement directly to school administrators. While there may have been some improvement in educational leadership since mid-century, it is difficult to credit any such improvement directly to our preparatory programs. And while there have been substantial changes in our programs within the period documented in this chapter, it is an act of faith to conclude that such changes have been improvements in any criterion-validated way. The fact is that we have not yet succeeded in determining measurable criteria of success in educational administration against which we can evaluate our programs.

Having recognized this lacking, however, we can take heart from two observations: (1) a claim that our preparatory programs have improved cannot validly be disproved; and (2) more seriously, as Deneen has noted,[7] it is possible to achieve some degree of content validity in evaluating our programs. This involves establishing a relationship (a "significant overlap") between the requirements of an administrative job and the content of a preparatory program; to the extent that such relationships can be identified, the program is evaluated positively in a content-validated way. If the apparent promise of competency-based approaches to administrative preparation is realized, we should reach a point where we are able to evaluate the effectiveness of our programs in this limited manner. About all that we can claim at present, however, is that our graduates know different things and can do different things with what they know than was the case when they entered our programs, that what they learn in our programs now is different from what their predecessors learned a quarter-century ago, and that most of them appear to be surviving professionally in a milieu that has changed drastically over that period. Even this is no small claim for the effects of developments in our preparatory programs.

Projection

It is not a primary task of this chapter to forecast the future of administrative preparation; that responsibility has been lodged elsewhere in this volume. Nevertheless, the interpretive comments in the foregoing section generate a few short-range projective observations that may be worth noting. Two basic assumptions underlie the following comments. First, while preparatory programs will continue to change throughout this decade, this change will take the form of evolutionary development rather than major reform. Nothing of the magnitude of the "theory movement" during the previous period is likely to occur during the 1970s. Rather, the trends characteristic at the middle of the decade will continue, but with some adaptations. The trend toward growth will be tempered by a slower rate of increase in the number of programs offered and degrees awarded and a stabilization (and, on some campuses, reduction) in the size of departments of educational administration and by efforts to control the proliferation of preparatory components and specializations through the further synthesis, consolidation, integration, and rationalization of program content and structure. The trend toward relevance will be tempered by the realizations that the university context is simply inappropriate as a setting for the attainment of many noncognitive competencies required by practicing administrators and that those elements of preparation that the university cannot perform well should become the primary responsibility of other agencies that can perform them better. The trend toward democratization will be tempered by the recognition that "accountability" is more than a hollow catchword when applied to universities, that departments of educational administration and their faculties can be held responsible for some of the behavior of their graduates, and that they cannot meet this responsibility without exercising considerable authority and control over the "who" and "why" of admissions and the "what" and "how" of program design. Second, increasingly central to program development decisions and the tempering of current trends will be the viewpoint, expressed by March, that "the advantage of the university in the training of administrators is primarily in the intellective domain."[8] Program designers will focus more intensively on the identification of the analytical competencies required in administrative behavior and will deemphasize the contemporary infatuation with skills of leadership that do not rely primarily on a capacity for intellectual analysis.

With these two assumptions in mind, one can comment briefly on the near future of preparatory programs within the interpretive frameworks employed in the previous section. The two basic thematic dichotomies will remain operant. On the "theory-practice" issue the quest for balance (in an almost mathematical sense—less theory, more practice) will be replaced by a more responsible and demanding effort to establish useable criteria by which one can distinguish between those concepts and theories that are essential to the intellectual analysis of contemporary problems in educational administration and those that are not. Toward this end, fewer courses will be taken in social science departments "across campus" and more multidisciplinary content (interactive concepts from several disciplines focused in an integrative way upon administrative problem analysis) will be presented in departments of educational administration; internships will decline in popularity as components of university programs and will be replaced with a variety of short-term assignments in which students work with practitioners on the examination and resolution of significant problems which are selected because of their susceptibility to intellectual analysis (the less cognitive learnings associated with internships will become viewed as more appropriately the domain of nonuniversity training agencies); and simulation and other reality-oriented instructional approaches will be incorporated more integrally into substantive seminars and treated less frequently as teaching aids for discrete workshop activities.

On the "freedom-control" issue, there will be some moderation of the "openness-flexibility" syndrome of the mid-1970s: the determination of analytical competencies crucial to administrative behavior should yield valid selection procedures that can replace open admissions policies; and student choice in building individualized programs from innumerable options (including independent study) will be constrained by recommended sets of offerings carefully selected in accordance with predetermined specializations and by firm faculty guidance. However, given these adaptations, the participation of students in departmental decision making will continue to be encouraged.

The framework of cause and effect for analysis also yields a few observations about the likely nature of administrative preparation in the near future. With respect to substantive and technological advances, new knowledge will continue to result from research and development in educational administration and related fields, and this will yield additional relevant content for preparatory programs. New content will likely be oriented more toward culture and less toward systems than was the case in the previous period, and emerging emphases on values, futurism, and inductively generated knowledge involving anthropological concepts and modes of inquiry will be strengthened. Related to this, and reflecting the view that educational administration should be a source of society's moral leadership, more attention will be paid during preparation to some of the most significant contemporary intellectual issues and value dilemmas —the polluted environment, the unstable economy, the energy crisis, artificial insemination, mind-controlling drugs, the personal privacy of individuals, the secrecy of public agencies, food shortages, and international relations—to name but a few topics on which educational leaders should have thoroughly conceived views but which we give them little opportunity to examine (despite the fact that the university campus is a uniquely appropriate setting for such examination). But of greater influence than new content will be the reorganization of existing knowledge and its consequent effect on program structure. Information technology will facilitate the identification, synthesis, and integration of knowledge from a variety of relevant fields in terms of contemporary problems and developing specializations in the study of educational administration.

Cultural and social pressures will also continue to influence preparatory programs. Whereas their impact in recent years has been reflected in growing openness, flexibility, and individualization, however, it now appears to be shifting toward the opposite direction. "Inhumane" schools in which many children learned little were viewed as a disgrace in the 1960s, but the public of the 1970s is even less satisfied with undisciplined students who don't know "the basics," regardless of how "humane" their schools might be. The contemporary pressure is for more structure and authority, and this pressure will be felt by university departments of educational administration; the result, as noted previously, will be the imposition of some constraints on the current freedom in admission of students and building of programs.

And the effects of economic and political forces will remain with us, although they will be less harsh than in the early and mid-1970s. As a prime target for efforts at retrenchment and charges of irrelevance, we have been required to react rather quickly, as indicated in the previous section. Because our reactions have been fairly visible, it is probable that the "heat" will come off toward the end of the decade. This does not mean that we shall be deluged with public confidence and financial support, as we were during the 1960s. Rather, we shall probably be left alone—neglected, if not ignored—to pursue our own objectives to the extent possible within resource limitations that will remain stringent.

Finally, given the above developments, the effects of our programs will likely become more demonstrable than they are at present. If our orientation toward performance continues, if we focus our content on administrative competencies involving the skills of intellectual analysis (as we in universities are uniquely able to do), and if we establish content-validated approaches to evaluating our programs, it should become possible to demonstrate that our graduates have learned something in our programs and to make a plausible case that what they have learned is influencing their behavior as educational administrators. Whether or not this behavior leads to superior performance will depend on our perspicacity in selecting competencies and on numerous personal and situational variables over which we have no control. And the effects of administrative performance on the quality of education, and ultimately on the quality of life in the nation, cannot legitimately be related to our programs in any direct way—although they represent pertinent questions of research for our attention as scholars. Thus, we must discourage ambitious expectations for the effects of our programs; but modest expectations, within the above parameters, are appropriate and our chances of meeting them as we approach the end of the decade seem reasonably good.

Conclusion

I conclude, then, on a note of cautious optimism. Our preparatory programs in the mid-1970s are in a state of some disarray, especially as compared with the relative excitement, united commitment,
and mutual support that characterized those of the 1960s. We are
now beset with fragmentation and diffusion internally and with en-
croachment and retrenchment emanating from without. Nevertheless, our present programs are very different from (and undoubtedly
better than) those of a quarter-century ago. We have demonstrated a
capacity to change and improve our offerings rather rapidly; in fact,
our responsiveness and progress are impressive when compared with
those of other fields of professional education.[9] These capabilities
should enable us to surmount the diversity and adversity we confront
at the three-quarter mark of the century. In doing so, we shall not
change dramatically. Rather, the short-range projections offered
herein suggest a rather deliberate extension and modification of contemporary trends; they are presented as realistic expectations which
are within our capability to achieve, barring unforeseen disaster. As
we pursue them, it can be hoped that we shall take a fresh look at
the gains we realized during our "golden age." The "relevance reaction" may have caused some of us to reject theory because it is
theoretical. This is an overreaction. The incorporation of social science theory into our programs is still the most significant improvement we have made. Perhaps, in light of our sobering experience
during the early 1970s, we can return with new insights and seasoned
maturity to our erstwhile endeavors at developing a unique discipline
(if not a science) of educational administration. In so doing, it is
probable that the generation of "grounded" theory will receive more
attention than it did in our earlier attempts.

By way of postscript, I feel compelled to note that the substance of this chapter is not novel, although it was prepared independently. The content of the first half is known history, and many
of the ideas in the second half appear in the work of Culbertson,
Silver, Willower,[10] and other leaders within the UCEA aegis. This is
taken as evidence that shared ideals and mutual commitment still
operate within the field of educational administration. These characteristics bode well for the future of preparatory programs.

Notes

1. Hollis A. Moore, Jr., "The Ferment in School Administration," in Daniel E. Griffiths (ed.), *Behavioral Science and Educational Administration* (Chicago: Sixty-third Yearbook of the National Society for the Study of Education, 1964), 11-32.

2. *Ibid.*, 14.

3. Roald F. Campbell and Russell T. Gregg (eds.), *Administrative Behavior in Education* (New York: Harper and Brothers, 1957); Andrew W. Halpin (ed.), *Administrative Theory in Education* (Chicago: Midwest Administration Center, University of Chicago, 1958); Daniel E. Griffiths, *Administrative Theory* (New York: Appleton-Century-Crofts, 1959).

4. *Behavioral Science and Educational Administration, op. cit.*

5. For a comprehensive treatment of this subject, see Jack Culbertson *et al., Preparing Educational Leaders for the Seventies* (Columbus, Ohio: UCEA, 1969)—especially Section IV, 181-268; for a brief synthesis, see Robin H. Farquhar, "Trends and Needs in Superintendent Preparation," *The School Administrator* (September 1969), 11-12.

6. University Council for Educational Administration, *The Preparation and Certification of Educational Administrators: A UCEA Commission Report* (Columbus, Ohio: UCEA, 1973); S. J. Knezevich, *Doctorate Needs in Educational Administration during the 1970's and 1980's: A Preliminary Analysis* (Columbus, Ohio: UCEA, 1975).

7. James R. Deneen, "Building Long Range Evaluation into New Models of Administrator Preparation" (unpublished paper presented at the annual meeting of the American Educational Research Association, Washington, D.C., April 1975).

8. James G. March, "Analytical Skills and the University Training of Educational Administrators," *The Journal of Educational Administration* XII, 1 (May 1974), 28.

9. See Lewis B. Mayhew, *Changing Practices in Education for the Professions* (Atlanta: Southern Regional Education Board, 1971).

10. Jack Culbertson, "The Changing Directions of UCEA," *UCEA Newsletter* XV, 4 (April 1974), 19-25; Paula Silver, "Some Apparent Trends in Preparatory Programs for Educational Administrators," *UCEA Newsletter*, XV, 5 (June 1974), 20-25; Donald J. Willower, "Educational Administration and the Uses of Knowledge," *UCEA Newsletter* XV, 4 (April 1974), 1-5.

Part V

THE FUTURE OF
THEORY AND PRACTICE

The final set of papers presented at the conference addressed the future of theory and practice in the field of educational administration. To this point, so much attention had been given to problems within the field and the slow pace of efforts to ameliorate them that some attendees wondered aloud whether the field had a future. The chapters included in Part V were prepared by people with diverse perspectives and emphasize different aspects of the field. For the most part, however, they offer a relatively optimistic view of the future.

W. W. Charters is most direct in rejecting much of what has been said by others about the development of research and theory during the past twenty years. Taking a position very close to that espoused by Getzels in the Keynote presentation, he asserts that the period from 1954 to 1974 was essentially one of growth in intellectual competence and interest across the field. He thus explicates the issue of how long a field might reasonably be expected to be in the process of growth from infancy to adulthood. A corollary question concerns the signs of maturation to be looked for as this process goes forward. The lack of clear answers to such questions helps account for the differences of opinion regarding the vitality of the field among those who attended the conference. Some suggested that the conference might mark the end of the era in which behavioral science was seen as the foundation of study and practice in educational administration. Charters disagrees and asserts that the study of educational administration in the future should emphasize the merits of replication, greater concern for dependability, and increased use of dynamic rather than static theories of behavioral science.

Wayne Carle addresses the future from the perspective of the practitioner. Taking note of contemporary problems and criticism, he nevertheless avers that administrators will preside over schools that have changed little by 1995. He also predicts that skillful administrators will be in short supply and that, while important theoretical developments will transpire, they will be of less importance to the field than basic human qualities. An important theme in Carle's chapter, as well as other conference deliberations, is that educational administration is a field of practice rather than a basic discipline. As he notes, an implication of this is that progress in the development and utilization of knowledge will require professors and practitioners to work together at points of application.

As background for discussing the future of preparation programs for administrators, Daniel Griffiths gives voice to another theme that recurred throughout the conference—the impact of societal developments upon administrative practice. In his view, major developments of this type culminated in the social revolution of the 1960s. The 1970s have become a period to comprehend these changes and establish stable new relationships which should endure and should make possible prediction of administrative needs for the next twenty years. For the administrator who will succeed during this period, preparation will emphasize "ability to see his job in a broader context, to understand the setting in which he works, his deep appreciation of the value of people, a well-thought-out philosophy of education, and an ability to work with and through people."

The final presentation of the conference was made by Mrs. Virla Krotz, a member of the California State Board of Education. Speaking from a citizen's perspective, Mrs. Krotz notes the crisis of public confidence in the schools and opines that the enduring qualities of leadership and concern for and attention to individuals will be essential in the future. She also indicates the need for increased cooperation between the school and the community and expresses concern that attention continue to focus on both equal and adequate educational opportunities. Noting that many positive things are now occurring in schools, she observes that even more must be done in order to achieve the standard of excellence necessary to restore public confidence.

15. The Future (and a Bit of the Past) of Research and Theory

W. W. CHARTERS, JR.

Before offering observations on the future, I feel I must comment on a pervasive theme I have encountered regarding the present and recent past of research and theory in educational administration. The theme is expressed through phrases and observations of the following sort: anti-intellectualism is rampant; the Ikon of theory is broken and stored away in the attic; the paradigm has run its course; only a fifth of the professors in the field even lay claim to engaging in research or scholarly writing; neither the quantity nor quality of published research has changed "all that much" in twenty years; the behavioral sciences have proven to be "a bust."

Observers of educational administration seem to have reached a definition so utterly discordant with my personal observations, that I begin to think either my senses have failed me or I am looking at a world different from that viewed by everyone else. I feel obliged to break the tacit unanimity before the study of administration is defined out of existence. The assumption that the New Look in educational administration is dead and awaiting burial is a self-fulfilling prophecy, which if unchallenged can induce us to spend the future mourning its passing rather than engaging in productive work.

362

Ingredients of the Movement

First of all, it is useful to consider the ingredients of the new movement that hit the field in 1954. I refuse to call it the "theory movement" except, perhaps, as a shorthand because it was considerably broader than the word *theory* normally intends. The new movement was carrying several intertwined but discernible messages to professors of administration:

1. The *study* of education is to be valued in its own right. One need not apologize for wondering about or trying to explain a puzzling phenomenon rather than teaching classes, advising school districts, or prompting panaceas. Research is good.

2. Explanations of things have to be checked against facts and, in doing so, unusual care must be exercised to protect oneself (and others) from mistaken inference. The road from observed facts back to the explanations they purport to test is strewn with hazards that only thoughtfully planned and carefully designed studies can hope to minimize. Not only is research good, but good research is essential.

3. The "is" must be separated from the "ought." Or, more precisely, special pains must be taken to prevent the "ought" from masquerading as the "is."[1]

4. It is useful for the professor of educational administration to formulate a particular phenomenon with which he is concerned in terms more abstract than those immediately given. To see his particular case as an instance of a general process or category may allow him to learn from other instances, even though they seem quite disparate when viewed at the superficial level. If the principal and his problems can be formulated as an instance of role conflict, there may be much to gain from examining domains in which conflict of roles has been better studied, as among proctors of college examinations at Harvard, Southern Protestant clergymen during the desegregation crisis of the 1950s, or policemen in the aftermath of a natural disaster in their community. Simply accessing *Educational Index* under "Principals, problems of," is not likely to get the investigator far into potentially relevant research literature.

5. The investigator should worry about his *explanation* for a set of facts. An explanatory system should be considered an object of worth of its own; it should be set forth explicitly, turned around,

held up to the light, inspected for hidden assumptions, ambiguous concepts, internal inconsistencies, and logically improper deductions. Moreover, the investigator should direct his research toward checking and perfecting the explanatory scheme, all the while recognizing that the perfect explanation, the final word, can never be achieved. It is a goal to be pursued, not one to be attained.

6. And finally, the behavioral sciences can be a help in getting the enterprise started. After all, behavioral scientists have been in the business of studying people and groups for a good many years, and the literature of sociology, social psychology, and the like can propose ways of formulating questions, suggest fruitful concepts and modes of abstraction, propose methodological approaches, and more generally furnish a model to emulate.

These ingredients, wrapped together, form a reasonably coherent perspective or point of view. This perspective offers a way of professional life for a segment of academic educators who are intent upon making the study of education a career, replete with values, activities, institutional supports, and social norms. I am not sure what I would call the movement, and its attached perspective, that began to emerge in the mid-1950s. "Theory" is only a part of the package, implicated most directly in point 5 above, but it is hardly the key ingredient; other parts of the package can (and do) survive quite well without it. The "behavioral science movement" was an apt label through most of the 1960s, but in recent years, as the field has developed its own ignition system, point 6 has diminished in prominence. It is perhaps enough to refer to the movement as the "serious study of educational administration."[2]

In any event, it would be helpful to know which ingredients the prophets of despair have in mind when they proclaim the demise of the movement, for then a challenge could be more pointed.

The Study of Administration *Circa* 1950

I also cannot bring myself to believe that there has been little change at the working and producing level in our field over the past twenty years or that an initial surge of sophisticated energy peaked sometime in mid-period and it has all been down hill since then. No one would claim, I am sure, that the movement has taken hold on an even front across all departments of educational administration in the nation, nor is there reason to doubt that some of our colleagues have exploited the symbols of the perspective without acknowledging its substance. The same can be said for any social movement from Marxism to Feminism. Clearly, fiscal support for the serious study of educational administration has come on hard times in recent years, but this too is not unique to our field.

I am one of the first to despair at the poverty of research and theorizing that appears in the journals and dissertations. The dross rate is high when one searches for dependable studies in a given area, perhaps as high as 85 to 90 percent of referenced titles. Yet, what is the standard of comparison? Might we be measuring the present against extravagant expectations of how far a field can move, starting virtually at ground zero, in a short period of history? My personal experience vivifies some profound contrasts and makes me take note of how far we have come.

I entered the educational field in 1950 (the Bureau of Educational Research at the University of Illinois) fresh from doctoral studies in social psychology. George Stoddard, president of Illinois, Willard Spalding, dean of the College of Education, and a few others had the view of creating in the Bureau a site for basic investigations into a range of educational problems, and F. G. Cornell had been brought in as director. Among those present in the early days were Lee Cronbach, N. L. Gage, David Ausubel, David Krathwohl, and William McLure, to mention some recognizable names.

What did the study of educational administration amount to in the early 1950s? For professional journals there were the slick covers, *School Executive* and *Nation's Schools* and the *American School Board Journal,* and a small magazine soon to expire called *Educational Administration and Supervision*—none exactly a medium of scholarly exchange. Once every three years the *Review of Educational Research* devoted an issue (typically thin) to "Administration, Organization, and Finance," and that was about the size of it.

Professional meetings? The American Educational Research Association (AERA) in those predivisional days met in Atlantic City with the American Association of School Administrators (AASA) and the school board association amidst the school bus and floor wax displays, and as far as administration was concerned, it was difficult to determine by content whether one was attending an AERA or an AASA session. Nearly anything submitted in the name of research would be accepted on the program, and if a paper took inquiry too seriously—by highlighting the evidentiary basis of conclusions rather than practical implications—the audience would drift away.

Where was the research of quality in administration? There was one major study: Mort and Cornell's *American Schools in Transition,* published in 1937, and a string of dissertations under Paul Mort's aegis at Teachers College, Columbia, that followed the pioneering work. There might have been some other studies, especially in the area of finance, but I was not acquainted with them. At one point before the mid-1950s, naively believing there *must* be unmined treasures in the mountains of dissertations and periodical articles from the past, the Bureau staked me to a grant to obtain every source I could find relating to research on school board personnel. Those were the days of strictly interlibrary loan, often with a signed promise to return unpublished dissertations within ten days. This project was a terrible mistake. I sifted through hundreds of references, the vast majority of which had no empirical evidence of any variety, and ended with eighty or ninety "studies," mostly dissertations, which contained numbers in them. The trouble was, they were exactly alike. With three or four exceptions, they were all status studies of school board characteristics (age, sex, occupation, marital status, children in school, hobbies—the standard list) in some corner of some state, patterned after George Counts's survey in 1927 but without the understanding that Counts had of why one might collect such information.[3] It was absolutely bad reading. The dross rate in this instance was in the neighborhood of 99 and 44/100s percent.

How about colleagueship in the early 1950s—people I could talk to about the relevance of the work of Chester Barnard, of Dorwin Cartwright on social power, of Robert Merton on professionals in bureaucracies, of Harold Lasswell, Muzafer Sherif, or Max Weber for the study of educational administration? Outside of my immediate surroundings there was no one. Of course I was young and new to the field at the time, and perhaps it was due to unfamiliarity, but the fact was that there was no generally known or readily identifiable circle of scholars of school administration with whom one could make a connection.

Contrast, 1975

That was the scene, as I experienced it, *circa* 1950. The contrast with 1975 is sharp. We have several professional journals, perhaps not outstanding in the world of scholarship but certainly devoted to the study of educational administration. No longer need we tailor research reports to an audience, say, of secondary school principals. The thirty or so Division A sessions at the annual AERA meeting would hardly be mistaken for an AASA program. Research articles, monographs, and reports on one's "must read" list have begun to outstrip available time, and I see no signs of this receding.

There is no doubt that a number of academics across the North American continent take the serious study of school administration as the focus of their careers. It may not be their only business, but it is their main business. Their commitment, moreover, is not likely to be turned off and on by fluctuations of federal money.[4]

When I attend conferences I find a substantial number of people who share my perspective on the study of educational administration, who talk the same language, who, in short, are colleagues. The circle is not alarmingly large, but it is identifiable and functional. Moreover, I am regularly struck by new doctorates entering the field who take for granted a point of view literally unheard of among administrative trainees twenty years ago, and some have intellectual competencies as well as research skills that put the most sophisticated among us to shame.

Quality research is waxing, not waning. There are half a dozen subareas of school administration and organization the literature of which I have tracked rather closely over the years, and in none of them do I detect a decline in production of research or conceptual development. One of them is school board research. Despite my disastrous encounter with the literature in my formative years, Jay Scribner and I returned to the topic a few years ago to see what had happened to the research between 1952 and 1968.[5] It is worth reporting our observations in a little detail, since they help give perspective to Immegart's review in chapter 13 of this volume of research production in educational administration generally.

For one thing, school board research shared in the publication boom of the period that Immegart has noted. In the postwar interval from 1950 through 1959, the raw number of empirical studies and dissertations held steady at about seven per year, but in the next four years, from 1960 through 1963, the rate went to twelve per year, followed by a steep increase to twenty-one from 1964 through 1967, the last year for which we had complete data. (The frequencies are shown in Figure 1.) The great majority of the citations were dissertations or articles based on dissertations, as Immegart's summary would lead us to expect, and not many investigators appeared on the list with second or third studies. (We disregarded multiple reports of the same study.) On the other hand, there were several clusters of dissertations from the same university connected by a common theme and, in two or three of such clusters, one study built on the next to form a cumulative series. While Immegart seems to discount the growth in publication as being due to larger numbers of people in the field, I am impressed by the sheer volume of the empirical studies and what they portend for our knowledge of the domain.

More revealing, though, is the other trend shown in the figure. Those ubiquitous surveys of board member characteristics that had

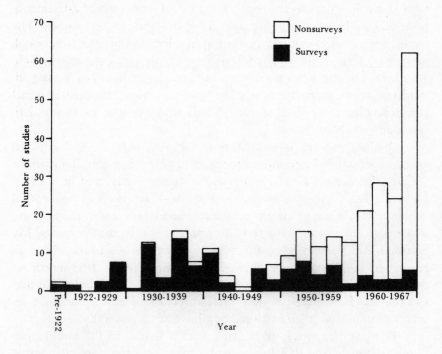

Figure 1. Studies of school board personnel, through 1967

dominated the literature for so long began to assume distinct minority status. Unlike the experience of my earlier review where I could predict with considerable confidence that the next interlibrary loan thesis would be a status study, Scribner and I, when we encountered a citation, could not firmly predict the quality or type of study. (By this time, of course, we were working with computerized searches and abstracts.) In that sense, the production of research associated with the New Look in educational administration certainly was not "more of the same."

Because of their great diversity, it is difficult to characterize succinctly the new generation of studies that began to appear. Some studies looked at the board's connection to the community, some its connection with the school bureaucracy, and some concentrated on its internal workings. Investigators examined how an individual gets on a school board, what he believes and does in office, and even what he does after he leaves.

It was abundantly clear from our review that the messages sent by leaders of the movement in educational administration had not been universally received by 1968 and that the espoused ideals had not been transformed suddenly into working skills and manifest research behavior. The newly born had not attained instant adulthood. Methodology, while proliferating in type, remained on a primitive level; questionnaires, cross-sectional designs, and one-way frequency distributions predominated. More often than not conclusions drawn were unrelated to evidence gathered, and much of the research was still painful to read for its want of purpose. It required little intuition to recognize that the majority of the authors did not regard themselves as researchers and that they were untrained for the role. Yet, there were signs of efforts to separate the is from the ought at least at the point of observation, and of efforts, no matter how feeble, to use more abstract concepts than the immediately given. Many concepts were drawn directly from the behavioral sciences of the day. Exceptional studies were more common than in my previous review and far more exceptional. The latter is an important point, since no field of scientific inquiry depends on its researcher from the rank and file for its advances but rather on the exceptional few with unique insight and skill.

School board research from 1952 to 1968 was heterogeneous in the extreme. While it would be a wild stretch of the imagination to read a deliberate strategy into it, it was as though investigators were trying on new ideas for size, probing for weak spots, seeking points that would yield to the tools of social science. The era was one of concepts, widely disparate and infirmly grasped, but decidedly not one of theories even in their weakest meaning. Since 1968, by my less systematic observation, matters have profoundly improved. Studies of the rank and file continue to be produced, to be sure, but truly exceptional studies, sophisticated in conceptualization, research methodology, and the development of bona fide theory, have also begun to appear. After seemingly exploring the environment at random, the infant is starting to learn to walk. The specialty is far from dead or dying.[6]

Another specialty the literature of which I have tracked for some time is the domain of turnover and mobility among teachers. Apart from a scattering of studies, such as Ward Mason's early investigation into the selectivity of beginning teachers, the specialty has been devoid of significant studies throughout the postwar period— until very recently. Among the several recent publications is George Pedersen's conceptually and methodologically sophisticated social-economic analysis of teacher migration.[7] This domain was virtually untouched by the New Look in educational administration but just now seems to be getting the benefit of it.

I could cite other contrasts and trends in the various working areas of educational administration to give credence to my difficulties in accepting the assessments of the prophets of gloom and demise, but these will suffice. Perhaps the problem lies in the prophets themselves—in their unrealistic expectations of what was required and how long it would take following insemination to move a field from birth to infancy to youth to adolescence and finally to adulthood. It does not happen overnight.

It is my faith in the present vigor of the field that makes it worth my while to turn to its future.

The Future of Research and Theory

Empiricist that I am, I find the future of anything a difficult subject with which to deal. Hard facts about it are rather scarce, and I do not choose to invent them, or alternative sets of them, as worthy as that enterprise might be in another context. I prefer rather to comment on several matters that periodically come to mind about the study of administration as I read in the field or help to plan projects.

The worth of replication. I am regularly surprised by how little attention we researchers pay to one another's work, or, more exactly, to the significant features of the work. It is certain that we are quick to pick up the new instruments that have been devised and to cite the more striking conclusions of studies, especially if they happen to support the position we are currently arguing. What I mean is, rarely do we attend to someone's study in *detail*. We are not inclined to fathom its line of reasoning, looking for the tacit but questionable assumptions, nor do we often make the effort to unravel the connections, loose or otherwise, between conceptual and operational definitions. Nor do we typically inspect the fall of the data in the tables to determine if they say more (or less) than the author sees in them, nor attempt to follow the line from the numbers back up the ladder of abstraction to the author's general allegations as certification that the leaps in logic do not challenge credence. What is more important, we rarely do these things with the intention in mind of correcting the obvious deficits or otherwise improving on the research in a study of our own. In short, we are uninclined to build on one another's work.

Closely associated with this observation, or perhaps another way of making it, is that replications of prior research are extremely rare in our field. Three times in my career I have been involved in a study designed to account for what seemed to be firm findings of an earlier investigation, but, before our nice explanatory scheme could be put to work, the original findings vanished. I am not sure to what degree the unfortunate injunction on doctoral candidates to produce an "original contribution" is responsible for our inclination to avoid the work of our colleagues, but I have nearly reached the point of *insisting* on replication in the doctoral thesis. It certainly would be "original" at this juncture.[8]

The paucity of dependable facts. Another matter that periodically concerns me is our curious tendency to glorify theory and high-flying conceptualization and to downplay fact. It is especially noticeable in a common type of AERA presentation in which three-quarters of the paper is devoted to words and phrases in which the empirical referents are utterly opaque, after which the operationally defined meanings and relationships are finally reached and are offered almost as an afterthought. I have always thought that theories are invented to explain puzzling facts and observed regularities, but our field seems to be long on theorizing and short on hard facts to be explained.

Some years ago I was present at a symposium on "adult socialization." Adult socialization is a set of more or less associated propositions designed to explain why people in a given role are more homogeneous in their values, motivations, and thoughtways than a random assortment of people from the population at large. It is, of course, just one explanation of the phenomenon of homogeneity, mechanisms of social selection being another. In any event, the reporting investigators were highly ingenious in using the ideas of adult socialization to guide their analyses of what happened to doctoral students going through the trauma of comprehensive examinations or to apprentice teachers undergoing one pattern or another of practice teaching. The studies all lacked one crucial thing, however—a phenomenon to explain. There was no firm evidence at the time, nor is there much more today, that academics who have survived the comprehensive exam or teachers who have emerged from their apprenticeships are more homogeneous than a random sample of the population, once age and sex are taken into account. Here was an elaborate theory in search of some facts to explain.

I am not one to advocate raw empiricism, but I sometimes believe that our priorities are lopsided, that instead of devoting so much time to spinning webs of abstruse concepts and propositions we should be paying closer heed to the problems of accurate description and measurement. Little of our research effort is directed toward examining the psychometric properties of the indexes and scales we invent or borrow. In the unlikely event that a previous investigator has made a quick check of split-half reliability on a measure and attaches a coefficient of, say, .70 to it, when we borrow the measure for our own research we rarely ask whether that value will stand up under more careful examination or even whether a split-half estimate is the relevant one for our intended use of the measure. We do not try to improve on the measure or subject it to scrutiny. Said generally, measurement technology is not a tradition in our field, and, without it, hard, dependable facts to which to address our explanatory schemes are few and far between.

The road to relevant theory. Finally, I would like to comment on the several expressions of disillusionment with the behavioral sciences so often heard these days. The New Look is on the wane, we are told, because the workers in the field have begun to realize that the issues addressed by inquiry based on disciplines are irrelevant to the problems of school administration. It is said that emphasis on the study of administration has led us away from the practical.

If much of the research that appears in our journals is impractical, as I believe it is, the reason is not that serious study, inquiry based on disciplines, or use of the behavioral sciences inherently makes it so. Rather, the problem resides in the particular analytical schemes and the particular concepts we have drawn from the behavioral sciences to apply to the issues of our field.

Consider for a moment the practical, everyday dilemmas of the working school administrator or, indeed, the working professor, consultant, or researcher. His basic question is, how can I get from here to there? What can I do this afternoon to affect the situation tomorrow, or what is going to come back to haunt me next fall if I take this step now? His dilemmas are ones of acts and their subsequent consequences, the focus is on events moving through time, the language is a language of verbs.

Now consider the character of research on educational administration that follows the sociological, or social-psychological, version of organizational theory, to take a currently prominent example. As I read it, I see nothing moving, no one acting, and no indications of how one gets from here to there. Time stands still. The underlying theory is essentially static. The propositions mainly concern the way various pieces of the organization are presumed to fit together to form a whole, and the central concepts directing the researcher's observations are nounlike typologies. The propositions read like this: If the organization is of such-and-such a type with respect to the service it renders, then its form will be decentralized (or centralized), power will rest on expertise (or legitimacy), channels of communication will be horizontal (or vertical), and competing interests will be resolved through consensus (or bargaining). Then the research follows suit. Twenty or fifty organizations are selected and classified by type, questionnaires are administered and correlations are run on the aggregated data. Given this kind of theory, correlations are perfectly satisfactory, since the propositions make no allegations of causality and nothing is claimed to be antecedent to anything else. It is simply a matter of establishing how well the data fit.

It is instructive to go through journals to examine the principal concepts used in this genre of administrative research. They are static concepts. Even when they refer to people rather than the organization as a whole, they refer to enduring attributes of people, such as job satisfaction, leadership style, or pupil control ideology, and it does not matter whether the researcher measures them today, tomorrow, or next month, for, short of measurement error, the score on the measure should be the same. They change glacially, if at all, and are presumed to vary only under massively disparate types of context.

Theories of behavioral science do not have to be static. Demography is not, nor is learning theory in psychology, whether Hullian or Skinnerian. In these domains it matters what comes before what. The time order of events is built into the very foundations of the explanatory systems and, for the most part, the research necessary to test the propositions could not get by with cross-sectional designs and correlational procedures. This is not to say that demography or learning theory would be relevant to the problems of educational administration but only that the particular behavioral science on which we have depended so heavily in certain realms of our field is ill suited to the task of illuminating practical affairs of the workaday world.

Relevance would be better served by theoretical schemes that permit us to talk about what tilts when you push in a certain place, how long it takes between push and tilt, whether the object is likely to right itself after the push, whether to push back, or knock into something else. Empirical investigation can lead to the development of such schemes. To do so, investigators must focus on acts rather than states, must keep an eye on the clock or calendar, and must be prepared to isolate sequences of cause and effect. Once a set of accurately measured, time-dependent regularities has been observed, and the observations replicated, theories will be invented to explain them, and the theories will be relevant to the practitioner.

Notes

1. I have long regarded the distinction between "is" and "ought" as misleading with respect to the task of research. A focus on studying what is seems to convey the idea that research ends with description. While some research may appropriately end with pure description, much seeks to go beyond that to explanation. A cumbersome but more accurate phrasing would pose the distinction as "the way things work" versus "the way they ought to work."

2. In no way can the perspective I have described be called a "paradigm," if one means the term as Thomas Kuhn used it in *The Structure of Scientific Revolutions* (Chicago, Ill.: University of Chicago Press, 1962). In his usage paradigms exist in fields of established scientific study once they have passed through a preparadigmatic epoch. The study of educational administration is still struggling to reach the preparadigmatic status.

3. It is fitting to mention one of the exceptions. I must say I dreaded receiving notices from the library that still another thesis had arrived and would have to be returned within *x* days, and notice Number 35 reporting the receipt of a Stanford dissertation was no different in that respect. But it soon became apparent that the study was different. Its author had actually read George Counts's monograph and understood the argument; he had gone beyond the conventional survey to collect additional data, voting records of the board members, with the view of testing a logical implication of the Counts position. His empirical procedures were shaky, but the author had a clear purpose for the study, and it was easily five standard deviations above the mean. I mention it because it was my first encounter with the name of Roald Faye Campbell.

4. The importance usually assigned to outside grants, incidentally, may lead us to overlook the major source of support for scholarly work in a field: the academic post itself. I suppose the several universities with which I have been associated during my life have contributed through regular department budgets over 80 percent of the funds necessary to keep me alive, well, and productive.

5. This work was never brought to fruition, due to the unexpected volume of studies we encountered and the competition of other commitments.

6. It is likely, though, that school board research will become a less distinct specialty as more abstract concepts or subsuming analytical schemes come to be applied to the study of the school. Scribner and I, in 1968, encountered a number of important contributions to board research that were parts of more encompassing studies—studies which never could be conceived (and were not referenced) as simply "school board research," and my impression is that the phenomenon is more pronounced now.

7. K. George Pedersen, *The Itinerant Schoolmaster* (Chicago, Ill.: University of Chicago Press, 1973).

8. My comment should not be taken as condoning the pointless *repetition* of earlier research, such as occurred in the endless surveys of board member characteristics from the late 1920s through the 1950s.

16. The Future of Practice

WAYNE M. CARLE

It has been said in this volume that gains in the development of research and theory in educational administration have fallen short of those envisioned twenty years ago. To blame, some have averred, are the social convulsions that disrupted the schools, the federal dollars that diverted college research efforts, and the affirmative actions that allegedly diluted selection standards of faculty and students. One could infer that professors, still smarting from forced engagement with the outside world of the 1960s, are eager to get back to their "real" world of study and contemplation.

I hope that this is no impulse toward aloofness, for American education needs a rebirth of philosophy and values, of ideas and inspiration, for which we traditionally have looked to the universities. Yet the distance between the scholarly world of the professor and the pragmatic world of the practitioner may constitute the gap between theory and practice we all say exists in our field.

Remoteness between actors in the public schools and observers on the university campus has undoubtedly minimized what we have been able to abstract and apply from the tumultuous past decade. What, for example, have we learned from the conflicts and commotion that can be applied to better school management? In what ways

will practitioners be better prepared and professors be better pre-
parers, to deal with tomorrow's equivalents of the desegregation,
militancy, social conflict, mobility, technology, and war that characterized the 1960s?

Would that we were armed by our experiences to lead the educational reformation for which so many are calling. Instead, we may
foresee with Lewis B. Mayhew that education "is moving into a
period of neglect." School administrators, he says, need "the art of
intelligently coping with an arbitrary fate."[1] Declines in enrollment,
school closings, collective bargaining and fiscal bankruptcy seemingly
are combining to give today's school manager little control over the
destiny of the educational institution, much less of the society it is
supposed to affect.

No, it is not the best of times for school administration. Aside
from college presidents, few educational administrators have won
widespread recognition for their leadership. When *Saturday Review/
World* named the preeminent educator of the past fifty years, it was
not a school administrator. Wrote James Cass of the magazine's
choice, John Dewey: "More than anyone else he made us aware—
luminously aware—of the students we teach as the alpha and omega
of our thinking about curriculum, methods, and the organization of
education. Indeed, I'd allege that he is the only *great* educator in our
history."[2] Far from being so praised, many administrators are dis-
tressed. For them maintaining a positive outlook has become difficult. Dwight Teel, who like James Redmond of Chicago was an acting superintendent for the 1974-1975 year while their boards of
education sought successors, took pains to urge his Milwaukee staff
to avoid cynicism: "One of the things that has disturbed me the most
in recent years is the lack of basic trust on the part of the community for the schools and sometimes on the part of the staff members
for the superintendency and with their colleagues."[3]

Thus, in this last quarter of the twentieth century, it does not
appear that there is much in which the practitioner of educational
administration can take heart. If not encouraging, however, it may at
least be instructive to note that the last twenty difficult years have
shown some signs of progress.

After the neglect of the Depression of the 1930s and the war-
time 1940s, the "frustrating 1950s" became a decade of search and
self-examination for the nation. For the schools it was a period of

rising demands and flaming disagreement about what the schools were and should be doing. Russia's orbiting of Sputnik in 1958 inflicted self-doubt on Americans for the first time in the steady rise by the United States to the pinnacle of world power.

For most of that decade the President's Commission on National Goals, appointed by President Eisenhower, struggled to define what our country should be about and doing. Their recommendations were published in 1960[4] and included these goals for education:

    • Education should be strengthened at every level and in every discipline;

    • A higher proportion of the gross national product should be devoted to educational purposes;

    • Small and inefficient school districts should be consolidated, reducing the number from 40,000 to 10,000;

    • Every state should have a high-level board of education;

    • Teachers' salaries must be improved;

    • Two-year colleges should be within commuting distance;

    • Graduate school capacity must be approximately doubled;

    • Adult education should stress education throughout life;

    • Financial support should increase from $20 billion to $40 billion by 1970;

    • The federal government should supplement state funds and offer matching grants to states.

To a considerable extent these goals have been addressed by our country. Attainment of some of them has escaped us, however. The number of school districts, for example, remains at more than 16,000, and some states still do not have boards of education. Although Senator Robert Taft, "Mr. Republican," advocated it at the time, there still is no program of general federal aid to education. Still, education is getting a larger share of the gross national product. For the first time, expenditures for schools and colleges are approaching the outlay for national defense.

The period also has seen passage of the National Defense Education Act, the Vocational Education Act, the Manpower Development and Training Act, the Elementary and Secondary Education Act, and unprecedented civil rights and equal opportunities legislation that have had lasting impact on public education. The schools have become a national priority.

Can the decades ahead be less eventful? Probably not, although to predict trends in this present period of worldwide economic, energy, and political stagnation seems more difficult than prophesying may have appeared to be in the expansive period just ended.

Nevertheless, here are some forecasts about the practice of school administration.

1. Schools, and school administration, will survive the next two decades. Despite efforts of the "deschoolers," the venerable institution of public education will continue to involve, as students or teachers, about one-fourth of all Americans. Despite gloomy "widespread pessimism about the ability of public schools to make rapid and adequate adaptation to our fast-changing times,"[5] schools will continue to move about as fast as the public will permit. Despite the doom implied in reports of a general decline in pupil achievement,[6] schools will continue to be viewed as the most efficient means of transmitting knowledge.

In saying this, I am not unaware of the severe limitations of public education that have been exposed in the past two decades. For those who idealize American schooling it is painful to have the eminent historian who told us in an unprecedented *Life* editorial in 1950 that "our schools have kept us free," later say: "To judge by results—the results of the past 40 years or so—this whole enterprise of relying on schools to reform society by direct teaching has been an unmitigated failure. After 40 years of exposure to world cultures, world politics, world geography, we have turned out to be culturally more alienated, politically more isolated, economically more reckless, and, on the world scene, more chauvinistic and militaristic than at any previous time in our history."[7] But these more recent words of Henry Steele Commager, written in the wake of Watergate, perhaps serve to remind us of the dual role of schools and society in education—and of the failure of the latter to provide examples from life of the values the former is expected to teach.

In spite of the myriad inadequacies of the present educational system, it will continue because of the universal human need that will not be better met. Formalized learning must be nearly as old as our species. "In man," writes Bronowski, "before the brain is an instrument for action, it has to be an instrument of preparation." He speculates that our ancestral cousin, *Australopithecus,* had many orphans who needed help through their long childhoods: "Therefore there must have been a social organization in which children were looked after and (as it were) adopted, were made part of the community, and so in some general sense were educated."[8] That formalized learning is a necessity of life also was stressed by Dewey: "The inequality of achievement between the mature and immature not only necessitates teaching the young, but the necessity of this teaching gives an immense stimulus to reducing experience to that order and form which will render it most easily communicable and hence most usable."[9] Thus, to assume that an institution as deeply rooted in human need and as durably planted in human society as American schools presently are, will be abandoned or replaced in the foreseeable future is as unrealistic as the revolutionaries who in recent years have proposed it. Administrators, while less durable, will still be needed.

2. *Administrative practitioners will be presiding over institutions that are little changed by 1995.* Although the past two decades have seen the emergence of the middle school and a substantial move toward open and individualized instruction in elementary schools, the American high school is largely unchanged. True, there has been a stampede toward vocational schools and magnet centers, but the comprehensive high school is largely traditional. In the North Central Association's national survey of twenty-seven important innovations reported in high schools eight years ago, Cawelti found not only low adoption rates but also high abandonment rates for new practices in most schools.

Reports that a closer working relationship between broadcasters and educators is foreseen in a study released by the Corporation for Public Broadcasting[10] do not assure that school administrators will make better use of new media than in the past. The lag that has existed between the schools and business and the armed services in the use of electronic, programmed, and laboratory technology can be expected to continue.

One even could speculate that schools may resort to past practices rather than to new forms in the future, what with former United States Commissioner of Education Terrell H. Bell's holding that "the key to dramatic progress in American education is to gain a rededication to learning in the home." Furthermore, after a decade of storefront, parkway, part-time, and magnet models, alternative school "father" Mario Fantini has advocated options *within* the American school.[12]

This is not to say that no new models will emerge. Recent reports from the United States Office of Education indicate student dissatisfaction with traditional school hours and subjects and interest in more work-study, volunteer and external learning opportunities. Briner and Sroufe predict that by 1985 administrators will be accounting for the quality of each school, and that differences among schools will become positive attributes. Nonetheless, Miller's observation about school administrators and the status quo is likely to persist in the foreseeable future: "In the main, those of us who are school practitioners dare not, and to be completely candid, we care not to serve as democratic change agents. Schools are organized and school people are appointed by boards of education to be followers, not leaders; to be defenders of the status quo, not agitators for reform. We obey the power structure in our communities, and the power structure wants no waves, no controversy, and no unnecessary budget hikes."[13]

3. *Administrators will be dealing with younger and older learners in the future.* Lifelong learning will be centered in schools as never before. From preschool through adult vocational and avocational classes, schools are going to serve a wider range of clients.

This is so not merely because of the growing interest in community school programs, but also—for the first time since World War II—because schools have surplus space and unemployed teachers. What better way to use them than to serve three- and four-year-olds (often while mother and dad work), the ungraduated, and the unfulfilled?

Perhaps it was with tongue only partly in cheek that "Doc" Howe reported—in *Saturday Review/World*'s look at the next half century—to "Madame" President on the White House Conference on Education of 2024, noting the decline of career education, the rise of lifelong learning, and the possibility of "the butcher with a Ph.D."[14]

4. *Fewer administrators will be employed.* Innumerable teachers have prepared for administration in the past and been disappointed at finding no openings. This situation will be exacerbated in the future.

Formerly, when teachers tired of waiting for an opening on what appeared to be a seniority basis in smaller systems, they moved to the city in search of opportunity. Now the chances for mobility are declining. A National School Boards Association survey[15] showed that for the decade ended in 1973 enrollments declined in forty-four

of the forty-eight largest cities. The drop showed up even in suburban districts, and staff cuts were made throughout the country.
Campbell and others suggest that there may be less than one-third
the present number of school districts in the future, although the loss
of superintendents and part-time principals from abolishing smaller
units may be offset by more central office administrators and full-
time principals.[16]

With reduction of teaching staffs and closing of buildings, however, the pattern at the moment is for principals and central office
personnel to be laid off or reassigned so as not to give the appearance
of favoring one group over another. This reduction is unfortunate,
for American schools traditionally have been undersupervised.

This condition was noted as long as twenty years ago by Sargent
and Belisle. They observed that "school systems in general and irrespective of size are basically suffering from a deprivation of administrative resources. . . ." Span of control from administrator to teacher
and other school employees is nowhere near as close as in business
and industry.

Moreover, schools have few external resources to which to turn.
". . . the structure of assistance and auxiliary aids at state and federal levels, or via other resource units available to and serving local
school systems, is relatively small and undeveloped in comparison."[17]
The limited growth of state education departments and regional service centers under federal stimulus the past decade have not filled the
breech. Perhaps it was this deprivation which led so many schools to
turn to consultants when federal money became available—an experience that often led to disappointment. "Many times, during the last
1960's," write Bonwit and Kirsch, "there were monies which had
been spent; and the hiring of a consultant was done without adequate needs assessment procedures."[18]

5. *Administrative talent will continue to be in short supply.* If
everyone who holds an administrator's license possessed the qualities
boards of education list on prospectuses for job openings, perhaps
there would be no shortage and little turnover in the school management field.

For a short time in the 1960s, the average tenure of superintendents in large cities was down to two years. It may have improved: the Indiana Association of School Administrators reported
for 1975 that the average experience of a superintendent in a larger
city was approximately the same as the average for all 305 Indiana

school districts—6.6 years.[19] On the other hand, although Cleveland Superintendent Paul Briggs observed his twelfth anniversary on the job in 1975, thereby becoming the dean of the largest city administrators, Ohio State Superintendent Martin Essex reported an unprecedented number of openings for school administrators in that state in 1975, many of them where school boards had fired the incumbent.[20]

This condition was echoed by former Commissioner Bell when he said, "Another thing I think needs our attention is the high turnover rate in school administration. . . . I know one city that is looking for its seventh superintendent in nine years."[21] George Brain and Paul Salmon of AASA planned a seminar for suburban superintendents in the summer of 1975 on "Everything you wanted to know about getting a job and were afraid to ask."

Leadership is in short supply worldwide. Combs observes that "because educational systems have become so complex, they need carefully recruited, well-trained modern managerial personnel of many sorts. ". . . since there is a world-wide shortage of such people, an educational system suffers from a self-inflicted wound if it denies itself a potential source of managerial talent lying beyond the products of its own inbreeding process. . . . because of the complex tasks now facing educational systems, they need not only 'administrators' in the narrow meaning of the term, but a diversified management team."[22] These needs are likely to increase the interdisciplinary approaches to the development of administrative talent.

6. *Professors and practitioners will be in closer liaison.* That there are at least ten times as many administrators in service as in preparation has dawned on many departments of educational administration. They are moving to serve in-service needs, much as the National Academy for School Executives and the School Management Institute have been providing education at midcareer.

This is as university programs should be, and as some have aspired to be. In fact, it may be less difficult to bring faculty and field together than some have assumed. Armour found that, as groups, superintendents and professors agreed to a high degree as to the personal and conceptual dimensions of administrative skills.[23] In other words, both groups had more in common than in disagreement about administration as art versus administration as science, practice versus theory, and subjectivity versus objectivity.

This joint concern for development at midcareer will focus new attention on the study of school administration by both practitioners and professors.

7. *Together they will evolve a theory of administration.* Many of the programs now underway in departments of administration are outgrowths of the research undertaken through the Cooperative Program in Educational Administration (CPEA) and the leadership of AASA's Committee for the Advancement of School Administration. They have given the practitioner more insight than ever before.

For example, when I was engaged in a graduate program twenty years ago, conventional wisdom focused on administrative roles, tasks, and processes. These did not seem complicated, since they essentially described the organization and operation of schools as they were.

It was possible to orient a student of school administration with considerable specificity. Reeder went so far as to include in his textbook a fold-out sample of a pupil's cumulative record. He illustrated an office desk, demonstrating how to organize the drawers (miscellaneous committee reports, lower left drawer).[24]

Hunt and Pierce lamented that administrative tasks pulled principals and superintendents away from the theoretical realm: "Administrators began to expend relatively less effort on systematic educational theory largely because of the increasing multiplicity and complexity of administrative problems attending urban development, and the phenomenal growth of professional literature produced in the main by staffs of teacher-training institutions, professional organizations and educational foundations."[25]

Eastmond hoped that through action research and the fading out of the line-staff structure into more democratic participation a profession unified on a solid base of research would emerge: "Unity within a profession and public confidence do not come automatically or easily; they must be sought for and honestly earned. For teaching this seeking and earning involves the long, slow process of research, of validating methods and procedures, and of grounding school programs in the findings of psychology, sociology, anthropology, and other behavioral sciences."[26]

It remained, however, for a series of endeavors by CPEA to move beyond practice to constructs of theory. The case study method was explored, by Sargent and Belisle with courses in cases and concepts at Harvard, by Culbertson and others growing out of the University of Oregon seminars, and by movement by Campbell, Gregg, and others into behavioral research. Beyond the in-basket simulation developed through CPEA, Boardman developed a model for computer simulation of administrative problem solving. Griffiths targeted on decision making as the central process of administration.[27]

Interest in the development of theory does not assure that housekeeping may not continue to preoccupy many practitioners. Principal Kimball Howes maintains that the proper utilization of time is "the key management problem school administrators face."[28] But for many administrators and professors the pursuit of theory will remain an absorbing intellectual pursuit: "Within a set of principles, yet to be formulated, it will be possible to predict the behavior of individuals within the organizational framework, and it will be possible to make decisions that will result in a more efficient and effective enterprise."[29]

8. *Personal, human qualities will dominate theoretical constructs.* Arriving at a theory of management that implies control of a democratic institution such as education sounds ominous, with Orwellian overtones, perhaps. Davies warns that, "The impending Breakthrough in educational administration, irresistibly carried along by a world rushing into ever vaster and more complex organization, can lead to the elimination of our current concepts of freedom."[30]

It would appear, however, that an understanding of behavior, of human relations and communication, is essential to the perpetuation of a democratic organization. Sachs maintains that the human side of administration, and human values, cannot be ignored. According to Sargent and Belisle, "Unless an administrator really understands and behaves in terms of the implications of the past quarter-century's accumulated knowledge and thinking about the nature and dynamics of social organization and human behavior, his awareness of the human aspects of administration is archaic, no matter how up-to-date his technical knowledge may be."[31]

Wiles holds that "In light of present data . . . the way to better schools seems to be in the decision of the official leadership to work within the group and the development of practices which implement that commitment." So important is an understanding of human relationships that Stoops and Rafferty say, "It is highly probable that the next great advance in education will have to wait on the development of a generation of administrators who know how to tap the vast unplumbed resources at present lying unused in the persons and intelligence of teachers, vice-principals, bus drivers, janitors and attendance clerks."[32]

Netzer and others claim that the new professionalism in school administration will be so oriented toward humans that it will be characterized by consumer control, indifference to credentials, superordinate purpose, an attitude of criticism, and impatience with rate of change: "the animus is compassion."[33] This degree of change seems unlikely, but humane qualities undoubtedly are being sought in persons filling administrative positions.

Indeed, as popularized in the press, today's successful school administrator must be almost charismatic. Item: Four months after devoting two articles to describing the chaos he saw in a Chicago high school, newspaper columnist Jack Mabley found a remarkable turnabout in school atmosphere and attitude with the appointment of a "determined, businesslike woman" as principal.[34]

In the years ahead, practitioners and theoreticians will be searching for the precise personal qualities that make leaders of administrators. Merrow, Foster, and Estes suggest that, "What is needed is integrity, the capacity for leadership, and an inclination toward a life of the mind. By life of the mind, we mean humane learning and the habits of reflection and introspection."[35]

9. *Administrators will be evaluated and paid on the criteria of performance.* School executives are increasingly being weaned away from ratios tied to the teaching salary schedule. This may work to the detriment of administrators as teacher pay rises. In fact, a national study for 1975 indicated that the highest salary paid an American school superintendent did not change from the previous year, and that the lowest salary dropped among the large cities group.[36]

As administrative theory becomes increasingly based on behavior, however, it seems likely that results will be able to be measured and documented. "One of the things that we will want to emphasize is to teach management by objectives and evaluation of education and how to tie that into a results-oriented management system," says former Commissioner Bell.[37] This is reinforced by the movement towards accountability and management systems expressed in acronyms such as MBO, PPBS, and PERT.

Spalding has proposed a scheme for rating administrative positions, based on quantitative and subjective measurements of eight factors (see Table I). For example, the impact on a school system of decisions made by a given position's incumbent and the exposure to risk inherent in those decisions are considered to be important measures of responsibility and, hence, of the accountability entailed in the position. Table II shows a matrix for measuring the level of impact, on one axis, and the frequency of exposure to risk, on the other. The various levels of impact on the school system range from the greatest at Level A down to a very minor impact at Level K. The exposure to risk ranges from constant, through frequent and infrequent, to seldom.

Table I. Proposed Administrators' Rating Plan[38]

Factors	Maximum points	Percent
1. Accountability—impact of decisions	300	25.0
2. Decision making	200	16.7
3. Knowledge and experience	175	14.6
4. Number of students	150	12.5
5. Number of staff	130	10.8
6. Working relationships	120	10.0
7. Public involvement	75	6.2
8. Amount of budget	50	4.2
Totals	1,200	100.0

Table II. Accountability—Impact of Decisions[39]

Level of impact of decisions on system	Constant	Frequent	Infrequent	Seldom
A	300	285	270	255
B	285	270	255	240
C	270	255	240	225
D	255	240	225	210
E	240	225	210	195
F	225	210	195	180
G	210	195	180	165
H	195	180	165	150
I	180	165	150	135
J	165	150	135	120
K	150	135	120	105

Similar matrixes are provided for each of the other factors involved in rating a position. Table III illustrates the application of the rating plan to the position of superintendent of schools. Table IV illustrates a position for the duties and responsibilities on which a position rating would be based.

Table III. Rating for position of superintendent of schools $(60:67)$[40]

Position Rating

Date: May, 1974

TITLE: SUPERINTENDENT	POINTS
1. Accountability-Impact of Decisions—Incumbent's decisions are of Level A impact on the school system and involve almost constant exposure to risks	300
2. Decision Making—Constantly makes decisions at Level A of complexity.	200
3. Knowledge and Experience—Superintendent's certificate which specifies a Master's degree plus 30 semester hours; ten years of combined teaching, supervisory and administrative experience. A-9	175
4. Number of Students—Responsible for the instructional achievements of all students in the school system.	230
5. Number of Staff—Responsible for entire school corporation staff.	130
6. Working Relationships—Directly accountable to the Board of School Trustees. Level A.	120
7. Public Involvement—Level A of involvement.	75
8. Amount of Budget—Responsible for the entire school corporation expenditures of approximately $27,000,000.	50
Total	1,280
Rate Group	——

Other work on behavioral descriptions of the work of school administration is proliferating. Ehrenberg has compiled an excellent set of criteria for evaluating specific competencies involved in instructional leadership.[41] This greater specificity in describing what administrators do, together with evaluation based on performance, will lead to more equitable rewards.

Table IV. Position description on which rating can be based. $(60:48)^{42}$

Position Description

Title	Date
Assistant Superintendent	May 15, 1974
For Curriculum and Instruction	

Division/Department	Written by
Curriculum and Instruction	R. O. Spalding & Associates

Basic Function—To develop and administer the instructional program, K through 12, for all schools in the School City of Hammond; to provide auxiliary instructional services, as needed.

Duties and Responsibilities—This position reports directly to the Superintendent and is responsible for:

• Supervising all Directors and Staff in the instructional area and all school Principals.

• Developing new curriculum based on appropriate research.

• Recommending all school staffing to the Superintendent.

• Developing instructional budgets in coordination with the Assistant Superintendent for Business and Management Services.

• Directing all special State and Federal programs.

• Providing special education classes for qualifying students.

• Providing pupil personnel services to students, as required.

• Providing adult and vocational education as needed.

• Recommending school boundary changes when necessary to spread the enrollment as equitably as possible.

• Providing proper inservice training for all instructional employees.

• Furnishing instructional specifications for new and renovated school facilities to the Assistant Superintendent for Business and Management Services.

• Supervising, through subordinates, textbook selection for all courses of study.

• Serving as a member of the Superintendent's Executive and the Rate Structure Committees and as an advisor in negotiations.

• Helping to maintain an effective public relations program for the corporation's schools and policies.

Job Qualifications and Related Facts

1. Master's degree required, Doctor's degree preferred; Administration and Supervision Certificate; nine years of combined teaching and administrative experience.

2. Length of Contract: Twelve months with four weeks vacation.

10. Middle management will assume increased authority and responsibility. A trend towards decentralization already is established. An Educational Research Service survey indicates that 42.6 percent of all school systems now have a policy encouraging decentralized decision making, and another 15.2 percent are in the process of developing one.[43] If the struggle between boards of education and teacher organizations does not bargain away all prerogatives of management, decentralization promises a greater voice to those who work closest to the line of action in schools.

In the administrative reorganization study cited earlier, Spalding recommended implementing an improved financial accounting package by cost centers and programs. Then, he urged, "expand the budget responsibility of Principals and Department Directors to encompass, eventually, all elements of cost, including staffing, maintenance, utilities, materials, supplies, etc."[44]

Whereas program planning and budgeting systems mandated by the state have met delay and controversy in many parts of the country, including reversal in California, I hope that one offshoot will be the hastening of universal conversion to Federal Handbook II accounting procedures. As such new financial systems are implemented—so definite costs can be determined in each school building and central office department area—more and more budget responsibility should be given to the principals and department heads.

With this authority, principals and department heads can effect a better match between available resources and needs. Overall guidelines would be required for their direction, and this expansion of responsibility would have to be accomplished in an orderly fashion, but school system management would be improved in direct relation to the flexibility permitted those who directly managed the instructional programs at the school level.

11. It is regrettable that blacks, Latinos, and women will be mostly in token roles and will not be involved in policy making in school administration for the foreseeable future. This is a prediction that I fervently wish would not be true twenty years from now, but past experience indicates otherwise.

An early mentor of mine was a superintendent in whose schools I not only grew up but was later hired. I recall his musing with me, circa 1955, that he thought the time had come to consider hiring a Polynesian in one of the elementary schools of our college town.

Parents of the school nearest the university campus might not object, he reasoned. I left town before this staff "integration" began but had occasion recently to check the latest federal figures for Provo, Utah. Two decades later there are now four minority teachers on a staff of 332—two Oriental and two Spanish. Little wonder that minority persons continue to shake their heads and say, "How long, O Lord, how long?"

I could not help recalling testimony in the Dayton, Ohio, desegregation case in Federal District Court. The former superintendent of schools, evidence showed, had assured the National Association for the Advancement of Colored People (NAACP), back in the mid-1950s, that Negro teachers would be hired "as we find community acceptance for them." A former personnel director who served during that period of time was asked about the slow pace of hiring blacks in the ensuing years. "Well," he said, "we were being cautious but moving forward in what our board of education called a policy of 'dynamic gradualism.'"

The DeFunis case and other resistance to affirmative action have disillusioned black Americans. As NAACP Attorney Nathanial Jones puts it:

As for the general mood of black people, I offer the following: Blacks feel themselves buffeted about on every front. It seems that as soon as progress appears realistically achievable, whether in housing, education or jobs, the whistle gets blown and the rules of the game are changed. In school desegregation, just as the HEW guidelines and Federal judges were getting down to business, the country elected and re-elected an anti-integration President, who fired Leon Panetta, made nationwide appeals against busing and instructed his Justice Department to intervene in desegregation cases against the interests of black children. As the moment of truth was about to appear for contractors and labor unions, the Secretary of Labor issued a memorandum defanging Home Town Plans.[45]

If we can be honest with ourselves, we will recognize that blacks who have been hired in school administration tend to be placed in "soft money" positions, rather than line assignments. Many are promoted and assigned to schools of turmoil. Theirs are the least desirable and least powerful roles. As Singleton observes: "Black educational administrators, like their black counterparts in practically every other municipal service, are inheriting the nation's cities at a time when concomitant forces are rendering them bankrupt areas."[46]

There is no reason to assume that all-white suburban and rural schools will not remain racially isolated for years to come and that two societies at war with each other, predicted by the Kerner Commission in 1968, will not continue to emerge in our country.

Nor can we speculate that schools will deal with sexism any more effectively than with racism. We are steeped in both. One of the widely used textbooks on school administration, in fact, titles a whole section on the educational administrator as an individual, as "The Man."[47]

At the root of school discrimination and separation, of course, is the political system which preaches equality of opportunity but provides unequal resources, support, and treatment of pupils. Carter states, "The fact that the public school system as it is now organized has evidenced little influence on the child's achievement, independent of background and social class, does not prove that social class determines educational achievement, but rather that social class —specifically the white middle class—has governed school organization, orientation, and methodology."[48] Educational administrators have shown little propensity to challenge or change the white middle class of which such an overwhelming proportion of them are members.

Maybe the only way to end intra- and interstate disparities in educational opportunity is to consider, as Rosenberg suggests, a constitutional amendment: "Section 1. Education in public schools is a fundamental right guaranteed to all the people of the United States; Section 2. The right to equality of educational opportunity in public schools shall not be denied or abridged by the United States or by any state on account of sex, religion, racial/ethnic background, economic condition, or place of birth or residence; Section 3. Congress shall have the power to enforce this article by appropriate legislation."[49] And add, with Rosenberg, that "At one point in our history we concluded that this country could not endure half slave and half free. Today we must conclude that this country cannot endure half well educated and half poorly educated." To the extent that we can give life to the concept of equal opportunity we will rectify longstanding discrimination against minorities and women in American education.

12. *The board-administration relationship will remain crucial in school management.* When Chicago Superintendent James Redmond announced in April 1975 that after nine years' service he would not

seek another term, he stated two reasons: a board of education that ventured beyond policy into administrative matters, and a board whose bickering members could not unify on solutions to the schools' pressing problems. His reasons can characterize the situation in many cities.

Ericson, in studying factors influencing morale of superintendents, listed the relationship with the board as paramount. "Although one would expect a superintendent to be concerned about his relationship with the board, its effect upon his morale is greater than might at first be surmised."[50]

The problem is multiplied by a public only half of which knows "there is a difference between a 'school board' and a 'school administration' and that the latter is legally subordinate to the former."[51] Furthermore, public pressure against secrecy in government will make it increasingly difficult for board and administration to meet informally to promote understanding. As Bagin predicts, "A few years from now, school officials will probably reflect on the recent past and remember executive sessions and the opportunities that once existed for private discussion of school matters. The way trends of complete openness are developing this kind of reflection might take place nearly everywhere."[52] Blurring of policy making and administration roles, politicized blocs on boards and public pressures do not augur well for future relationships between boards and superintendents.

13. Power brokering will continue to limit administrative effectiveness. Depolitization of the schools at the turn of the century was intended to professionalize the management of schools. But the very reforms that paved the way for the superintendency and principalship also led to expansion of staff, formation of unions, contracts, and teachers' virtual power of veto over school board policy making. Thus came the rise of "teacher power" as an outgrowth of earlier designs to "limit citizen participation and to improve the schools."[53]

Today, on the one hand, boards are being warned of giving away too much to teachers, while, on the other hand, being demanded to include parents and the public in the process. Says a nationally active board member, Robert L. Ridgley: "One can reasonably accept collective bargaining for public employees without opening the floodgates on scope of negotiations. . . . The ultimate scope in bargaining will be elimination of the principal as an educa-

tional leader and subversion of citizen rights." To which Carl Mar-
burger, former New Jersey Commissioner of Education now senior
associate of the National Committee for Citizens in Education, adds:
"If the public is expected to pay through its taxes for the outcomes
of bargaining, it rightfully has a voice in the process, whether the
conclusions result in dollar costs, or revised policies, or the redistri-
bution of power." And Don Davies of the new Institute for Responsive Education says: "Decisions made at the bargaining table have
profound implications for educational policy. The absence of public
voice in the process is a clear violation of the basic American belief
of 'no taxation without representation,' and it runs counter to the
principle that those who are directly affected by public agency decisions should participate in making those decisions."[54]

With pressures mounting from within and without the education establishment, what decision making will be left to school management? Maybe more will be left than appears at the present. Only
partly facetiously, apparently, Illinois Commissioner of Education
Joseph Cronin sees a future coalition of teachers and administrators,
public school people, and public workers generally, men and women
listening to each other and to everyone else—from young athletes to
older Americans—all because of the changing economics of education: fewer students, higher costs, surplus teachers, shortages of federal dollars, new alliances—and the ending of the old feuds once a
federal public bargaining bill is signed![55]

14. *In the future, as in the past, courage will contrast with conservatism in school administration.* In our era after Watergate, school
executives share with other leaders of the establishment in the distrust of youth. Writing about the young, Griffith says "their most
charitable assumption about anyone in power is that he has been
compromised, where he has not been corrupted; and his role is seen
to be, in one of their favorite words, manipulative."[56]

We who supposedly espoused Dewey most ardently may be
most vulnerable to the scorn of those who see schools as flawed
exemplars of democracy. Yet educational management clearly is
needed if schools are to change. Whether management can change is
the crucial question. "The managerial arrangements typical of educational systems," says Combs, "are grossly inadequate to deal with a
crisis-ridden set of new challenges and are, themselves, a crucial part
of the educational crisis." The change agent is not welcome: "The

conservative nature of the system, moving by the momentum of its own mass . . . grinds down even a would-be bold administrative innovator until even he is absorbed into the conservative mass and reflects its conservative behavior."[57]

With Flynn we can wonder about the attitudes of superintendents to functions of the schools oriented toward the future, but Culbertson and others see the problem of change as not the responsibility of the creative leader alone.[58] A creative staff and community also are involved. "In the place of utopianism and opportunism, responsible leadership and action are needed," Culbertson maintains.

To the extent that leaders cast their shadows on institutions, however, American schools clearly need strong administrators, ones whose intelligence, broad cultural background, and administrative training equip them to stand tall.

Griffiths would not have the school administrator shy away from the demands a troubled society is making: "The personal courage of the superintendent must be of the highest level. His is a role that requires taking positions on controversial issues. He must be able to withstand the many pressures which will be exerted on him. Courage is a *sine qua non* of the superintendent."[59]

I have said that schools and their administrators will be more constant than changed twenty years from now. There will be fewer administrators but a continued shortage of talent. Administrative theory will advance, and humane qualities will be emphasized. Performance will be rewarded, but authority probably will not be commensurate with responsibility in the changing power structure. Schools will continue to discriminate and resist change. But courage occasionally will triumph.

Eighteen years ago Morphet, Johns, and Reller undertook to define scores of issues confronting school administration.[60] As we attempt to foresee the practice of school administration two decades from now, it may provide perspective to recall the issues they raised in just one chapter, on improving educational administration, and to assess what progress has been made in resolving them:

· How can the contributions of fields such as sociology, social psychology, and anthropology best be utilized in programs for the preparation of educational administrators?

· Should the number of institutions preparing superintendents of schools be sharply limited?

• Should the completion of specified courses be the basis for the issuance of administrative credentials?

• Should the program of preparation and the credentials be the same for principals and superintendents?

• Is the internship the most promising method of preparing administrators?

• Is the development of programs for the improvement of administration through the preparation of administrators a responsibility of the colleges and universities or of the local school systems? The list seems all too current in terms of problems yet to be resolved. Twenty years passes very quickly.

Whether or not the next score of years brings the boycotts, strikes, violence, riots, litigation, racial conflict, and vandalism with which many administrators have lived in the past decade or whether the skills needed are in the realms of politics, conflict management, value clarification, desegregation, integration, or negotiation—principals and superintendents will need all the help they can get.

I hope that together professors and practitioners can work for:

• Development of a process for documenting and extrapolating from current issues and controversies in school administration, both to inform and alert practitioners and to stimulate development of research and theory.

• Strengthening ties of the University Council for Educational Administration with the National Academy of School Executives, the School Management Institute, and organizations of state administrators both for communication and for in-service program development.

• Retrenching on the number of institutions offering graduate programs in administration, to assure greater quality of staff, program and facilities.

• Establishment of more relationships for professors to work in the field and practitioners to teach on the campus.

• Increased participation by practitioners in state and national meetings of professors of educational administration.

• Increased participation by professors of educational administration in state and national meetings of school administrators.

As Roald Campbell reminded us at the conference on which this book is based, ours is more a field of practice than a discipline or profession. To me this suggests that both professors and practitioners must focus their study and their work on action. Let us work for the close and continuous tie that will make such a relationship possible in the years ahead.

Notes

1. Reported in "Previews," *Education U.S.A.* 17, 15 (December 9, 1974), 88.

2. James Cass, "Education," in "Giants of the Half-Century," *Saturday Review/World* (August 10, 1974), 84.

3. "Avoid Cynicism, Teel Cautions Staff," *Milwaukee Public Schools Staff Bulletin* 24, 5 (October 2, 1974), 1.

4. President's Commission on National Goals, *Goals for Americans* (Englewood Cliffs, N.J.: Prentice-Hall, 1960), 6-7.

5. Richard O. Carlson, "Barriers to Change in Public Schools," *Change Processes in the Public Schools* (Eugene, Ore.: Center for the Advanced Study of Educational Administration, University of Oregon, 1965), 3.

6. "Science Knowledge Declines," *National Assessment of Educational Progress Newsletter* 8, 2 (March-April 1975), 1.

7. Henry Steele Commager, "Our Schools Have Kept Us Free," *Life* 19, 16 (October 16, 1950), 46-47; "The School as Surrogate Conscience," *Saturday Review* (January 11, 1975), 56.

8. J. Bronowski, *The Ascent of Man* (Boston: Little, Brown, 1973), 424, 40.

9. John Dewey, *Democracy and Education* (New York: Macmillan, 1916), 7.

10. Gordon Cawelti, "Innovative Practices in High Schools: Who Does What—And Why—and How," *Nation's Schools* 79, 4 (April 1967), 58.

11. "Closer Ties Predicted Between Education and Public Broadcasting," *The School Administrator* (March 1975), 5.

12. "Bell: Parents Are the Key; Help Them Help You," *AASA Convention Reporter* (Arlington, Va.: American Association of School Administrators, 1975), 10; Mario Fantini, "Options Within the Public School System," speech to Ohio Department of Education Division of Planning and Evaluation Spring Conference, Columbus, Ohio, March 28, 1975.

13. Conrad Briner and Gerald Sroufe, "Organization for Education in 1985," *Educational Futurism 1985: Challenges to Schools and Their Administrators* (Berkeley, Cal.: McCutchan, 1971), 90; Bernard S. Miller, "A Brief Trip to the Schools of the Eighties," *North Central Association Quarterly* 49, 4 (Spring 1975), 357.

14. Harold Howe II, "Report to the President," *Saturday Review/World* (August 24, 1974), 130.

15. "School Size Drops in Big Cities," *Chicago Tribune* (April 21, 1975), Section 2, 8.

16. Roald F. Campbell, Luvern L. Cunningham, Raphael O. Nystrand, and

Michael D. Usdan, *The Organization and Control of American Schools* (Columbus, Ohio: Merrill, 1975), 243.

17. Cyril G. Sargent and Eugene L. Belisle, *Educational Administration: Cases and Concepts* (Boston: Houghton Mifflin, 1955), 444, 445.

18. Toby D. Bonwit and Myra K. Kirsch, "Catalogue of Inservice Education," *Teacher Education Forum* 3, 6 (February 1975), 8 (Bloomington: Indiana University Division of Teacher Education).

19. "Superintendents Salary Survey," Indiana Association of Public School Administrators, March 1975 (Bloomington: The Association, mimeographed), 3.

20. Martin W. Essex, "The State Department of Education and the Local School District: A Coalition for Educational Progress," speech to the North Central Association of Schools and Colleges Annual Meeting, Chicago, April 8, 1975.

21. "Commissioner Bell Calls for Upgrading of Educational Leadership and Greater Effort from State Legislatures," *The School Administrator* 31, 10 (November 1974), 4.

22. Philip H. Combs, *The World Educational Crisis* (New York: Oxford University Press, 1968), 123.

23. James D. Armour, "Personal and Conceptual Knowledge in Education and Administration," unpublished dissertation, University of Oklahoma, Norman, 1974.

24. Ward G. Reeder, *The Fundamentals of Public School Administration* (New York: Macmillan, 1951), 676, 727.

25. Herold G. Hunt and Paul R. Pierce, *The Practice of School Administration, A Cooperative Professional Enterprise* (Cambridge, Mass.: The Riverside Press, 1958), 318-318.

26. Jefferson N. Eastmond, *The Teacher and School Administration* (Boston: Houghton Mifflin, 1959), 73, 177-178, 444.

27. See Sargent and Belisle, *Educational Administration*; Jack Culbertson, Paul B. Jacobsen, and Theodore L. Reller, *Administrative Relationships, a Casebook* (Englewood Cliffs, N.J.: Prentice-Hall, 1960); Roald F. Campbell and Russell T. Gregg (eds.), *Administrative Behavior in Education* (New York: Harper & Row, 1957); Gerald R. Boardman, "A Computer-Based Simulation Model for the Feedback and Analysis of the Administrative In-Basket Exercise," *Educational Administration Quarterly* 11, 1 (Winter 1975), 55-71; Daniel E. Griffiths, *Administrative Theory* (New York: Appleton-Century-Crofts, 1959).

28. Kimball L. Howes, "Time: The Administrator's Most Precious Resource," *North Central Association Quarterly* 49, 2 (Fall 1974), 277.

29. Campbell and Gregg, *Administrative Behavior*, 388.

30. Daniel R. Davies, "The Impending Breakthrough," *Phi Delta Kappan* 37, 7 (April 1956), 275.

31. Benjamin M. Sachs, *Educational Administration, A Behavioral Approach* (Boston: Houghton Mifflin, 1955); Sargent and Belisle, *Educational Administration*, 438.

32. Kimball Wiles, *Supervision for Better Schools* (Englewood Cliffs, N.J.: Prentice-Hall, 1950), 286; Emery Stoops and M. L. Rafferty, Jr., *Practices and Trends in School Administration* (Boston: Ginn, 1961), 542.

33. Lanore Netzer and others, *Educational Administration and Change* (New York: Harper and Row, 1970), 23-35.

34. Jack Mabley, "Phillips High Chaos Replaced by Respect," *Chicago Tribune* (April 3, 1975), Section 1, 4.

35. John Merrow, Richard Foster, and Nolan Estes, *The Urban School Superintendent of the Future* (Durant, Okla.: Southeastern Foundation, 1974), 92-93.

36. "ERS Study Draws Comprehensive Picture of 1974-75 School Personnel Salaries," *The School Administrator* (April 1975), 1f.

37. "Commissioner Bell Calls for Upgrading."

38. R. O. Spalding and Associates, *Report on an Administrative Reorganization and Rate Structure Study for the School City of Hammond* (Freemont, Ind.: Spalding, 1974), 31.

39. *Ibid.*, 61.

40. *Ibid.*, 67.

41. Sydella D. Ehrenberg, *A Taxonomy of Educational Competencies: For Classroom Instruction, For Instructional Leadership* (Miami, Fla.: Institute for Staff Development, 1974).

42. Spalding, *Report*, 48.

43. "Decentralized Decision Making," *ERS Information Aid*, March 1975 (Arlington, Va.: Educational Research Service, Inc.).

44. Spalding, *Report on Administrative Reorganization*, 19.

45. Nathanial R. Jones, "The Future of Black-Jewish Relations," *The Crisis* 82, 1 (January 1975), 25.

46. Robert Singleton, "The School Financial Crisis and the Black Educational Administrator," *Leadership and Change in Educational Administration* 2, 1 (Winter 1974), 14.

47. Roald F. Campbell, John E. Corbally, Jr., and John A. Ramseyer, *Introduction to Educational Administration* (Boston: Allyn and Bacon, 1965), 266.

48. Robert L. Carter, "The Right to Equal Educational Opportunity" in *The Rights of Americans*, Norman Dorsen (ed.) (New York: Random House, 1971), 15.

49. Max Rosenberg, "Proposed: An Equal Opportunity Amendment to the U.S. Constitution," *Phi Delta Kappan* 55, 7 (March 1974), 442.

50. Robert C. Ericson and Charles E. Kline, "Measuring School Superintendent Morale," *ISBA Journal* 21, 1 (January-February 1975), 18.

51. Harold V. Webb, "A New Gallup Study: What the Public Really Thinks of Its School Boards," *The American School Board Journal* 162, 4 (April 1975), 37.

52. Don Bagin, *How to Start and Promote a P.R. Program* (Evanston, Ill.: National School Boards Association, 1975), 39.

53. James W. Guthrie, "Public Control of Public Schools: Can We Get It Back?" *Public Affairs Report* 15, 3 (June 1974) (Berkeley, Cal.: Institute of Governmental Studies, University of California).

54. "Shooting Away Management and Public Rights," *Successful School Administration* 2, 14 (April 7, 1975), 82; "Parent Power: New Bargaining

Force?" *Nation's Schools and Colleges* (April 1975), 68; "Collective Bargaining: Bringing Citizens to the Round Table," *Citizen Action in Education* 2, 1 (Fall 1974), 1.

55. Joseph M. Cronin, "School Unity: The Year the School People Finally Got It All Together," *Phi Delta Kappan* 56, 7 (March 1975), 448f.

56. Thomas Griffith, "Reshaping the American Dream," *Fortune* (April 1975), 90.

57. Combs, *World Educational Crisis*, 120, 121.

58. Richard Flynn, "Attitudes of Indiana School Superintendents Regarding the Effects of Futurology on Selected Public School Functions," unpublished doctoral dissertation, Ball State University, 1975; Culbertson, Jacobsen, and Reller, *Administrative Relationships*, 455.

59. Daniel E. Griffiths, *The School Superintendent* (New York: Center for Applied Research in Education, 1966), 105.

60. Edgar L. Morphet, Roe L. Johns, and Theodore L. Reller, *Educational Administration Concepts, Practices and Issues* (Englewood Cliffs, N.J.: Prentice-Hall, 1959).

17. Preparation Programs for Administrators

DANIEL E. GRIFFITHS

Even though the years since 1954 have been times of great activity in the preparation of administrators, the content and methodology of ideal training programs remain uncertain. Indeed, complicating factors have been introduced since 1954, which have caused concern about program elements that were considered certainties. Whereas administrators were once prepared only in accredited universities, there is now an array of competitors. Whereas the significance and nature of the job of the administrator was once largely taken for granted, there are now doubts as to whether schools should have principals and questions as to the role of the superintendent. Whereas the power and authority of boards was once undeniable, most boards are now paper tigers. A short twenty years following the administrative renaissance, the field is again at a crossroads, and it is again necessary to rethink the preparation of educational administrators.

The organization of this chapter is straightforward. The first section discusses the social setting in which educational administrators must function. The second presents the tasks of the administrator—that is, what he does as he performs his job. The third section deals with two issues confronting those who prepare educational administrators, and the last section presents some ideas on the preparation of administrators.

I do not view this chapter as an exercise in futurism but believe that the basic trends for the next twenty-five years are now quite evident. I believe that the 1960s were the time of social revolution both for individuals and organizations. The 1970s are a period in which attempts are being made to understand and rationalize the changes and to build a new set of relationships. This chapter should be seen as an effort to state the direction in which educational administration is moving and what this means for the preparation of administrators.

The New Setting

The major reason for the changes in educational administration is the fractured and fractious setting in which the administrator functions. While the setting in which he works has particular meaning for the educational administrator, the factors contributing to the setting are general in nature, affecting all institutions in the Western world.

At the root of the present disorder of American institutions is a trend that can be called "the collapse of consensus." Whatever its name, it effects deep erosion of the political base upon which government rests and alienation of individuals from the basic institutions of society.

In this country, sociologist Robert Nisbet has given considerable thought to the results of the loss of social coherence and has expressed it this way: "There is every reason for concluding that we are living in one of history's twilight periods; in our time a twilight of politics. It is the fate of all civilizations to outgrow the system of power that binds them. This, quite clearly, is happening in the West today, not least in the United States. I believe the waning of the political order . . . is a fact of highest significance, and far too little noted."[1] Historian Henry Steele Commager believes there is less harmony in American society now than at any time since Reconstruction. He calls the 1960s and 1970s "a great divide—the divide of disillusionment."[2] Lord Morris, a noted English philosopher and university administrator concerned with the practicalities of governance, makes this observation: "The people do not want to be governed, and clearly they do not believe that there is any real and final necessity to be governed. Their political posture is no longer very far removed from that of the hippies and the flower people; and the signs are that it is getting not further away but nearer to it."[3]

Not all observers are alarmed at the fading away of unanimity. Some say that complete harmony is incompatible with democracy and that what appears as consensus in American history books has been only the pretense of national harmony or the imposition of those in power on the populace.[4] Others view lack of consensus as highly desirable. For example, Richard Sennett in his book *The Uses of Social Disorder* argues that in societies in which there is social conformity the members actively seek their own enslavement. He believes that disorder is basic to a social system in which people will become more in control of themselves and more aware of each other, that disorder is a positive development that must precede social progress. Strikes by public employees in the vital services are welcome expressions of human need. The school serves as the focus for conflict and conciliation for the parents and as a place to demonstrate to children that there is an equilibrium of disorder in the lives of adults and, indeed, in the children themselves.[5] To accept this thesis is to countenance permanent disorder as a social goal.

Causes of the Collapse

Social scientists and humanists have examined and reexamined the causes of the collapse of consensus in the Western world in the context of societal changes since World War II. We once held to the ideal of America as a melting pot. Now ethnic identification is basic to most minorities. A recent manifestation of this trend is bilingual education, which was spurred by the desire to maintain cultural pluralism. There is a growing loyalty to one's neighborhood. In large cities this is apparent in decentralization of school systems and in the formation of neighborhood associations.

In a related development, it is said that there are now more than 2,500 communes, which are characterized by a withdrawal from political society. Then there is the rediscovery of religion, mostly of a fundamentalist or mystical character, which leads their patrons to singular, private views. Perhaps at the base of these trends are what futurologists call "increasingly sensate cultures," which they characterize as expressing protest or revolt, extreme, sensation-seeking, vulgar, ugly, and nihilistic.[6]

Another divisive course is the acceptance by many people of the philosophy of phenomenology, which holds that organizations are "invented social reality," that they have no goals of their own and serve only as vehicles for the achievement of the goals of their members.[7]

Many people not swept up by these waves have been made so cynical and become so demoralized by Vietnam, Watergate, revelations of CIA activity, inflation, and the "energy crisis" that they have given up on government entirely. Forty-five percent of registered voters did not vote in the 1976 election; 91 percent did not bother to cast ballots in 1975 for district school boards in New York City. The view of most people appears to coincide with that of Governor Edmund G. Brown, Jr., of California, who remarked during his campaign, "I take a somewhat jaundiced view of the ability of government to perform."[8] That this is so is revealed in a 1975 Harris Poll that confirmed an all-time low public confidence in key institutions. Only 18 percent of the population had faith in Congress, organized labor, and law firms; 25 percent in the press; 33 percent in the military; 40 percent in colleges. A full 67 percent of the people felt that "what you think doesn't count much anymore."

An additionally disturbing fact for educators is a general downgrading of schooling on the list of national priorities. It may be that education is so commonplace in America that it is no longer treasured, as gold had for the asking would be worthless. Or it may be that parents, particularly the middle and upper-middle classes, believe that they can do a better job than the schools. College degrees have depreciated in value, as corroborated by the Freeman-Holloman study published in September 1975, which shows that in the last five years college graduates suffered an unprecedented loss in their economic advantage over less educated Americans. In the same period, the proportion of eighteen- and nineteen-year-old males in college dropped from 44 percent to 33.4 percent. The researchers conclude: "Large numbers of young people, for the first time, are likely to obtain less schooling and potentially lower occupational status than their parents."[9]

The sense of national cohesiveness that provided values to which large majorities could subscribe is gone. The Horatio Alger ideal, the dominance of the Protestant work ethic, and the morality of the McGuffey Readers have all disappeared. While many say good riddance, the fact is that criteria of success that support the common good have been replaced by other values that hold self-actualization and personal goals uppermost. As a result, we are living with, or being dominated by, a new kind of politics that has repercussions on all who aspire to govern, to administer, or simply to live in our modern institutions. As Lord Morris put it, "The new Machiavelli can no longer make up his mind what he wants to do and then bring the people around to putting up with it. His primary problem, almost it seems his whole problem, is to find some act of government, or any act of government, which is acceptable."[10]

Disagreement on School Governance

There is no clear agreement between constituents on the governance of education in this country. Students and their parents are at odds with administrators; administrators are in conflict with school boards; and there is even crippling disunity within institutions.

In a 1974 Gallup Poll, only one of ten issues in education claimed the support of two-thirds of the respondents, and that was equalization of expenditures for education within states. The public was opposed—often overwhelmingly—to the present practices of automatic promotion, tenure, unisex athletic teams, no aid to parochial schools, no prayers in schools, and busing to achieve racial mixing. There was no agreement at all on how to handle recalcitrant students or on whether the schools were innovating too slowly or too quickly. It is obvious that the public does not subscribe to all the policies endorsed by the education establishment, by the courts, or by legislation.

Such disagreement is not restricted to polls. It has been expressed by gunfire and arson in such places as Kanawha County, West Virginia, and Pontiac, Michigan. The focal points of the conflict vary. Sometimes it is "dirty books" or sex education; other times it is liberal politics or unpopular court orders.

Although there is no definitive study available, conflicts between boards of education and their superintendents are on the rise, as is evidenced by the firing or resignation in 1975 of a dozen superintendents in large cities. There are numerous reasons for the friction, but a basic cause lies with board members who agree neither among themselves nor with educators on what the schools should be doing. Yet, not content with a policy-making role, they aim to run the schools.

Collective Bargaining

The single factor that has most changed the job of the educational administrator is the unionization of teachers with the resulting collective bargaining.[11] Not only are teachers unionized, but school principals, vice-principals, central office supervisors, and other middle managers have also joined collective bargaining units. Cooper reports that some 30,000 public school administrators currently bargain through unions and he believes the number will increase.[12]

Once collective bargaining is introduced into an organization the process of decision making, allocation of resources, and working conditions change. The first step taken is agreement on a contract—usually an elaborate set of rules governing the relationships among board, superintendent, middle managers, teachers, and students. Positions (chapter chairmen) are established to see that the contract conditions are lived up to, and mechanisms (grievance procedures) are devised for use when teachers or administrators feel the rules are not being administered fairly. The administrator must work within the contract; he must find ways of developing a warm climate within the school while enforcing those rules on which there is mutual agreement and ignoring others.[13] Any deviation from the contract must be carefully negotiated, and the administrator finds himself initiating plans that he feels will be accepted by the union members. He is, then, functioning as predicted by Lord Morris.

The Administrator's Job

How does the administrator—who alone remains responsible for solving the problems confronting his institution—cope, if not lead? The answer is that he must function within a new context. As Lord Morris said, "The professional administrator must research the facts and devise an operable scheme. And by the same token it is his task to present an *acceptable* scheme; for today only acceptable schemes are operable."[14] Not only will the administrator have to see that his methods are acceptable, he will have to make everything that he does comprehensible to the various publics. It will be very difficult to be an administrator in these circumstances. "Acceptable" government policies, including those of boards of education, will perforce be very changeable, and the circumstances that affect policy will affect administration.

Today public school administrators work in a climate that varies greatly from that of twenty years ago. They are selected in different ways—often by "the community," as in New York City, or with the participation of teachers, students, and parents, as in the suburbs. They have little of the authority of their predecessors, and they have great difficulty making their decisions stick. Policies that were once considered educational are now often made without reference to professional expertise. This is especially true of appointments to teaching and administrative positions and, in some cases, of selection of educational materials. With the advent of collective bargaining many areas of decision making were taken away from administrators altogether; those that dealt with the reward system decreased the power of the administrator even further.

It is not surprising that school principals now feel that they do not have clearly defined jobs. Similarly, most deans and college presidents find themselves stripped of authority, some because of contracts, others because of the power of faculties, senates, or other governing bodies. One must look still deeper to understand what has happened to make the administrator's job so difficult. What is the role of the administrator, given a society that values education less than it did previously and does not want to be administered in any event? Leadership is possible only in the context of shared goals. How does one lead an organization when its members do not acknowledge its goals? Management by objectives becomes an empty cliché when each person or group seeks its own objectives to the exclusion of others.

We are at the stage in our practice described by Lord Morris, but our theory has not caught up. The nature of administration is changing because the way people see their organization is changing. Faculties really do not want deans. Public school teachers do not want principals or superintendents. But these administrators are necessary if the institutions are going to operate.

New Theories of Administration Needed

Accepted theories of administration assume that organizations are essentially directed by the goals they strive for, with the members committed to achieving the goals. These theories derive from the study of organizations that are oriented toward rules, relatively stable, fulfilling legitimate (i.e., publicly sanctioned) purposes, and that exist in a world in which most members agree on values and ends. The administrative process is viewed as essentially orderly and rational.

These accepted theories are essentially "Great Man" theories, which also assume that if the administrator is capable enough he will be able to comprehend and resolve all situations in a satisfactory manner. A number of recent studies, however, lead to precisely the opposite conclusion: namely, that there are situations that no administrator, however capable, can comprehend and resolve unless the environment or the organization is changed in fundamental ways. The situation may be more powerful than the administrator. In the face of such developments, present theories for educational administration are inadequate; they need to be conceptualized anew.

It would appear that the real world is much more as it is perceived by the phenomenologists than by the more traditional philosophers. This means that all administrators should recognize that a large number of the people in an organization have little concern for the professed goals of the organization and that they are there to achieve their own goals. An administrator who recognizes this as a fact will proceed differently from one who does not. The kind of leader likely to emerge in this case is one who is a genius at forecasting what is practical (fundamentally, what is acceptable) in government.

To create schemes that are more acceptable, the administrator must be aware that personal values are most important to many, if not most, people who work in the schools. He must propose ways in which the individual can attain his own goals while working to achieve the goals of the schools. When these goals are in conflict, the administrator will need to work out a creative compromise. The major task for the administrator is, then, the reestablishment of congruence of individual and organizational goals.

Corporate Management

The English and the Scots are trying out a new approach to governance that has great implications for the administration of education in the United States. Their plan calls for corporate management of city and county services. Members of the management team are heads of the service departments—like development, housing, amenity services (parks, libraries, etc.), public services (transport, refuse collection, etc.), education, health, social work, and police—led by a chief executive who has no direct responsibility for any individual department. Each department head on that team must be concerned not only with his own department but with the wider objectives of the whole local authority, and he will have to accept limitations on his own departmental plans in the interests of coordination.

The significance of corporate management rests on the fact that education does not exist apart from all other governmental services. As research on such topics as nutrition, health, environment, and family living mounts, formal education is seen more clearly as a contributing rather than a dominant factor in human development. Indeed, if the work of Mort, Coleman, and Jencks is to be given any credence at all, one might reasonably come to the conclusion that success in educating children is more dependent on what happens outside the classroom than on what happens inside.

The corporate management plan is particularly appropriate for American schools. Educational institutions here—originally the universities, then the public schools—were among the first to experience the new politics because their political bases were so weak. In the past, public schools operated quite successfully apart from the established political structure. In New York State all of the school districts except those in the six largest cities are fiscally independent and politically separate. Even in these, the educational structure is separate from the municipal government, though the governmental structures are parallel. Elections are held in the summer, and candidates for boards of education do not run with labels of a particular political party. We profess that education is apolitical, but persistence in this illusory stance heightens the schools' vulnerability to the frequent and disruptive demands of a variety of factions. Closer ties to the regular political structure are required, for education is a governmental function, inevitably and unavoidably in politics.

It is now time to give serious consideration to the proposal that education abandon its traditional status as a separate, autonomous branch of government and consider joining with the regular political structure. Max Rubin advocated this stimulating idea for New York City. He advocated the abolition of the board of education, the position of chancellor, and the small Office of Education and their replacement with a commissioner of education appointed by the mayor subject to the approval of the city council. As a member of the mayor's board of commissioners, the commissioner of education would have more authority, more support for his actions.[15] This would also be the case with his administrators.

Moving education into the mayor's cabinet would mean that there could be the closest possible cooperation of the central educational agency with other municipal offices such as police, welfare, parks, correction, health, sanitation, environmental protection, and municipal services. It would facilitate accountability, because it would focus the currently diffused responsibility for educational performance on the mayor, the highest elected officer in the city. It would make clear and legitimize what is now the mayor's sub-rosa practice of making all important decisions, such as the size of the money settlement in union contracts after the pretenses of collective bargaining have been exhausted. It would execute the coup de grace on the central board of education, which is now an anachronism in most large cities.

We have lost the traditional American idea of a board of education composed of lay people who volunteer their time to develop policies for the management of education. We have, instead, amateurs who attempt to administer the schools. In New York City this has become a full-time, paid job. The proper place for lay citizens in education is at the building level. There should be a board of education for each sizable school building (600 or more students), and the board should work with the principal and staff in constructing educational programs appropriate to the population served by the school.

Corporate management will not, in itself, reverse the collapse of consensus, but it will force educational administrators to come to terms with those who administer all of the other services on which success is based. It should tend to cut down some of the wide variation in goals held by the numerous publics and make possible the setting of acceptable objectives.

Tasks of the Educational Administrator

The objective of this section is the presentation of an overview of what administrators do.[16] Since it is an overview, it is general and does not get to the nitty-gritty of administrative life. It does, however, present a framework comprising five administrative tasks which can be embellished in the preparation program. Further, each of these tasks is discussed through one or more research studies. These studies might be the vehicle used by professors for teaching the tasks. The studies are, of course, illustrative, not exhaustive.

One of the most succinct frameworks for a discussion of the work of the administrator has been developed by Paul Lazarsfeld. He contends that the administrator of any organization is confronted with four major tasks:

1. *The administrator must fulfill* the goals *of the organization.*

2. *The administrator must make use of* other people *in fulfilling these goals, not as if they were machines, but rather in such a way as to release their initiative and creativity.*

3. *The administrator must also face the humanitarian aspects of his job. He wants people who work for him to be happy. This is* morale—*the idea that under suitable conditions people will do better work than they will under unsuitable conditions.*

4. *The administrator must try to build into his organization* provisions for innovation, *for change, and for development. In a changing world, people and organizations must adjust to changing conditions. The conditions for change must be incorporated into the organization so that there may be a steady process of development rather than a series of sudden disruptive innovations.*

In summary, the administrator attempts to fulfill the goals of the organization, with the help of people, in a setting which increases the possibility for creativity, for development, and for change. [17]

To these four must be added another task, *organizational analysis*, through which the administrator will develop an understanding of his institution that will enable him to perform the tasks laid out by Lazarsfeld.

Organizational Analysis

The setting in which administrators work has not been given the emphasis it deserves. The research has focused almost exclusively on the administrator as a person, and it was assumed that he functioned independent of his environment. A little known study by Nicholas and his associates is the first to point up the extreme importance of the setting and the effect it could have on the behavior of the administrator and his ability to perform his tasks. [18]

The Nicholas study was ingenious in its design and implementation. The purpose of the study was to determine the effect of environmental differences on the frequency, type, and initiation of problems brought to the principal's office. Four elementary schools were selected: two schools with relatively "open" organizational climates, one of them in a "high" and one in a "low" socioeconomic setting; and two schools with relatively "closed" organizational climates, one in a high and one in a low socioeconomic setting. The schools were almost completely segregated with the low socioeconomic settings being 99 percent black and the high socioeconomic settings, 100 percent white. The students in the low-setting schools were well below city norms in academic achievement, the high-setting schools well above. The delinquency rate was three times as great in schools at the low socioeconomic level than at the high level. It would seem that the locating of schools that varied in environment to test the basic purpose of the study was achieved. Two miniature transistorized video cameras were installed in each principal's office, and everything that happened was recorded for six and one-half hours, from 8:15 a.m. to 3:45 p.m., with an hour off for lunch, on a six-week schedule. Each school was actually filmed for three weeks, since two schools were filmed each week. A total of 450 hours of recorded experience was obtained. These data were analyzed by teams of trained observers.

The researchers reported that the most striking difference between schools in a high socioeconomic setting and those in a low one was "the quality of the impact upon principals made by the pupil-behavior problems brought to the office."[19] This conclusion did not come from the results of coding the problems seen in the videotapes, rather it came as a general impression gained from viewing hours of tapes. The low-setting schools seemed characterized by urgency, crisis, and harrassment. On the other hand, the high-setting schools seemed to be routine, businesslike operations. This was in spite of the fact that there were more problems handled in the high-setting schools. The reason was that the highest frequency of problems in the low-setting schools were pupil's behavior problems. The researchers observed that in the low-setting schools, the large number of behavior problems resulted in principals losing the initiative in deciding what they would work on; they were put in the position of constantly reacting to the demands of others. If the school was in both a low socioeconomic setting and a closed climate, the situation was worse. In fact, Nicholas and associates characterized such a case as "untenable." They contended further that the high incidence of pupil's behavior problems might well have caused the closed climate rather than the closed climate being the result of the personality or administrative setting of the principal.[20] If they are correct in this conclusion (and they might well be), it is one of the most significant findings in the past decade. What they are saying is that the behavior of the students is so powerful a factor that it outweighs all other factors and determines the climate of the school. More research must be done to confirm this conclusion, but it does appear to be one that must be seriously considered at the present time.

The pressure or "press" on principals in low-setting schools was from the inside, while in high socioeconomic settings it was from the outside. In the low-setting schools the compounded aggravation of pupils' behavior problems was so great that it consumed the time of principals, assistant principals, the attendance agent, nurse, and police. All were so busy treating symptoms, they could do little to prevent the problems from occurring. Furthermore, both problems of behavior and other types were brought to the principal's office *in person*. It is virtually impossible for one to ignore problems or even to put them in order when the initiator of the problem is present. In contrast to problems in the low-setting schools, those in the high-setting schools came largely from parents and other citizens, very often by telephone. The problems were, in effect, placed in order automatically, since the phone would be busy when many parents called, thus forcing them to take their turn.

While the researchers had only one large school with which to work, and it was a low-setting, closed-climate school, it appears that they were convinced that the concentration of large numbers of children in such a school contributed to the high frequency of behavior problems. Nicholas and his associates do believe, without doubt, that large size contributed to a chaotic environment.

No other study has so dramatically emphasized the significance of the environment in which the administrator attempts to function. Unless the administrator thoroughly comprehends his surroundings, and, further, unless these surroundings are congenial to the administrator, he will be unable to perform his tasks. While the study has some obvious flaws, notably the small number of cases, it should be replicated. It is one of the few studies that gathered data in a form not reduced to symbols, and it does enable the student to grasp the essence of administration—people in constant interaction within an institution.

Goal Determination and Achievement

The first task of the administrator, as described by Lazarsfeld, comprises two components: goals must be determined, and then they must be achieved. There is little research on either of these steps, but something can be said about the establishment of goals.

It is the responsibility of administrators to see that a clear set of operationally defined goals is developed and that they are achieved. It is not the administrator's job to develop the goals himself but rather to guide in the process of their definition. If members of the faculty participate in defining goals, there is some evidence to suggest that they will be more open to accepting these goals and aiding in their achievement.

The goals should be written, and there should be formal action by the faculty to accept them. Once adopted, the goals serve to help the administrator set priorities in all areas: selection of staff, purchase of equipment, courses offered, faculty load, and on and on.

As an approach to the nature of goals in an educational organization, consider the McGrath Report on the mission of departments in schools of home economics.[21] The chief value of the McGrath Report was its presentation and discussion of goals. McGrath contended that "Its [home economics'] central mission has been and must continue to be that of family service." It can be argued, however, that this contention is somewhat less than useful.[22] At this level of abstraction virtually every profession can be said to have family service as its goal. Questions must be raised at a more meaningful level, and the report does this, for example: What direction will the home economics unit take to make its information available to more people? Should the unit have a doctoral program? (The answers appear to be "no" for most universities.) How can the home economics unit effect a more satisfactory distribution of services? What can be done to develop a capability for research in the unit? Should the unit be activist in seeking certain goals in society?

While setting goals is a different and little understood process, implementing goals is equally difficult but, fortunately, better understood. The development of systems theory presented the administrator with the management tools needed to achieve specific goals.[23] It is not the theory that is useful to the administrator, however, it is the large number of specific applications that are available. Some of these are operations analysis, cost-effectiveness, PERT, and input-output analysis, all generally subsumed under the name, planning-programming-budgetary system (PPBS).[24]

Command of the concepts of PPBS enables an administrator to focus the resources of the institution on a specific goal, to make allocations of money, materials, and manpower, and then to monitor progress towards the goal. The difficulties that are apt to arise come not from the lack of management tools, but from the lack of consensus on goals. If the people in the school system—board members, teachers, students, and parents—do not agree on the goal being sought by the administrator, he is going to have great difficulty achieving it. The modern administrator, however, does have management tools not possessed by his predecessors.

Making Use of Other People

The third task of the administrator is to make use of other people in fulfilling the goals of the organization. He must use them not as if they were machines, but rather in such a way as to release their initiative and creativity. One of the many ways to do this is to build a climate or environment in which participants can work at the highest levels. Frederiksen and his associates have researched this problem in a highly significant study.[25] They did an experiment using four types of climates to simulate business environments and studied the effects of the climates on a wide range of variables. The climates are: (1) innovative with global supervision, (b) innovative with detailed supervision, (c) rules with global supervision, and (d) rules with detailed supervision.

It will be noted that (a) and (d) contain consistent climates. That is, *innovative* is consistent with *global supervision* and *rules* is consistent with *detailed supervision*. Likewise, it should be noted that (b) and (c) are inconsistent climates: *innovative* is inconsistent with *detailed supervision* and *rules* with *global supervision*.

The major finding is that the mean *productivity* score, that is, the amount of work completed, is significantly affected by the consistency of the climate conditions. Putting it a bit differently, productivity is increased when climate conditions are consistent and decreased when climate conditions are inconsistent. The negative effect of inconsistency is greatest in the combination of innovation and detailed supervision, which might mean that this type of inconsistency is most enervating. Administrators would be well advised to avoid urging subordinates to be innovative while at the same time enforcing detailed supervision.

The findings of the study might be extrapolated to say that consistency of environment extends to other variables such as salary increments, promotions, allocation of released time, travel funds, and extra secretarial help. These benefits should be dispersed to those who are meeting the goals of the unit. Consistency in allocating benefits is necessary to maximize productivity and attainment of goals.

Morale

The fourth task that the administrator must be concerned with is building morale and the idea that under suitable conditions people will do better work. The task must be construed broadly and must take cognizance of the fact that most people are in organizations to achieve their own goals, not necessarily those of the organization. It also implies that negotiation is a way of life for the administrator, since he must resolve situations of conflict with a minimum of authority and power. And, last, is the obvious point that the behavior of the administrator affects the attitudes and behavior of others. Only two aspects of morale will be dealt with here: the resolution of conflicts through game theory and the office behavior of the administrator.

There are two major uses of game theory which can be employed by administrators, namely: Classifying situations in a way that helps clarify the kind of action that should be taken and suggesting specific solutions to conflict situations. To use game theory efficiently the administrator has to retreat from the situation sufficiently and reflect upon what is happening. He has to adopt an analytical, reasoned approach, and he cannot allow himself to become as emotionally involved as those directly in the conflict. Game theory provides the administrator with the concepts he needs to find solutions to conflicts. Once he has analyzed a situation, the administrator can use game theory to decide the strategy and tactics to be used, together with some indication of outcomes. Administrators now and in the future will have to become skilled in the use of game theory.

Through the use of game theory all conflict situations may be classified as "game" and "nongame." A nongame conflict situation is one to which a rule applies. Whenever a conflict occurs, the administrator's first action is to search for a rule covering the situation. If there is a rule, he should apply it as judiciously as possible. At other times no appropriate rule exists, but the administrator must realize that a rule is obviously needed to fit the situation. For example, a conflict might arise over a newly adopted sick-leave policy, and the administrator knows that the same kind of situation will arise continuously. He may have to resort to game theory to solve the immediate problem, but he should also develop a rule that can be adopted when the situation recurs.

If the conflict situation cannot be solved by applying a rule, it most likely has game characteristics. As Ohm says: "If the situation involves a conflict of interest for which no decision rule exists, and/or a discretionary decision is required within a framework of a general rule or policy, the situation may be classified as an . . . event to which game models of interaction can be applied. Such situations may have one or more of the characteristics of games: namely, opposing sets of interests, a set of choices of strategies, interdependence, change, imperfect information, and a preferred ordering of outcomes."[26]

Once a situation is determined to be a game, it can be further classified as to what type of game it is. There are four categories of games:

1. *Two-person, zero sum.* In this type of game, there are two conflicting interests. In every game of this type, one of the interests wins and the other loses to the same extent; that is, the gains of player X equal the losses of player Y.

2. *Two-person, non-zero sum.* This is a somewhat more common administrative situation than the two-person, zero sum, in that the sum of gains and losses does not equal zero; in other words, one side does not win or lose everything. The losing party may be allowed to save face by having the winner grant a small concession.

3. *N-person, zero sum.* (The n-person concept in this type means more than two sets of interests.) This game category probably does not exist in real life since the n-sides generally form coalitions and so become a number of two-person, zero sum games.

4. *N-person, non-zero sum.* In organizations this is by far the most common type of game. The administrative conflict situations

generally involve the administrator as the third person. Generally winning or losing is not complete and cannot be considered as zero-sum.

Since most of the conflict situations the administrator is called upon to solve are n-person, non-zero sum, this type of game is most significant. Some of the difficulties included in this category are arguments between two or more professors and a student involving a grade and conflicts among sections over the use of facilities or equipment. There is no end to the n-person, non-zero sum conflict situations that might turn up in an academic setting.

The most suitable role for the administrator in this type of conflict is that of mediator. As Ohm says: "The perception of and capacity to mediate conflicts or discontinuities has become a primary administrative task. Balancing, mediating, or relating individual needs and organizational demands or rationalizing (conflicts in) organizational structure are crucial administrative functions."[27]

When confronted with an n-person, non-zero sum situation, the administrator should know that the players will attempt to form a coalition with him and to move the conflict to a two-person, zero sum game. It will work to the advantage of one set of players, and to the disadvantage of the administrator over the long term, if he is forced to side with one or the other sets of players. His fundamental strategy must be to mediate, that is to see that all sides win to some extent and lose to some extent. In terms of game theory, he must keep an n-person, non-zero sum game going as an n-person, non-zero sum game.

The administrator's strategy should be one in which he tries to find a new set of boundaries for the problem. Examples of this are numerous, but one will suffice. If the administrator can get the combatants to accept referral of the argument, he has changed the boundaries. This is the advantage of a grievance procedure, which moves the conflict into an agreed upon process. When the combatants agree to "to do grievance" they agree to accept a set of rules and standards, and they agree to abide by the final judgment. This conflict is bounded and generally is resolved to at least the partial satisfaction of those involved.

It has long been speculated that the administrator's nonverbal behavior affects the morale of those who work with him. Lipham and Francke designed two studies to test this idea and published them in a single article.[28] Since Lipham studied school principals and Francke studied naval officers, this paper deals only with Lipham's research. He interviewed forty-two principals, half of whom had been evaluated as "promotable" and half as "unpromotable" by central office personnel. The principals were, of course, not notified of their ratings, and the researcher did not have this information prior to the interviews.

The first set of findings concerned how principals structured interaction with the visitor. Lipham looked for answers to the questions: How do principals greet visitors? Where do visitors sit? At what distance? How are their visits terminated?

Lipham found significant differences between the two groups in the way they greeted visitors. Promotables typically greeted visitors at the doors to their offices and even, on occasion, in the outer office. Unpromotables tended to stay at their desks and only occasionally shook hands. Lipham even noted a difference in the way the two groups of principals dealt with the visitor's hat and coat. If the secretary failed to take the hat and coat, the promotable principal did so himself. Lipham noted that unpromotables often had to be asked, "May I put my hat and coat somewhere?"

Lipham found that the placement of the visitor's chair and its distance from the principal differed between groups. The promotables tended to seat the visitors alongside their desks or on their side of the desk at a distance of three to four feet. This was in marked contrast to the unpromotables, who placed the visitor in front and at the center of the desk at distances of five to twelve feet from them. In addition, promotable principals adjusted the blinds and regulated the temperature.

Promotables also behaved differently as the conferences ended. As Lipham says, "Almost without exception, promotables offered to take the visitor on a tour of the school; to serve coffee, refreshments, or simply a drink of water; or, since some of the conferences terminated near noon, to have lunch in the school cafeteria."[29] Promotables often checked to see whether the interviewer knew his way to the next school. Unpromotables rarely behaved in this way. Promotables differed from unpromotables in the way they parted with visitors, often walking to the door of the office, or the door of the outer office, or even to the door of the building.

The second set of findings resulted from Lipham's attempt to answer the question: How does the working environment feel? He made systematic notes on decor, working order, noise, and the use of status symbols.

The only differences in the decor of offices was that promotables had more personal items in their offices. Pictures of the family, paintings, figurines, and citations were types of personal articles seen in the offices of promotables. Unpromotables had more nonpersonal articles in their offices, generally calendars, official notices, plaques, and flags.

There was no correlation with promotability and neatness or lack of neatness of the administrator's desk. Lipham reports, however, that offices of unpromotables were noisier than promotables. He observed more students in their offices, as many as a dozen at one time, either for disciplining or running errands. Unpromotables also tended to be interrupted more often; they answered their own phones, responded to the intercom, and answered knocks on doors even when a secretary was present.

The nameplates of unpromotable principals tended to be larger, more expensive, and displayed more prominently than those of promotable principals.

In general, the nonverbal behavior of promotable principals revealed a warmer and more considerate feeling for people than that of the unpromotables. Promotables also seemed to have their working environment better organized. While yielding few specifics, Lipham's study demonstrates that nonverbal behavior does make a difference.

Providing for Change

The fifth task calls for the administrator to build into his organization provision for innovation, change, and development. Two studies throw a great deal of light on building change into an organization, one by Heathers on introducing the dual progress plan, an innovative method for the organization of elementary schools, and the other by Gross and his associates on a change in the teacher's role (from traditional to catalytic) in the Cambire School, an elementary school.[30]

The two studies form the basis for the following generalizations about the implementation of change in educational organizations.

1. *The typical view of administrators concerning the process of*

change is erroneous. Gross contends that school administrators typically view the process of promoting successful change in the schools as having three components: a promising new educational idea must be located or developed; the necessary money must be found to finance the idea; and the staff must be willing to change.

Gross seriously questions the validity of these points of view. All three were present at the Cambire School, yet the innovation under study was not fully implemented. The three components were also present for the dual progress plan; certainly the first two were fully present, and the teachers were at least ready to try it. Gross concluded that the three conditions may constitute the necessary prerequisites for the initiation of innovations, but they do not represent a sufficient set of requirements for the successful implementation of innovations. In fact, Gross and his associates feel strongly that one of the reasons why so many innovations are not fully implemented is that administrators hold such an overly simplified and inadequate version of the change process. Both Heathers and Gross are convinced that bringing major change to a school is a far more difficult and complex task than has been realized to date.

2. *Feedback mechanisms must be built into the innovation.*

One thing that is certain about change is that it cannot be fully planned. It is not possible for anyone to foresee all of the problems that are going to occur. It is therefore imperative that workable systems of feedback be built in from the start. There must be carefully worked out methods whereby teachers can let administrators know what is going right, and, particularly, what is going wrong. Several unanticipated problems developed in the Cambire School which prevented imple. ientation of the innovation. When teachers acted as catalytic agents, the children began acting in ways described by teachers as wild, rude, or unmotivated. Unable to feed back their anxieties, teachers reverted to their former roles, ones in which they felt more secure. It is clear that feedback mechanisms must be provided.

3. *The leadership role of the administrator is crucial.*

Gross apparently feels that the crucial role in the success or failure to implement an innovation is played by the administrator. First of all, he points out that administrators typically assign the responsibility for carrying out an innovation to subordinates or an outside agency. This, he believes, is a major error. Innovations cannot be left to teachers or to assistants who may not be as convinced as the administrator of the worth of an innovation. The chief administrator must hold on to an innovative project and give it the overall guidance that only he is able to supply. Building in adequate feedback is one way of holding on.

More than this is necessary, however. Following is a set of "musts" for administrative performance.

The administrator must make the innovation clear to the staff. Observations of teachers in the Cambire School indicated that many of them did not have a clear picture of how they were to behave in their new roles. Gross believes that the reason for this was that the administrators did not have a good understanding of the innovation. With no one knowing exactly what the new role for teachers was to be, it can be seen that it would be difficult to bring the new plan off. While it seems trite to say it, an innovation must be clearly understood by all in order for it to be fully implemented.

The administrator must provide the experience that will retrain the staff. The teachers on the Cambire staff reported that they lacked the skills and knowledge necessary to function in the new role. As a result, they soon gave up trying. If staff members are to perform differently, they must be retrained. Experiences must be provided whereby new skills and knowledge can be learned. Only the administrator can provide these experiences.

The administrator must make certain that the staff is willing to make the necessary effort. The administrator must, as far as possible, see to it that those who work to make the change successful are rewarded. Rewards of all sorts, ranging from oral or written notes of congratulations to promotions and salary increments, should be used. If administrators do not do this, they lead staff members to feel that the innovation is not important and that they would be better off doing something else. The reward system should support the process of implementation.

The administrator must make available the materials necessary to implement the innovation. Both Gross and Heathers reported that necessary materials and equipment were lacking in the innovations, and the lack was demoralizing to the teachers. For example, mastery tests for each grade level and mastery tests for nongraded curricular sequences were essential for the implementation of the dual progress plan but were not provided to teachers. Highly motivating self-instructional materials were central to the new role that teachers were to assume at the Cambire School, yet they were not provided. Teachers cannot be expected to invent such sophisticated materials; it is the job of the administrator to provide them.

The administrator must make the necessary organizational adjustments. Any major innovation normally requires that many changes be made in the organization. If these are not made, the innovation may not be implemented. In the Cambire School, for instance, neither the rigid school schedule nor the requirement that teachers give grades was altered. The dual progress plan called for promotion on the basis of mastery of the grade-basic curriculum, yet the schools retained their general standards of promotion. On the other hand, Heathers reported that changes in scheduling and facilities were made, and this aided implementation. This serves to emphasize that órganizational arrangements must be compatible with the innovation.

In addition, it may be that roles of administrators as well as teachers must change. For instance, administrators in the Cambire School continued to make decisions on the purchase of materials, but it would have been more appropriate for teachers to do so. Roles of administrators should also be compatible with the desired change.

These two studies present realistic pictures of the difficulties involved in implementing change in schools. Unlike most research studies, they offer many recommendations to practicing administrators, and the advice appears to be carefully drawn from the data.

Issues in the Preparation of Educational Administrators

There are two major issues in the preparation of educational administrators: should administrators be educated solely in bona fide universities, and should preparation programs be shaped into the competency mode?

Nonresidential University Programs

Three new nonresidential universities, all located in Florida—Nova, Walden, and Laurence—are heavily engaged in EdD programs in educational administration. According to Morland, Nova is the only one of the three to hold regional accreditation; Laurence and Walden hold only temporary licenses to operate issued by the Florida Board of Independent Colleges and Universities. These three institutions have tremendous appeal and do not lack for applicants. In 1973 Morland estimated that by 1975 Nova would have some 2400 candidates in two programs, one for educational administrators and the other for community college faculty, and that Laurence and Walden would each produce between 200 and 250 doctorates a year.[31] Morland's estimates, however, appear to be highly inflated in light of Graham's cohort study of students entering Walden in 1971-1973.[32] Of the 449 doctoral candidates who enrolled in 1971, 1972, and 1973, only 206, or 46 percent, had received the degree by July 1974. When it is realized that only thirteen traditional universities granted 100 or more doctorates in 1971, the output is still impressive.

These institutions are clearly different from other universities granting the doctorate. There are few of the external manifestations of traditional universities—no faculties in residence, no research libraries, no campuses. Their attraction is that the candidate can earn a doctorate while living at home and keeping his job. The candidate must spend four weeks at Walden, five weeks at Laurence, and two weeks at Nova for institutes and courses. Whatever else is required can be done at home. The doctor's degree can be gained in one year from Walden and Laurence and in three years from Nova. The quality of lecturers, field advisors, and summer school faculty who instruct in the various programs is impressive. They are among the best professors at the leading universities in the country. This combination of moonlighting professors, brief periods in Florida, and short time span, capped by a doctorate has tremendous appeal. In addition, there are some aspects of the Nova program that have particular appeal to practitioners, since instruction takes place throughout the year in what are called "clusters," groups of some twenty-five educators, generally practicing administrators. The clusters meet monthly to work on their practicums or to discuss with "national lecturers." There is interaction among peers, and this is seen as highly desirable by the students.

The Nova approach appears to have much to offer as an inservice program and, in fact, is somewhat similar to The Superintendents' Network, another plan featuring peer discussions.[33] The Walden program does not appear to be the "easy" doctorate that so many of their enrollees expected. The data that Graham collected led him to conclude: "First, the chances of a Walden student obtaining the doctorate decreased markedly after the first year. Second, the percentage graduating in one year declined over the period 1972 to 1974. Third, the institution does not seem to be a 'diploma mill,' as that term is generally construed."[34] None of the programs, however, seem to be sufficient when held up against criteria that must be met by a first-rate residential university wishing to grant a doctorate, including adequate faculty in administration, cognate, and supporting subjects; a research library; student and faculty facilities; admissions standards; and a high level of student performance. One is led to the conclusion that preparation for the superintendency should be restricted to the more traditional universities until the time when the new nonresidential universities demonstrate that they can produce equally capable graduates.

Competency-Based Administration Programs

It is indeed unfortunate that at a time when the country needs intelligent, creative administrators universities are being pressured by state education departments, federal agencies, and some educational spokesmen to develop programs in the competency mode. These programs are takeoffs on competency-based teacher education. Rosner defined the approach when he wrote that it "requires the explication of the specific knowledge and skills that comprise the teacher education program. It requires systematic assessment of the prospective teacher's performance at various levels of training until a desired level of mastery is achieved."[35] This statement does not hold true for administrators and, to a large extent, teachers, because it is not possible to specify the knowledge and skills that make up programs to educate administrators—at least not if the program is to bear any relation to the work of an administrator. I am in full agreement with Hills when he says: "Looking over the agenda for the board meeting, it occurs to me that the variety of subjects, issues and problems that arises is so great that there isn't a ghost of a chance of preparing administrators to deal with the content of their job."[36]

He goes on to say that administrators need to know processes, i.e., how to solve problems—something quite the opposite of a specific competency. While there are some skills that all administrators need and that should be taught in preparation programs, these skills are not crucial to the success of the administrator. What is crucial is the administrator's ability to see his job in a broader context, understand the setting in which he works, appreciate the true value of people, develop a well-thought-out philosophy of education, and work with and through people. In no way can these abilities be called competencies.

Many educators appear to be fascinated with the idea that people can be taught by having the subject matter broken up into specific pieces that can be easily learned. It is expected that the learner will then put the pieces together into useful wholes. During the 1920s, for example, there was a movement called elementist psychology, which took teacher education by storm. As an example, in geometry a theorem was divided into as many as a hundred bits and each was taught to the child. The approach probably had its origins in factories where difficult tasks performed by skilled mechanics were subdivided into little pieces which were taught to unskilled laborers. While the work got done, no one expected the unskilled laborers to become skilled mechanics. But in education it was anticipated that children taught by methods of elementalist psychology would become mathematicians, historians, and the like. It was quickly found that, after they had learned all the bits, children had no idea what the total concept meant. The sum of the parts did not equal the whole. As could be expected in a field that had and still has no theoretical base, professional education swung to an opposite and equally fruitless approach to teaching—one employing Gestalt psychology.[37]

Educational administration has also tried a competency approach to teaching administration. The Southern States Cooperative Program in Educational Administration spent a great deal of money in the 1950s in an attempt to utilize this approach.[38] The fact that virtually no university other than Tennessee adopted this approach is perhaps the best indication that the approach was a failure.

It is incorrect, however, to discuss the competency movement only in terms of competencies. There are aspects of the movement that have value and that can and should be utilized in university programs. These include: close relationships with practicing administrators that would result in cooperative planning; lengthy field experiences; evaluation of both the program and the products; and the use of this information in program revision. It would certainly seem that activities of this sort should be performed in revising any program of preparation, while the pressure to devise and teach competencies should be resisted.

The Preparation Program

A great deal can be learned about the preparation of potential administrators if one observes the way professional football teams are developed. First of all, each team has an extensive network of scouts who search for talent. They attend as many high school and college games as possible, take extensive notes (and often pictures) on the players, and feed this information into the team's computer. When the player draft takes place, the general manager has a vast amount of data on each player. Since he knows what he wants—a strong tight end, a field goal kicker, a kick-off returner who can run the 100 in 9.5 seconds—he puts needs together with talents and drafts players who fit. When the team is assembled for practice, the coach must perfect each player's known skills and build teamwork and morale. As each game approaches, he develops a strategy that maximizes his team's strengths and minimizes his opponents' skills.

It should be noted that there are many characteristics that the players must possess before they are chosen. There is no effort made to teach slow runners to become fast, or short players to grow tall, or clumsy men to be agile, or weak players to become strong, although the training program is designed both to improve their good qualities and to utilize them in optimum ways.

The same principle should apply in the preparation of educational administrators. First of all, there should be extensive and rigorous selection. People should be chosen for the basic qualities that make good administrators; these qualities either cannot be developed or are so expensive to develop that it is not worth the effort.

Selection

While there is little disagreement on what characteristics are essential for a successful administrator, knowledge of these characteristics is rarely applied. The following qualifications should be sought in selecting students for preparation programs in educational administration:

Intellect. The basic quality that must be possessed by administrators if they are to succeed is *intellect*. I use the term as defined by English and English: "1. The *mental faculty* by means of which man (and man alone) can think. 2. A class name for *cognitive* processes, esp. those of thinking (i.e. relating, judging, conceiving). 3. Ability, esp. high ability, to think."[39]

Many people have discussed the need for administrators to have great intellectual powers, but few have done it more eloquently than Adams:

Administration is the capacity of coordinating many, often conflicting, social energies in a single organism so adroitly that they shall operate as a unity. This presupposes the power of recognizing a series of relations between numerous special social interests, with all of which no single man can be intimately acquainted. Probably no very highly specialized class can be strong in this intellectual quality because of the intellectual isolation incident to specialization; and yet administration or generalization is not only the faculty upon which social stability rests, but is, possibly, the highest faculty of the human mind.[40]

Moore, in describing the experience at Stanford University in selecting administrators quotes Tyler, Briner, and Campbell, Corbally, and Ramseyer as nominating intelligence first among varying sets of qualities.[41] Moore also reported that those who emerged as principals from a lengthy selection procedure had higher intelligence.

The selection procedure should place intellect first; however, it should be pointed out that what is being sought is not simply a high IQ, but a high level of intelligence that can be used in administrative situations. In other words, candidates must display high intelligence plus judgment.

Standardized tests can and should be used to provide information on the candidates' intellectual ability.[42] Either the *Miller Analogies Test* or the *Graduate Record Examination* Verbal and Quantitative Sections are appropriate. These tests should be used in conjunction with a test composed of practical problems to determine the candidate's ability to make judgments. The test could be composed of short cases or a portion of a simulation.

Other Characteristics. There are several other personal characteristics which should be considered in the selection process. The method of selection is suggested by the characteristic, so evidence should be collected on the following questions. Does the candidate: Speak well? Write? Have a history of leadership? (Has the candidate been a leader in the Boy Scouts or Girl Scouts? class officers in high school or college? captain of athletic teams?) Have good interpersonal skills? Have ability to live with ambiguity? Have ability to make decisions with little data? Have courage?

While there is no general agreement on desirable personality traits, at least one study has related a number of personality attributes of administrators to positive ratings by teachers and superiors. These attributes are described as sociable, sensitive, trusting, confident, relaxed, mature, lively, and dependent.[43] In addition, some factors were related to negative ratings by teachers and superiors. These are described as aloof, shy, practical, skeptical, independent, insecure, unstable, dominant, and tense.[44] *The Sixteen Personality Factor Questionnaire* was used to determine the personality traits, and it can be recommended to those who wish to use a personality measure in the selection process. Lipham described six personality variables of effective administrators: activity drive, achievement drive, mobility drive, social ability, feelings of security, and emotional control.[45]

An adequate selection procedure for administrators should include measures of personality. While it is not necessary to base selection on all the personality variables related to effective administrators, those thought to be most relevant to program objectives should be used.

Every effort should also be made to recruit women as administrators. Meskin reviewed the literature on women in administration and found five studies comparing men and women in elementary school principalships.[46] Her conclusion should be cause for concern to those who head university programs for the preparation of administrators: "When we highlight some of the specific findings concerning women administrators in these studies—their propensity toward democratic leadership, thoroughness of approach to problem solving, and bent toward instructional leadership, as well as the general effectiveness of their performance as rated by both teachers and superiors —we puzzle over the small number of women administrators employed by school districts and especially over the decline of women in the elementary principalship."[47]

The quickest way to upgrade the quality of people entering educational administration might be to increase the number of women in preparation programs.

The Program

The major goal of a program preparing administrators is to develop in each person in the program something that has been given different names. Hills says, "I'm inclined now to say that one constructs some sort of generalized synthesis out of his experience and study that determines, not specific courses of action in specific cases, but the pattern of action over time."[48] He also paraphrases Getzels on the same point by saying that a person's education and experience come together to form "the context for administrative practice."[49] Levine uses the term "theory of practice" which he says "seeks to give the administrator reliable means for using diverse research findings to create system-specific courses of action."[50] Others have referred to a philosophy of administration. What they all seem to be saying is that administrators must develop what was called around the turn of the century an "apperceptive mass"—the term I prefer. The administrator should have certain skills and a knowledge of research and theory, combined with experience, so that when he is confronted with a situation or problems needing to be resolved he has a basis for action. The preparation program enables the administrator to act in an effective way when called upon. At times he must act immediately, at other times he will need to consult, while at still other times it would be prudent for him to commission a study of the problem. It is necessary then for the administrator to have not only a substantive background but a sense of timing as well. He should know when to do what it is that should be done.

Since the goal of the program is to produce people who will act, not merely think, both intellectual and clinical elements must be blended in such a way that each student administrator has an internalized set of guides to action.

Intellectual Elements

Preparation programs for administrators should have a general and a specialized component. The general part should be of value regardless of the position for which the student is preparing, while the specialized part should be directed toward the position he wishes to occupy for a major portion of his career. The chief source of substance should be the conception of the administrator held by the university department of educational administration. One such conception was presented earlier in the section called "The Tasks of the Administrator," in which the various tasks were defined, and one or more research studies were cited to provide a knowledge base. This approach—that is, definition of tasks supported by evidence from research—is an effective way to teach people how to become administrators.

Using the tasks as an organizing theme for preparation programs solves the major problem of what concepts from the behavioral sciences should be taught.[51] The concepts, research findings, and theories selected from the behavioral sciences should be those that help an administrator to analyze the setting in which he works, establish goals, make use of other people in meeting these goals, develop morale, and build into the organization provisions for change. Most help in this undertaking comes from research done in educational administration and the behavioral sciences and relatively little from theories of administration or organization.

The view that theories are of less value than research findings is contrary to the current tenets of professors. A Campbell and Newell study, for example, showed that 76 percent of professors in the University Council for Educational Administration (UCEA) responded "strongly agree" or "tend to agree" to the statement, "The literature of educational administration should be theory-based."[52] In reality, it would be difficult, if not impossible, to base the literature of educational administration on theory. The point to be made is that there is not enough theory with a clear and demonstrated relationship to educational administration on which to base a program of preparation. If professors believe that they can adequately base programs on present theories, they have overestimated the power of theories.

The proper place of theory in preparation programs is when they are used to give administrators insight into how theoreticians think about administration and organizational behavior, to understand and interpret research based on theory, and to provide a frame of reference in which to conceptualize problems. In order to accomplish these outcomes, theory should be read and discussed in the context of specific cases, situations, and problems. The study of theory is, however, of major value to researchers rather than administrators. In programs for practitioners more time should be devoted to the study of research findings, whether or not they are related to theory. An analogy might serve here: A general knowledge of the theory of optics combined with intensive knowledge based on research which informs him of those lenses that remedy particular eye dysfunctions is of more value to an optometrist than in-depth knowledge of theory alone.

I favor preparation programs in which potential practitioners and researchers would initially study together in a foundations core based upon the tasks of administration clarified by research and theory. Then each group would branch off, with administrators having a highly clinical program and researchers a more theoretical curriculum.[53]

What should be taught as specialization is less of a problem. It is not controversial, nor is it likely to be so in the future. There should be a course in problems encountered in particular positions—be it superintendent, principal, or business manager. While the content of the course will change over time, the course title should stay the same. There should be course work in particular aspects of each position. Using the superintendency as an example, these aspects would include finance, school board relations, collective bargaining, and the role of the state and federal governments in education.

There is always the question of how much education (i.e., reading, counseling, and curriculum) should be taught. Because there is so much to learn, it is obvious that all of it cannot be taught. Even a sampling is too much. The clue, however, is not that there is too much to learn and so one learns nothing; rather one must realize that it is not the job of the administrator to be an expert in curriculum or reading. It is, however, the administrator's responsibility to recognize the need for expertise and to get it either through consultants or curriculum specialists attached to the school. The implication for the university preparation program is that the student should have the opportunity to study a sufficient number of courses so that he can become familiar with the educational program.

Skills. There are a number of skills that an administrator should possess. Since some students will have skills and others will not, they should be taught on an individualized basis. While the selection procedure might well weed out those with very poor skills, most candidates will need to have some skills strengthened.

It is suggested that each department of educational administration create an administrative skills center that would have personnel and equipment to test and teach the desired skills. The skills should include speaking, writing, working with computers, dealing with groups, interpersonal relations, budget making, and negotiating, Once a student's skills have been assessed, there should be instructional modules that he can take on his own. Each student, then, would have his skills appraised and would take instruction to strengthen weak ones.

Methods of Instruction. Since the purpose of the program is to prepare administrators who can act when confronted with problems or situations, the instructional program should stress "doing" rather than passive listening. This means that the substance of the program should be taught through or concurrently with appropriate cases, games, simulations, role playing, and other activities. Teaching should be such that potential administrators constantly use what they are being taught. There are now enough materials available from UCEA to make the recommended approach feasible. It is also quite possible to create materials of one's own; in fact, most of what UCEA has for sale was originally made by a professor for his own use.

Clinical Experiences. A well planned series of clinical experiences should extend throughout the entire preparation program. Beginning with the first course, there should be experiences such as observation of school board and other public meetings, interviews with administrators, and minisurveys of school buildings and of public and student opinion on school issues.

These experiences should be followed by several short internships. Each internship should have a single, limited objective to be attained. As examples, the student might work with a high school principal to build a class schedule, be a member of a team of interns working with a superintendent to pass a board issue, work with a school business manager to develop specifications for new school furniture, or be a member of the management team as it engages in collective bargaining.

Clinical experiences should be capped with a lengthy (either one or two semesters) internship with a skilled practitioner. While the short internship has a single specific objective, the long internship serves a different purpose. Here the student gets to learn about the constant pressure under which administrators function, about the informal organization of a school, and about community pressures. In fact, it is only in the long internship that the student really begins to get the "feel" of administration. Clinical experiences should be the focus for the preparation program. The program should be field-centered, in the sense that so much time would be spent observing and working in practical situations.

The clinical experience is expensive for the university, since a great deal of faculty time must be spent in developing contacts with practicing administrators, setting up schedules, and, in particular, in supervising the interns. Without extensive clinical experience, however, the preparation program is merely academic and does not sufficiently prepare the student to be an effective administrator.

Integrative Seminar

The final activity should be an integrative seminar in which the student puts together all aspects of his program—builds his "apperceptive mass." The student should examine what he has learned from research and theory, and he should match this with his clinical experiences. A large case study or a computer based simulation might serve as the vehicle for the seminar. The professor should be well experienced and have a good grasp of administrative content, but he might bring teams of professors and practitioners to the seminars to discuss points of concern to the students, thus supplementing his own expertise. The university has improperly left this integration of knowledge and experience to the student; the integrative seminar should remedy that shortcoming.

Notes

1. Robert Nisbet, "The Decline of Academic Nationalism," *Change* (Summer 1974), 26.

2. *Time* (July 15, 1974), 23.

3. Lord Morris, Opening Address, International Intervisitation Programme, 1974, Bristol, England. For additional information contact Professor George Baron, Institute of Education, University of London.

4. See, for example, Irving Kristol, "American Historians and the Democratic Idea," *American Scholar* (Winter 1969-1970), 89-104; Colin Greer, *The Great School Legend: A Revisionist Interpretation of American Public Education* (New York: Basic Books, 1972); Michael Katz, *Class Bureaucracy and Schools: The Illusion of Educational Change in America* (New York: Praeger, 1971).

5. Richard Sennett, *The Uses of Social Disorder* (New York: Knopf, 1970).

6. Herman Kahn and Anthony J. Wiener, "The Next Thirty-three Years: A Framework of Speculation," *Daedalus* (Summer 1967), 707-708.

7. T. Barr Greenfield, "Organizations as Social Inventions: Rethinking Assumptions about Change," *Applied Behavioral Science* 9, 1 (1973), 551-574.

8. *Time* (October 21, 1974), 27.

9. Richard Freeman and J. Herbert Holloman, "The Declining Value of College Going," *Change* 7, 7 (September 1975), 24-31, 62.

10. Morris, Opening Address.

11. Unionization is here meant the organizing of teachers for purposes of collective bargaining regardless of whether they are affiliated with the American Federation of Teachers, National Education Association, or any other organization, or whether they are independent.

12. Bruce Cooper, "Middle Management Unionization in Education," *Administrators Notebook* XXIII, 6 (1975).

13. Frank Lutz, *The Union Contract as it Affects Principal Leadership Behavior in Urban Schools* (Institute for Staff Relations, School of Education, New York University, 1968).

14. Morris, Opening Address.

15. Max J. Rubin, "New York City Needs a Commissioner of Education," *New York University Education Quarterly* (Winter 1972), 2-7.

16. For a more detailed discussion of this topic see Daniel E. Griffiths, "The Tasks of the Administrator," *Studies in Educational Administration and Organization* 1, 1 (Spring 1973), 7-20 (in Hebrew). English copies may be obtained from the Center for Educational Administration, Haifa, Israel.

17. Paul Lazarsfeld, "The Social Sciences and Administration: A Rationale," in Lawrence W. Downey and Frederick Enns (eds.), *The Social Sciences and Educational Administration* (Edmonton: University of Alberta, 1963), 3-4.

18. Lynn N. Nicholas, Helen E. Virjo, and William W. Wattenburg, *Effect of Socio-economic Setting and Organizational Climate on Problems Brought to Elementary School Offices* (Detroit: Wayne State University, 1965). U.S. Office of Education Contract No. 2394 (OE4-10-084).

19. *Ibid.*, 121.

20. *Ibid.*, 122.

21. Earl J. McGrath, "The Changing Mission of Home Economics," *Journal of Home Economics* 60, 2 (February 1968), 85-92.

22. *Ibid.*, 87.

23. Glenn L. Immegart and Francis J. Pilecki, *An Introduction to Systems for the Educational Administrator* (Reading, Mass.: Addison-Wesley, 1973).

24. Harry J. Hartley, *Educational Planning-Programming-Budgeting* (Englewood Cliffs, N.J.: Prentice-Hall, 1968). See also portions of American Association of School Administrators, *Administrative Technology and the School Executive* (Washington, D.C.: The Association, 1969).

25. N. Frederiksen, O. Jenson, and A. E. Beaton, *Organizational Climates and Administrative Performance* (Princeton, N.J.: Educational Testing Service, 1968).

26. Robert E. Ohm, *Leadership Game—Secondary Principalship Instructors Manual* (Columbus, Ohio: University Council for Educational Administration, 1968), 12.

27. *Ibid.*, 17.

28. James M. Lipham and Donald C. Francke, "Nonverbal Behavior of Administrators," *Educational Administration Quarterly*, II, 2 (Spring, 1966), 101-109.

29. *Ibid.*, 105.

30. Glen Heathers, *Organizing Schools through the Dual Progress Plan* (Danville, Ill.: Interstate, 1967); Neal Gross, Joseph B. Giacquinta, and Marilyn Bernstein, *An Attempt to Implement a Major Educational Innovation: A Sociological Inquiry* (Cambridge, Mass.: Harvard University, Center for Research and Development on Educational Differences, 1968).

31. Richard B. Morland, "The External Doctorate in Education: Blessing or Blasphemy?" *Phi Delta Kappan* LV, 3 (November 1973), 163-168. For other views, see Donald P. Mitchell, "Let's Set the Record Straight: A Case For Nova University's External Doctorate in Education"; John Mahoney, "Open is Open, For Heaven's Sake," *Phi Delta Kappan* LV, 6 (February 1974), 370-375; Gerald E. Sroufe, "Nova's Ed.D. Program for Educational Leaders: Looking Backward, Looking Forward," *Phi Delta Kappan* LVI, 6 (February 1975), 402-405.

32. Robert H. Graham, "The Walden University External Doctorate," *Phi Delta Kappan* 57, 7 (March 1976), 474-475.

33. John Merrow, Richard Foster, and Nolan Estes, *The Urban School Superintendent of the Future* (Durant, Okla.: Southeastern Foundation, 1974).

34. Graham, "Walden University External Doctorate."

35. Benjamin Rosner, "The Promise of Competency-Based Teacher Education," *New York University Education Quarterly* IV, 3 (Spring 1973), 2-6.

36. Jean Hills, "Preparation for the Principalship: Some Recommendations from the Field," *Administrator's Notebook* XXIII, 9.

37. Daniel E. Griffiths, "Intellectualism and Professionalism," *New York University Education Quarterly* V, 1 (Fall 1973), 1-6.

38. *Better Teaching in School Administration*, Southern States Cooperative Program in Educational Administration, 1955.

39. Horace B. English and Ava Champney English, *A Comprehensive Dictionary of Psychological and Psychoanalytical Terms* (New York: Longmans, Green, 1958), 267.

40. Brooks Adams, *The Theory of Social Revolutions* (New York: Macmillan, 1914), 207-208.

41. Robert B. Moore, "Selecting Administrators through Testing," *Administrator's Notebook* X, 8 (April 1962).

42. The author agrees with the point-of-view set forth by Kenneth E. McIntyre in *UCEA Review* XVI, 4 (April 1975), 14, 22, 23.

43. John Hemphill *et al.*, *Administrative Performance and Personality* (New York: Teachers College Press, 1962), 328.

44. *Ibid.*

45. James M. Lipham, "Personal Variables of Effective Administrators," *Administrator's Notebook* IX, 1 (September 1960).

46. Joan D. Meskin, "The Performance of Women School Administrators: A Review of the Literature," *Administrator's Notebook* XXIII, 1 (1974).

47. *Ibid.*

48. Jean Hills, "The Preparation of Administrators: Some Observations from the 'Firing Line,' " *Educational Administration Quarterly* 11, 3 (Autumn 1975), 3.

49. *Ibid.*

50. Donald Levine, "Response to Some Thoughts about Theory in Educational Administration—1975," *UCEA Review* (November 1975).

51. Jack Culbertson *et al., Social Science Content for Preparing Educational Leaders* (Columbus, Ohio: Merrill, 1973). This volume indicates the difficulties in deciding what should be used from the behavioral sciences.

52. Roald F. Campbell and L. Jackson Newell, *A Study of Professors of Educational Administration* (Columbus, Ohio: University Council for Educational Administration, 1973), 88.

53. For a more complete discussion of the argument over theory in preparation programs, see Daniel E. Griffiths, "Some Thoughts about Theory in Educational Administration—1975," *UCEA Review* (November 1975).

18. Emerging Educational Leadership:
A Citizen's Perspective

VIRLA R. KROTZ

Citizens are becoming more concerned with education—not only as parents or taxpayers, but as members of the community—and are deeply concerned with the future of this nation and world. Educators are beginning to realize the necessity of involving citizens in planning goals and objectives, assisting schools in implementing these objectives, and monitoring their achievements. Around 400 BC Isocrates offered the following description of educated men:

Whom, then, do I call educated? First, those who manage well the circumstances which they encounter day by day and who possess a judgment which is accurate in meeting occasions as they arise and rarely miss the expedient course of action; next, those who are decent and honorable in their intercourse with all men, bearing easily and goodnaturedly what is unpleasant or offensive in others, and being themselves as agreeable and reasonable to their associates as it is humanly possible to be; furthermore, those who hold their pleasure always under control and are not unduly overcome by their misfortunes, bearing up under them bravely and in a manner worthy of our common nature; finally, and most important of all, those who are not spoiled by their successes and who do not desert their true selves, but hold their ground steadfastly as wise and soberminded men, rejoicing no more in the good things which have come to them through chance than in those which through their own nature and intelligence are theirs since birth. Those who have a character which is in accord, not with one of these things, but

with all them—those I maintain are educated and whole men, possessed of all the
virtues of a man.

That is quite a definition of education. It would take the combined efforts and talents of professional educators and citizens to
achieve these goals in education.

Education, as well as many other phases of life, swings like a
pendulum. It moved from the extreme of strict discipline to complete permissiveness and is now, I hope, reaching a balance between
the two. It moved from emphasis on memorization and the "three
Rs" to complete disregard for them and instead stressed the development of self-awareness. I hope we are now realizing that both are
important and should be incorporated into our curriculum.

To assume leadership one must be aware of emerging trends in
education. What are some of the trends that we as citizens and educators see in education? I believe there are five that are of immediate
and long-range importance to our schools and to society in general.
They are: (1) Treating the child, the adolescent, or the young adult
who comes to our schools as an individual rather than as a unit of
attendance or some other statistical abstraction; (2) Involving the
school in the community and the community in the school; (3) Concern for affective as well as cognitive skills; (4) A realistic, pragmatic
concern with evaluation and accountability; and (5) Equal and adequate educational opportunities for all children.

All of these trends are recognizable, because they are happening
in school systems everywhere. Let me share some experiences with
these trends in California and the manner in which the public is becoming increasingly involved.

Let me start with the trend toward treating the child as an individual rather than as a statistic. It is now recognized that the public
school system has been contributing to student failure through its
insistence that the child fit the system or fail. For too many generations of children, teachers and administrators have sorted youngsters
into slow, average, or advanced groups the day that they start school
and have tracked them from first to twelfth grades in those groups. If
a child has not met the group standard, he has dropped back,
dropped out, or both.

Schools have failed to recognize what every parent of more than
one child has always known—no two children are alike. Every child

enters school with his own learning style and pace and particular set of needs to be met. Every child enters school as an individual, eager to learn and running over with the excitement of joining those who know—how to read, how to count, how to do all of the things big people do. What did the requirement of "fit the system or fail" do to that child? It frustrated him, it forced him into a uniform mold, and, finally, it turned his eagerness into boredom or bitterness.

In California we are getting away from that narrow view of education. We are now adapting the system to the individual child. In all of our new programs adopted in the past six years, there is one recurrent requirement—treat the child as an individual. In our Early Childhood Education program, for example, we insist that, before a school can be funded for participation, some essential elements must be present in the project plan:

Personalization of instruction to meet each child's capabilities and needs with ongoing evaluation of each pupil's progress;

Reduction of the adult-pupil ratio to at least 1:10 through the use of aides and tutors;

Organization of the learning experience to allow each child to make continuous progress at his own rate and to develop positive attitudes and feelings of self-worth;

Active partnerships among the school, parents, and the community and local autonomy;

Locally defined goals and objectives expressed in measurable terms;

Ongoing evaluation and accountability of local school and district programs; and

Coordination of all resources—district, community, state, and federal—available to the school in order to avoid fragmentation of effort while focusing on the needs of all students.

Although the Early Childhood Education program is only in its fourth year of operation, previous years' results indicate that significant changes in the learning climate and solid gains in pupil achievement have already been made.

We are also making the individual child and his needs the basic concern of our new special education master plan. No longer will a child have to bear the stigma of some label in order to receive the kinds of attention and education he needs.

The child who has been sidetracked into some isolated setting will now be part of mainstream education as much as possible. Special education teachers will remain on the staff as resource teachers to meet the needs not met by regular classroom teachers. Children—all children—have individual needs. The handicapped child must not be made to feel that he is somehow less wanted because his needs are different. That same concern for the individual characterizes our efforts to reform intermediate and secondary education.

Increasing attention is being given to career education. Students are often more interested in learning the basics if they can see some practical value in a course. Awareness about careers and the exploration of opportunities in all fields are being included in our curriculum. A well planned curriculum also includes cultural development. In addition, students are being taught available options and are being encouraged to include training that will enable them to fill jobs at an opening level no matter when they leave school. This does not threaten higher education for that opening level applies to everyone, even the student who continues in school for his doctorate. The student is learning the possibilities for upward mobility. Business and community leaders are becoming involved in assisting schools in curriculum planning and job counseling and are serving on career advisory committees.

The second trend emerging in the 1970s is the one toward involving the school in the community and the community in the school. We have finally realized that the school is not and cannot be an enclave isolated from the cultural context of the community. Man no longer divides life into three discrete parts—one for learning, one for working, and one for retirement. We are all learning and all teaching throughout our lives.

We have come to realize in this era of finite resources that we can no longer afford the luxury of ignoring the resources for learning available in our communities. We are involving parents as aides in our Early Childhood Education and our special education programs. We are involving business and industry in our career education programs.

But more than that, we are finding ways to use our schools as centers for a wide range of community activities. In many districts, schools are not used for school events only but serve as community centers for citizens in the evenings, on weekends, and during vacations. They are a part of the community.

The classroom teacher is now assuming a new role in the educational process. The teacher is now a team leader, a facilitator of learning. The teacher is not merely a teacher, but the linchpin that holds the learning process together. The teacher is a learner as well as a teacher. Learning a new role is a difficult process, but our teachers are doing it, and they are doing it well. They have given up the isolation of the self-contained classroom and are enthusiastically welcoming team teachers, parents, and paid aides. They are sharing the autonomy they used to enjoy behind those closed doors. And our students and our schools are benefiting from the thousands of volunteers who are helping in the classrooms.

We are involving students in a role of leadership. For the past eight years, a student selected by the California Association of Student Councils has sat with the State Board of Education as a participating member. The input has been tremendous and very worthwhile. Many local boards of education have also adopted the practice of involving a student member.

The third emerging trend—related closely to the involvement of the school with the community—is the concern for developing affective as well as cognitive skills. As schools have become part of the real world, teachers and administrators have come to realize the need to develop in each student the ability to live as a participating member of the larger society. We know now that, if we are to have more than a mere tolerance of others, we must learn that differences in life styles, skin color, and values are not important. Our school board members, administrators, and teachers are aware that through their actions they transmit to the generations that follow a genuine respect for, not merely a tolerance of, differences.

Inherent in that respect for differences is the need to develop in the individual a respect for himself and a sense of responsibility for his actions. We know that we cannot promote moral development through teaching maxims of right and wrong from copybooks. We tried that with previous generations and harvested violence, vandalism, and crime not only in our schools, but in our communities as well.

The public is equally concerned about discipline and problems related to discipline in our schools and reading, computing, busing, and other issues. We are responding to that concern by including in curriculum guidelines for all subject areas development of self-esteem, self-responsibility and self-discipline. Development of these values is not something that can be accomplished by a twenty-minute lecture once a week; it must permeate everything that happens in the school.

Again, school board members, administrators, teachers, and adults in general have become aware that, through their actions, they transmit these values to the students. If we want a child to have self-respect, we must respect him. If we want him to achieve self-discipline, we must permit him to learn through actual experience how to make decisions and assume responsibility for his own actions. And as we teach students to be responsible, we see an emerging trend toward accepting responsibility for our own actions as well.

Let us not forget, however, that the public is increasingly demanding a return to the basics. More and more publicity is being given to the poor preparation our students are receiving in communicative and computational skills. These must not be neglected.

There is a trend toward a realistic and pragmatic concern with evaluation and accountability. As resources for public services shrink under the impact of inflation and recession, the public is going to demand ever greater accountability for our use of those dollars allocated to education. We are not going to receive generous sums or even miserly pittances for continuation of such programs as Early Childhood Education and Career Education unless we can show, through actual evaluation of results, that they are increasing in effectiveness.

It is not only teachers and administrators who must accept the public demand for accountability. School board members, too, are accountable to the parents and the taxpayers for how effectively educational programs meet the objectives of the community.

That is why in California local school board members are encouraged by our State Board of Education to set practical standards for graduation from high school—standards that establish minimum levels of proficiency in basic skills rather than some arbitrary collection of units or amount of time spent in the classroom. The suggested standards require that students be able to do such things as read a newspaper and understand what they have read, be able to apply for a job and meet the entry qualifications, be able to fill out an income tax return and compute the tax due, understand contracts and interest on installment purchases, and so on.

Parents like that kind of accountability. They have had enough of their children being pushed through school and turned out unable to function in today's world. As taxpayers become more critical of how the educational dollar is used, university research must be concerned with this criticism.

The fifth trend concerns equal and adequate educational opportunities for all children. The impetus toward insistence that equal opportunities also include adequate educational opportunities is coming from those who are determined that "equality" will not be used as an excuse to make all districts equally poor. I count myself among that number.

If there are to be sufficient funds for support of programs that incorporate the trends I have mentioned, taxpayers must be assured—no, that is not strong enough—they must be guaranteed that the education provided our students will be far better than that which they are receiving today. The economically disadvantaged and minorities are not going to—nor should they be expected to—accept a double standard for the quality of educational programs.

Now we educators, board members, and citizens concerned with education must assure that these emerging trends which hold so much promise for a better education for all children will not fade away, victims of shrinking dollars and misjudged priorities.

We must give that assurance because there is a crisis of public confidence in all of our cherished institutions. Schools are not in some favored position, isolated and remote from the hostility that thrives in the swamp of distrust. A hostile public, lacking confidence in the effectiveness of public schools to support its cherished dream of upward mobility, is going to demand alternatives. Unless we restore that confidence, the twenty-first century may well see the end of free public education for every child.

Thus all of us in education—whether in California or in Ohio, whether professional educators or involved citizens—must meet these emerging trends with bold leadership and clarity of purpose. I have faith that we will meet them as opportunities for improved education, because we are preparing ourselves and we are trying.

We are moving forward with positive programs in schools all across this nation. We are embarking on new programs to reform our educational processes to meet the individual needs of the children and the adults in our communities. We are working to make our school finance structures more equitable for both children and taxpayers. We are involving more citizens in order to utilize their expertise and make them aware of educational problems and development.

But even more effort is necessary if we are to restore confidence in our schools, if we are to assure that there will be public education for all children in the next century.

We must tolerate no deviation from a standard of excellence for ourselves as leaders, the staff we employ, our administrators and teachers, and every child entrusted to our care.

Excellence depends upon our acceptance of responsibility for results, for student outcomes. It depends upon our willingness to put the needs of the child, adolescent, or adult before the needs of the profession or the institution.

A commitment to excellence is perhaps the greatest challenge of all. Could it be that, when we have met this last and greatest challenge, we will have at last created the kinds of schools that will renew us eternally as a great nation?

I believe that this cannot be realized through leadership in one segment of education alone. Professional educators must have the cooperation of informed and concerned lay citizens. Both need the advice and stimulation of student involvement. Successful leadership of the future must be a team effort.

Early in the fifteenth century, Martin Luther said "The prosperity of a country depends, not on the abundance of its revenues, nor on the strength of its fortifications, nor on the beauty of its public buildings; but it consists in the number of its cultivated citizens, in its men of education, enlightenment and character." Working together, we can furnish the leadership to attain this goal.